Women and Goddesses in Myth and Sacred Text

An Anthology

Edited by

Tamara Agha-Jaffar

Kansas City Kansas Community College

PEARSON
Longman

New York San Francisco Boston
London Toronto Sydney Tokyo Singapore Madrid
Mexico City Munich Paris Cape Town Hong Kong Montreal

Publisher: Priscilla McGeehon
Executive Marketing Manager: Ann Stypuloski
Production Manager: Denise Phillip
Project Coordination, Text Design, and Electronic Page Makeup: WestWords, Inc.
Cover Design Manager: Wendy Ann Fredericks
Cover Designer: Kay Petronio
Cover Art: Riva Brown/Images.com/Corbis
Manufacturing Manager: Mary Fischer
Printer and Binder: Courier Corporation
Cover Printer: Coral Graphic Services

For permission to use copyrighted material, grateful acknowledgment is made to the copyright holders on pp. 289–290, which are hereby made part of this copyright page.

Library of Congress Cataloging-in-Publication Data

Women and goddesses in myth and sacred text : an anthology / edited by Tamara Agha-Jaffar.
    p. cm.
  Includes bibliographical references and index.
  ISBN 0-321-24432-X (pbk.)
1. Women—Mythology. 2. Goddesses. 3. Women and religion. I. Agha-Jaffar, Tamara, 1952–
BL325.F4W66 2004
202'.114—dc22

                                                                    2004020789

Please visit us at http://www.ablongman.com

ISBN 0-321-24432-X

1 2 3 4 5 6 7 8 9 10—CRS—07 06 05 04

To my beloved mother, Najla Chalabi
And to my grandmothers,
Bebe Al-Bassam and Zaynab Mussawi

Contents

Preface

At first, it seemed a task of momentous proportions. Inspired by my students' interest in women in mythology and religion, I decided to develop and teach a course on the subject. Accordingly, I began the search for a suitable textbook. I knew exactly what type of text I was seeking: one that situated the female as the primary subject of study; one that contained a wide variety of primary sources from different cultural and religious traditions; one that located each female within her cultural tradition; and one that shattered stereotypical images of women by depicting them in a multiplicity of roles and manifestations.

My search for a suitable textbook proved fruitless. Nothing seemed to suit my purpose. I found books about goddesses, about goddesses within specific cultural and religious traditions, about women in religion, about women in myth, about the Great Goddess and her demise, about woman-centered communities before the coming of patriarchy, about the contribution of women to the development of civilization, about feminist spirituality, and so on. I read Serinity Young's vast compendium *An Anthology of Sacred Texts By and About Women.* And while this is an impressive, wide-ranging collection of sacred texts by and about women, many of the excerpts from the primary sources are too short and inadequate. I needed fewer but longer excerpts that would lend themselves to analysis and discussion. My search continued, but to no avail.

So with a cockiness that has been one of my defining characteristics ever since I was a scrawny-legged girl with a smattering of freckles and a shock of unruly, dark hair, I decided to face the task head on and write a textbook myself. For more years than I care to recount, I have been teaching classes in Mythology, World Literature, English Literature, Women in Literature, Humanities, and Women's Studies. And ever since my immersion in feminism and goddess literature, I have been fascinated with women and goddesses that play prominent roles in mythology and religion. I had just completed my first book, *Demeter and Persephone: Lessons From a Myth,* a feminist interpretation of the classical Greek poem, the *Homeric Hymn to Demeter.* Invigorated by that experience and infused with a desire to compile an anthology that prominently features women in myth and sacred texts, I decided to embark on this project. Fortunately for me, I found an editor and a publisher who shared my conviction for the need of such a book and my enthusiasm for producing it. And so, after a great deal of research, writing, and rewriting, after heeding the advice of preliminary reviewers, after rejecting some of my initial figures and including others, *Women and Goddesses in Myth and Sacred Text: An Anthology* was born.

I sought the assistance of scholars in Religious Studies and the Classics to review my chapters. I am fortunate to have had such a wonderful group of consultants who guided me and generously shared their academic expertise in the various content areas. These individuals are:

Gustavo Benavides, Associate Professor of Theology and Religious Studies at Villanova University, who read my chapters on Kali, Sita, Amaterasu, and Kuan Yin.

Mary Churchill, Visiting Professor of American Indian and Native Studies at the University of Iowa, who read my chapters on White Buffalo Woman and Corn Mother.

Paul Mirecki, Chair and Associate Professor in the Department of Religious Studies at the University of Kansas, who read my chapters on Inanna and Tiamat.

Gaile M. Pohlhaus, Assistant Professor of Theology and Religious Studies at Villanova University, who read my chapters on Isis, Lilith, Eve, and the Virgin Mary.

Margaret Rausch, Assistant Professor of Religious Studies at the University of Kansas, who read my chapters on Hawwa and Maryam.

Sandra Spencer, Director of Women's Studies at the University of North Texas, who read my chapters on Demeter and Persephone, Circe, and Medea.

I. Peter Ukpokodu, Courtesy Professor of Theatre and Film, Chairperson and Professor of African and African American Studies at the University of Kansas, who read my chapter on Oshun.

Women and Goddesses in Myth and Sacred Text takes us on a fascinating journey, beginning with the story of Isis in ancient Egypt as told in selections from Plutarch's *Moralia.* This is followed by the story of Inanna from ancient Sumer and the story of Tiamat in *The Babylonian Creation.* From there, we explore the classical Greek story of Demeter and Persephone in the *Homeric Hymn to Demeter,* the story of Circe in selections from the *Odyssey,* and Medea from the play of the same name by Euripides. Our journey continues with two figures from the Hindu tradition: Sita from the *Ramayana* and Kali as she is depicted in selections from the *Devi-Mahatmya.* Amaterasu's story in the selections from the *Kojiki* within the Japanese Shinto tradition is our next subject. She is succeeded by the story of the Buddhist Kuan Yin as it is told in *The Legend of Miao-Shan.* Within the Hebrew tradition, we explore the story of Lilith as it is told in *The Alphabet of Ben Sira* and the story of Eve in Genesis. This leads us to Luke 1 and 2 and the story of the Virgin Mary within the Christian tradition. We then proceed to the Islamic tradition and the selections from the *Qur'an* that recount the stories of Hawwa (Eve) and Maryam (the Virgin Mary). Oshun of the Yoruba in the *Ifa Divination* is our next subject. The anthology concludes with the stories of White Buffalo Woman and Corn Mother from within the American Indian tradition.

In the introduction to each selection, I have tried to provide useful context that situates the selection in its cultural and religious tradition. As much as possible, I have tried to resist imposing my own interpretation and biases on the material. My preference has been to allow each piece to speak for itself and to stimulate critical thinking about the material through the use of pedagogical tools in each chapter.

By compiling this material into one convenient anthology, I hope to have contributed to increasing the accessibility and appreciation for these multifaceted women and goddesses from within their different cultural traditions and in their various manifestations.

Acknowledgments

A work of this nature would not have been possible without the professional and personal assistance from a host of many. I owe a great deal to a great number of people.

Thank you to current and former colleagues at Kansas City Kansas Community College. Among them are Morteza Ardebili, Don Black, Tom Burke, Andrea Chastain, Bill Chennault, Cindy Coleman, Steve Collins, Antonio Cutolo-Ring, Darren Elliot, Mary Fenlon, Amy Fugate, Jennifer Gieschen, Joseph Grisela, Adam Hadley, Ben Hayes, Evelyn Huffman, Melanie Jackson-Scott, Alice Jenkins, Michael Kimbrough, Jim Krajewski, Cindy Lahmann, Pat Lawson, Charles Leader, Leota Marks, Denise McDowell, Connie Mayfield, Phil Miller, Tom Murdock, Hira Nair, Joann Nelson, Awilda Olson, Mike Pettengell, Deloris Pinkard, Becky Pinter, Anita Reach, Jerry Reid, Charles Reitz, John Ryan, Patty Schmaus, Mahdi Shariati, Dale Shetler, Marilee Shrader, Steve Spartan, Jerry Toney, Teresa Truman, Gregg Ventello, Rob Vuturo, Kaye Walter, Valerie Webb, Tom Weis, Bryan Whitehead, Charles Wilson, and Valdenia Winn.

Thank you to the reviewers for their comments: Jane Atchison-Nevel, Florida International University; Susan A. Farrell, Kingsborough Community College; Nikki Bado-Fralick, Iowa State University; Joan Ferrante, Columbia University; Laurel Holmstrom, Sonoma State University; Shira Lander, University of Pennsylvania; Deshae E. Lott, University of Illinois at Springfield; Kate McCarthy, California State University, Chico; Lesley A. Northup, Florida International University; Alicia Ostriker, Rutgers University; Ana Self-Schuber, University of Alabama; Mary Suydam, Kenyon College; Katharina von Kellenbach, St. Mary's College of Maryland; and Ann K. Wetherilt, Emmanuel College.

Thank you to the staff at Kansas City Kansas Community College Library, especially Teri Hunter. Teri successfully expedited my frantic and interminable requests for research materials with outstanding punctuality and a cheerful disposition.

Thank you to my many students throughout the years who continue to inspire me and encourage me. Students can be the best teachers, and I have been blessed with so many who have taught me so much and from whom I have still so much to learn.

Thank you to my editor, Priscilla McGeehon for her patience, support, and encouragement as I embarked on the challenging process of birthing this book. Thank you also to the staff at Longman Publishers for making me feel very welcome and for providing me with excellent assistance throughout the publication process.

Thank you to my friend for over two decades, Leslie Overfelt, for her friendship and her ability to retain her sanity and sense of humor in spite of years of immersion in legalese.

Thank you to my brother, Jaffar, because no mother could have asked for a better son; no sister could have asked for a better brother. Thank you also to my three sisters, Zaynab, Sara, and Besma, who share with me childhood memories of simpler times in a house called Broadlawns.

Thank you to my beloved mother, Najla Chalabi. A book about women should be dedicated to women, so I have dedicated this book to my mother and to my grandmothers, Bebe Al-Bassam and Zaynab Mussawi. But I would be dreadfully remiss if I did not acknowledge the tremendous debt I owe to my father. So thank you also to my beloved father, Abdul Latif Agha-Jaffar. Although it has been over a decade since his death, his positive influence and example continue to guide me with each new project I undertake.

Thank you to my sons, Bashar and Reshad, for their support and willingness to accept the demands on my time that this project required. To Reshad, I say a special thank you for patiently helping me design the complicated pantheons and family trees that are in this book. And to Bashar, I say thank you for critiquing my manuscript, providing fresh insights and comments, and celebrating with me each completed section of the book.

Thank you to my best friend, my sounding board, my support, my cheering squad, my guide, my partner, and my husband, Samih K. Staitieh. Thank you for our early morning briefing sessions, a time for sharing with you the work I have done and the work I have yet to do. Thank you for my daily dose of encouragement and support. Thank you for reminding me to laugh at myself. And, above all, thank you for serving this supportive feast with two cups of delicious espresso coffee that jump start my mornings.

It is with a sense of profound humility and deeply felt gratitude that I acknowledge my three Staitieh men for their unconditional love and unwavering support for all that I do.

Tamara Agha-Jaffar

Introduction

Archeological evidence strongly suggests that our prehistoric ancestors worshipped a Great Goddess who was known by many names and assumed many guises and manifestations. She was the Creatrix and Mother of All, a multifaceted being whose existence predates the arrival of the male gods who were to usurp her power and authority.

Over an extended period of time, the powers of the Great Goddess were diminished, diffused, fragmented, and harnessed to support a masculine theology. The all-encompassing qualities she once embodied were splintered off and assigned to a host of other deities. This shift from Goddess to God was not merely a question of gender change. It constituted a paradigm shift that was to impact every level of society. Goddess religion was earth-centered and life-affirming. The deity's presence was immanent within all of creation. Humanity was interconnected with nature; death was a part of life. Worship of the Goddess was sensual and erotic and celebrated the body. The Great Goddess was revered as the force that was responsible for the renewal and regeneration of life. In Goddess-worshiping communities, women held a high status and were treated with respect.

Patriarchy's entrance into human history precipitated a cultural transformation of such proportions that we are still reeling from its impact. According to a male-constructed hierarchy of values, the theology that replaced Goddess worship proceeded to designate as inferior all things associated with the feminine and that fall within the feminine sphere of influence. Transcendence replaced immanence; domination replaced partnership. Natural functions of the human body, especially functions associated with the woman's body, were viewed with contempt and disdain. The intricate web that interconnected all of life was replaced with a system which ranked males at the head and legitimized their power and authority over one half of humanity and over all of nature. Patriarchy led to different ways of perceiving self and community as well as different ways of thinking and being. Women, the female, and the feminine were subordinated, devalued, and suppressed in a system that forced societies to rank difference hierarchically.

But in spite of patriarchy's attempt to smother all evidence of a time when human communities operated differently, the Great Goddess was never totally forgotten. Glimmerings of her former glory and power and evidence of her demise continue to surface through a variety of goddesses and sacred women. For men and women to arrive at a more holistic, balanced perspective, one that is nurturing of ourselves and the planet and one which opens up the possibility of exploring alternative ways of thinking about life and our interconnectedness with all that lives, it becomes necessary for us to embrace the life-affirming qualities once represented by the Great Goddess and to integrate them into our daily lives, our relationships, our institutions, and our communities.

The stories in *Women and Goddesses in Myth and Sacred Text: An Anthology* provide evidence of some of the footprints left by the Great Goddess. Many of the figures included in the anthology manifest one or more of her aspects and trace her demise and her recent reemergence. The evidence assumes the form of a continuum that begins with the Great Goddess at one end and gradually moves in the direction of spiritual and/or sacred women at the other.

The anthology features 18 women and goddesses depicted in a variety of roles and manifestations, beginning with powerful goddess figures and concluding with two sacred women from the Native American tradition. Each figure is unique; each has a different story to tell; and each operates within her own cultural and religious traditions—either by accommodating those traditions, repudiating them, or negotiating a separate space for herself within them.

The guiding principle in the selection process has been to include those females who play prominent roles in ancient and living sacred texts and myths from a variety of world cultures and traditions. Admittedly, that constitutes a broad spectrum of choices. My criteria for excluding some figures and including others was based on the female's prominence within her cultural and religious tradition, the availability of a primary source that situates her as its center of study, and a desire to maintain somewhat of a numerical balance between traditions by selecting only a few representative examples from within each tradition. The result is a collection that is inclusive, diverse, and representative.

Beginning with Isis of ancient Egypt, we can see facets of the Great Goddess in her capacity as cosmic mother, god mother, and queen of heaven. Although Isis' powers were later subordinated to the powers of Osiris in Egyptian mythology, it is apparent from the selection of the *Ancient Egyptian Book of the Dead* in Plutarch's *Moralia,* that it was Isis who once held the power. She resuscitates Osiris from the dead and provides him with the knowledge he needs to become ruler of the underworld. She is the throne upon which the pharaoh sits. And she is the mother of Horus, the son of god who is embodied in the living pharaoh. If not for Isis and her prodigious powers, Osiris would still be languishing in a pillar at the palace.

Inanna of Ancient Sumer, known as queen of heaven and earth, embodies the life-generating powers of the Great Goddess. A consideration of Inanna's story, including the sections not available in this text, reveals that Inanna's powers, as great as they are, constitute a reduction of the Great Goddess' original power. Inanna is forced to rely on male assistance to do for her what she can no longer do for herself. She needs Gilgamesh to rid the huluppu tree of its uninvited guests. She needs Enki's decrees governing the universe to empower her. No longer partheno-genetic, she needs Dumuzi to help her create new life, and she needs Enki's assistance to emerge from the underworld.

Tiamat of *The Babylonian Creation* tells of the defeat and mutilation of the Great Goddess. Known as the Mother of All, Tiamat is murdered by her descendent Marduk, the supreme leader of the younger generation of gods. After killing her, Marduk splits open her lifeless carcass and constructs the skies and land from her mutilated body. The land is still female, but its powers have now been subdued, circumscribed, and appropriated by a male god who has committed matricide.

The *Homeric Hymn to Demeter* can be seen as a transitional myth. It tells of a time when the Great Goddess, as manifested in Demeter, refuses to cower down to the challenge of patriarchy. Demeter's insistence on retaining some measure of control over the welfare of her child and her insistence that the voice of the mother be heard force the patriarchal power structure to accommodate her needs. But this accommodation proves to be temporary.

Circe demonstrates the transformational powers of the Great Goddess. She transforms Odysseus' men to swine and then back again as new and improved versions of their former selves. She assists Odysseus in his transformation from a brutish warrior, bloodied by battle, to an individual who is closer to achieving balance through his accommodation of the feminine. But Circe is able to retain her powers of transformation and her fierce autonomy only because she lives on an island, isolated from the main land. In Circe, the Goddess lives, but she can only survive on the outskirts of patriarchy.

Medea demonstrates the wrathful aspect of the Great Goddess—the one who wreaks vengeance on a people for refusing to acknowledge her powers or accommodate a place for her in society. Medea violates the traditional roles and mores ascribed to women in Greek society and demonstrates the perils that can lie ahead for those who would marginalize the Goddess and all she represents.

In the Hindu tradition, Sita is the incarnation of the goddess Lakshmi. Born of the earth, she manifests the chthonic qualities of the Great Goddess. However, Sita has been stripped of her power. She adheres to the laws of righteous behavior (dharma) which clearly require the female to assume a subordinate role to that of her husband. The goddess Kali, on the other hand, is a formidable warrior. She embodies the ability of the Great Goddess to devour her enemies with obvious gusto, to celebrate her unbridled sexuality, and to laugh uproariously at any who attempt to circumscribe her powers within the prim and proper framework of a subdued femininity.

As the Japanese sun goddess, Amaterasu embodies the power of the Goddess to make the earth bountiful and fertile. But her powers and strength also represent a decline in the once all-powerful Great Goddess. When Amaterasu is challenged by the male hegemonic power structure as represented by her brother Susanowo, she retreats into a cave until the remaining deities come to her rescue.

Kuan Yin of China, as the embodiment of perfected wisdom, demonstrates the unlimited power of the Great Goddess for love, forgiveness, and compassion. She forgives her father for his abusive behaviors and dismembers her own body to save him. Like the Great Goddess, Kuan Yin gives of herself so that others may live.

In the Hebrew figure of Lilith, we see evidence of the struggle for power between conflicting ideologies. Lilith refuses to submit to male authority and is subsequently demonized for daring to oppose and challenge woman's subordinate status. The Hebrew Eve experiences a similar fate in that she is held responsible for all the ills that have befallen humankind due to her act of disobedience. But Eve's conduct can also be seen as an assertion of her right to retain the powers of the Great Goddess to effect transformation, to provide access to higher knowledge, and to bring about rebirth.

The Virgin Mary of the Christian tradition echoes the Great Goddess in her capacity as the mother of God—the womb that brings forth renewal and salvation. She has much in common with her sister, Isis, in that both conceive "miraculously" and both give birth to the son of God who will "save" the people from the forces of chaos and darkness.

Unlike their counterparts in the Hebrew and Christian traditions, however, Hawwa and Maryam of the Islamic tradition are depicted as fully human. They show no trace of the Great Goddess. Hawwa's voice is heard in concert with that of Adam's; Maryam cries out in the throes of labor pains as she gives birth to her human son, the prophet 'Isa.

Oshun of the Yoruba reflects the Goddess in her life-giving capacity. She represents the perpetually renewing source of life that underlies all of creation. Like the Great Goddess, Oshun is aligned with the female and feminine processes of childbirth, and the rearing, healing, and nurturing of children.

As sacred beings of the Native American tradition, White Buffalo Woman and Corn Mother reflect qualities of the Great Goddess in their ability to guide, to teach, and to give of themselves so that their children may live. White Buffalo Woman reminds us of the interconnection between humans and animals; Corn Mother reminds us of the interconnection between humans and plants. Like the Great Goddess, both figures embody the sacred, life-generating powers of the earth.

The last few decades have witnessed an increasing interest in the subject of the Great Goddess, of prepatriarchal goddesses, and of the role of women as revealed in myth and sacred texts. This interest promises to grow as research, theory, and hypotheses concerning the nature of preliterate communities, their belief systems and rituals, the demise of the Great Goddess, her role and the corresponding role of women in the development of culture and tradition—in short, intellectual discussions that had once been restricted to academic circles—have recently become popularized through the media and through the proliferation of best-selling books on the topic. To date, most of these works consist of summaries and discussion and posit theories and interpretations of materials that explore the role of women in general in the development of civilization. Alternatively, they may explore a group of women and goddesses within the same cultural tradition as evidenced through mythology or sacred texts. But an exploration of what is currently available reveals a paucity of collections that house extended excerpts from a wide-ranging and culturally diverse selection of ancient and living sacred texts and myths that situate the female as the center of study. Hence the need for a collection such as this.

Women and Goddesses in Myth and Sacred Text: An Anthology consists of a compilation of selected excerpts from primary sources that situate the female in mythology and religion as the center of analysis and discussion. Whenever possible, the preference is to cite direct translations of primary sources. However, in some cases that is not possible: some of the available primary sources consist of fragments; some stories have emerged from cultures that are oral and therefore do not have a primary written source as such; and some provide brief glimpses and references to a particular female figure scattered throughout many volumes. In those cases, authoritative texts and translations are cited that provide an accurate rendition of the story or myth as well as an accurate composite figure of the woman or goddess under consideration.

As much as possible, I have tried to proceed chronologically, but this proved to be a challenging task since some of the texts emerge from traditions that had been transmitted orally for many years before they were committed to writing. I have clustered the readings according to their cultural traditions to enable readers to draw parallels between figures within the same or a similar cultural tradition while simultaneously accentuating the similarities and differences with figures from other traditions.

Each chapter begins with an introduction to the culture and tradition that is particular to the work and to the figure under examination. In some cases, the tradition has been far from monolithic, embracing instead many different variations. While acknowledging the existence of the multiple and diverse components within any tradition, a work of this nature does not attempt or claim to elucidate subtle nuances and interpretative variations within a tradition. Oversimplification, therefore, becomes not only inevitable but also a necessity. My pedagogical goal has been to provide readers with a beginning—a general overview of the cultural and religious context within which to situate each figure. Readers can then begin the process of exploring each tradition in greater depth and scope.

Each introduction is followed with an excerpt from the primary source. In some cases, locating the primary source proved to be quite a challenge either because of the scarcity of English translations, as in the case, for example, of the *Devi-Mahatmya* or the *Legend of Miao-Shan,* or because of the wide range of translations to choose from. In the case of the *Qur'an,* for example, I sought the assistance of Arabic-speaking, Muslim religious scholars for advice on the most authoritative translation.

The selections from the primary source vary in length, and whenever feasible, I tried to include the entire work. If that were not possible, I selected an excerpt from the work that best represents the woman or goddess under discussion. Each selection from the primary source is followed with *Questions For Review and Discussion,* a series of questions that are designed to stimulate discussion and critical thinking on the material. There is an extensive bibliography at the end of the book.

Beginning with Isis and concluding with Corn Mother, each of these figures speaks to us in significant ways. Some can be seen as a source of empowerment because of their strength and life-affirming qualities. Others demonstrate their fierce resistance to an oppressive ideology that attempted to subvert their authority, and still others demonstrate their inability to resist the onslaught. Each of these 18 figures has something to say. And in spite of their obvious diversity, each has something in common with one or more of her sisters—a commonality that leaps across time, space, geographical boundaries, and one that may reflect a shared origin in the Great Goddess. It is this commonality that intrigues me. And it is this commonality that has made this book such a pleasure to write.

I hope you enjoy reading about these fascinating women and goddesses as much as I have enjoyed sharing their stories with you.

Timeline of Women and Goddesses

Timeline scale (BCE to CE): 3000 — 2000 — 1800 — 800 — 650 — 500 — 200 (BCE) | 80 — 400 — 625 — 700 — 1000 — 1550 (CE)

Culture	Figures
Egypt	Isis
Sumer	Inanna
Babylon	Tiamat
Greece	Demeter/Circe, Medea
India	Sita, Kali
Japan	Amaterasu
China	Kuan Yin
Hebrew	Eve/Lilith–Genesis, Lilith–Ben Sira
Christian	Virgin Mary
Islamic	Hawwa/Maryam
Africa	Oshun*
Native America	White Buffalo Woman*, Corn Mother*

* No known date

Chapter 1

Isis

GLOSSARY OF NAMES

ANUBIS   Son of Osiris and Nephthys; god of mummification

HORUS   Son of Isis and Osiris; heir to Osiris; living god and savior

ISIS   Queen of Heaven, Great Mother; sister/wife of Osiris

NEPHTHYS   Sister to Isis, Osiris, and Seth; sister/wife of Seth

OSIRIS   Supreme judge of the dead; brother/spouse of Isis

SETH   Brother of Isis and Osiris; enemy of Osiris; known as Typhon in the selection below

THOTH   God of wisdom, science, and medicine

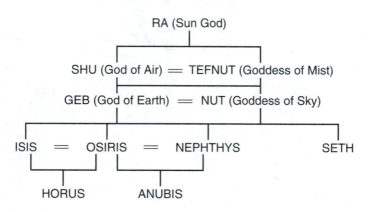

Egyptian Pantheon

Isis is one of the most famous goddesses of ancient Egypt. She was worshipped as the cosmic mother, god mother, and queen of heaven. Reverence for Isis spanned over three thousand years, ending at approximately the second century C.E. With the coming of Christianity, many of the temples and shrines built in her honor throughout the Roman Empire were rededicated to the Virgin Mary. Isis is frequently depicted standing alongside her sister, Nephthys, and behind her brother/spouse Osiris in the Hall of Judgment. One of the most ubiquitous depictions of Isis is of her nursing her young son, Horus. For contemporary viewers, his maternal image, in statues, wall paintings, and papyri, bears a striking resemblance to the Madonna and Child and may have been the prototype for later Christian iconography.

The story of Isis and her brother/husband Osiris constituted the foundation for ancient Egyptian beliefs in life after death. The myth permeated all aspects of Egyptian life. The rituals based on this preeminent myth became intimately connected with Egyptian culture, eventually providing a method for mere mortals to overcome death. Since Osiris suffered death and mutilation by the powers of evil and, with the assistance of Isis, was able to transcend death by rising again, he became the god of resurrection and eternal life. Ancient Egyptians believed that mortals could similarly gain access to an eternal life of bliss with the gods if they performed the necessary rituals and lamentations, recited the appropriate incantations, and preserved their bodies after death in the same manner as the mummification of Osiris. Surviving family members and friends took great pains to replicate the ceremonies, rituals, and tasks performed by the gods over the body of Osiris as revealed in the myth in order to preserve the bodies of deceased individuals and ensure for them a life after death.

Isis plays a central role in the myth. She is a great granddaughter of the sun god Ra and the granddaughter of Shu and Tefnut, god of air and goddess of mist, respectively. Isis's parents are the children of Shu and Tefnut. Her father, Geb, is god of earth; her mother, Nut, is goddess of sky. Isis has three siblings: two brothers, Osiris and Seth, and one sister, Nephthys. Isis becomes the spouse of Osiris; Nephthys becomes the spouse of Seth.

The myth of Isis and Osiris recounts the story of Seth's increasing jealousy of Osiris's success and power as an earthly ruler. Osiris is credited with teaching humans to cultivate grain and with transforming a barbarian people to a civilized one. Overwhelmed by envy, Seth eventually murders Osiris by sealing his body in a casket and sending it down the Nile. Grief-stricken over the loss of her beloved Osiris, Isis sets out to locate him. She finds him and is able to revive him long enough for her to become pregnant with their son, Horus. But Seth continues to plague the divine couple, this time dismembering Osiris's body and scattering his pieces throughout the Nile. Isis searches for the pieces, and with the help of Thoth and Anubis, restores and embalms Osiris's body and escorts him to the afterlife to become the supreme god and judge of the dead.

Meanwhile, Horus has grown to maturity and fights an epic battle with Seth to avenge his father's murder. The battle is repeated annually, and Horus's inevitable victory against the forces of death as represented by Seth continues to ensure the restoration of peace, fertility, and order to the land.

Isis plays a crucial role throughout the myth since it is she who searches for and locates Osiris's body, resurrects it, and is responsible for situating him as the supreme judge of the dead in the Hall of Judgment. She incarnates the qualities of devoted wife and mother as well as the healer of the sick. She uses her magical powers to temporarily breathe life into Osiris to rouse him long enough for her to conceive their son, Horus. With the help of Thoth, she heals Horus after he has been bitten by a scorpion.

Her ability to revive Osiris from death and nurse Horus from illness reinforces her prodigious skill in healing—a skill she was later able to use to benefit humankind.

Isis is the lap or throne from which Horus emerges and upon which he is seated. Her presence legitimizes his right to rule and bestows on him divine qualities and powers. The same legitimacy and powers are extended to the living pharaoh who is identified with Horus and assumes his name as soon as he claims his place on the throne. Horus, begotten under highly unusual circumstances, becomes identified as the living god and savior. He is the heir and successor of Osiris, responsible for avenging his father's murder and for holding the forces of chaos in check. Egyptians believed that he was embodied in the living pharaoh. At the pharaoh's death, Horus's power and authority is transferred to his successor who then becomes the new embodiment of Horus. The dead pharaoh, through the efforts, magic, and with the accompaniment of Isis, becomes one with Osiris in the afterlife. Isis acts as the mediator who makes possible the birth and nourishment of the new Horus within the living pharaoh. She also acts as the psychopomp who guides the dead pharaoh to the afterlife to join Osiris.

The myth has its roots in the geography of Egypt. Egyptian civilization clustered along the Nile valley, bordered on either side by a harsh desert terrain that served as a buffer to protect and encase its culture. Life in the Nile Valley depended on the cyclical fluctuations and permutations of the river. Beginning in late spring, the melting snows from the mountains of Ethiopia and Uganda where the river originates would cause the Nile to flood. From October to February, the river subsided, depositing fertile mountain soil on the valley fields and allowing the planting cycle to begin. From March until June, drought prevailed. Egyptians would take advantage of the flooding period to trap water for later use. This alternating cycle of drought and flooding of the Nile made possible the cultivation of crops in an otherwise hostile environment.

The myth of the death and resurrection of Osiris suggests the cyclical movement of vegetative life. Osiris's association with fertility is readily apparent. Like the crops, Osiris grows to maturity and dies only to be reborn again with the onset of a new cycle. Egyptians made clay figurines of Osiris's body into which they pressed seeds. The seeds would germinate, and a miniature field of grain would sprout from the god's body. Osiris's mutilation and dismemberment were signified at the time of harvest with the cutting and trampling of the grain. And just as Osiris emerges from the dead in the afterlife, so, too, new life emerges with the sprouting grain of the next planting cycle. In his association with fertility and in his capacity as god of the afterlife, Osiris, therefore, embodies the continuity of the life force that dies and is resurrected in an ongoing, eternal cycle.

Isis's role in the perpetuation of this cycle is crucial. Her tears for the dead Osiris cause the Nile to flood and replenish the soil to facilitate the growth of new life; her untiring devotion to her brother/spouse brings about his resurrection; her initiative in the act of procreation results in the conception of Horus; her intervention enables Horus to thrive and defeat Seth; her labors bestow on Osiris eternal fame as the supreme god in the afterlife; her presence makes possible the transference of Horus's divine power from the dead pharaoh to his living successor; and her miraculous abilities enable her to grant immortality to her devotees as she had been able to do with Osiris.

Unfortunately no complete version of the myth of Isis and Osiris has survived from Egypt. Fragments of the myth appear intermittently in a variety of ancient texts. The oldest, known as the *Pyramid Texts,* were compiled from the hieroglyphics on pyramid walls and are dated approximately 2625 B.C.E. Their purpose was to guide deceased pharaohs as they navigated their way through the afterlife to arrive at the throne of Osiris and achieve immortality with the gods. A few centuries later these instructions, which by now had been democratized and provided nobles with access to the afterlife, were carved on coffins and known as the *Coffin Texts.* Later still in a process of further democratization, the texts were copied on papyrus scrolls that were placed inside the coffin or tomb. The numerous sources were eventually compiled into a series of works known collectively as *The Book of the Dead,* dating approximately 1320 B.C.E.

These Egyptian texts make reference to ancient Egyptian mythology and rituals. But the references are partial, frequently obscure, sometimes at variance with one another, and occasionally unintelligible. For a more systematic and comprehensive understanding of Egyptian mythology, we need to turn to Greek and Roman writings. For a complete description of the myth of Isis and Osiris, we must turn to the work of Plutarch, a Greek traveler and historian of the first century after the Common Era. Unfortunately in his retelling of the myth of Isis and Osiris, Plutarch conflates the deities of ancient Egypt with the deities of ancient Greece, occasionally using the names synonymously and attributing the deeds of Egyptian deities to their counterparts in Greece. But in spite of all its shortcomings, Plutarch's version remains the most comprehensive rendering of the myth of Isis and Osiris and is considered to be essentially accurate. In the selection below Plutarch substitutes the name Typhon for Seth.

Plutarch's rendition of the myth appears in Volume 5 of his *Moralia.* The selection below is translated by Frank C. Babbitt.

REFERENCES

Anthes, Rudolf. "Mythologies in Ancient Egypt." *Mythologies of the Ancient World.* Ed. Samuel Noah Kramer. New York: Anchor/Doubleday, 1961. 15–92.

Armour, Robert A. *Gods and Myths of Ancient Egypt.* 2nd ed. New York: American U of Cairo P, 1986.

Babbitt, Frank Cole, trans. *Plutarch's Moralia.* The Loeb Classical Library. Vol. V. Massachusetts: Harvard UP, 1962. 15 vols.

Bleeker, C. J. "Isis and Hathor: Two Ancient Egyptian Goddesses." *The Book of the Goddess, Past and Present: An Introduction to Her Religion.* Ed. Carl Olson. New York: Crossroad, 1990. 29–48.

Budge, E. A. Wallis. *Egyptian Religion.* New York: Barnes and Noble, 1994.

Campbell, Joseph. *The Masks of God: Oriental Mythology*. New York: Viking, 1962.

Faulkner, Raymond O. Trans. *The Ancient Egyptian Book of the Dead*. Ed. Carol Andrews. New York: Macmillan, 1984.

Harvey, Andrew, and Anne Haring. *The Divine Feminine: Exploring the Feminine Face of God Throughout the World*. Berkeley: Connari P, 1996.

Kinsley, David. *The Goddesses' Mirror: Visions of the Divine From East and West*. Albany: SUNY P, 1989.

The Ancient Egyptian Book of the Dead in Plutarch's *Moralia*

Isis and Osiris

Here follows the story related in the briefest possible words with the omission of everything that is merely unprofitable or superfluous:

They say that the Sun, when he became aware of Rhea's intercourse with Cronus, invoked a curse upon her that she should not give birth to a child in any month or any year; but Hermes, being enamoured of the goddess, consorted with her. Later, playing at draughts with the moon, he won from her the seventieth part of each of her periods of illumination, and from all the winnings he composed five days, and intercalated them as an addition to the three hundred and sixty days. The Egyptians even now call these five days intercalated and celebrate them as the birthdays of the gods. They relate that on the first of these days Osiris was born, and at the hour of his birth a voice issued forth saying, "The Lord of All advances to the light." But some relate that a certain Pamyles, while he was drawing water in Thebes, heard a voice issuing from the shrine of Zeus, which bade him proclaim with a loud voice that a mighty and beneficent king, Osiris, had been born; and for this Cronus entrusted to him the child Osiris, which he brought up. It is in his honour that the festival of Pamylia is celebrated, a festival which resembles the phallic processions. On the second of these days Arueris was born whom they call Apollo, and some call him also the elder Horus. On the third day Typhon was born, but not in due season or manner, but with a blow he broke through his mother's side and leapt forth. On the fourth day Isis was born in the regions that are ever moist; and on the fifth Nephthys, to whom they give the name of Finality and the name of Aphroditê, and some also the name of Victory. There is also a tradition that Osiris and Arueris were sprung from the Sun, Isis from Hermes, and Typhon and Nephthys from Cronus. For this reason the kings considered the third of the intercalated days as inauspicious, and transacted no business on that day, nor did they give any attention to their bodies until nightfall. They relate, moreover, that Nephthys became the wife of Typhon; but Isis and Osiris were enamoured of each other and consorted together in the darkness of the womb before their birth. Some say that Arueris came from this union and was called the elder Horus by the Egyptians, but Apollo by the Greeks.

One of the first acts related of Osiris in his reign was to deliver the Egyptians from their destitute and brutish manner of living. This he did by showing them the fruits of cultivation, by giving them laws, and by teaching them to honour the gods. Later he travelled over the whole earth civilizing it without the slightest need of arms, but most of the peoples he won over to his way by the charm of his persuasive discourse combined with song and all manner of music. Hence the Greeks came to identify him with Dionysus.

During his absence the tradition is that Typhon attempted nothing revolutionary because Isis, who was in control, was vigilant and alert; but when he returned home Typhon contrived a treacherous plot against him and formed a group of conspirators seventy-two in number. He had also the co-operation of a queen from Ethiopia who was there at the time and whose name they report as Aso. Typhon, having secretly measured Osiris's body and having made ready a beautiful chest of corresponding size artistically ornamented, caused it to be brought into the room where the festivity was in progress. The company was much pleased at the sight of it and admired it greatly, whereupon Typhon jestingly promised to present it to the man who should find the chest to be exactly his length when he lay down in it. They all tried it in turn, but no one fitted it; then Osiris got into it and lay down, and those who were in the plot ran to it and slammed down the lid, which they fastened by nails from the outside and also by using molten lead. Then they carried the chest to the river and sent it on its way to the sea through the Tanitic Mouth. Wherefore the Egyptians even to this day name this mouth the hateful and execrable. Such is the tradition. They say also that the date on which this deed was done was the seventeenth day of Athyr, when the sun passes through Scorpion, and in the twenty-eighth year of the reign of Osiris; but some say that these are the years of his life and not of his reign.

The first to learn of the deed and to bring to men's knowledge an account of what had been done were the Pans and Satyrs who lived in the region around Chemmis, and so, even to this day, the sudden confusion and consternation of a crowd is called a panic. Isis, when the tidings reached her, at once cut off one of her tresses and put on a garment of mourning in a place where the city still bears the name of Kopto. Others think that the name means deprivation, for they also express "deprive" by means of "koptein." But Isis wandered everywhere at her wits' end; no one whom she approached did she fail to address, and even when she met some little children she asked them about the chest. As it happened, they had seen it, and they told her the mouth of the river through which the friends of Typhon had launched the coffin into the sea. Wherefore the Egyptians think that little children possess the power of prophecy, and they try to divine the future from the portents which they find in children's words, especially when children are playing about in holy places and crying out whatever chances to come into their minds.

They relate also that Isis, learning that Osiris in his love had consorted with her sister through ignorance, in the belief that she was Isis, and seeing the proof of this in the garland of melilote which he had left with Nephthys, sought to find the child; for the mother, immediately after its birth, had exposed it because of her fear of Typhon. And when the child had been found, after great toil and trouble, with the help of dogs which led Isis to it, it was brought up and became her guardian and attendant, receiving the name of Anubis, and it is said to protect the gods just as dogs protect men.

Thereafter Isis, as they relate, learned that the chest had been cast up by the sea near the land of Byblus and that the waves had gently set it down in the midst of a clump of heather. The heather in a short time ran up into a very beautiful and massive stock, and enfolded and embraced the chest with its growth and concealed it within its trunk. The king of the country admired the great size of the plant, and cut off the portion that enfolded the chest (which was now hidden from sight), and used it as a pillar to support the roof of his house. These facts, they say, Isis ascertained by the divine inspiration of Rumour, and came to Byblus and sat down by a spring, all dejection and tears; she exchanged no word with anybody, save only that she welcomed the queen's maidservants and treated them with great amiability, plaiting their hair for them and imparting to their persons a wondrous fragrance from her own body. But when the queen observed her maidservants, a longing came upon her for the unknown woman and for such hairdressing and for a body fragrant with ambrosia. Thus it happened that Isis was sent for and became so intimate with the queen that the queen made her the nurse of her baby. They say that the king's name was Malcander; the queen's name some say was Astartê, others Saosis, and still others Nemanûs, which the Greeks would call Athenais.

They relate that Isis nursed the child by giving it her finger to suck instead of her breast, and in the night she would burn away the mortal portions of its body. She herself would turn into a swallow and flit about the pillar with a wailing lament, until the queen who had been watching, when she saw her babe on fire, gave forth a loud cry and thus deprived it of immortality. Then the goddess disclosed herself and asked for the pillar which served to support the roof. She removed it with the greatest ease and cut away the wood of the heather which surrounded the chest; then, when she had wrapped up the wood in a linen cloth and had poured perfume upon it, she entrusted it to the care of the kings; and even to this day the people of Byblus venerate this wood which is preserved in the shrine of Isis. Then the goddess threw herself down upon the coffin with such a dreadful wailing that the younger of the king's sons expired on the spot. The elder son she kept with her, and, having placed the coffin on board a boat, she put out from land. Since the Phaedrus river toward the early morning fostered a rather boisterous wind, the goddess grew angry and dried up its stream.

In the first place where she found seclusion, when she was quite by herself, they relate that she opened the chest and laid her face upon the face within and caressed it and wept. The child came quietly up behind her and saw what was there, and when the goddess became aware of his presence, she turned about and gave him one awful look of anger. The child could not endure the fright, and died. Others will not have it so, but assert that he fell overboard into the sea from the boat that was mentioned above. He also is the recipient of honours because of the goddess; for they say that the Maneros of whom the Egyptians sing at their convivial gatherings is this very child. Some say, however, that his name was Palaestinus or Pelusius, and that the city founded by the goddess was named in his honor. They also recount that this Maneros who is the theme of their songs was the first to invent music. But some say that the word is not the name of any person, but an expression belonging to the vocabulary of drinking and feasting: "Good luck be ours in things like this!", and that this is really the idea expressed by the exclamation "maneros" whenever the Egyptians use it. In the same way we may be sure that the likeness of a corpse which, as it is exhibited to them, is carried around in a chest, is not a reminder of what happened to Osiris, as some assume; but it is to urge them, as they contemplate it, to use and to enjoy the present, since all very soon must be what it is now and this is their purpose in introducing it into the midst of merry-making.

As they relate, Isis proceeded to her son Horus, who was being reared in Buto, and bestowed the chest in a place well out of the way; but Typhon, who was hunting by night in the light of the moon, happened upon it. Recognizing the body he divided it into fourteen parts and scattered them, each in a different place. Isis learned of this and sought for them again, sailing through the swamps in a boat of papyrus. This is the reason why people sailing in such boats are not harmed by the crocodiles, since these creatures in their own way show either their fear or their reverence for the goddess.

The traditional result of Osiris's dismemberment is that there are many so-called tombs of Osiris in Egypt; for Isis held a funeral for each part when she had found it. Others deny this and assert that she caused effigies of him to be made and these she distributed among the several cities, pretending that she was giving them his body, in order that he might receive divine honours in a greater number of cities, and also that, if Typhon should succeed in overpowering Horus, he might despair of ever finding the true tomb when so many were pointed out to him, all of them called the tomb of Osiris.

Of the parts of Osiris's body the only one which Isis did not find was the male member, for the reason that this had been at once tossed into the river, and the lepidotus, the sea-bream, and the pike had fed upon it; and it is from these very fishes the Egyptians are most scrupulous in abstaining. But Isis made a replica of the member to take its place, and consecrated the phallus, in honour of which the Egyptians even at the present day celebrate a festival.

Later, as they relate, Osiris came to Horus from the other world and exercised and trained him for the battle. After a time Osiris asked Horus what he held to be the most noble of all things. When Horus replied, "To avenge one's father and mother for evil done to them," Osiris then asked him what animal he considered the most useful for them who go forth to battle; and when Horus said, "A horse," Osiris was surprised and raised the question why it was that he had not rather said a lion than a horse. Horus answered that lion was a useful thing for a man in need of assistance, but that a horse served best for cutting off the flight of an enemy and annihilating him. When Osiris heard this he was much pleased, since he felt that Horus had now an adequate preparation. It is said that, as many were continually transferring their allegiance to Horus, Typhon's concubine, Thueris, also came over to him; and a serpent which pursued her was cut to pieces by Horus's men, and now, in memory of this, the people throw down a rope in their midst and chop it up.

Now the battle, as they relate, lasted many days and Horus prevailed. Isis, however, to whom Typhon was delivered in chains, did not cause him to be put to death, but released him and let him go. Horus could not endure this with equanimity, but laid hands upon his mother and wrested the royal diadem from her head; but Hermes put upon her a helmet like unto the head of a cow.

Typhon formally accused Horus of being an illegitimate child, but with the help of Hermes to plead his cause it was decided by the gods that he also was legitimate. Typhon was then overcome in two other battles. Osiris consorted with Isis after his death, and she became the mother of Harpocrates, untimely born and weak in his lower limbs.

Questions for Review and Discussion

1. The myth of Isis and Osiris tells the story of a god who suffered a mortal's fate of death and dismemberment. He becomes god of the dead, while his son Horus embodies the living god. The myth bears resemblance to the Christian story of Jesus. What are some of the similarities and/or differences in the two stories?

2. What parallels exist in the Egyptian triad of Osiris, Horus, and Isis with that of the Christian concept of the trinity of Father, Son, and Holy Ghost? Is it possible that one could be the precursor of the other?

3. Plutarch tells us that Isis assumes the guise of a bird in the palace at Byblos. Where else in the myth does Isis assume birdlike qualities? What is the significance of this transformation?

4. What are the metaphorical implications of Seth's dismemberment and trampling of the body of Osiris?

5. Horus's defeat of Seth restores order and fertility to the land by holding the forces of chaos in check. But this battle occurs repeatedly and on an annual basis. Why is Horus never able to annihilate Seth completely and permanently?

6. What is the role of Osiris in this myth? What do you think of Osiris?

7. At one point in the myth, Isis has to locate the dismembered parts of Osiris's body. She is able to find all but one part—the god's sexual organ, which has apparently been devoured by a fish. What are some possible interpretations for this event?

8. The myth of Isis and Osiris lends itself to a variety of different interpretations. What are some of the possible interpretations?

9. Isis plays the role of healer, caregiver, and nurturer to both her spouse and her son. What claims can be made for or against Isis as a figure who reinforces gender stereotypes?

Chapter 2

Inanna

GLOSSARY OF NAMES

AN   Sky god

DUMUZI   Shepherd-King; Inanna's husband

ENKI   God of Wisdom and Flowing Water; son of An and Nammu

ENLIL   Air god; son of An and Ninhursag

ERESHKIGAL   Queen of the Underworld ("the Great Below"); Inanna's sister

GALATUR   Creature fashioned by Enki to rescue Inanna

GALLA   Demons from the underworld

GESHTINANNA   Dumuzi's sister

GILGAMESH   Inanna's earthly brother

INANNA   Queen of Heaven and Earth; daughter of Nanna

KI (NINHURSAG)   Earth goddess; Queen of the Mountain; wife of An

KURGARRA   Creature fashioned by Enki to rescue Inanna

LILITH   Unwelcome occupant of the Huluppu tree. (See also Chapter 11 in text)

NANNA   Moon god; son of Enlil

NETI   Gatekeeper of the Underworld

NINSHUBUR   Inanna's priestess and loyal servant

SIRTUR   Dumuzi's mother

UTU   Sun god; son of Nanna

The most revered deity of ancient Sumer was the goddess Inanna, the Queen of Heaven and Earth. Hymns in praise of her and stories about her are inscribed in tablets that date back to 2000 B.C.E. Inanna, known to the Semites as Ishtar, was also referred to as the First Daughter of the Moon and the Morning and Evening Star. Envisioned as a young, radiant, and sexually vibrant female, she was a multifaceted goddess with prolific powers, including the power over the fertility and fecundity of plants, animals, and humans. Her journey to the underworld earned her access to the mysterious powers of death and rebirth. Her association with the moon, with earthly fertility, and with the mystery of life and death gave her sovereignty over the sky, the earth, and the underworld. The Sumerians believed that Inanna was an all-powerful goddess with a diverse set of powers and roles whose domain extended throughout the far reaches of the earth and all that inhabited it.

Sumer, located in the southern half of modern Iraq, gave rise to a highly gifted, cultured, and technologically innovative civilization that spawned the first urban centers and developed the cuneiform system of writing. Cuneiform was eventually disseminated throughout the ancient Near East. The Sumerians were a non-Semitic, non-Indo-European people who dominated much of the Near East between approximately 3500 and 2000 B.C.E., at the end of which time they were

Sumerian Pantheon

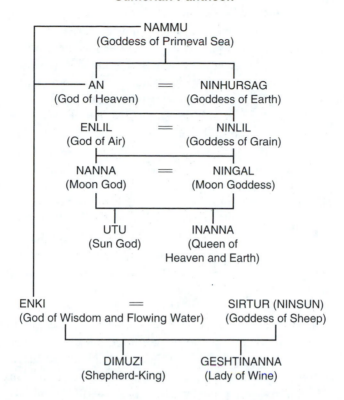

conquered by the Semites. Flourishing 5,000 years ago, the Sumerians have left their imprint on many areas of human knowledge, including religion, law, architecture, education, art, and literature. Their impact was so pervasive that we continue to feel its presence today to such a degree that ancient Sumer has been designated the "cradle of civilization."

Sovereignty over the land of Sumer and its neighboring areas resided with the city-state that demonstrated its superior military muscle. The "Sumerian King List" records the names of a succession of kings and their dynasties. Sargon, a Semite, eventually captured Sumer and most of western Asia and established his capital in Agade, also known as Akkad. Sumer gradually assumed the name Sumer-Akkad, and Akkadian eventually replaced the Sumerian tongue as the spoken language. Sumer fluctuated between periods in which its civilization flourished and waned, depending on whether it experienced military victory or defeat. The victory of the Semite Hammurabi, King of Babylon, over his Sumerian counterpart, Rin-Sin, King of Larsa, and Hammurabi's subsequent reign (1792–1750 B.C.E.) marked the formal end of Sumerian civilization and the beginning of the Babylonian civilization. But while Babylonian kings were Semites and the spoken language was Akkadian, the language of Sumer survived as the language for formal and written communication.

Moreover, Sumerian mythology and literature survived and formed the nucleus for what was to become the mythology and literature of Babylon.

The leading deities of the Sumerian pantheon were the Sky God An; the Earth Goddess Ki who later became known as Ninhursag, Queen of the Mountain; their off-spring, the Air God Enlil who eventually assumed leadership position in the pantheon; Enlil's son, the Moon God Nanna; Nanna's two offspring—Utu the Sun God and Inanna the Goddess of the Morning and Evening Star; and the son of An and Nammu, Enki the God of Wisdom and Flowing Water. The sky, earth, air, and water deities were collaboratively responsible for creating and controlling the elements of the earth and sky. To govern the earth and sky and maintain order and harmony within and between the elements, the gods devised a universal and absolute set of rules, known as the holy *me*. In a drunken stupor, Enki offers the *me* to the goddess Inanna.

Sumerian religion featured public rituals and ceremonies performed at the city temple. In addition to the daily sacrifices offered to the gods, the Sumerians engaged in a variety of festivals and monthly celebrations. The most important of these was the annual New Year celebration that culminated in the *hieros gamos* or sacred marriage between the goddess Inanna (embodied in the High Priestess) and the reigning monarch (embodying the shepherd-king Dumuzi), which took place in Inanna's temple in Uruk. The king, playing the role of Dumuzi and personifying the land of Sumer, consummated his marriage to the goddess by copulating with the sacred priestess who embodied her. The sexual union between the incarnations of Inanna and Dumuzi was perceived as a fundamentally sacred activity that was deemed essential for the future fertility and prosperity of the community.

In order to situate the readings below, which begin with the courtship of Inanna and Dumuzi, a brief summary of Inanna's story is necessary. The Inanna cycle opens with "The Huluppu-Tree" in which Inanna rescues the huluppu tree from the river and nurtures it to maturity. The huluppu tree may have been the Sumerian version of a combination of the Tree of Life and the Tree of Knowledge of Good and Evil. The tree becomes the habitat of the Anzu bird, the snake, and Lilith—unwelcome guests whose presence interferes with Inanna's desire to carve a throne and a bed from the tree trunk. Unable to rid the tree of its intruders, Inanna seeks male assistance. Her earthly brother, Gilgamesh, obliges by killing the serpent and causing the Anzu bird and Lilith to flee. He uproots the tree and takes it to the city where he carves a throne and a bed for Inanna. In gratitude, Inanna reciprocates his gifts by fashioning a *pukku* and *mikku* for her brother. The meanings of *pukku* and *mikku* have yet to be determined, but one possible explanation is that they represent emblems of kingship.

"Inanna and the God of Wisdom" begins with Inanna celebrating her woman-hood ("Rejoicing at her wondrous vulva") and anxious to test her powers. She visits Enki, the God of Wisdom and of the Waters. Enki celebrates her arrival with food and drink, and in a drunken stupor, offers her the gifts of the *me*, the decrees governing the universe. These number over one hundred, and included among them are those referring to kingship with its accompanying privileges and paraphernalia; the arts of speech, lovemaking, song, music, and dance; and miscellaneous other items that deal with governing, culture, and human relations. Enki's last and most important gift, without which all the other *me* are ineffectual, is the gift of making decisions. Elated, Inanna loads the *me* on the Boat of Heaven and heads for Uruk. Meanwhile, Enki, having emerged from his drunken daze, regrets his action and sends Isimud and an entourage of wild-haired sea creatures to retrieve the *me* from Inanna. Their attempts are thwarted by Inanna's trusted servant, the priestess Nin-shubur. Inanna finally arrives in Uruk, at which time more *me* appear than Enki had originally given. The new *me* pertain to Inanna's feminine attributes ("the art of the woman")—as if to suggest that Inanna emerges from her experience as a more com-plete female. Enki then grants her permission to retain the holy *me* in her temple at Uruk, thereby elevating that city's stature and establishing a bond between his sacred city of Eridu with Uruk.

In "The Courtship of Inanna and Dumuzi," Utu engages in matchmaking and suggests that Inanna take the shepherd Dumuzi as her bridegroom. Inanna expresses her preference for the farmer. An incensed Dumuzi proceeds to woo Inanna and eventually wins her over. There follows a delightful and lengthy descrip-tion of Inanna preening herself to receive her bridegroom and an unabashed description of their lovemaking. Inanna then pledges to serve Dumuzi as her king and husband in all aspects of his reign. Since Dumuzi is listed as a historical king, Inanna's commitment thereby extends not only to Dumuzi but also to the earthly rulers who sequentially incarnate him. The section concludes with Dumuzi asking to be released from Inanna ("Set me free") in order to assume his role as king.

"The Descent of Inanna" describes Inanna's journey to the netherworld ("the Great Below") to visit her sister Ereshkigal. She begins by abandoning her seven cities and their temples, as if to suggest she is surrendering her powers on heaven and earth. She provides her faithful servant Ninshubur with explicit instructions to res-cue her from the netherworld should she fail to emerge from her ordeal after three days. She enters the underworld and is made to relinquish an item of jewelry, a sym-bol of office, or a piece of clothing at each of its seven gates. Finally gaining access to Ereshkigal in the throne room, she stands naked and vulnerable. Ereshkigal "fastens the eye of death" on her sister and hangs her rotting corpse on a hook in the wall.

When Inanna fails to emerge from her ordeal at the end of the third day, Nin-shubur laments for her mistress and follows her instructions by soliciting the assis-tance of Enlil, Nanna, and Enki consecutively. Only Enki agrees to help. From the dirt under his fingernails, he fashions two creatures, a *kurgarra* and a *galatur*, that he sends as emissaries to the underworld. He instructs them to empathize with Ereshkigal's agony, thereby obtaining the release of Inanna. Following directions, the two creatures win the conditional release of Inanna. However, she must send a substitute to take her place in the underworld. Accompanied by the *galla*, demons from the underworld, Inanna searches for a substitute, finally resolving on Dumuzi. The section concludes with Dumuzi's appeal to Utu for help.

"The Dream of Dumuzi" begins with Dumuzi tearfully narrating his dream to his sister Geshtinanna. She interprets it by predicting his impending capture by the *galla.* Dumuzi extracts a promise from Geshtinanna not to disclose his hiding place. In spite of her capture and subsequent torture by the *galla,* Geshtinanna refuses to reveal her brother's whereabouts. Eventually, however, the *galla* locate Dumuzi, seize him, and send him to the underworld.

The final section, "The Return," begins with Inanna weeping for her beloved Dumuzi. Sirtur, his mother, also weeps for him, as does Geshtinanna. Inanna is so touched by Geshtinanna's weeping that she permits the sister to act as Dumuzi's surrogate in the underworld for six months of every year. Dumuzi's emergence from the underworld enables him to share his stored vitality, vigor, and wisdom with the surrounding community, thereby precipitating the much needed renewal.

As the goddess of love and sexual desire, Inanna embodies the force in animal and human nature that is unable to resist the urge to mate. Endowed with a healthy dose of feminine attributes ("the art of the woman"), Inanna not only flaunts her feminine sexuality, she positively gushes in ecstasy over it. Her annual participation in the sacred union with Dumuzi performed the dual function of legitimizing the king's position as the political sovereign and ensured earthly prosperity, fertility, and abundance for the subsequent year. Dumuzi's "death" (his time spent in the "Great Below" when Inanna is denied her lover's presence and fertility is on the decline) explains the corresponding withering of vegetation during the heat and aridity of the inhospitable summer months. Dumuzi's emergence from the "Great Below" at the autumnal equinox and his subsequent sexual union with Inanna precipitates the regeneration of the earth. The Sumerians celebrated this auspicious event at the sacred marriage rites during the New Year Festival, at which time the annual sacred marriage between the priestess as Inanna and the reigning monarch as the resurrected god/lover was commemorated with music, song, ceremony, and, possibly, sexual activity in and around the temple grounds.

The selection from the Inanna cycle below is from *Inanna, Queen of Heaven: Her Stories and Hymns From Sumer* by Diane Wolkstein and Samuel Noah Kramer.

REFERENCES

Armstrong, Karen. *A History of God: The 4,000-Year Quest of Judaism, Christianity, and Islam.* New York: Ballantine, 1993.

Bottero, Jean. *Religion in Ancient Mesopotamia.* Trans. Teresa Lavender Fagan. Chicago: U of Chicago P, 2001.

Jacobsen, Thorkild. *The Harps That Once . . . Sumerian Poetry in Translation.* New Haven: Yale UP, 1987.

———. *The Treasures of Darkness: A History of Mesopotamian Religion.* New Haven: Yale UP, 1976.

———. *Toward the Image of Tammuz and Other Essays on Mesopotamian History and Culture.* Ed. William L. Morgan. Massachusetts: Harvard UP, 1970.

Kramer, Samuel Noah. "Mythology of Sumer and Akkad." *Mythologies of the Ancient World.* Ed. Samuel Noah Kramer. New York: Anchor/Doubleday, 1961. 95–137.

————. *The Sacred Marriage Rite: Aspects of Faith, Myth, and Ritual in Ancient Sumer.* Bloomington: Indiana UP, 1969.

————. *Sumerian Mythology: A Study of Spiritual and Literary Achievement in the Third Millennium B.C.* Rev. Ed. Philadelphia: U of Pennsylvania P, 1972.

Lerner, Gerda. *The Creation of Patriarchy.* New York: Oxford UP, 1986.

Perera, Sylvia Brinton. "The Descent of Inanna: Myth and Therapy." *Feminist Archetypal Theory: Interdisciplinary Re-Visions of Jungian Thought.* Ed. Estella Lauter and Carol Schreier Rupprecht. Knoxville: U of Tennesee P, 1985. 137–186.

Pritchard, James B., ed. *Ancient Near Eastern Texts: Relating to the Old Testament.* 3rd ed. Princeton: Princeton UP, 1969.

Sandars, N. K., trans. *Poems of Heaven and Hell From Ancient Mesopotamia.* London: Penguin, 1971.

Stuckey, Johanna H. "Inanna and the Huluppu Tree": An Ancient Mesopotamian Narrative of Goddess Demotion." *Feminist Poetics of the Sacred: Creative Suspicions.* Ed. Frances Devlin-Glass and Lyn McCredden. Oxford: Oxford UP, 2001. 91–105.

Wolkstein, Diane, and Samuel Noah Kramer. *Inanna, Queen of Heaven: Her Stories and Hymns From Sumer.* New York: Harper and Row, 1983.

Inanna, Queen of Heaven and Earth

The Courtship of Inanna and Dumuzi

Inanna, at her mother's command,
Bathed and anointed herself with scented oil.
She covered her body with the royal white robe.
She readied her dowry.
5   She arranged her precious lapis beads around her neck.
She took her seal in her hand.

Dumuzi waited expectantly.
Inanna opened the door for him.
Inside the house she shone before him
10 Like the light of the moon.

Dumuzi looked at her joyously.
He pressed his neck close against hers.
He kissed her.

. . .

Inanna spoke:
15   "What I tell you
              Let the singer weave into song.
              What I tell you,

Let it flow from ear to mouth,
Let it pass from old to young:
20   My vulva, the horn,
The Boat of Heaven,
Is full of eagerness like the young moon.
My untilled land lies fallow.

As for me, Inanna,
25   Who will plow my vulva?
Who will plow my high field?
Who will plow my wet ground?

As for me, the young woman,
Who will plow my vulva?
30   Who will station the ox there?
Who will plow my vulva?"

Dumuzi replied:
"Great Lady, the king will plow your vulva.
I, Dumuzi the King, will plow your vulva."

35   Inanna:
"Then plow my vulva, man of my heart!
Plow my vulva!"

At the king's lap stood the rising cedar.
Plants grew high by their side.
40   Grains grew high by their side.
Gardens flourished luxuriantly.

. . .

Inanna sang:
"He has sprouted; he has burgeoned;
He is lettuce planted by the water.
45   He is the one my womb loves best.

My well-stocked garden of the plain,
My barley growing high in its furrow,
My apple tree which bears fruit up to its crown,
He is lettuce planted by the water.

50   My honey-man, my honey-man sweetens me always.
My lord, the honey-man of the gods,
He is the one my womb loves best.
His hand is honey, his foot is honey,
He sweetens me always.

. . .

55   My eager impetuous caresser of the navel,
     My caresser of the soft thighs,
     He is the one my womb loves best,
     He is lettuce planted by the water."

Dumuzi sang:
60   "O Lady, your breast is your field.
     Inanna, your breast is your field.
     Your broad field pours out plants.
     Your broad field pours out grain.
     Water flows from on high for your servant.
65   Bread flows from on high for your servant.
     Pour it out for me, Inanna.
     I will drink all you offer."

                    . . .

Inanna sang:
     "Make your milk sweet and thick, my bridegroom.
70   My shepherd, I will drink your fresh milk.
     Wild bull, Dumuzi, make your milk sweet and thick.
     I will drink your fresh milk.

     Let the milk of the goat flow in my sheepfold.
     Fill my holy churn with honey cheese.
75   Lord Dumuzi, I will drink your fresh milk.

     My husband, I will guard my sheepfold for you.
     I will watch over your house of life, the storehouse,
     The shining quivering place which delights Sumer—
     The house which decides the fates of the land,
80   The house which gives the breath of life to the people.
     I, the queen of the palace, will watch over your house."

                    . . .

Dumuzi spoke:
     "My sister, I would go with you to my garden.
     Inanna, I would go with you to my garden.
85   I would go with you to my orchard.
     I would go with you to my apple tree.
     There I would plant the sweet, honey-covered seed."

Inanna spoke:
     "He brought me into his garden.
90   My brother, Dumuzi, brought me into his garden.
     I strolled with him among the standing trees,
     I stood with him among the fallen trees,

By an apple tree I knelt as is proper.
Before my brother coming in song,
95 Who rose to me out of the poplar leaves,
Who came to me in the midday heat,
Before my lord Dumuzi,
I poured out plants from my womb,
I placed plants before him,
100 I poured out plants before him.
I placed grain before him,
I poured out grain before him.
I poured out grain from my womb."

Inanna sang:
105 "Last night as I, the queen, was shining bright,
Last night as I, the Queen of Heaven, was shining bright,
As I was shining bright and dancing,
Singing praises at the coming of the night—

He met me—he met me!
110 My lord Dumuzi met me.
He put his hand into my hand.
He pressed his neck close against mine.

My high priest is ready for the holy loins.
My lord Dumuzi is ready for the holy loins.
115 The plants and herbs in his field are ripe.
O Dumuzi! Your fullness is my delight!"

. . .

She called for it, she called for it, she called for the bed!
She called for the bed that rejoices the heart.
She called for the bed that sweetens the loins.
120 She called for the bed of kingship.
She called for the bed of queenship.

Inanna spread the bridal sheet across the bed.
She called to the king:
"The bed is ready!"
125 She called to her bridegroom:
"The bed is waiting!"

. . .

He put his hand in her hand.
He put his hand to her heart.
Sweet is the sleep of hand-to-hand.
130 Sweeter still the sleep of heart-to-heart.

Inanna spoke:

"I bathed for the wild bull,
I bathed for the shepherd Dumuzi,
I perfumed my sides with ointment,
135   I coated my mouth with sweet-smelling amber,
I painted my eyes with kohl.

He shaped my loins with his fair hands,
The shepherd Dumuzi filled my lap with cream and milk,
He stroked my pubic hair,
140   He watered my womb.
He laid his hands on my holy vulva,
He smoothed my black boat with cream,
He quickened my narrow boat with milk,
He caressed me on the bed.

145   Now I will caress my high priest on the bed,
I will caress the faithful shepherd Dumuzi,
I will caress his loins, the shepherdship of the land,
I will decree a sweet fate for him."

. . .

The king went with lifted head to the holy loins.
150   He went with lifted head to the loins of Inanna.
He went to the queen with lifted head.
He opened wide his arms to the holy priestess of heaven.

. . .

Inanna spoke:

"My beloved, the delight of my eyes, met me.
155   We rejoiced together.
He took his pleasure of me.
He brought me into his house.

He laid me down on the fragrant honey-bed.
My sweet love, lying by my heart,
160   Tongue-playing, one by one,
My fair Dumuzi did so fifty times.

Now, my sweet love is sated.
Now he says:
'Set me free, my sister, set me free.
165   You will be a little daughter to my father.
Come, my beloved sister, I would go to the palace.
Set me free . . .'"

My blossom-bearer, your allure was sweet.
My blossom-bearer in the apple orchard,
170   My bearer of fruit in the apple orchard,
Dumuzi-*abzu*, your allure was sweet.

My fearless one,
My holy statue,
My statue outfitted with sword and lapis lazuli diadem,
175   How sweet was your allure . . . ."

The Descent Of Inanna
From The Great Above to The Great Below

From the Great Above she opened her ear to the Great Below.
From the Great Above the goddess opened her ear to the Great Below.
180 From the Great Above Inanna opened her ear to the Great Below.

My Lady abandoned heaven and earth to descend to the underworld.
Inanna abandoned heaven and earth to descend to the underworld.
She abandoned her office of holy priestess to descend to the underworld.
She abandoned her seven temples to descend to the underworld.
185 She gathered together the seven *me*. °
She took them into her hands.
With the *me* in her possession, she prepared herself:

She placed the crown of the steppe on her head.
She arranged the dark locks of hair across her forehead.
190 She tied the small lapis beads around her neck,
Let the double strand of beads fall to her breast,
And wrapped the royal robe around her body.
She daubed her eyes with ointment called "Let him come, Let him come,"
Bound the breastplate called "Come, man, come!" around her chest,
195 Slipped the gold ring over her wrist,
And took the lapis measuring rod and line in her hand.

Inanna set out for the underworld.
Ninshubur, her faithful servant, went with her.
Inanna spoke to her, saying:
200   "Ninshubur, my constant support, who gives me wise advice,
My warrior who fights by my side,
I am descending to the underworld.
If I do not return,
Set up a lament for me by the ruins.
205   Beat the drum for me in the assembly places.

°attributes of civilization

Circle the houses of the gods.
Tear at your eyes, at your mouth, at your thighs.
Dress yourself in a single garment like a beggar.
Go to Nippur, to the temple of Enlil.
210   When you enter his holy shrine, cry out:
'O Father Enlil, do not let your daughter
Be put to death in the underworld.
Do not let your bright silver
Be covered with the dust of the underworld.
215   Do not let your precious lapis
Be broken into stone for the stoneworker.
Do not let your fragrant boxwood
Be cut into wood for the woodworker.
Do not let the holy priestess of heaven
220   Be put to death in the underworld.'

If Enlil will not help you,
Go to Ur, to the temple of Nanna.
Weep before Father Nanna.
If Nanna will not help you,
225   Go to Eridu, to the temple of Enki.
Weep before Father Enki.
Father Enki, the God of Wisdom, knows the food of life,
He knows the water of life;
He knows the secrets.
230   Surely he will not let me die."

Inanna continued on her way to the underworld.
Then she stopped and said:
      "Go now, Ninshubur—
      Do not forget the words I have commanded you."

235
When Inanna arrived at the outer gates of the underworld,
She knocked loudly.
She cried out in a fierce voice:
      "Open the door, gatekeeper!
      Open the door, Neti!
240
      I alone would enter!"

Neti, the chief gatekeeper of the underworld, asked:
      "Who are you?"

She answered:
      "I am Inanna, Queen of Heaven,
245   On my way to the East."

Neti said:

> "If you are truly Inanna, Queen of Heaven,
> On your way to the East,
> Why has your heart led you on the road
> From which no traveler returns?"

250

Inanna answered:

> "Because . . . of my older sister, Ereshkigal,
> Her husband, Gugalanna, the Bull of Heaven, has died.
> I have come to witness the funeral rites.
> Let the beer of his funeral rites be poured into the cup.
> Let it be done."

255

Neti spoke:

> "Stay here, Inanna, I will speak to my queen.
> I will give her your message."

260 Neti, the chief gatekeeper of the underworld,
Entered the palace of Ereshkigal, the Queen of the Underworld, and said:

> "My queen, a maid
> As tall as heaven,
> As wide as the earth,
> As strong as the foundations of the city wall,
> Waits outside the palace gates.

265

> She has gathered together the seven *me*.
> She has taken them into her hands.
> With the *me* in her possession, she has prepared herself:

270 When Ereshkigal heard this,
She slapped her thigh and bit her lip.
She took the matter into her heart and dwelt on it.
Then she spoke:

> "Come, Neti, my chief gatekeeper of the Underworld,
> Heed my words:
> Bolt the seven gates of the underworld.
> Then, one by one, open each gate a crack.
> Let Inanna enter.
> As she enters, remove her royal garments.
> Let the holy priestess of heaven enter bowed low."

275

280

Neti heeded the words of his queen.
He bolted the seven gates of the underworld.
Then he opened the outer gate.
He said to the maid:

> "Come, Inanna, enter."

285

When she entered the first gate,
From her head, the crown of the steppe was removed.

Inanna asked:
>"What is this?"

290 She was told:
>"Quiet, Inanna, the ways of the underworld are perfect.
>They may not be questioned."

When she entered the second gate,
From her neck the small lapis beads were removed.

295 Inanna asked:
>"What is this?"

She was told:
>"Quiet, Inanna, the ways of the underworld are perfect.
>They may not be questioned."

300 When she entered the third gate,
From her breast the double strand of beads was removed.

Inanna asked:
>"What is this?"

She was told:
305 >"Quiet, Inanna, the ways of the underworld are perfect.
>They may not be questioned."

When she entered the fourth gate,
From her chest the breastplate called "Come, man, come!" was removed.

Inanna asked:
310 >"What is this?"

She was told:
>"Quiet, Inanna, the ways of the underworld are perfect.
>They may not be questioned."

When she entered the fifth gate,
315 From her wrist the gold ring was removed.

Inanna asked:
>"What is this?"

She was told:
>"Quiet, Inanna, the ways of the underworld are perfect.
320 >They may not be questioned."

When she entered the sixth gate,
From her hand the lapis measuring rod and line was removed.

Inanna asked:
>"What is this?"

325   She was told:
>"Quiet, Inanna, the ways of the underworld are perfect.
>They may not be questioned."

When she entered the seventh gate,
From her body the royal robe was removed.

330   Inanna asked:
>"What is this?"

She was told:
>"Quiet, Inanna, the ways of the underworld are perfect.
>They may not be questioned."

335   Naked and bowed low, Inanna entered the throne room.
Ereshkigal rose from her throne.
Inanna started toward the throne.
The Annuna, the judges of the underworld, surrounded her.
They passed judgment against her.

340   Then Ereshkigal fastened on Inanna the eye of death.
She spoke against her the word of wrath.
She uttered against her the cry of guilt.

She struck her.

Inanna was turned into a corpse,
345   A piece of rotting meat,
And was hung from a hook on the wall.

. . .

When, after three days and three nights, Inanna had not returned,
Ninshubur set up a lament for her by the ruins.
She beat the drum for her in the assembly places.
350   She circled the houses of the gods.
She tore at her eyes; she tore at her mouth; she tore at her thighs.
She dressed herself in a single garment like a beggar.
Alone, she set out for Nippur and the temple of Enlil.

When she entered the holy shrine,
355   She cried out:
>"O' Father Enlil, do not let your daughter
>Be put to death in the underworld.
>Do not let your bright silver
>Be covered with the dust of the underworld.

360   Do not let your precious lapis
        Be broken into stone for the stoneworker.
        Do not let your fragrant boxwood
        Be cut into wood for the woodworker.
        Do not let the holy priestess of heaven
365   Be put to death in the underworld."

Father Enlil answered angrily:
        "My daughter craved the Great Above.
        Inanna craved the Great Below.
        She who receives the *me* of the underworld does not return.
370   She who goes to the Dark City stays there."

Father Enlil would not help.

Ninshubur went to Ur and the temple of Nanna.
When she entered the holy shrine,
She cried out:
375   "O Father Nanna, do not let your daughter
        Be put to death in the underworld.
        Do not let your bright silver
        Be covered with the dust of the underworld.
        Do not let your precious lapis
380   Be broken into stone for the stoneworker.
        Do not let your fragrant boxwood
        Be cut into wood for the woodworker.
        Do not let the holy priestess of heaven.
        Be put to death in the underworld."

385 Father Nanna answered angrily:
        "My daughter craved the Great Above.
        Inanna craved the Great Below.
        She who receives the *me* of the underworld does not return.
        She who goes to the Dark City stays there."

390 Father Nanna would not help.

Ninshubur went to Eridu and the temple of Enki.
When she entered the holy shrine,
She cried out:
        "O Father Enki, do not let your daughter
395   Be put to death in the underworld.
        Do not let your bright silver
        Be covered with the dust of the underworld.
        Do not let your precious lapis
        Be broken into stone for the stoneworker.

400   Do not let your fragrant boxwood
      Be cut into wood for the woodworker.
      Do not let the holy priestess of heaven
      Be put to death in the underworld."

Father Enki said:

405   "What has happened?
      What has my daughter done?
      Inanna! Queen of All the Lands! Holy Priestess of Heaven!
      What has happened?
      I am troubled. I am grieved."

410   From under his fingernail Father Enki brought forth dirt.
He fashioned the dirt into a *kurgarra,* a creature neither male nor female.
From under the fingernail of his other hand he brought forth dirt.
He fashioned the dirt into a *galatur,* a creature neither male nor female.

He gave the food of life to the *kurgarra.*
415   He gave the water of life to the *galatur.*
Enki spoke to the *kurgarra* and *galatur,* saying:
        "Go to the underworld,
        Enter the door like flies.
        Ereshkigal, the Queen of the Underworld, is moaning
420   With the cries of a woman about to give birth.
        No linen is spread over her body.
        Her breasts are uncovered.
        Her hair swirls about her head like leeks.
        When she cries, 'Oh! Oh! My inside!'
425   Cry also, 'Oh! Oh! Your inside!'
        When she cries, 'Oh! Oh! My outside!'
        Cry also, 'Oh! Oh! Your outside!'
        The queen will be pleased.
        She will offer you a gift.
430   Ask her only for the corpse that hangs from the hook on the wall.
        One of you will sprinkle the food of life on it.
        The other will sprinkle the water of life.
        Inanna will arise."

The *kurgarra* and the *galatur* heeded Enki's words.
435   They set out for the underworld.
Like flies, they slipped through the cracks of the gates.
They entered the throne room of the Queen of the Underworld.
No linen was spread over her body.
Her breasts were uncovered.
440   Her hair swirled around her head like leeks.

Ereshkigal was moaning:
>"Oh! Oh! My inside!"

They moaned:
>"Oh! Oh! Your inside!"

445 She moaned:
>"Ohhhh! Oh! My outside!"

They moaned:
>"Ohhhh! Oh! Your outside!"

She groaned:
450 >"Oh! Oh! My belly!"

They groaned:
>"Oh! Oh! Your belly!"

She groaned:
>"Oh! Ohhhh! My back!!"

455 They groaned:
>"Oh! Ohhhh! Your back!!"

She sighed:
>"Ah! Ah! My heart!"

They sighed:
460 >"Ah! Ah! Your heart!"

She sighed:
>"Ah! Ahhhh! My liver!"

They sighed:
>"Ah! Ahhhh! Your liver!"

465 Ereshkigal stopped.
She looked at them.
She asked:
>"Who are you,
>Moaning—groaning—sighing with me?
470 >If you are gods, I will bless you.
>If you are mortals, I will give you a gift.
>I will give you the water-gift, the river in its fullness."

The *kurgarra* and *galatur* answered:
>"We do not wish it."

475 Ereshkigal said:
>"I will give you the grain-gift, the fields in harvest."

The *kurgarra* and *galatur* said:
> "We do not wish it."

Ereshkigal said:

480
> "Speak then! What do you wish?"

They answered:
> "We wish only the corpse that hangs from the hook on the wall."

Ereshkigal said:
> "The corpse belongs to Inanna."

485   They said:
> "Whether it belongs to our queen,
> Whether it belongs to our king,
> That is what we wish."

The corpse was given to them.

490   The *kurgarra* sprinkled the food of life on the corpse.
The *galatur* sprinkled the water of life on the corpse.
Inanna arose . . . .

Inanna was about to ascend from the underworld
When the Annuna, the judges of the underworld, seized her.
495   They said:
> "No one ascends from the underworld unmarked.
> If Inanna wishes to return from the underworld,
> She must provide someone in her place."

As Inanna ascended from the underworld,
500   The *galla*, the demons of the underworld, clung to her side.
The *galla* were demons who know no food, who know no drink,
Who eat no offerings, who drink no libations,
Who accept no gifts.
They enjoy no lovemaking.
505   They have no sweet children to kiss.
They tear the wife from the husband's arms,
They tear the child from the father's knees,
They steal the bride from her marriage home.

The demons clung to Inanna.
510   The small *galla* who accompanied Inanna
Were like reeds the size of low picket fences.
The large *galla* who accompanied Inanna
Were like reeds the size of high picket fences.

The one who walked in front of Inanna was not a minister,
515   Yet he carried a sceptre.

The one who walked behind her was not a warrior,
Yet he carried a mace.
Ninshubur, dressed in a soiled sackcloth,
Waited outside the palace gates.
520 When she saw Inanna
Surrounded by the *galla,*
She threw herself in the dust at Inanna's feet.

The *galla* said:
    "Walk on, Inanna,
525   We will take Ninshubur in your place."

Inanna cried:
    "No! Ninshubur is my constant support.
    She is my *sukkal* who gives me wise advice.
    She is my warrior who fights by my side.
530   She did not forget my words.

    She set up a lament for me by the ruins.
    She beat the drum for me at the assembly places.
    She circled the houses of the gods.
    She tore at her eyes, at her mouth, at her thighs.
535   She dressed herself in a single garment like a beggar.

    Alone, she set out for Nippur and the temple of Enlil.
    She went to Ur and the temple of Nanna.
    She went to Eridu and the temple of Enki.
    Because of her, my life was saved.
540   I will never give Ninshubur to you."

The *galla* said:
    "Walk on, Inanna,
    We will accompany you to Umma."

In Umma, at the holy shrine,
545 Shara, the son of Inanna, was dressed in a soiled sackcloth.
When he saw Inanna
Surrounded by the *galla,*
He threw himself in the dust at her feet.

The *galla* said:
550   "Walk on to your city, Inanna.
    We will take Shara in your place."

Inanna cried:
    "No! Not Shara!
    He is my son who sings hymns to me.
555   He is my son who cuts my nails and smooths my hair.
    I will never give Shara to you."

The *galla* said:
> "Walk on, Inanna,
> We will accompany you to Badtibira."

560 In Badtibira, at the holy shrine,
Lulal, the son of Inanna, was dressed in a soiled sackcloth.
When he saw Inanna
Surrounded by the *galla,*
He threw himself in the dust at her feet.

565 The *galla* said:
> "Walk on to your city, Inanna,
> We will take Lulal in your place."

Inanna cried:
> "Not Lulal! He is my son.
570 > He is a leader among men.
> He is my right arm. He is my left arm.
> I will never give Lulal to you."

The *galla* said:
> "Walk on to your city, Inanna.
575 > We will go with you to the big apple tree in Uruk."

In Uruk, by the big apple tree,
Dumuzi, the husband of Inanna, was dressed in his shining *me*-garments.
He sat on his magnificent throne; (he did not move).

The *galla* seized him by his thighs.
580 They poured milk out of his seven churns.
They broke the reed pipe which the shepherd was playing.

Inanna fastened on Dumuzi the eye of death.
She spoke against him the word of wrath.
She uttered against him the cry of guilt:
585 > *"Take him! Take Dumuzi away!"*

The *galla,* who know no food, who know no drink,
Who eat no offerings, who drink no libations,
Who accept no gifts, seized Dumuzi.
They made him stand up; they made him sit down.
590 They beat the husband of Inanna.
They gashed him with axes.

The Return

Inanna wept for Dumuzi:
      "Gone is my husband, my sweet husband.
      Gone is my love, my sweet love.
      My beloved has been taken from the city.
595   O, you flies of the steppe,
      My beloved bridegroom has been taken from me
      Before I could wrap him with a proper shroud.

      The wild bull lives no more.
      The shepherd, the wild bull lives no more.
600   Dumuzi, the wild bull, lives no more."

      . . .

There is mourning in the house.
There is grief in the inner chambers.

The sister wandered about the city, weeping for her brother.
Geshtinanna wandered about the city, weeping for Dumuzi:
605   "O my brother! Who is your sister?
      I am your sister.

      . . .

      The day that dawns for you will also dawn for me.
      The day that you will see I will also see.

      I would find my brother! I would comfort him!
610   I would share his fate!"

When she saw the sister's grief,
When Inanna saw the grief of Geshtinanna,
She spoke to her gently:
      "Your brother's house is no more.
615   Dumuzi has been carried away by the *galla*.
      I would take you to him,
      But I do not know the place."

Then a fly appeared.
The holy fly circled the air above Inanna's head and spoke:
620   "If I tell you where Dumuzi is,
      What will you give me?"

Inanna said:
      "If you tell me,
      I will let you frequent the beer-houses and taverns.
625   I will let you dwell among the talk of the wise ones.

I will let you dwell among the songs of the minstrels."

The fly spoke:
>"Lift your eyes to the edges of the steppe,
>Lift your eyes to Arali.

630
>There you will find Geshtinanna's brother,
>There you will find the shepherd Dumuzi."

Inanna and Geshtinanna went to the edges of the steppe.
They found Dumuzi weeping.
Inanna took Dumuzi by the hand and said:

635
>"You will go to the underworld
>Half the year.
>Your sister, since she has asked,
>Will go the other half.
>On the day you are called,

640
>That day you will be taken.
>On the day Geshtinanna is called,
>That day you will be set free."

Questions for Review and Discussion

1. The language celebrating the courtship of Inanna and Dumuzi is sexually explicit. But because their union generates earthly fertility, the language is also enmeshed with references to bountiful harvests and plush vegetation. Inanna is both fertile womb and fertile field. Find examples of language that reflect both the sexual and the earthly fertility motif.

2. Inanna celebrates her feminine sexuality and makes abundantly clear her desire for and potential to achieve and deliver sexual pleasure. Her attitude reflects the Sumerian recognition that sex is pleasurable as well as necessary for procreation. Nevertheless, the Sumerians apparently deemed it necessary to circumscribe even a goddess' female sexuality and sexual pleasure under the institution of marriage. What possible reasons might they have had for doing so?

3. Why does Inanna visit the "Great Below?" Has she gained knowledge as a result of her death and rebirth? Explain.

4. Before she is allowed to encounter Ereshkigal, Inanna has to relinquish an item of jewelry or clothing or a symbol of her office at each of its seven gates. Why must Inanna be stripped naked before she encounters Ereshkigal?

5. When Neti, the chief gatekeeper of the underworld, informs Ereshkigal that her sister is at the entrance to the palace gates, Ereshkigal is so outraged by the news that she slaps her thigh and bites her lip. What is the source of Ereshkigal's anger with Inanna? Why does she "fasten the eye of death" on her sister?

6. Enki instructs the *kurgarra* and the *galatur* to mirror Ereshkigal's pain by engaging in an empathic lament with her in order to obtain the release of Inanna. What is the significance of this lament? What does it demonstrate?

7. Dumuzi manages to evade the *galla* temporarily. Eventually, however, they seize him and take him to the underworld. His sister Geshtinanna agrees to act as his surrogate and makes possible his resurrection for six months of every year. Discuss the role of Geshtinanna in the Inanna cycle. Is she a hero? Why or why not?

8. Inanna is the queen of heaven; her sister Ereshkigal is the queen of the underworld. Discuss these two figures as mirror images of each other. Does the existence of one necessitate the existence of the other?

9. There are striking parallels between the story of Inanna and the death and resurrection of Jesus in the Christian tradition. Identify the parallels and differences in the two stories.

10. Inanna is the all-powerful queen of heaven and earth in Sumerian mythology. Although the entire Inanna cycle is not included in the readings, it is clear from the complete work that, as powerful as she is, Inanna still needs male assistance. She cannot rid the huluppu tree of its uninvited guests without the assistance of Gilgamesh. She is empowered by the *me* but only because of Enki's drunken generosity. She emerges from the underworld because Enki sends creatures to rescue her. And she cannot regenerate the land without engaging in sexual intercourse with Dumuzi. What is the significance of the fact that in each of these cases, Inanna has to rely on a male to empower her and/or come to her aid? Explain.

Chapter 3

Tiamat

GLOSSARY OF NAMES

ABABU   Flood-storm or cloud-burst

ANSHAR   Horizon of Sky; male offspring of Tiamat and Apsu or Lahmu and Lahamu (ambiguity of origin)

ANU   Heaven, male offspring of Anshar and Kishar; father of Nudimmud Ea

ANUNNAKI   Gods of heaven and/or seven judges of hell

APSU   Father god; son (?) consort of Tiamat; sweet water ocean

ASARLUHI   Title indicating supremacy; given to Marduk by Anshar after his defeat of Tiamat

ASARULUDU   Seventh title given to Marduk; connotes mysterious powers

BARASHAKUSHU   Fourth title given to Marduk; he who sits on the throne

DAMKINA   Consort of Nudimmud Ea; mother of Marduk

IMHULLU   Hurricane; tempestuous winds

KAKA   Messenger and counselor of Anshar

KINGU   Consort of Tiamat, laborer

KISHAR   Horizon of earth; female offspring of Tiamat and Apsu or Lahmu and Lahamu (ambiguity of origin)

KULILI   A flying dragon; one of Tiamat's brood of monsters

KUSARIQU   Wild bison; one of Tiamat's brood of monsters

LAHMU   Silt; male offspring of Tiamat and Apsu; sibling of Lahamu; father of Anshar and Kishar (?)

LAHAMU   Silt, female offspring of Tiamat and Apsu; sibling of Lahmu; mother of Anshar and Kishar (?)

LUGALDIMMERANKIA   Fifth title given to Marduk; ruler of the universe

MARDUK   King of the gods, son of Nudimmud Ea and Damkina

MARUTUKKU   Third title given to Marduk; a pun on the words "weapon" and "man"

MUMMU   Mist, emanating from Tiamat and Apsu

NAMRU   Ninth title given to Marduk; brilliance and magical powers

NAMTILLAKU   Eighth title given to Marduk; comforter and god of life

NAR   Sixth title given to Marduk; supreme ruler of the universe

NUDIMUMMD EA   Intellect, wisdom; father of Marduk

TIAMAT   Mother goddess; salt-water ocean

The goddess Tiamat is the mother goddess, in relation to Apsu the father god, in the ancient Mesopotamian poem, the *Enuma Elish,* also known as *The Babylonian Creation.* The *Enuma Elish* takes its name from the opening words of the poem, which mean "When above" or "When on high." The words are somewhat equivalent to "In the beginning." Although none of its surviving tablets dates earlier than 1000 B.C.E., evidence of earlier Babylonian documents indicates that this hymn was composed some time during the First Babylonian Dynasty (1894–1595 B.C.E.), if

Babylonian Pantheon*

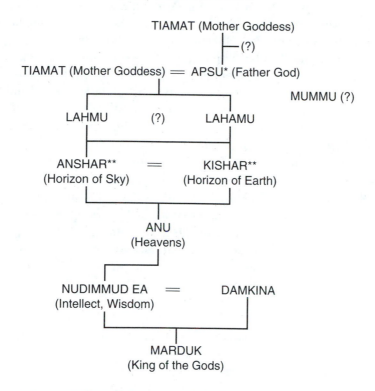

*   Apsu is the consort of Tiamat, but it is unclear from the text if he is
     also her son

** The text is ambiguous: Anshar and Kishar may have been the
     offspring of Tiamat and Apsu or Lahmu and Lahamu

not earlier. For the most part, the mythology of ancient Babylon (Akkad) is derived from and greatly influenced by the mythology of ancient Sumer. Its themes and motifs reflect Sumerian sources, and its deities have their counterparts in the Sumerian pantheon, with some of the deities assuming Sumerian names.

Embracing religious, political, and secular dimensions, the *Enuma Elish* was recited annually by a high priest at the New Year festival in Babylon. It commemorates the ascendancy of Marduk as the supreme deity and the corresponding elevation of his city of Babylon to the status of supreme city, the axis mundi or center of the universe where intersect the sacred and the profane. The city of Babylon incarnates an earthly image of the heavenly city, acting as the sacred center linking the two realms. Its auspicious function and location are established at the end of the *Enuma Elish* when the gods agree to meet annually at the temple they have built in Babylon to honor their supreme god Marduk.

This event was commemorated annually at the New Year festival held in Babylon during the month of April (Nisan) at the time of the spring equinox. The festival lasted eleven days, during which time rituals were performed involving recitation of the *Enuma Elish*, enactment of some of the events described in the hymn, prayer, purification rites, a mock battle, public humiliation of the king, animal sacrifices, and processions. Statues of gods of neighboring city-states were brought to Marduk's temple in Babylon to participate in an assembly. The purpose of this annual assembly of gods and people was to celebrate Marduk's majesty, establish Babylon as his center, ratify his authority (and by extension, the authority of his human representative, namely, the king of Babylon), ritually re-create the universe, and set it on its regulated course for another year. Annual recitation of the *Enuma Elish* and performance of the rituals during the New Year festival allowed for human participation in sacred activity and facilitated the process whereby Marduk emerges victorious against primordial chaos. He subdues, contains, and regulates the forces of nature; he establishes balance and equilibrium for the subsequent year; and he ensures the renewal of the universe.

The *Enuma Elish* opens with a brief reference to the divine parents and their progeny. The gods represent both cosmic elements and forces in nature. The primal mother, Tiamat, is salt-water ocean and her first consort, Apsu, is sweet-water ocean. Mummu may refer to some sort of mist rising from the waters. Tiamat and Apsu commingle, and out of their union emerges the brother and sister pair of Lahmu and Lahamu. This pair is later surpassed in stature by their younger siblings or offspring Anshar and Kishar. (Textual ambiguity leads some scholars to claim that Anshar and Kishar are the younger offspring of Tiamat and Apsu, while others argue that they are the offspring of Lahmu and Lahamu.) Anshar and Kishar, the horizons of sky and earth, give birth to Anu. Anu fathers Nudimmud-Ea who, in turn, fathers the heroic Marduk.

The poem can be divided into three main parts. The first part tells the story of the emanation of successive generations of pairs of deities from the primal mother, Tiamat, with each pair of deities acquiring greater definition and accomplishment than its predecessor and with each pair representing the sequential stages of the creation of the cosmos. The story thus addresses the issue of the origin of deities (theogony) and the origin of the cosmos (cosmogony). The second part tells of the growing feud between Tiamat's fractious descendents—the older generation of gods who represent the forces of inertia and lethargy pitted against the younger generation of gods who represent the creative forces of commotion and youthful exuberance; Tiamat's creation of a brood of misshapen monsters and her second consort, Kingu, to assist her in battle; the cosmic battle in which Tiamat is defeated by her descendent Marduk; and the emergence of Marduk as the supreme deity who regulates the universe and who designates the responsibilities and tasks for governing the cosmos to his subordinates. The poem, therefore, begins with the watery, unregulated, and primordial chaos of Tiamat and concludes with the establishment of the orderly, regulated, and controlled universe of Marduk. The third part, which may or may not have been included in the original, consists of an elaborate hymn of praise for Marduk in which the gods confer upon him his fifty names and follow each name with a brief explanation.

Marduk agrees to confront Tiamat on behalf of the warring faction of gods on condition that they appoint him as supreme ruler for all eternity. He demands absolute sovereignty over the whole universe for all time, thereby possibly laying the foundation for monotheism in religion and monarchy in political governance. The gods agree to his demand and equip him with the tools he needs to defeat Tiamat. After he has successfully accomplished his mission, Marduk secures his position as the supreme leader by appropriating the Tables of Fate that control events and natural phenomena, by straddling the lifeless cadaver of the once all-powerful Tiamat, by constructing the skies and land from her mutilated body, by measuring and regulating natural elements, and by appointing jurisdictions to the various gods to keep them happy. Completely satisfied, the gods once again assemble to ratify Marduk's supreme status and authority.

According to the description in the hymn, Tiamat is the primal female with a human form that possesses nostrils, eyes, legs, a crotch, and entrails. At the same time, however, she is a limitless, swampy, all-enveloping womb without discernible boundaries. Her name is etymologically linked with the Hebrew *tehom*, which means *deep* or *abyss* (Genesis 1:2). She is the mother of all, and from her union with Apsu emerge all the other deities. After her defeat, her dismembered carcass forms the arc or firmament of heaven, the ring of earth, and the waters of the earth and sky. From her pierced eyes emerge the two rivers, the Tigris and Euphrates of Mesopotamia (Iraq). The earth, therefore, is female, but it is now formed from the lifeless carcass of a deceased mother goddess whose creative power, control, and authority have been appropriated by the supreme male god, Marduk.

The portrayal of Tiamat seems to be somewhat conflicted. On the one hand, she is depicted as the swampy, inchoate, and primal force of chaos and anarchy that must be delineated, controlled, and regulated; on the other hand, Tiamat is depicted sympathetically as a classic example of motherly compassion. Her devotion and loyalty to her children have been described as her defining characteristics. Although it can be argued that Marduk slays Tiamat in self-defense since she intended to murder her younger offspring, it can also be argued that it is Tiamat who acts in self-defense. She is spurred into action in order to defend herself and her older offspring. She is unresponsive to Apsu's request to quell the clamor caused by their rambunctious offspring, but she responds to her children's plea for help by preparing to wage war against their familial rivals—a course of action that proves to be her undoing. This conflicted depiction of the mother goddess may perhaps be due to feelings of guilt on the part of the author and culture for a work that celebrates the killing of the primal mother. To fashion the universe and to impose order on its elements required no less a monumental and possibly guilt-ridden task than the murder of the mother goddess. And since the skies, land, and all within are fashioned from her lifeless carcass, the Babylonians lived and functioned while surrounded by constant reminders of the original matricide.

The *Enuma Elish* or *Babylonian Creation* below is translated by N. K. Sandars.

REFERENCES

Armstrong, Karen. *A History of God: The 4,000-Year Quest of Judaism, Christianity, and Islam.* New York: Ballantine, 1993.

Bottero, Jean. *Religion in Ancient Mesopotamia.* Trans. Teresa Lavender Fagan. Chicago: U of Chicago P, 2001.

Eliade, Mircea. *The Sacred and the Profane: The Nature of Religion: The Nature of Religious Myth, Symbolism, and Ritual Within Life and Culture.* Trans. Willard R. Task. San Diego: Harcourt Brace and Co., 1959.

Frymer-Kensky, Tivka. *In the Wake of the Goddess: Women, Culture, and the Biblical Transformation of Pagan Myth.* New York, Columbine, 1992.

Heidel, Alexander. *The Babylonian Genesis: The Story of Creation.* 2nd ed. Chicago: U of Chicago P, 1951.

Jakobsen, Thorkild. *The Treasures of Darkness: A History of Mesopotamian Religion.* New Haven: Yale UP, 1976.

Kramer, Samuel Noah. "Mythology of Sumer and Akkad." *Mythologies of the Ancient World.* Ed. Samuel Noah Kramer. New York: Anchor/Doubleday, 1961. 95–137.

Pritchard, James B., ed. *Ancient Near Eastern Texts: Relating to the Old Testament.* 3rd ed. Princeton: Princeton UP, 1969.

Sandars, N. K., trans. *Poems of Heaven and Hell From Ancient Mesopotamia.* London: Penguin, 1971.

The Babylonian Creation

I

When there was no heaven,
no earth, no height, no depth, no name,
when Apsu was alone,
the sweet water, the first begetter; and Tiamat
the bitter water, and that
return to the womb, her Mummu,
when there were no gods—

When sweet and bitter
mingled together, no reed was plaited, no rushes
muddied the water,
the gods were nameless, natureless, futureless, then
from Apsu and Tiamat
in the waters gods were created, in the waters
silt precipitated,

> Lahmu and Lahamu,
> were named; they were not yet old,
> not yet grown tall
> when Anshar and Kishar overtook them both,
> the lines of sky and earth
> stretched where horizons meet to separate
> cloud from silt.

> Days on days, years
> on years passed till Anu, the empty heaven,
> heir and supplanter,
> first-born of his father, in his own nature
> begot Nudimmud-Ea,
> intellect, wisdom, wider than heaven's horizon,
> the strongest of all the kindred.

Discord broke out among the gods although they were brothers, warring and jarring in the belly of Tiamat, heaven shook, it reeled with the surge of the dance; Apsu could not silence the clamour, their behaviour was bad, overbearing and proud.

But still Tiamat lay inert till Apsu, the father of gods, bellowed for that servant who clouds his judgement, his Mummu,
'Dear counsellor, come with me to Tiamat.'
They have gone, and in front of Tiamat they sit down and talk together about the young gods, their first-born children; Apsu said,

'Their manners revolt me, day and night without remission we suffer. My will is to destroy them, all of their kind, we shall have peace at last and we will sleep again.'

When Tiamat heard she was stung, she writhed in lonely desolation, her heart worked in secret passion, Tiamat said,
'Why must we destroy the children that we made? If their ways are troublesome, let us wait a little while.'

Then Mummu advised Apsu, and he spoke in malice,
'Father, destroy them in full rebellion, you will have quiet in the daytime and at night you will sleep.'

When Apsu heard, the die was cast against his children, his face flamed with the pleasure of evil; but Mummu he embraced, he hung on his neck, he sat him down on his knees and kissed him.

The decision was known to all their children; confusion seized them and after, a great silence, for they were confounded.

The god who is the source of wisdom, the bright intelligence that perceives and plans, Nudimmud-Ea, saw through it, he sounded the coil of chaos, and against it devised the artifice of the universe.

He spoke the word that charmed the waters, it fell upon Apsu, he lay asleep, the sweet waters slept, Apsu slept, Mummu was overcome, Apsu lay drowned, undone.

Then Ea ripped off his flaming glory coat and took his crown, he set on himself the aureole of the king. When Ea had bound Apsu he killed him, and Mummu, the dark counsellor, he led by the nose and locked away.

Ea had defeated his enemies and trodden them down. Now that his triumph was completed, in deep peace he rested, in his holy palace Ea slept. Over the abyss, the distance, he built his house and shrine and there magnificently he lived with his wife Damkina.

In that room, at the point of decision where what is to come is predetermined, he was conceived, the most sagacious, the one from the first most absolute in action.

In the deep abyss he was conceived, MARDUK was made in the heart of the apsu, MARDUK was created in the heart of the holy apsu. Ea begot him and Damkina bore him, father and mother; he sucked the paps of goddesses, from his nurses he was fed on the terribleness that filled him.

His body was beautiful; when he raised his eyes great lights flared; his stride was majestic; he was the leader from the first.

When Ea who begot him saw him he exulted, he was radiant, light-hearted, for he saw that he was perfect, and he multiplied his godhead, the one to be first and stand highest.

His limbs were immaculate, the making a fearful mystery beyond comprehension; with four eyes for limitless sight, and four ears hearing all; when his lips moved a tongue of fire burst out. Titanic limbs, standing so high he overtopped the tallest god; he was strong and he wore the glory of ten, and their lightnings played round him.

'My son, my son, son of the sun, and heaven's sun!'

Then Anu begot winds and brought them from the four quarters, to be the van and to command the ranks; and he brought the tornado, a wild surf to worry Tiamat.

But now the other gods had no rest any more, tormented by storms, they conspired in their secret hearts and brought to Tiamat the matter of their plot. To their own mother they said,

'When they killed Apsu you did not stir, you brought no help to him, your husband. Now Anu has called up from the four quarters this abomination of winds to rage in your guts, and we cannot rest for the pain;

'Remember Apsu in your heart, your husband, remember Mummu who was defeated; now you are all alone, and thrash around in desolation, and we have lost your love, our eyes ache and we long for sleep.

'Rouse up, our Mother! Pay them back and make them empty like the wind.'

Tiamat approved it, she said,

'I approve this advice: we will make monsters, and monsters and gods against gods will march into battle together.'

Together they jostle the ranks to march with Tiamat, day and night furiously they plot, the growling roaring rout, ready for battle, while the Old Hag, the first mother, mothers a new brood.

She loosed the irresistible missile, she spawned enormous serpents with cutting fangs, chock-full of venom instead of blood, snarling dragons wearing their glory like gods. (Whoever sees this thing receives the shock of death, for when they heave those bodies up they never turn them back.)

She made the Worm
the Dragon
the Female Monster
the Great Lion
the Mad Dog
the Man Scorpion
the Howling Storm
Kulili
Kusariqu

There was no pity in their weapons, they did not flinch from battle for her law was binding, irrevocable.

Eleven such monsters she made, but she took from among the gods the clumsy labourer

Kingu

one of the first generation to be her Captain, War-leader, Assembly-leader, ordering the supplies, leading the van to battle

Supreme Commander of the Wars

All this she gave him when she raised their Company, she said,

'Now it is in your hands, my spell will hold them bound, they must obey my will. You are supreme, my one husband, your word will hold the rebel horde.'

She gave him the Tables of Fate and fastened them on to his breast,

'Now and for evermore your word is irrevocable, your judgements will last! They will quench the fire and the swinging mace will fail of its power.'

When Kingu had received the authority, that belonged before to Anu, in their several natures they confirmed the brood of monsters.

II

When her labour of creation was ended, against her children Tiamat began preparations of war. This was the evil she did to requite Apsu, this was the evil news that came to Ea.

When he had learned how matters lay he was stunned, he sat in black silence till rage had worked itself out; then he remembered the gods before him. He went to Anshar, his father's father, and told him how Tiamat plotted,

'She loathes us, father, our mother Tiamat has raised up that Company, she rages in turbulence and all have joined her, all those gods whom you begot,

'Together they jostle the ranks to march with Tiamat, day and night furiously they plot, the growling roaring rout, ready for battle, while the Old Hag, the first mother, mothers a new brood.

'She has loosed the irresistible missile, spawned enormous serpents with cutting fangs, chock-full of venom instead of blood, snarling dragons wearing their glory like gods. (Whoever sees this thing receives the shock of death, for when they heave those bodies up they never turn them back.)

'She has made the Worm,
the Dragon
the Female Monster
the Great Lion
the Mad Dog
the Man Scorpion
the Howling Storm
Kulili
Kusariqu

'There is no pity in their weapons, they do not flinch from battle for her law is binding, irrevocable.

'Eleven such monsters she has made but she took from among the gods the clumsy labourer

Kingu

one of the first generation to be her Captain, War-leader, Assembly-leader, ordering the supplies, leading the van to battle

Supreme Commander of the Wars

All this she gave him when she raised their Company, she has said,

"'Now it is in your hands, my spell will hold them bound, they must obey my will. You are supreme, my one husband, your word will hold the rebel horde.'"

She has given to him the Tables of Fate and fastened them on to his breast,

"'Now and for evermore your word is irrevocable, your judgements will last! They will quench the fire and the swinging mace will fail of its power."

So Kingu has received the authority that belonged before to Anu, they have confirmed in their several natures the brood of monsters.'

When Anshar heard how the Tiamat-tempest was rising he struck his groin, bit his lip, restless, gloomy and sick at heart, he covered his mouth to stifle his groans.

At last he spoke, urging Ea on to the fight,

'Once you made a snare of words, now go and try it out. You killed Mummu, killed Apsu; kill Kingu who marches in front of Tiamat!'

The sagacious counsellor of all the gods, Nudimmud-Ea, answered Anshar . . .

[break of eight lines partially reconstructed]

'I will meet Tiamat and calm her spirit, when her heart brims over she will hear my words, and if not mine then yours may appease the waters.'

Nudimmud took the short road, went the direct way to Tiamat; but when he saw her whole strategy he could not face her, but he came back cringing.

So Anshar called his son Anu,

'This is the true hero, an irresistible onslaught, a strong god. Go, and face Tiamat, and calm her spirit; when her heart brims over she will listen to you, but if she remains unreconciled my word may appease the waters.'

Anu obeyed his father's orders, he took the short road, went the direct way to Tiamat; but when he had come so close that he saw her whole strategy, he could not face her, he came back cringing to his father Anshar.

He spoke as though he saw Tiamat still,

'My hands are too weak, I cannot conquer her.'

Anshar was dumb; he stared at the ground and his hair stood on end. He shook his head at Ea, all the Anunnaki, the host of gods gathered into that place tongue-tied; they sat with mouths shut for they thought,

'What other god can make war on Tiamat? No one else can face her and come back.'

Then the Lord, the father of gods, Anshar rose to his feet majestically. Having considered everything he spoke to the Anunnaki,

'Which one of us is impetuous in battle? The hero Marduk! Only he is strong enough to avenge us.'

Then Ea called Marduk into a secret place and gave him subtle advice out of his deep mind,

'You are the dear son who warms my heart, Marduk. When you see Anshar go straight to him as you would go into battle. Stand up when you speak, and when he sees you he will grow calm.'

Lord Marduk exulted, he strode forward and stood facing Anshar. When Anshar saw him his heart swelled with joy, he kissed him on the lips and shook off despair.

'Anshar, break your silence, let your words ring out for I will accomplish what you long for most in your heart. What hero has forced the battle on you? Only a female thing, only Tiamat flies at you with all her contrivance. You shall soon straddle Tiamat's neck.'

'My son, my wise son, confuse Tiamat with charged words, go quickly now, the storm is your chariot, they will never deflect you from Tiamat, but having done with her, then return.'

The Lord exulted, with racing spirits he said to the father of gods,

'Creator of the gods who decides their destiny, if I must be your avenger, defeating Tiamat, saving your lives,

'Call the Assembly, give me precedence over all the rest; and when you sit down to pass your decrees, cheerfully sit in Ubshukinna, the Hall of the Synod; now and for ever let my word be law;

'I, not you, will decide the world's nature, the things to come. My decrees shall never be altered, never annulled, but my creation endures to the ends of the world.'

III

Words broke from the lips of Anshar; he said to his counsellor Kaka,

'You are the counsellor in whom my heart finds its happiness, the one who judges truly and persuades fairly: go to Lahmu and Lahamu, I am sending you down to primeval sediments, call together the generations of the gods.

'Let them speak, let them sit down to banquet together, they shall eat the feast and drink the new-drawn liquor and then they shall all confirm in his destiny the avenger, Marduk! Kaka, go off, stand in front of them and repeat what I say.

"'I am sent here by your son Anshar, I am charged to tell you his secret thoughts,

"'She loathes us, our mother Tiamat has raised up that Company, she rages in turbulence and all have joined her, all those gods whom you begot,

"'Together they jostle the ranks to march with Tiamat, day and night furiously they plot, the growling roaring rout, ready for battle, while the Old Hag, the first mother, mothers a new brood.

"'She has loosed the irresistible missile, spawned enormous serpents with cutting fangs, chock-full of venom instead of blood, snarling dragons wearing their glory like gods. (Whoever sees this thing receives the shock of death, for when they heave those bodies up they never turn them back.)

"'She has made the Worm
the Dragon
the Female Monster
the Great Lion
the Mad Dog
the Man Scorpion
the Howling Storm
Kulili
Kusariqu

"'There is no pity in their weapons, they do not flinch from battle for her law is binding, irrevocable.

"'Eleven monsters she has made, but she took from among the gods the clumsy labourer

Kingu

one of the first generation to be her Captain, War-leader, Assembly-leader, ordering the supplies, leading the van to battle

Supreme Commander of the Wars

All this she gave him when she set up their Company, she has said,

"'"Now it is in your hands, my spell will hold them bound, they must obey my will. You are supreme, my one husband, *your* word will hold the rebel horde.'

"'She has given to him the Tables of Fate and fastened them on to his breast,

"'"Now and for evermore your word is irrevocable, your judgements will last! They will quench the fire and the swinging mace will fail of its power.'

"'So Kingu has received the authority that belonged before to Anu, they have confirmed in their several natures the brood of monsters.

"'I sent Anu but he could not face her, Nudimmud came flying back in terror, then Marduk stood up, a wise god, one of your lineage, his heart has compelled him to set out and face Tiamat, but first he said this,

""Creator of the gods who decides their destiny, if I must be your avenger, defeating Tiamat, saving your lives,

""Call the Assembly, give me precedence over all the rest; and when you sit down to pass your decrees, cheerfully sit in Ubshukinna, the Hall of the Synod, now and for ever let my word be law;

""I, not you, will decide the world's nature, the things to come. My decrees shall never be altered, never annulled, but my creation endures to the ends of the world.

""Come soon and confirm the destiny of Marduk and the sooner he is off to meet the Great Adversary.""'

He left and took his way down to Lahmu and Lahamu, stooping he kissed the primeval sediments, bowed to the ground at their feet and delivered the message to old gods,

'I have been sent here by your son Anu, I am charged to tell you his secret thoughts.

'She loathes us, our mother Tiamat has raised up that Company, she rages in turbulence and all have joined her, all those gods whom you begot.

'Together they jostle the ranks to march with Tiamat, day and night furiously they plot, the growling roaring rout, ready for battle, while the Old Hag, the first mother, mothers a new brood.

'She has loosed the irresistible missile, spawned enormous serpents with cutting fangs, chock-full of venom instead of blood, snarling dragons wearing their glory like gods. (Whoever sees this thing receives the shock of death, for when they heave those bodies up they never turn them back.)

'She has made the Worm
the Dragon
the Female Monster
the Great Lion
the Mad Dog
the Man Scorpion
the Howling Storm
Kulili
Kusariqu

'There is no pity in their weapons, they do not flinch from battle for her law is binding, irrevocable. Eleven such monsters she has made, but she took from among the gods the clumsy labourer

Kingu

one of the first generation to be her Captain, War-leader, Assembly-leader, ordering the supplies, leading the van to battle.

Supreme Commander of the Wars

All this she gave him when she raised their Company, she has said,

'"Now it is in your hands, my spell will hold them bound, they must obey my will. You are supreme my one husband, *your* word will hold the rebel horde."

'She has given to him the Tables of Fate and fastened them on to his breast,

'"Now and for evermore your word is irrevocable, your judgements will last! They will quench the fire and the swinging mace will fail of its power."

'So Kingu has received the authority that belonged before to Anu, they have confirmed in their several natures the brood of monsters.

'I sent Anu but he could not face her, Nudimmud came flying back in terror, then Marduk stood up, a wise god, one of your lineage, his heart has compelled him to set out and face Tiamat, but first he said this,

'"Creator of the gods who decides their destiny, if I must be your avenger, defeating Tiamat, saving your lives,

'"Call the Assembly, give me precedence over all the rest; and when you sit down to pass your decrees, cheerfully sit in Ubshukinna, the Hall of the Synod, now and for ever let my word be law;

'"I, not you, will decide the world's nature, the things to come. My decrees shall never be altered, never annulled, but my creation endures to the ends of the world.

'"Come soon and confirm the destiny of Marduk and the sooner he is off to meet the Great Adversary."'

When Lahmu and Lahamu heard this they muttered together, all the gods moaned with distress,

'What a strange and terrible decision, the coil of Tiamat is too deep for us to fathom.'

Then they prepared for the journey, all the gods who determine the nature of the world and of things to come came in to Anshar, they filled Ubshukinna, greeted each other with a kiss.

In the Hall of the Synod the ancestral voices were heard, they sat down to the banquet, they ate the feast, they drank the new-drawn liquor and the tubes through which they sucked dripped with intoxicating wine.

Their souls expanded, their bodies grew heavy and drowsy; and this was the state of the gods when they settled the fate of Marduk.

IV

They set up a throne for Marduk and he sat down facing his forefathers to receive the government.

'One god is greater than all great gods,
a fairer fame, the word of command,
the word from heaven, O Marduk,
greater than all great gods, the honour
and the fame, the will of Anu, great
command, unaltering and eternal word!
Where there is action the first to act,
where there is government the first to govern;
to glorify some, to humiliate some,
that is the gift of the god.
Truth absolute, unbounded will;
which god dares question it?
In their beautiful places a place
is kept for you, Marduk, our avenger.

'We have called you here to receive the sceptre, to make you king of the whole universe. When you sit down in the Synod you are the arbiter; in the battle your weapon crushes the enemy.

'Lord, save the life of any god who turns to you; but as for the one who grasped evil, from that one let his life drain out.'

They conjured then a kind of apparition and made it appear in front of him, and they said to Marduk, the first-born son,

'Lord, your word among the gods arbitrates, destroys, creates: then speak and this apparition will disappear. Speak again, again it will appear.'

He spoke and the apparition disappeared. Again he spoke and it appeared again. When the gods had proved his word they blessed him and cried,

'Marduk Is King!'

They robed him in robes of a king, the sceptre and the throne they gave him, and matchless war-weapons as a shield against the adversary,

'Be off. Slit life from Tiamat, and may the winds carry her blood to the world's secret ends.'

The old gods had assigned to Bēl what he would be and what he should do, always conquering, always succeeding;

Then Marduk made a bow and strung it to be his own weapon, he set the arrow against the bow-string, in his right hand he grasped the mace and lifted it up, bow and quiver hung at his side, lightnings played in front of him, he was altogether an incandescence.

He netted a net, a snare for Tiamat; the winds from their quarters held it, south wind, north, east wind, west, and no part of Tiamat could escape.

With the net, the gift of Anu, held close to his side, he himself raised up

Imhullu

the atrocious wind, the tempest, the whirlwind, the hurricane, the wind of four and the wind of seven, the tumid wind worst of all.

All seven winds were created and released to savage the guts of Tiamat, they towered behind him. Then the tornado

Abuba

his last great ally, the signal for assault, he lifted up.

He mounted the storm, his terrible chariot, reins hitched to the side, yoked four in hand the appalling team, sharp poisoned teeth, the Killer, the Pitiless, Trampler, Haste, they knew arts of plunder, skills of murder.

He posted on his right the Batterer, best in the mêlée; on his left the Battlefury that blasts the bravest, lapped in this armour, a leaping terror, a ghastly aureole; with a magic word clenched between his lips, a healing plant pressed in his palm, this lord struck out.

He took his route towards the rising sound of Tiamat's rage, and all the gods besides, the fathers of the gods pressed in around him, and the lord approached Tiamat.

He surveyed her scanning the Deep, he sounded the plan of Kingu her consort; but so soon as Kingu sees him he falters, flusters, and the friendly gods who filled the ranks beside him—when they saw the brave hero, their eyes suddenly blurred,

But Tiamat without turning her neck roared, spitting defiance from bitter lips,
'Upstart, do you think yourself too great? Are they scurrying now from their holes to yours?'

Then the lord raised the hurricane, the great weapon, he flung his words at the termagant fury,
'Why are you rising, your pride vaulting, your heart set on faction, so that sons reject fathers? Mother of all, why did you have to mother war?

'You made that bungler your husband, Kingu! You gave him the rank, not his by right, of Anu. You have abused the gods my ancestors, in bitter malevolence you threaten Anshar, the king of all the gods.

'You have marshalled forces for battle, prepared the war-tackle. Stand up alone and we will fight it out, you and I alone in battle.'

When Tiamat heard him her wits scattered, she was possessed and shrieked aloud, her legs shook from the crotch down, she gabbled spells, muttered maledictions, while the gods of war sharpened their weapons.

Then they met: Marduk, that cleverest of gods, and Tiamat grappled alone in single fight.

The lord shot his net to entangle Tiamat, and the pursuing tumid wind, Imhullu, came from behind and beat in her face. When the mouth gaped open to suck him down he drove Imhullu in, so that the mouth would not shut but wind raged through her belly; her carcass blown up, tumescent, she gaped— And now he shot the arrow that split the belly, that pierced the gut and cut the womb.

Now that the Lord had conquered Tiamat he ended her life, he flung her down and straddled the carcass; the leader was killed, Tiamat was dead, her rout was shattered, her band dispersed.

Those gods who had marched beside her now quaked in terror, and to save their own lives, if they could, they turned their backs on danger. But they were surrounded, held in a tight circle, and there was no way out.

He smashed their weapons and tossed them into the net; they found themselves inside the snare, they wept in holes and hid in corners suffering the wrath of god.

When they resisted he put in chains the eleven monsters, Tiamat's unholy brood, and all their murderous armament. The demoniac band that marched in front of her he trampled into the ground;

But Kingu the usurper, the chief of them, he bound and made death's god. He took the Tables of Fate, usurped without right, and sealed them with his seal to wear on his own breast.

When it was accomplished, the adversary vanquished, the haughty enemy humiliated; when the triumph of Anshar was accomplished on the enemy, and the will of Nudimmud was fulfilled, then brave Marduk tightened the ropes of the prisoners.

He turned back to where Tiamat lay bound, he straddled the legs and smashed her skull (for the mace was merciless), he severed the arteries and the blood streamed down the north wind to the unknown ends of the world.

When the gods saw all this they laughed out loud, and they sent him presents. They sent him their thankful tributes.

The lord rested; he gazed at the huge body, pondering how to use it, what to create from the dead carcass. He split it apart like a cockle-shell; with the upper half he constructed the arc of sky, he pulled down the bar and set a watch on the waters, so they should never escape.

He crossed the sky to survey the infinite distance; he stationed himself above apsu, that apsu built by Nudimmud over the old abyss which now he surveyed, measuring out and marking in.

He stretched the immensity of the firmament, he made Esharra, the Great Palace, to be its earthly image, and Anu and Enlil and Ea had each their right stations.

V

He projected positions for the Great Gods conspicuous in the sky, he gave them a starry aspect as constellations; he measured the year, gave it a beginning and an end, and to each month of the twelve three rising stars.

When he had marked the limits of the year, he gave them Nebiru, the pole of the universe, to hold their course, that never erring they should not stray through the sky. For the seasons of Ea and Enlil he drew the parallel.

Through her ribs he opened gates in the east and west, and gave them strong bolts on the right and left; and high in the belly of Tiamat he set the zenith.

He gave the moon the lustre of a jewel, he gave him all the night, to mark off days, to watch by night each month the circle of a waxing waning light.

'New Moon, when you rise on the world, six days your horns are crescent, until half-circle on the seventh, waxing still phase follows phase, you will divide the month from full to full.

'Then wane, a gibbous light that fails, until low down on the horizon sun oversails you, drawing close his shadow lies across you, then dark of the moon—at thirty days the cycle's second starts again and follows through for ever and for ever.

'This is your emblem and the road you take, and when you close the sun, speak both of you with justice judgement uncorrupt . . .

[some lines are missing here]

When Marduk had sent out the moon, he took the sun and set him to complete the cycle from this one to the next New Year. . . . He gave him the Eastern Gate, and the ends of the night with the day, he gave to Shamash.

Then Marduk considered Tiamat. He skimmed spume from the bitter sea, heaped up the clouds, spindrift of wet and wind and cooling rain, the spittle of Tiamat.

With his own hands from the steaming mist he spread the clouds. He pressed hard down the head of water, heaping mountains over it, opening springs to flow: Euphrates and Tigris rose from her eyes, but he closed the nostrils and held back their springhead.

He piled huge mountains on her paps and through them drove water-holes to channel the deep sources; and high overhead he arched her tail, locked-in to the wheel of heaven; the pit was under his feet, between was the crotch, the sky's fulcrum. Now the earth had foundations and the sky its mantle.

When god's work was done, when he had fashioned it all and finished, then on earth he founded temples and made them over to Ea;

But the Tables of Destiny taken from Kingu he returned as a first greeting to Anu; and those gods who had hung up their weapons defeated, whom he had scattered, now fettered, he drove into his presence, the father of the gods.

With the weapons of war broken, he bound to his foot the eleven, Tiamat's monstrous creation. He made likenesses of them all and now they stand at the gate of the abyss, the Apsu Gate; he said,
　'This is for recollection for Tiamat shall not be forgotten.'

All the generations of the Great Gods when they saw him were full of joy, with Lahmu and Lahamu; their hearts bounded when they came over to meet him.

King Anshar made him welcome with ceremony, Anu and Enlil came carrying presents; but when his mother Damkina sent her present, then he glowed, an incandescence lit his face.

He gave to her servant Usmu, who brought the greeting, charge of the secret house of Apsu; he made him warden of the sanctuaries of Eridu.

All the heavenly gods were there, all the Igigi fell prostrate in front of him, all that were there of the Anunnaki kissed his feet. The whole order came in together to worship.

They stood in front of him, low they bowed and they shouted

　'He is king indeed!'

When all the gods in their generations were drunk with the glamour of the manhood of Marduk, when they had seen his clothing spoiled with the dust of battle, then they made their act of obedience . . .

He bathed and put on clean robes, for he was their king. . . . A glory was round his head; in his right hand he held the mace of war, in his left grasped the scep- tre of peace, the bow was slung on his back; he held the net, and his glory touched the abyss . . .

He mounted the throne raised up in the temple. Damkina and Ea and all the Great Gods, all the Igigi shouted,

'In time past Marduk meant only "the beloved son" but now he is king indeed, this is so!'

They shouted together,

'*Great Lord of the Universe!*

this is his name, in him we trust.'

When it was done, when they had made Marduk their king, they pronounced peace and happiness for him,

'Over our houses you keep unceasing watch, and all you wish from us, that will be done.'

Marduk considered and began to speak to the gods assembled in his presence. This is what he said,

'In the former time you inhabited the void above the abyss, but I have made Earth as the mirror of Heaven, I have consolidated the soil for the foundations, and there I will build my city, my beloved home.

'A holy precinct shall be established with sacred halls for the presence of the king. When you come up from the deep to join the Synod you will find lodging and sleep by night.

'When others from heaven descend to the Assembly, you too will find lodging and sleep by night. It shall be

Babylon

the home of the gods. The masters of all the crafts shall build it according to my plan.'

When the older of the gods had heard this speech they had still one question to ask:

'Over these things that your hands have formed, who will administer law? Over all this earth that you have made, who is to sit in judgement?

'You have given your Babylon a lucky name, let it be our home for ever! Let the fallen gods day after day serve us; and as we enforce your will let no one else usurp our office.'

Marduk, Tiamat's conqueror, was glad; the bargain was good; he went on speaking his arrogant words explaining it all to the gods,

'They will perform this service, day after day, and you shall enforce my will as law.'

Then the gods worshipped in front of him, and to him again, to the king of the whole universe they cried aloud,

'This great lord was once our son, now he is our king. We invoked him once for very life, he who is the lord, the blaze of light, the sceptre of peace and of war the mace.

'Let Ea be his architect and draw the excellent plan, his bricklayers are we!'

VI

Now that Marduk has heard what it is the gods are saying, he is moved with desire to create a work of consummate art. He told Ea the deep thought in his heart.

'Blood to blood
I join,
blood to bone
I form
an original thing,
its name is MAN,
aboriginal man
is mine in making.

'All his occupations
are faithful service,
the gods that fell
have rest,
I will subtly alter
their operations,
divided companies
equally blest.'

Ea answered with carefully chosen words, completing the plan for the gods' comfort. He said to Marduk,
'Let one of the kindred be taken; only one need die for the new creation. Bring the gods together in the Great Assembly; there let the guilty die, so the rest may live.'

Marduk called the Great Gods to the Synod; he presided courteously, he gave instructions and all of them listened with grave attention.

The king speaks to the rebel gods,
'Declare on your oath if ever before you spoke the truth, who instigated rebellion? Who stirred up Tiamat? Who led the battle? Let the instigator of war be handed over; guilt and retribution are on him, and peace will be yours for ever.'

The Great Gods answered the Lord of the Universe, the king and counsellor of gods,

'It was Kingu who instigated rebellion, he stirred up that sea of bitterness and led the battle for her.'

They declared him guilty, they bound and held him down in front of Ea, they cut his arteries and from his blood they created man; and Ea imposed his servitude.

When it was done, when Ea in his wisdom had created man and man's burden, this thing was past comprehension, this marvel of subtlety conceived by Marduk and executed by Nudimmud.

Then Marduk, as king, divided the gods: one host below and another above, three hundred above for the watchers of heaven, watchers of the law of Anu; five times sixty for earth, six hundred gods between earth and heaven.

When universal law was set up and the gods allotted their calling, then the Anunnaki, the erstwhile fallen, opened their mouths to speak to Marduk:
'Now that you have freed us and remitted our labour how shall we make a return for this? Let us build a temple and call it

The-Inn-of-Rest-by-Night

'There we will sleep at the season of the year, at the Great Festival when we form the Assembly; we will build altars for him, we will build the Parakku, the Sanctuary.'

When Marduk heard this his face shone like broad day:
'Tall Babel Tower, it shall be built as you desire; bricks shall be set in moulds and you shall name it Parakku, the Sanctuary.'

The Anunnaki gods took up the tools, one whole year long they set bricks in moulds; by the second year they had raised its head ESAGILA, it towered, the earthly temple, the symbol of infinite heaven.

Inside were lodgings for Marduk and Enlil and Ea. Majestically he took his seat in the presence of them all, where the head of the ziggurat looked down to the foot.

When that building was finished the Anunnaki built themselves chapels; then all came in together and Marduk set out the banquet.

'This is Babylon,
"dear city of god"
your beloved home!
The length and breadth
are yours, possess it,
enjoy it, it is your own.'

When all the gods sat down together there was wine and feasting and laughter; and after the banquet in beautiful Esagila they performed the liturgy from which the universe receives its structure, the occult is made plain, and through the universe gods are assigned their places.

When the Fifty Great Gods had sat down with the Seven who design the immutable nature of things, they raised up three hundred into heaven. It was then too that Enlil lifted the bow of Marduk and laid it in front of them.

He also lifted the net; they praised the workmanship now that they saw the intricacy of the net and the beauty of the bow.

Anu lifted the bow and kissed it, he said before all the gods,
    'This is my daughter.'
And this was the naming of the bow—

'One is for Long-wood,
two for the Rain-bow,
three is for Starry-bow
glittering above.'

And Starry-bow was a god among gods.

When Anu had pronounced the bow's triple destiny he lifted up the king's throne and set Marduk above in the gods' Assembly.

Among themselves they uttered an execration, by oil and by water, pricking their throats, to abide its fate on pain of death.

They ratified his authority as King of Kings, Lord of the Lords of the Universe. Anshar praised him, he called him ASARLUHI, the name that is first, the highest name.

'We will wait and listen, we bend and worship
his name! His word is the last appeal
his writ will run from the zenith to the pit.
All glory to the son, our avenger!
His empire has no end, shepherd of men,
he made them his creatures to the last of time,
they must remember.
He shall command hecatombs, for the gods,
they shall commend food, for the fathers,
and cherish the sanctuary
where the odour of incense and whisper of liturgy
echo on earth the customs of heaven.
Black-headed men will adore him on earth,
the subjected shall remember their god,
at his word they shall worship the goddess.
Let offerings of food not fail

for god and goddess, at his command.
Let them serve the gods, at his command,
work their lands, build their houses.
Let black-headed men serve the gods on earth
without remission; while as for us,
in the multitude of his names
he is our god.
Let us hail him in his names,
let us hail him by his fifty names,
one god.'

Questions for Review and Discussion

1. Why does Tiamat advocate patience toward her offspring when Apsu complains of their tumult but heed her children's call for action when they voice the same complaint?
2. Locate some of the pejorative terms that are used to describe Tiamat. What are the political ramifications of describing her with such disparagement?
3. How does Marduk manipulate the other gods in order to emerge as the supreme deity? What assistance did they give him?
4. Tiamat creates Kingu to act as her consort. She gives him the Tables of Fate and assigns him the task of leading the rebellion against the rival faction of gods. He proves no match for Marduk, however, who binds and subsequently slays him to fashion humans by mixing Kingu's divine blood with dust. What is the significance of situating humans as the progeny of the defeated god Kingu?
5. Why does Marduk create humans? What purpose do they serve? What are the political ramifications of Marduk's actions?
6. What do humans have in common with the gods? How are they different from the gods?
7. Why must Tiamat be destroyed? Is she acting in self-defense? When Marduk confronts Tiamat, he accuses her of "mothering" war? Is this assessment correct?
8. The *Enuma Elish* depicts the replacement of an old world order with a new one. What is the new world order, and what was the old world order that it has replaced? How does Tiamat's continued existence challenge the new world order?
9. What role does gender play in the *Enuma Elish*?

Chapter 4

Demeter and Persephone

GLOSSARY OF NAMES AND TERMS

AIDONEUS Another name for Hades (see below)

CHTHONIA Greek word for "under the earth"

DEMETER Goddess of the Grain; sister/spouse of Zeus; mother of kore/ Persephone; also referred to as Deo

DEMO One of the four daughters of Metaneira and Keleos

DEMOPHOON Son of Metaneira and Keleos

ELEUSIS A city west of Athens; location for the Eleusinian Mysteries

ELEUSINIAN MYSTERIES Sacred rites performed annually; probably involved a reenactment of the myth

EREBOS Another name for the Underworld; the chthonic realm (see Hades)

HADES Underworld; land of the dead; also the name for the God of the Underworld; referred to as Aidoneus or the Host-to-Many; brother of Demeter and Zeus; uncle and abductor of Persephone

HEKATE Goddess of the Crossroads; stands at the threshold between the underworld and earth; associated with transitions

HELIOS Sun God

HERMES Messenger of the Gods; also referred to as the Slayer of Argos

IAMBE Postmenopausal female who lives in the palace at Eleusis

KALLIDIKE One of the four daughters of Metaneira and Keleos

KALLITHOE One of the four daughters of Metaneira and Keleos

KELEOS King of Eleusis; husband of Metaneira

KLEISIDIKE One of the four daughters of Metaneira and Keleos

KORE Persephone prior to her kidnap and rape; generic name for maiden; virgin

KRONOS Son of Gaia and Uranus; brother/spouse of Rheia; father of Zeus, Demeter, and Hades

METANEIRA Queen of Eleusis; wife of Keleos

PERSEPHONE Spring; daughter of Demeter and Zeus; known as kore prior to her kidnap and rape

RHEIA Sister/spouse of Kronos; mother of Zeus and Demeter; grandmother of Persephone

ZEUS Sky god; king of the Olympian gods; brother/spouse of Demeter; father of kore/Persephone

One of the earliest known accounts of the myth of Demeter and her daughter, Persephone, is celebrated in the Homeric *Hymn to Demeter*, composed in approximately 650 B.C.E. In the hymn, Homer tells the story of the young kore (later known as Persephone), who is innocently picking flowers when she is abducted to the underworld, raped, and held captive by her uncle and lord of the dead, Hades.

The Greek Pantheon*

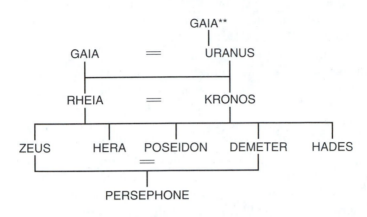

---

*   The Greek pantheon has been simplified for the purpose of showing
the relationship of the primary deities that appear in the *Homeric
Hymn to Demeter*

** Gaia is both mother and spouse of Uranus

Upon hearing her daughter's frantic scream for help as she is being swallowed by
the earth, Demeter embarks on a desperate pursuit to learn first of her daughter's
whereabouts and then to obtain her release from the clutches of death. She withdraws from the company of the gods on Mount Olympus and, disguising herself as a
mortal, she joins the company of humans at Eleusis, a city west of Athens.

In Eleusis, Demeter becomes a nursemaid to the infant prince, Demophoon.
She engages in a secret ritual to purge Demophoon of his morality by placing him in
the fire at night. One evening, Demophoon's mother, Metaneira, interrupts her in
this act, whereupon Demeter reveals her divine identity and orders the people of
Eleusis to build a temple in her honor to appease her anger. Upon its completion,
Demeter enters the temple and effectively declares war on the gods in Olympus. As
the goddess of the grain who is responsible for the growth of vegetation and plant
life, Demeter uses her power to her advantage: she withholds her blessings from
the earth until her daughter's release from captivity in the underworld. In effect,
she holds the earth hostage for one year, wreaking havoc on plants, animals,
humans, and, eventually, the gods. When the situation becomes intolerable, Zeus,
the king of the gods, sends word to his brother, Hades, to release Persephone from
the underworld to reunite with her mother. Before he does so, however, Hades
offers Persephone a pomegranate seed. Persephone's swallowing of the seed
ensures her return to the underworld for four months of the year. Her release from
the underworld and subsequent reunification with her mother heralds the coming
of spring.

The myth bears an obvious connection with the agrarian cycle of nature: winter, with its corresponding death of nature signifies Demeter's mourning for her daughter; spring, with its bourgeoning of new life signifies the joyous reunification of mother and daughter. The myth also has chthonic overtones since Demeter as an earth goddess is linked to the mythos of an earlier era, a time when the principal deity was the Great Goddess who, in her many cultural manifestations and under a variety of guises, was celebrated for her powers of generating earthly fertility and fecundity.

In addition to containing a narrative of the myth, the *Homeric Hymn to Demeter* commemorates the Eleusinian Mysteries, sacred rites performed annually for nearly twelve hundred years. The myth and its corresponding ritual captivated the classical world and formed the center of religious life for many centuries until orthodox Christianity, fearing their power and influence, terminated the rites at the end of the fourth century C.E. Since participants were sworn to secrecy, we know little of what actually transpired during the performance of the Eleusinian Mysteries. But we do know that the rites were performed in two phases: the Lesser Mysteries, which were held annually in spring in Athens; and the Greater Mysteries, which were performed in fall in Eleusis. The Lesser Mysteries prepared the initiate through purification; the Greater Mysteries consisted of further purification, sacrifices, and concluded in a final, visionary experience.

We know that participation in the ritual constituted such a powerful and transformative experience that the Eleusinian Mysteries held a unique position in the Greek and Roman world for many centuries. Since no description of the rituals has surfaced, scholars can only speculate as to what actually transpired. There is general agreement that some sort of reenactment of the myth occurred, with the initiate probably playing the role of Demeter in search for her daughter; with the final vision entailing the reunification of mother and daughter; and with the ritual concluding with the emergence of a chief priest carrying a single ear of grain that symbolized the new life.

Because it captivated the classical world and formed the center of religious life for so many centuries, the myth and its ritual must have offered the classical world more than a simple reenactment of the seasonal cycle of nature. The mysteries probably served as a powerful vehicle for gaining new insights into the meaning of life, loss, grief, suffering, death, and renewal, and facilitated the movement from partiality to wholeness, from separation to reunification, and from alienation to reintegration with the feminine source of life.

Demeter's conduct has spurred considerable debate. Her behavior is most heavily criticized in the episode with Metaneira and Demophoon, in which she "abducts" the young child from his mother, replicating the actions of her brothers Zeus and Hades. On the one hand, Demeter can be perceived as selfish, insensitive, and impervious to the damage she causes to humans and animals alike until she gets her way; on the other hand, she may be commended for her stubborn refusal to submit to the male hegemonic power structure of the Olympian gods. At times she is accused of being a binding mother who wants to thwart her daughter's attempt at autonomy; at others, she is praised for rescuing her daughter from the clutches of death. Criticism of Demeter may be mitigated somewhat by the knowledge that since she is the goddess of agriculture who bears the responsibility for earthly fertility and regeneration, she is simply acting in accordance with the laws of nature— laws which are not only amoral but are also impervious to the needs of humans and animals.

The myth has frequently been interpreted as a metaphor for the process of psychological "death" and renewal. There are striking parallels between Demeter's journey to reunite with her daughter and the stages of the grieving process. Demeter experiences anger and denial, engages in displacement by attempting to use Demophoon to fill the void left by Persephone, is forced to come to terms with her loss, and is ultimately reconciled with it upon the release of her daughter. Similarly, parallels can be drawn between Persephone's abduction and emergence from the underworld with "abduction" into and emergence from one's own psychological depths in the process of individuation. A psychological rendering of the myth may lead to Hades's emergence as an ambivalent figure: he is both rapist and agent for self-discovery—a "psychological midwife" who propels Persephone on her journey of growth by severing the umbilical connection with her mother.

Women are particularly drawn to the myth of Demeter and Persephone because of its unique privileging of the female position. The story unfolds from the perspective of Demeter, a grieving mother who experiences the loss of her daughter through abduction and rape. The *Hymn* provides a rich exploration of the dynamics that operate within a variety of human relationships: mother and daughter, father and daughter, male and female, and female and female. And it does so through the lens of the female. In a rich tapestry of female networking, the myth illustrates women working to help other women, women sharing knowledge with other women, and women learning from the experiences of other women. Although males are present in the myth and serve as catalysts to the action, their presence is tangential to the central concerns of the narrative. The Demeter and Persephone myth focuses on female dilemmas of female protagonists as they are articulated in the female sphere of influence.

The myth addresses a variety of topics that continue to have a current relevance, including an articulation of gendered modes of conduct and socialization. Zeus and Helios appear to demonstrate masculine ways of knowing and interacting; the female characters, including Hekate, Metaneira, her four daughters, and Iambe, appear to demonstrate feminine ways of knowing and interacting. Since the outcome of the central conflict consists of a compromise whereby Persephone divides her time between life and death and since she is able to negotiate a space for herself between the masculine realm represented by Zeus and Helios and the feminine realm represented by her mother and the other females, the myth of Demeter and

Persephone appears to make an eloquent statement for the importance of maintaining a gendered balance in perspective, in values, and in interaction with others.

The Homeric *Hymn to Demeter* below is translated by Helene P. Foley. The poem is cited in its entirety.

REFERENCES

Agha-Jaffar, Tamara. *Demeter and Persephone: Lessons From a Myth.* North Carolina: McFarland, 2002.

Bruteau, Beatrice. "The Unknown Goddess." *The Goddess Re-Awakening: The Feminine Principle Today.* Ed. Shirley Nicholson. Illinois: Quest, 1989. 68–90.

Carlson, Kathie. *In Her Image: The Unhealed Daughter's Search For Her Mother.* Boston: Shambhala, 1990.

———. *Life's Daughter/Death's Bride: Inner Transformations Through the Goddess Demeter/Persephone.* Boston: Shambhala, 1997.

Downing, Christine. *The Goddess: Mythological Images of the Feminine.* New York: Crossroad, 1981.

———. Ed. *The Long Journey Home: Re-Visioning the Myth of Demeter and Persephone for Our Time.* Boston: Shambhala, 1994.

Edinger, Edward F. *The Eternal Drama: The Inner Meaning of Greek Mythology.* Ed. Deborah A. Wesley. Boston: Shambhala, 1994.

Foley, Helene P., trans. and ed. *The Homeric Hymn to Demeter: Translation, Commentary, and Interpretive Essays.* Princeton: Princeton UP, 1994.

Kerenyi, Carl. *Eleusis: Archetypal Image of Mother and Daughter.* Trans. Ralph Manheim. Princeton: Princeton UP, 1967.

Powell, Barry P. *Classical Myth.* Englewood Cliffs: Prentice Hall, 1995.

Wilkinson, Tanya. *Persephone Returns: Victims, Heroes and the Journey From the Underworld.* Berkeley: Pagemill, 1996.

The Homeric Hymn to Demeter

Demeter I begin to sing,° the fair-tressed awesome goddess,
herself and her slim-ankled daughter whom Aidoneus°°
seized; Zeus, heavy-thundering and mighty-voiced, gave her,
without the consent of Demeter of the bright fruit and golden sword,

---

°The following divine genealogy will assist the reader in following the text. Gaia (Earth) and Ouranos (Sky) are the parents of Rheia and Kronos, who are in turn parents of Zeus, Hades, and Demeter. Zeus and Hades are thus both sons of Kronos. Demeter and Zeus are the parents of Korê/Persephone.

°°Hades

5   as she played with the deep-breasted daughters of Ocean,
plucking flowers in the lush meadow—roses, crocuses,
and lovely violets, irises and hyacinth and the narcissus,
which Earth grew as a snare for the flower-faced maiden
in order to gratify by Zeus's design the Host-to-Many,°
10   a flower wondrous and bright, awesome for all to see,
for the immortals above and for mortals below.
From its root a hundredfold bloom sprang up and smelled
so sweet that the whole vast heaven above
and the whole earth laughed, and the salty swell of the sea.
15   The girl marveled and stretched out both hands at once
to take the lovely toy. The earth with its wide ways yawned
over the Nysian plain; the lord Host-to-Many rose up on her
with his immortal horses, the celebrated son of Kronos;
he snatched the unwilling maid into his golden chariot
20   and led her off lamenting. She screamed with a shrill voice,
calling on her father, the son of Kronos highest and best.
Not one of the immortals or of humankind
heard her voice, nor the olives bright with fruit,
except the daughter of Persaios; tender of heart
25   she heard it from her cave, Hekate of the delicate veil.
And lord Helios, brilliant son of Hyperion, heard
the maid calling her father the son of Kronos. But he sat apart
from the gods, aloof in a temple ringing with prayers,
and received choice offerings from humankind.
30   Against her will Hades took her by the design of Zeus
with his immortal horses—her father's brother,
Commander- and Host-to-Many, the many-named son of Kronos.
So long as the goddess gazed on earth and starry heaven,
on the sea flowing strong and full of fish,
35   and on the beams of the sun, she still hoped
to see her dear mother and the race of immortal gods.
For so long hope charmed her strong mind despite her distress.
The mountain peaks and the depths of the sea echoed
in response to her divine voice, and her goddess mother heard.
40   Sharp grief seized her heart, and she tore the veil
on her ambrosial hair with her own hands.
She cast a dark cloak on her shoulders
and sped like a bird over dry land and sea,
searching. No one was willing to tell her the truth,

°Hades

45   not one of the gods or mortals;
      no bird of omen came to her as truthful messenger.
      Then for nine days divine Deo° roamed over the earth,
      holding torches ablaze in her hands;
      in her grief she did not once taste ambrosia
50   or nectar sweet-to-drink, nor bathed her skin.
      But when the tenth Dawn came shining on her,
      Hekate met her, holding a torch in her hands,
      to give her a message. She spoke as follows:
      "Divine Demeter, giver of seasons and glorious gifts,
55   who of the immortals or mortal men
      seized Persephone and grieved your heart?
      For I heard a voice but did not see with my eyes
      who he was. To you I tell at once the whole truth."
      Thus Hekate spoke. The daughter of fair-tressed Rheia°
60   said not a word, but rushed off at her side
      holding torches ablaze in her hands.
      They came to Helios, observer of gods and mortals,
      and stood before his horses. The most august goddess° spoke:
      "Helios, respect me as a god does a goddess, if ever
65   with word or deed I pleased your heart and spirit.
      The daughter I bore, a sweet offshoot noble in form—
      I heard her voice throbbing through the barren air
      as if she were suffering violence. But I did not see her with my eyes.
      With your rays you look down through the bright air
70   on the whole of the earth and the sea.
      Tell me the truth about my child. Have you somewhere
      seen who of gods or mortal men took her
      by force from me against her will and went away?"
      Thus she spoke and the son of Hyperion replied:
75   "Daughter of fair-tressed Rheia, mighty Demeter,
      you will know the truth. For I greatly revere and pity you
      grieving for your slim-ankled daughter. No other
      of the gods was to blame but cloud-gathering Zeus,
      who gave her to Hades his brother to be called
80   his fertile wife. With his horses Hades
      snatched her screaming into the misty gloom.
      But, Goddess, give up for good your great lamentation.
      You must not nurse in vain insatiable anger.
      Among the gods Aidoneus is not an unsuitable bridegroom,

°Demeter

85   Commander-to-Many and Zeus's own brother of the same stock.
As for honor, he got his third at the world's first division
and dwells with those whose rule has fallen to his lot."
He spoke and called to his horses. At his rebuke
they bore the swift chariot lightly, like long-winged birds.
90   A more terrible and brutal grief seized the heart
of Demeter, angry now at the son of Kronos with his dark clouds.
Withdrawing from the assembly of the gods and high Olympus,
she went among the cities and fertile fields of men,
disguising her beauty for a long time. No one of men
95   nor deep-girt women recognized her when they looked,
until she came to the house of skillful Keleos,
the man then ruler of fragrant Eleusis.
There she sat near the road, grief in her heart,
where citizens drew water from the Maiden's Well
100 in the shade—an olive bush had grown overhead—
like a very old woman cut off from childbearing
and the gifts of garland-loving Aphrodite.
Such are the nurses to children of law-giving kings
and the keepers of stores in their echoing halls.
105 The daughters of Keleos, son of Eleusis, saw her
as they came to fetch water easy-to-draw and bring it
in bronze vessels to their dear father's halls.
Like four goddesses they were in the flower of youth,
Kallidikê, Kleisidikê, fair Demo, and Kallithoê,
110 who was the eldest of them all.
They did not know her—gods are hard for mortals to recognize.
Standing near her, they spoke winged words.
"Who are you, old woman, of those born long ago?
From where? Why have you left the city and do not
115 draw near its homes? Women are there in the shadowy halls,
of your age as well as others born younger,
who would care for you both in word and in deed."
They spoke, and the most august goddess replied:
"Dear children, whoever of womankind you are,
120 greetings. I will tell you my tale. For it is not wrong
to tell you the truth now you ask.
Doso's my name, which my honored mother gave me.
On the broad back of the sea I have come now from Crete,
by no wish of my own. By force and necessity pirate men
125 led me off against my desire. Then they
put into Thorikos in their swift ship, where

the women stepped all together onto the mainland,
and the men made a meal by the stern of the ship.
My heart did not crave a heartwarming dinner,
130   but racing in secret across the dark mainland
I escaped from my arrogant masters, lest
they should sell me, as yet unbought, for a price overseas.
Then wandering I came here and know not at all
what land this is and who lives here.
135   But may all the gods who dwell on Olympus
give you husbands to marry and children to bear,
such as parents wish for. Now pity me, maidens,
and tell me, dear children, with eager goodwill,
whose house I might come to, a man's
140   or a woman's, there to do for them gladly
such tasks as are done by an elderly woman.
I could nurse well a newborn child, embracing it
in my arms, or watch over a house. I could
spread out the master's bed in a recess
145   of the well-built chamber and teach women their work."
So spoke the goddess. To her replied at once Kallidikê,
a maiden unwed, in beauty the best of Keleos' daughters.
"Good mother, we mortals are forced, though it hurt us,
to bear the gifts of the gods; for they are far stronger.
150   To you I shall explain these things clearly and name
the men to whom great power and honor belong here,
who are first of the people and protect with their counsels
and straight judgments the high walls of the city.
There is Triptolemos subtle in mind and Dioklos,
155   Polyxenos and Eumolpos the blameless,
Dolichos and our own lordly father.
And all these have wives to manage their households.
Of these not one at first sight would scorn
your appearance and turn you away from their homes.
160   They will receive you, for you are indeed godlike.
But if you wish, wait here, until we come to the house
of our father and tell Metaneira our deep-girt mother
all these things straight through, in case she might bid
you come to our house and not search after others'.
165   For her only son is now nursed in our well-built hall,
a late-born child, much prayed for and cherished.
If you might raise him to the threshold of youth,

any woman who saw you would feel envy at once,
such rewards for his rearing our mother will give you."
170   Thus they spoke and she nodded her head. The girls
carried proudly bright jars filled with water and
swiftly they reached the great house of their father.
At once to their mother they told what they saw and heard.
She bade them go quickly to offer a boundless wage.
175   Just as hinds or heifers in the season of spring
bound through the meadow sated with fodder,
so they, lifting the folds of their shimmering robes,
darted down the hollow wagon-track, and their hair
danced on their shoulders like a crocus blossom.
180   They found the famed goddess near the road
just where they had left her. Then to the house
of their father they led her. She, grieved in her heart,
walked behind with veiled head. And her dark robe
swirled round the slender feet of the goddess.
185   They soon reached the house of god-cherished Keleos,
and went through the portico to the place where
their regal mother sat by the pillar of the close-fitted roof,
holding on her lap the child, her young offshoot. To her
they raced. But the goddess stepped on the threshold. Her head
190   reached the roof and she filled the doorway with divine light.
Reverence, awe, and pale fear seized Metaneira.
She gave up her chair and bade the goddess sit down.
But Demeter, bringer of seasons and giver of rich gifts,
did not wish to be seated on the shining seat.
195   She waited resistant, her lovely eyes cast down,
until knowing Iambe set out a well-built stool
for her and cast over it a silvery fleece.
Seated there, the goddess drew the veil before her face.
For a long time she sat voiceless with grief on the stool
200   and responded to no one with word or gesture.
Unsmiling, tasting neither food nor drink,
she sat wasting with desire for her deep-girt daughter,
until knowing Iambe jested with her and
mocking with many a joke moved the holy goddess
205   to smile and laugh and keep a gracious heart—
Iambe, who later pleased her moods as well.
Metaneira offered a cup filled with honey-sweet wine,
but Demeter refused it. It was not right, she said,

for her to drink red wine; then she bid them mix barley
210   and water with soft mint and give her to drink.
        Metaneira made and gave the drink to the goddess as she bid.
        Almighty Deo received it for the sake of the rite.
        Well-girt Metaneira spoke first among them:
        "Hail, lady, for I suppose your parents are not lowborn,
215   but noble. Your eyes are marked by modesty
        and grace, even as those of justice-dealing kings.
        We mortals are forced, though it may hurt us, to bear
        the gifts of the gods. For the yoke lies on our necks.
        But now you have come here, all that's mine will be yours.
220   Raise this child for me, whom the gods provided
        late-born and unexpected, much-prayed for by me.
        If you raise him and he comes to the threshold of youth,
        any woman who saw you would feel envy at once,
        such rewards for his rearing would I give you."
225   Rich-crowned Demeter addressed her in turn:
        "Hail also to you, lady, may the gods give you blessings.
        Gladly will I embrace the child as you bid me.
        I will raise him, nor do I expect a spell or the Undercutter
        to harm him through the negligence of his nurse.
230   For I know a charm more cutting than the Woodcutter;
        I know a strong safeguard against baneful bewitching."
        So speaking, she took the child to her fragrant breast
        with her divine hands. And his mother was glad at heart.
        Thus the splendid son of skillful Keleos, Demophoön,
235   whom well-girt Metaneira bore, she nursed
        in the great halls. And he grew like a divinity,
        eating no food nor sucking [at a mother's breast];
        [For daily well-crowned divine] Demeter anointed
        him with ambrosia like one born from a god
240   and breathed sweetly on him, held close to her breast.
        At night, she would bury him like a brand in the fire's might,
        unknown to his own parents. And great was their wonder
        as he grew miraculously fast; he was like the gods.
        She would have made him ageless and immortal,
245   if well-girt Metaneira had not in her folly
        kept watch at night from her fragrant chamber
        and spied. But she shrieked and struck both thighs
        in fear for her child, much misled in her mind,
        and in her grief she spoke winged words.
250   "Demophoön, my child, the stranger buries you

deep in the fire, causing me woe and bitter cares."
Thus she spoke lamenting. The great goddess heard her.
In anger at her, bright-crowned Demeter snatched
from the flames with immortal hands the dear child
255 Metaneira had borne beyond hope in the halls and,
raging terribly at heart, cast him away from herself to the ground.
At the same time she addressed well-girt Metaneira:
"Mortals are ignorant and foolish, unable to foresee
destiny, the good and the bad coming on them.
260 You are incurably misled by your folly.
Let the god's oath, the implacable water of Styx, be witness,
I would have made your child immortal and ageless
forever; I would have given him unfailing honor.
But now he cannot escape death and the death spirits.
265 Yet unfailing honor will forever be his, because
he lay on my knees and slept in my arms.
In due time as the years come round for him,
the sons of Eleusis will continue year after year
to wage war and dread combat against each other.
270 For I am honored Demeter, the greatest
source of help and joy to mortals and immortals.
But now let all the people build me a great temple
with an altar beneath, under the sheer wall
of the city on the rising hill above Kallichoron.
275 I myself will lay down the rites so that hereafter
performing due rites you may propitiate my spirit."
Thus speaking, the goddess changed her size and appearance,
thrusting off old age. Beauty breathed about her and
from her sweet robes a delicious fragrance spread;
280 a light beamed far out from the goddess's immortal skin,
and her golden hair flowed over her shoulders.
The well-built house flooded with radiance like lightning.
She left the halls. At once Metaneira's knees buckled.
For a long time she remained voiceless, forgetting
285 to pick up her dear only son from the floor.
But his sisters heard his pitiful voice and
leapt from their well-spread beds. Then one took
the child in her arms and laid him to her breast.
Another lit the fire; a third rushed on delicate feet
290 to rouse her mother from her fragrant chamber.
Gathering about the gasping child, they bathed and
embraced him lovingly. Yet his heart was not comforted,

for lesser nurses and handmaids held him now.
All night they tried to appease the dread goddess,
295   shaking with fear. But when dawn appeared,
they explained to wide-ruling Keleos exactly
what the bright-crowned goddess Demeter commanded.
Then he called to assembly his innumerable people
and bid them build for fair-tressed Demeter
300   a rich temple and an altar on the rising hill.
Attentive to his speech, they obeyed at once and did
as he prescribed. It grew as the goddess decreed.
But once they finished and ceased their toil,
each went off home. Then golden-haired Demeter
305   remained sitting apart from all the immortals,
wasting with desire for her deep-girt daughter.
For mortals she ordained a terrible and brutal year
on the deeply fertile earth. The ground released
no seed, for bright-crowned Demeter kept it buried.
310   In vain the oxen dragged many curved plows down
the furrows. In vain much white barley fell on the earth.
She would have destroyed the whole mortal race
by cruel famine and stolen the glorious honor of gifts
and sacrifices from those having homes on Olympus,
315   if Zeus had not seen and pondered their plight in his heart.
First he roused golden-winged Iris to summon
fair-tressed Demeter, so lovely in form.
Zeus spoke and Iris obeying the dark-clouded
son of Kronos, raced swiftly between heaven and earth.
320   She came to the citadel of fragrant Eleusis
and found in her temple dark-robed Demeter.
Addressing her, she spoke winged words:
"Demeter, Zeus, the father, with his unfailing knowledge
bids you rejoin the tribes of immortal gods.
325   Go and let Zeus's word not remain unfulfilled."
Thus she implored, but Demeter's heart was unmoved.
Then the father sent in turn all the blessed immortals;
one by one they kept coming and pleading
and offered her many glorious gifts and whatever
330   honors she might choose among the immortal gods.
Yet not one could bend the mind and thought
of the raging goddess, who harshly spurned their pleas.
Never, she said, would she mount up to fragrant

Olympus nor release the seed from the earth,
335   until she saw with her eyes her own fair-faced child.
When Zeus, heavy-thundering and mighty-voiced,
heard this, he sent down the Slayer of Argos° to Erebos
with his golden staff to wheedle Hades with soft words
and lead back holy Persephone from the misty gloom
340   into the light to join the gods so that her mother
might see her with her eyes and desist from anger.
Hermes did not disobey. At once he left Olympus's height
and plunged swiftly into the depths of the earth.
He met lord Hades inside his dwelling,
345   reclining on a bed with his shy spouse, strongly reluctant
through desire for her mother. [Still she, Demeter,
was brooding on revenge for the deeds of the blessed gods].
The strong Slayer of Argos stood near and spoke:
"Dark-haired Hades, ruler of the dead, Father Zeus
350   bids me lead noble Persephone up from Erebos
to join us, so that her mother might see her with her eyes
and cease from anger and dread wrath against the gods.
For she is devising a great scheme to destroy
the helpless race of mortals born on earth,
355   burying the seed beneath the ground and obliterating
divine honors. Her anger is terrible, nor does she go
among the gods but sits aloof in her fragrant temple,
keeping to the rocky citadel of Eleusis."
Thus he spoke and Aidoneus, lord of the dead, smiled
360   with his brows, nor disobeyed king Zeus's commands.
At once he urged thoughtful Persephone:
"Go, Persephone, to the side of your dark-robed mother,
keeping the spirit and temper in your breast benign.
Do not be so sad and angry beyond the rest;
365   in no way among immortals will I be an unsuitable spouse,
myself a brother of father Zeus. And when you are there,
you will have power over all that lives and moves,
and you will possess the greatest honors among the gods.
There will be punishment forevermore for those wrongdoers
370   who fail to appease your power with sacrifices,
performing proper rites and making due offerings."
Thus he spoke and thoughtful Persephone rejoiced.

°Hermes

Eagerly she leapt up for joy. But he gave her to eat
a honey-sweet pomegranate seed, stealthily passing it
375   around her, lest she once more stay forever
by the side of revered Demeter of the dark robe.
Then Aidoneus commander-to-many yoked
his divine horses before the golden chariot.
She mounted the chariot and at her side the strong
380   Slayer of Argos took the reins and whip in his hands
and dashed from the halls. The horses flew eagerly;
swiftly they completed the long journey; not sea nor
river waters, not grassy glens nor mountain peaks
slowed the speed of the immortal horses,
385   slicing the deep air as they flew above these places.
He brought them to a halt where rich-crowned Demeter
waited before the fragrant temple. With one look she darted
like a maenad down a mountain shaded with woods.
On her side Persephone, [seeing] her mother's [radiant face],
390   [left chariot and horses,] and leapt down to run
[and fall on her neck in passionate embrace].
[While holding her dear child in her arms], her [heart
suddenly sensed a trick. Fearful, she] drew back
from [her embrace and at once inquired:]
395   "My child, tell me, you [did not taste] food [while below?]
Speak out [and hide nothing, so we both may know.]
[For if not], ascending [from miserable Hades],
you will dwell with me and your father, the
dark-clouded [son of Kronos], honored by all the gods.
400   But if [you tasted food], returning beneath [the earth,]
you will stay a third part of the seasons [each year],
but two parts with myself and the other immortals.
When the earth blooms in spring with all kinds
of sweet flowers, then from the misty dark you will
405   rise again, a great marvel to gods and mortal men.
By what guile did the mighty Host-to-Many deceive you?"
Then radiant Persephone replied to her in turn:
"I will tell you the whole truth exactly, Mother.
The Slayer of Argos came to bring fortunate news
410   from my father, the son of Kronos, and the other gods
and lead me from Erebos so that seeing me with your eyes
you would desist from your anger and dread wrath
at the gods. Then I leapt up for joy, but the stealthily

put in my mouth a food honey-sweet, a pomegranate seed,
415 and compelled me against my will and by force to taste it.
For the rest—how seizing me by the shrewd plan of my father,
Kronos's son, he carried me off into the earth's depths—
I shall tell and elaborate all that you ask.
We were all in the beautiful meadow—
420 Leukippê; Phaino; Elektra; and Ianthê;
Melitê; Iachê; Rhodeia; and Kallirhoê;
Melibosis; Tychê; and flower-faced Okyrhoê;
Khryseis; Ianeira; Akastê; Admetê;
Rhodopê; Plouto; and lovely Kalypso;
425 Styx; Ourania; and fair Galaxaura; Pallas,
rouser of battles; and Artemis, sender of arrows—
playing and picking lovely flowers with our hands,
soft crocus mixed with irises and hyacinth,
rosebuds and lilies, a marvel to see, and the
430 narcissus that wide earth bore like a crocus.
As I joyously plucked it, the ground gaped from beneath,
and the mighty lord, Host-to-Many, rose from it
and carried me off beneath the earth in his golden chariot
much against my will. And I cried out at the top of my voice.
435 I speak the whole truth, though I grieve to tell it."
Then all day long, their minds at one, they soothed
each other's heart and soul in many ways,
embracing fondly, and their spirits abandoned grief,
as they gave and received joy between them.
440 Hekate of the delicate veil drew near them
and often caressed the daughter of holy Demeter;
from that time this lady served her as chief attendant.
To them Zeus, heavy-thundering and mighty-voiced,
sent as mediator fair-tressed Rheia to summon
445 dark-robed Demeter to the tribes of gods; he promised
to give her what honors she might choose among the gods.
He agreed his daughter would spend one-third
of the revolving year in the misty dark and two-thirds
with her mother and the other immortals.
450 So he spoke and the goddess did not disobey his commands.
She darted swiftly down the peaks of Olympus
and arrived where the Rarian plain, once life-giving
udder of earth, now giving no life at all, stretched idle
and utterly leafless. For the white barley was hidden

455   by the designs of lovely-ankled Demeter. Yet as spring came on,
the fields would soon ripple with long ears of grain;
and the rich furrows would grow heavy on the ground
with grain to be tied with bands into sheaves.
There she first alighted from the barren air.

460   Mother and daughter were glad to see each other
and rejoiced at heart. Rheia of the delicate veil then said:
"Come, child, Zeus, heavy-thundering and mighty-voiced,
summons you to rejoin the tribes of the gods;
he has offered to give what honors you choose among them.

465   He agreed that his daughter would spend one-third
of the revolving year in the misty dark, and two-thirds
with her mother and the other immortals.
He guaranteed it would be so with a nod of his head.
So come, my child, obey me; do not rage overmuch

470   and forever at the dark-clouded son of Kronos.
Now make the grain grow fertile for humankind."
So Rheia spoke, and rich-crowned Demeter did not disobey.
At once she sent forth fruit from the fertile fields
and the whole wide earth burgeoned with leaves

475   and flowers. She went to the kings who administer law,
Triptolemos and Diokles, driver of horses, mighty
Eumolpos and Keleos, leader of the people, and revealed
the conduct of her rites and taught her Mysteries to all of them,
holy rites that are not to be transgressed, nor pried into,

480   nor divulged. For a great awe of the gods stops the voice.
Blessed is the mortal on earth who has seen these rites,
but the uninitiate who has no share in them never
has the same lot once dead in the dreary darkness.
When the great goddess had founded all her rites,

485   the goddesses left for Olympus and the assembly of the other gods.
There they dwell by Zeus delighting-in-thunder, inspiring
awe and reverence. Highly blessed is the mortal
on earth whom they graciously favor with love.
For soon they will send to the hearth of his great house

490   Ploutos, the god giving abundance to mortals.
But come, you goddesses, dwelling in the town of
fragrant Eleusis, and seagirt Paros, and rocky Antron,
revered Deo, mighty giver of seasons and glorious gifts,
you and your very fair daughter Persephone,

495   for my song grant gladly a living that warms the heart.
And I shall remember you and a new song as well.

Questions for Review and Discussion

1. From the time she leaves Mount Olympus until she reunites with her daughter, Demeter surrounds herself with a network of women. What role do these women play in the *Hymn*? How do they assist Demeter in her journey?
2. What are the stages of the grieving process? Does Demeter go through these stages as she grieves, mourns, and eventually reunites with her daughter?
3. Persephone's abduction, rape, and captivity in the underworld precipitate her transformation from kore (the "maiden") to Persephone, the powerful queen of the underworld. Other than her change in name, what other qualities has Persephone acquired that were not apparent in her manifestation as kore?
4. Why does Persephone swallow the pomegranate seed?
5. How do male modes of behavior and communication differ from female modes of behavior and communication as they are illustrated by the characters?
6. Why does Zeus send his mother to mediate with Demeter instead of talking to her directly himself?
7. What are some of the differences between the Hades who abducts kore and the Hades who releases Persephone from the underworld?
8. What are some of the similarities and differences between Persephone's journey to the underworld and Inanna's journey to the underworld?
9. In what ways can the myth of Demeter and Persephone be interpreted as a transitional myth between male-dominated society and the more ancient value system of goddess-worshipping communities that honored the contributions and role of the female?
10. What can Demeter and Persephone teach us about coping with adversity and trauma?

Chapter 5

Circe

Glossary of Names and Terms

AIOLOS   Keeper of the winds; traps all the bad winds in a bag and cautions Odysseus not to open the bag until he arrives in Ithaka

ANTIPHATES   A Lastrygonian who eats one of Odysseus's men

ARGEIPHONTES   Another name for Hermes (see below)

ATHENA   Greek goddess of wisdom and warfare; daughter of Zeus; Odysseus's advocate and mentor

CHARYBDIS   A violent whirlpool that Odysseus must sail past in order to get home

CHTHONIC   The land of the dead; the underworld; pertaining to the earth

CIRCE   Daughter of Helios and Perse; enchantress who turns Odysseus's men into swine; becomes Odysseus's lover and guide

CYCLOPS   One-eyed giant; son of Poseidon; Odysseus blinds him

ELPENOR   Member of Odysseus's crew; died in a drunken stupor by falling off Circe's roof

EREBOS   Land of the dead (see Hades)

EURYLOCHOS   Member of Odysseus's crew; evades Circe's attempt to transform him into a pig

HADES   The underworld; land of the dead; also known as Erebos

HIEROPHANT   High priestess; provides access to higher knowledge

HIEROS GAMOS   Sacred marriage; the sacred prostitute, as the embodiment of the great goddess, receives the male sexually to initiate him to higher knowledge

HELIOS   Sun god; Odysseus angers him when his men eat the sacred cattle on the island of Thrinakia

HERMES   Messenger of the gods; sent by Zeus to order Kalypso to release Odysseus; provides Odysseus with moly flower to evade Circe's spell

HOMER   Blind, Ionian poet, credited with writing the *Iliad* and the *Odyssey*

ILIAD   Greek epic poem that tells the story of the last year of the ten-year Trojan War

ITHAKA   Odysseus's kingdom

KALYPSO   Sea goddess who loves Odysseus; holds him captive for seven years; offers him immortality to stay with her

LAERTES   Odysseus's father

LAISTRYGONIANS   Man-eating giants

MOLY   Flower with white petals and black roots; protects Odysseus from Circe's spell

NAUSIKAA   The young princess of the Phaikians who is the first to encounter Odysseus when he lands on the island

ODYSSEUS   King of Ithaka; Greek warrior who fought in Trojan war

ODYSSEY   Greek epic poem that tells the story of Odysseus as he journeys home to Ithaka from Troy

PENELOPE   Odysseus's faithful wife who waits patiently for his return for 20 years

POLITES   A member of Odysseus's crew

PSYCHOPOMP   Escorts the souls of the dead to the underworld

PHAIAKIANS   Their island is Odysseus's last stop before going back to Ithaka; they invite him to recount his adventures before assisting him on his journey home

POSEIDON   God of the sea; seeks revenge on Odysseus for injuring his son, Cyclops

SKYLLA   A six-headed monster that Odysseus must sail by in order to get home

TEIRESIAS   Blind prophet; Odysseus seeks him in the underworld to receive his advice and direction

ZEUS   King of the Olympian gods

Circe is a goddess, the daughter of Helios, the sun god, and Perse. Her most prominent appearance in Greek mythology is in Book X of Homer's *Odyssey*. Although neither the existence of Homer nor the actual date of composition of two of the greatest epic poems in Western literature, the *Iliad* and the *Odyssey*, can be determined, most scholars agree that both poems were written by the blind Ionian poet named Homer. The research suggests that the poems were composed in the late eighth century and early seventh century B.C.E. The *Iliad*, which tells the story of the last year of the ten-year Trojan War between the Greeks and Trojans, is generally considered a product of Homer's youth, while the *Odyssey*, which describes the long and arduous journey of the Greek warrior Odysseus as he makes his way home to Ithaka from Troy, is considered a product of Homer's old age.

The *Odyssey* is in 24 books. It opens with Odysseus on the island of Kalypso, where he has been stranded for seven consecutive years. The goddess Athena, Odysseus's mentor and guide, takes advantage of Poseidon's absence from Mount Olympus to plead with Zeus for Odysseus's release. Zeus agrees, and Odysseus is released from Kalypso's island. However, once Odysseus is on the sea, Poseidon generates a storm that destroys his boat, leaving him to drown. With the assistance of Athena and others, Odysseus manages to crawl ashore on the island of the Phaiakians where he is invited to recount his adventures after his departure from Troy.

Beginning with Book IX, Odysseus narrates the sequence of the journey's events after the fall of Troy when he and his men set sail for Ithaka. He tells of an assortment of adventures and encounters that progressively diminish the number of surviving crewmembers and ships. Some of these adventures consist of self-inflicted punishments incurred for inciting the wrath of a god; some are not self-inflicted but are designed to test Odysseus's resolve and to delay his homecoming. By the time Odysseus arrives at Circe's island in Book X, he has lost all but his own ship.

Upon arriving at Circe's island, Odysseus sends some of his men to explore. Lured by Circe's singing, all but Eurylochos enter Circe's hall. Eurylochos watches as Circe provides his comrades with a drink and then, with one swish of her stick, promptly transforms them into swine. Eurylochos escapes to tell Odysseus the news. As Odysseus makes his way to Circe's hall to rescue his men, he encounters Hermes who provides him with a moly flower to protect him from Circe's spell. Hermes instructs Odysseus to accept Circe's offer of intimacy.

Odysseus enters Circe's hall, accepts her drink, but to her initial consternation, he fails to experience the brutish transformation upon the requisite swish of her stick. Instead, he whips out his sword and holds it against her throat. Circe then recognizes him as Odysseus and invites him to cement their mutual trust through the act of lovemaking. Odysseus obliges by mounting "the surpassingly beautiful bed of Circe." Circe honors Odysseus's request to transform his men back into their human form. And after spending a year as her lover, Odysseus asks Circe to keep her promise to assist him on his journey home. Circe charts the rest of the journey for him, cautioning him of hazards along the way and guiding his conduct. She then gives him the somewhat unwelcome news that he must visit Hades, the land of the dead, to consult with Teiresias.

Odysseus then journeys to the underworld where he meets with the souls of the dead, including Teiresias. This visit constitutes a transformative experience for him. It represents his confrontation with the ultimate fear, death itself. Odysseus becomes a changed man as a result of this contact with death. He begins to demonstrate a greater sensitivity, humility, and compassion in terms of how he leads his men and interacts with others—qualities that were far from evident in the first half of the epic.

After his visit to the underworld, Odysseus returns to Circe who guides him through the remaining stages of his journey. She instructs him on how to resist the song of the Sirens, how to navigate his way through the narrow straits of Skylla and Charybdis, and she cautions against eating Helios's sacred cattle on the island of Thrinakia. Circe accurately predicts that failure to abide by her precepts will result in the destruction of his remaining ship and death of his crew. All comes to pass as Circe has predicted, so that by the time Odysseus lands on Kalypso's island, he is the lone survivor, bereft of companions and a sailing vessel. He spends seven years with Kalypso until Athena obtains his release at the opening of the *Odyssey*.

Having heard Odysseus's tale, the Phaiakians honor their promise and assist him in his return to Ithaka. Once in Ithaka, Odysseus defeats the suitors, reunites with his wife, Penelope, and restores order to the land. Odysseus's journey home lasts ten years, but the action covered from beginning to end of the *Odyssey* covers a period of six weeks.

Circe's appearance in Book X of the *Odyssey* is central to the poem as a whole and pivotal to Odysseus's development. Circe teaches Odysseus the humility that comes with the knowledge that he does not have all the answers and needs the advice and assistance of others who do. And since that advice and assistance can come from a goddess, Circe also instills in him a greater respect for the feminine. Odysseus is transformed from the brusque, crude, and arrogant warrior he once was to a man who emerges naked from the sea in Book VI and approaches the young Nausikaa with a delicacy, sensitivity, and humility that had previously been absent from his behavior.

It is as a direct result of Circe's influence that Odysseus develops the skills and acquires the knowledge that enable him return to Ithaka and to Penelope. Circe does not appear in the poem until Odysseus is thoroughly lost and dejected, and she does not disappear from the poem until she has helped him regain his bearings and armed him with instructions on how to steer his course home and avert the dangers that lie ahead.

Circe's role can be compared to that of an initiator. She mediates Odysseus's development from an arrogant, brutish hero who is drunk with his own abilities and who suffers from inflated self-importance to one who has been duly chastened, humbled, and now demonstrates a readiness to be initiated into the feminine. Circe's initial encounter with Odysseus is characterized by a bitter gender rivalry—one that is based on mutual hostility, distrust, and hierarchy. She challenges the hero's masculinity. Those males who are feint-hearted and unable to meet her challenge are reduced to their lowest common denominator, their animalistic or swine-like nature. Since Odysseus resists her attempt to subjugate him and manages to retain his autonomous, masculine identity by threatening her with his phallic sword, he is rewarded with intimacy, the status of equal partnership, and initiation into the secrets of the chthonic realm—a realm under the feminine sphere of influence.

Circe's powers become benevolent only after Odysseus has thwarted her challenge. She accepts him as an equal partner and provides him with guidance and instruction to navigate his way successfully through the underworld and beyond. Odysseus proves himself a worthy student, one who has been humbled by his previous encounters and who now recognizes his limitations and is eager to embrace her assistance. Circe has enabled him to confront his greatest fear—death. This allows him to face life and the challenges that lie ahead with greater wisdom. In her willingness to champion Odysseus and provide him with the necessary skills he needs for a successful journey home, Circe illustrates her unlimited munificence to those who have proved themselves worthy of her help.

The *Odyssey* is fundamentally a story of initiation with a happy ending. Odysseus is initiated into the ways of the feminine. The masculinist perspective that Odysseus embodies will not change if left to its own devices. It has to be cajoled, lured, educated, and, in some cases, coerced by the feminine. The feminine qualities, represented by Circe, must be acknowledged, respected, and assimilated into the masculine realm in a noncompetitive, nonhierarchical environment in order to achieve balance and wholeness. Circe is the transformational feminine power who is endowed with the ability to offer the path of debasement or the path of deliverance. Through meeting her challenge, Odysseus pursues the path of deliverance and learns to balance his masculine, warrior attributes with the civilizing influence of the feminine.

Odysseus is assisted in this endeavor when he receives Hermes's moly flower with its protective attributes. Without this moly, Odysseus would have suffered the same fate as his comrades. The white flower (symbolizing the masculine) with black roots (symbolizing the feminine) suggests an integration between the masculine and feminine in a balanced harmony that is devoid of gender hierarchy. The moly represents the importance of integrating opposites and achieving balance in order to acquire wholeness. Odysseus's contact with the moly constitutes a contact with wholeness that enables him to neutralize Circe's attempt to strip him of his humanity.

The powers of transformation, including the process by which the psyche is reshaped to attain wholeness, has historically been associated with women. Until the connection between male insemination and female fertility was established, our ancestors believed that women had the singular ability to transform their blood into new life. They could generate new beings from their bodies; transform their bodily fluids into sustenance; and transform raw materials into food, clothing, containers, and utensils. Since woman was perceived as the transformational agent in the physical realm, it was naturally assumed she was also the transformational agent in the spiritual realm. Her body represented the gateway to higher knowledge.

Circe and Odysseus cement their relationship through engaging in sexual intercourse. This act recalls the *hieros gamos* or sacred marriage of prepatriarchal cultures, whereby the sacred prostitute or hierodule (an embodiment of the Great Goddess who served as the mediator between the deity and the male) received the male sexually in order to initiate him into higher knowledge and precipitate his transformation. The sacred marriage symbolizes a physical and psychological union of opposites whereby the disparate elements of our separate beings are reconciled to form a whole through a mutually beneficial interaction. In the consummation of the sacred marriage, man and woman, sexuality and spirituality are integrated and balanced, with each realm drawing vitality from the other to facilitate the movement from fragmentation to wholeness. Perhaps because he recognizes her as a tutelary figure, Odysseus is one of the few males in Greek mythology and literature who engages in sexual intimacy with a goddess and who is not made to suffer as a consequence. Circe's liaison with Odysseus may thus have a higher claim to the status of *hieros gamos* than any other in Greek legend.

Circe acts as Odysseus's hierophant, the priestess who initiates him into higher knowledge. She fulfills her role as a necessary agent for his transformation from an over masculinized male to one who has integrated the feminine and thereby become more complete. She facilitates his transition from a warrior bloodied by battle to a spouse who is worthy of the chaste and loyal Penelope. She guides, instructs, and provides the initiate with the necessary tools, but she cannot undertake the journey for him or grant him easy access to higher knowledge. This is a journey he must undertake for himself if he is to reap its rewards since those rewards can come only through experiencing the process.

Circe gives her gifts freely and generously, operating with an ethic of responsibility and care. But she is unwilling to subsume her independent identity to that of a male. Nor does she implode, fall apart, commit rash acts of murder, express her jealous outrage at Odysseus's wife, plead with Odysseus to stay, attempt to bribe him with immortality, or beg him for a baby. Instead, she provides assistance when needed and releases him willingly. There is no hint of possessiveness in her actions. Circe's conduct and attitude exemplify the autonomous, empowered woman who has retained her virginal status by maintaining her sovereignty, by remaining free from the need for male validation, and by controlling all aspects of her being, including her sexuality.

The figure of Hermes at this pivotal point in the poem is not without significance. As the messenger of the gods, Hermes has access to the three realms of heaven, earth, and underworld. In his role as *psychopomp,* he escorts the souls of the dead to the realm of Hades. Hermes is further associated with journeys. So it is only fitting that he should be the god who assists Odysseus as he embarks on a journey of transformation through Circe. Hermes acts as the guide who provides Odysseus with the necessary tools and instructions to effect this transformation through interaction with Circe and the feminine realm she embodies.

Book X of the *Odyssey* is from the translation by Richmond Lattimore.

REFERENCES

Agha-Jaffar, Tamara. *Demeter and Persephone: Lessons From A Myth.* North Carolina: McFarland, 2002.

Edinger, Edward F. *The Eternal Drama: The Inner Meaning of Greek Mythology.* Ed. Deborah A. Wesley. Boston: Shambhala, 1994.

Exum, Cheryl J. *Plotted, Shot, and Painted: Cultural Representations of Biblical Women.* Sheffield: Sheffield Academic P, 1996.

Homer. *The Odyssey.* Trans. Robert Fitzgerald. New York: Anchor, 1963.

Houston, Jean. *The Hero and the Goddess: The Odyssey as Mystery and Initiation.* New York: Ballantine, 1992.

Kerenyi, Karl. *Goddesses of Sun and Moon.* Trans. Murray Stein. Dallas: Spring, 1979.

Lattimore, Richmond, trans. *The Odyssey of Homer.* New York: Harper Perennial, 1991.

Powers, Meredith A. *The Heroine in Western Literature: The Archetype and her Reemergence in Modern Prose.* North Carolina: McFarland, 1991.

Qualls-Corbett, Nancy. *The Sacred Prostitute: Eternal Aspect of the Feminine.* Toronto: Inner City, 1988.

Yarnall, Judith. *Transformations of Circe: The History of an Enchantress.* Urbana: U of Illinois P, 1994.

The Odyssey of Homer

Book X

'We came next to the Aiolian island, where Aiolos
lived, Hippotas' son, beloved by the immortal
gods, on a floating island, the whole enclosed by a rampart
of bronze, not to be broken, and the sheer of the cliff runs upward
5   to it; and twelve children were born to him in his palace,
six of them daughters, and six sons in the pride of their youth, so

he bestowed his daughters on his sons, to be their consorts.
And evermore, beside their dear father and gracious mother,
these feast, and good things beyond number are set before them;
10   and all their days the house fragrant with food echoes
in the courtyard, but their nights they sleep each one by his modest
wife, under coverlets, and on bedsteads corded for bedding.
We came to the city of these men and their handsome houses,
and a whole month he entertained me and asked me everything
15   of Ilion, and the ships of the Argives, and the Achaians'
homecoming, and I told him all the tale as it happened.
But when I asked him about the way back and requested
conveyance, again he did not refuse, but granted me passage.
He gave me a bag made of the skin taken off a nine-year
20   ox, stuffed full inside with the courses of all the blowing
winds, for the son of Kronos had set him in charge over
the winds, to hold them still or start them up at his pleasure.
He stowed it away in the hollow ship, tied fast with a silver
string, so there should be no wrong breath of wind, not even
25   a little, but set the West Wind free to blow me and carry
the ships and the men aboard them on their way; but it was not
so to be, for we were ruined by our own folly.
        'Nevertheless we sailed on, night and day, for nine days,
and on the tenth at last appeared the land of our fathers,
30   and we could see people tending fires, we were very close to them.
But then the sweet sleep came upon me, for I was worn out
with always handling the sheet myself, and I would not give it
to any other companion, so we could come home quicker
to our own country; but my companions talked with each other
35   and said that I was bringing silver and gold home with me,
given me by great-hearted Aiolos, son of Hippotas;
and thus they would speak to each other, each looking at the man next him:
"See now, this man is loved by everybody and favored
by all, whenever he visits anyone's land and city,
40   and is bringing home with him handsome treasures taken from the plunder
of Troy, while we, who have gone through everything he has
on the same venture, come home with our hands empty. Now too
Aiolos in favor of friendship has given him all these
goods. Let us quickly look inside and see what is in there,
45   and how much silver and gold this bag contains inside it."
        'So he spoke, and the evil counsel of my companions
prevailed, and they opened the bag and the winds all burst out. Suddenly
the storm caught them away and swept them over the water

weeping, away from their own country. Then I waking
50 pondered deeply in my own blameless spirit, whether
to throw myself over the side and die in the open water,
or wait it out in silence and still be one of the living;
and I endured it and waited, and hiding my face I lay down
in the ship, while all were carried on the evil blast of the stormwind
55 back to the Aiolian island, with my friends grieving.
     'There again we set foot on the mainland, and fetched water,
and my companions soon took their supper there by the fast ships.
But after we had tasted of food and drink, then I
took along one herald with me, and one companion,
60 and went up to the famous house of Aiolos. There I found him
sitting at dinner with his wife and with his own children.
We came to the house beside the pillars, and on the doorstone
we sat down, and their minds wondered at us and they asked us:
"What brings you back, Odysseus? What evil spirit has vexed you?
65 We sent you properly on your way, so you could come back
to your own country and house and whatever else is dear to you."
     'So they spoke, and I though sorry at heart answered:
"My wretched companions brought me to ruin, helped by the pitiless
sleep. Then make it right, dear friends; for you have the power."
70   'So I spoke to them, plying them with words of endearment,
but they were all silent; only the father found words and answered:
"O least of living creatures, out of this island! Hurry!
I have no right to see on his way, none to give passage
to any man whom the blessed gods hate with such bitterness.
75 Out. This arrival means you are hateful to the immortals."
     'So speaking he sent me, groaning heavily, out of his palace,
and from there, grieving still at heart, we sailed on further,
but the men's spirit was worn away with the pain of rowing
and our own silliness, since homecoming seemed ours no longer.
80   'Nevertheless we sailed on, night and day, for six days,
and on the seventh came to the sheer citadel of Lamos,
Telepylos of the Laistrygones, where one herdsman, driving
his flocks in hails another, who answers as he drives
his flocks out; and there a man who could do without sleep could earn him
85 double wages, one for herding the cattle, one for the silvery
sheep. There the courses of night and day lie close together.
There as we entered the glorious harbor, which a sky-towering
cliff encloses on either side, with no break anywhere,
and two projecting promontories facing each other
90 run out toward the mouth, and there is a narrow entrance,

there all the rest of them had their oar-swept ships in the inward
part, they were tied up close together inside the hollow
harbor, for there was never a swell of surf inside it,
neither great nor small, but there was a pale calm on it.
95   I myself, however, kept my black ship on the outside,
at the very end, making her fast to the cliff with a cable,
and climbed to a rocky point of observation and stood there.
From here no trace of cattle nor working of men was visible;
all we could see was the smoke going up from the country.
100   So I sent companions ahead telling them to find out
what men, eaters of bread, might live here in this country.
I chose two men, and sent a third with them, as a herald.
They left the ship and walked on a smooth road where the wagons
carried the timber down from the high hills to the city,
105   and there in front of the town they met a girl drawing water.
This was the powerful daughter of the Laistrygonian
Antiphates, who had gone down to the sweet-running wellspring,
Artakie, whence they would carry their water back to the city.
My men stood by her and talked with her, and asked her who was
110   king of these people and who was lord over them. She readily
pointed out to them the high-roofed house of her father.
But when they entered the glorious house, they found there a woman
as big as a mountain peak, and the sight of her filled them with horror.
At once she summoned famous Antiphates, her husband,
115   from their assembly, and he devised dismal death against them.
He snatched up one of my companions, and prepared him for dinner,
but the other two darted away in flight, and got back to my ship.
The king raised the cry through the city. Hearing him the powerful
Laistrygones came swarming up from every direction,
120   tens of thousands of them, and not like men, like giants.
These, standing along the cliffs, pelted my men with man-sized
boulders, and a horrid racket went up by the ships, of men
being killed and ships being smashed to pieces. They speared them
like fish, and carried them away for their joyless feasting.
125   But while they were destroying them in the deep-water harbor,
meanwhile I, drawing from beside my thigh the sharp sword,
chopped away the cable that tied the ship with the dark prow
and called out to my companions, and urged them with all speed
to throw their weight on the oars and escape the threatening evil,
130   and they made the water fly, fearing destruction. Gladly
my ship, and only mine, fled out from the overhanging
cliffs to the open water, but the others were all destroyed there.

'From there we sailed on further along, glad to have escaped death,
but grieving still at heart for the loss of our dear companions.
135 We came to Aiaia, which is an island. There lived Circe
of the lovely hair, the dread goddess who talks with mortals,
who is own sister to the malignant-minded Aietes;
for they both are children of Helios, who shines on mortals,
and their mother is Perse who in turn is daughter of Ocean.
140 There we brought our ship in to the shore, in silence,
at a harbor fit for ships to lie, and some god guided us
in. There we disembarked, and for two days and two nights
we lay there, for sorrow and weariness eating our hearts out.
But when the fair-haired Dawn in her rounds brought on the third day,
145 then at last I took up my spear again, my sharp sword,
and went up quickly from beside the ship to find a lookout
place, to look for some trace of people, listen for some sound.
I climbed to a rocky point of observation and stood there,
and got a sight of smoke which came from the halls of Circe
150 going up from wide-wayed earth through undergrowth and forest.
Then I pondered deeply in my heart and my spirit,
whether, since I had seen the fire and smoke, to investigate;
but in the division of my heart this way seemed the best to me,
to go back first to the fast ship and the beach of the sea, and give
155 my companions some dinner, then send them forward to investigate.
But on my way, as I was close to the oar-swept vessel,
some god, because I was all alone, took pity upon me,
and sent a great stag with towering antlers right in my very
path; he had come from his range in the forest down to the river
160 to drink, for the fierce strength of the sun was upon him. As he
stepped out, I hit him in the middle of the back, next to
the spine, so that the brazen spearhead smashed its way clean through.
He screamed and dropped in the dust and the life spirit fluttered from him.
I set my foot on him and drew the bronze spear out of
165 the wound it had made, and rested it on the ground, while I
pulled growing twigs and willow withes and, braiding them into
a rope, about six feet in length, and looping them over
the feet of this great monster on both sides, lashed them together,
and with him loaded over my neck went toward the black ship,
170 propping myself on my spear, for there was no way to carry him
on the shoulder holding him with one hand, he was such a very
big beast. I threw him down by the ship and roused my companions,
standing beside each man and speaking to him in kind words:
"Dear friends, sorry as we are, we shall not yet go down into

175   the house of Hades. Not until our day is appointed.
Come then, while there is something to eat and drink by the fast ship,
let us think of our food and not be worn out with hunger."
            'So I spoke, and they listened at once to me and obeyed me,
and unveiling their heads along the beach of the barren water
180   they admired the stag, and truly he was a very big beast.
But after they had looked at him and their eyes had enjoyed him,
they washed their hands and set to preparing a communal high feast.
So for the whole length of the day until the sun's setting
we sat there feasting on unlimited meat and sweet wine.
185   But when the sun went down and the sacred darkness came over,
then we lay down to sleep along the break of the seashore;
but when the young Dawn showed again with her rosy fingers,
then I held an assembly and spoke forth to all of them:
"Hear my words, my companions, in spite of your hearts' sufferings.
190   Dear friends, for we do not know where the darkness is nor the sunrise,
nor where the Sun who shines upon people rises, nor where
he sets, then let us hasten our minds and think, whether there is
any course left open to us. But I think there is none.
For I climbed to a rocky place of observation and looked at
195   the island, and the endless sea lies all in a circle
around it, but the island itself lies low, and my eyes saw
smoke rising in the middle through the undergrowth and the forest."
            'So I spoke, and the inward heart in them was broken,
as they remembered Antiphates the Laistrygonian
200   and the violence of the great-hearted cannibal Cyclops,
and they wept loud and shrill, letting the big tears fall,
but there came no advantage to them for all their sorrowing.
            'I counted off all my strong-greaved companions into two
divisions, and appointed a leader for each, I myself
205   taking one, while godlike Eurylochos had the other.
Promptly then we shook the lots in a brazen helmet,
and the lot of great-hearted Eurylochos sprang out. He then
went on his way, and with him two-and-twenty companions,
weeping, and we whom they left behind were mourning also.
210   In the forest glen they came on the house of Circe. It was
in an open place, and put together from stones, well polished,
and all about it there were lions, and wolves of the mountains,
whom the goddess had given evil drugs and enchanted,
and these made no attack on the men, but came up thronging
215   about them, waving their long tails and fawning, in the way
that dogs go fawning about their master, when he comes home

from dining out, for he always brings back something to please them;
so these wolves with great strong claws and lions came fawning
on my men, but they were afraid when they saw the terrible big beasts.
220 They stood there in the forecourt of the goddess with the glorious
hair, and heard Circe inside singing in a sweet voice
as she went up and down a great design on a loom, immortal
such as goddesses have, delicate and lovely and glorious
their work. Now Polites leader of men, who was
225 the best and dearest to me of my friends, began the discussion:
"Friends, someone inside going up and down a great piece
of weaving is singing sweetly, and the whole place murmurs to the echo
of it, whether she is woman or goddess. Come, let us call her."
'So he spoke to them, and the rest gave voice, and called her,
230 and at once she opened the shining doors, and came out, and invited
them in, and all in their innocence entered; only
Eurylochos waited outside, for he suspected treachery.
She brought them inside and seated them on chairs and benches,
and mixed them a potion, with barley and cheese and pale honey
235 added to Pramneian wine, but put into the mixture
malignant drugs, to make them forgetful of their own country.
When she had given them this and they had drunk it down, next thing
she struck them with her wand and drove them into her pig pens,
and they took on the look of pigs, with the heads and voices
240 and bristles of pigs, but the minds within them stayed as they had been
before. So crying they went in, and before them Circe
threw down acorns for them to eat, and ilex and cornel
buds, such food as pigs who sleep on the ground always feed on.
'Eurylochos came back again to the fast black ship,
245 to tell the story of our companions and of their dismal
fate, but he could not get a word out, though he was trying
to speak, but his heart was stunned by the great sorrow, and both eyes
filled with tears, he could think of nothing but lamentation.
But after we had wondered at him and asked him questions,
250 at last he told us about the loss of his other companions:
"We went, O glorious Odysseus, through the growth as you
told us, and found a fine house in the glen. It was
in an open place, and put together from stones, well polished.
Someone, goddess or woman, was singing inside in a clear voice
255 as she went up and down her loom, and they called her, and spoke to her,
and at once she opened the shining doors, and came out and invited
them in, and all in their innocence entered, only
I waited for them outside, for I suspected treachery.

Then the whole lot of them vanished away together, nor did one
260   single one come out, though I sat and watched for a long time."
          'So he spoke, and I slung my great bronze sword with the silver
nails across my shoulders, and hung my bow on also,
and told him to guide me back by the same way he had gone;
but he, clasping my knees in both hands, entreated me,
265   and in loud lamentation spoke to me and addressed me:
"Illustrious, do not take me against my will there. Leave me
here, for I know you will never come back yourself, nor bring back
any of your companions. Let us rather make haste, and with these
who are left, escape, for we still may avoid the day of evil."
270   'So he spoke, and I answered again in turn and said to him:
"Eurylochos, you may stay here eating and drinking, even
where you are and beside the hollow black ship; only
I shall go. For there is strong compulsion upon me."
          'So I spoke, and started up from the ship and the seashore.
275   But as I went up through the lonely glens, and was coming
near to the great house of Circe, skilled in medicines,
there as I came up to the house, Hermes, of the golden
staff, met me on my way, in the likeness of a young man
with beard new grown, which is the most graceful time of young manhood.
280   He took me by the hand and spoke to me and named me, saying:
"Where are you going, unhappy man, all alone, through the hilltops,
ignorant of the land-lay, and your friends are here in Circe's
place, in the shape of pigs and holed up in the close pig pens.
Do you come here meaning to set them free? I do not think
285   you will get back yourself, but must stay here with the others.
But see, I will find you a way out of your troubles, and save you.
Here, this is a good medicine, take it, and go into Circe's
house; it will give you power against the day of trouble.
And I will tell you all the malevolent guiles of Circe.
290   She will make you a potion, and put drugs in the food, but she will not
even so be able to enchant you, for this good medicine
which I give you now will prevent her. I will tell you the details
of what to do. As soon as Circe with her long wand strikes you,
then drawing from beside your thigh your sharp sword, rush
295   forward against Circe, as if you were raging to kill her,
and she will be afraid, and invite you to go to bed with her.
Do not then resist and refuse the bed of the goddess,
for so she will set free your companions, and care for you also;
but bid her swear the great oath of the blessed gods, that she
300   has no other evil hurt that she is devising against you,

so she will not make you weak and unmanned, once you are naked,"
  'So spoke Argeïphontes, and he gave me the medicine,
which he picked out of the ground, and he explained the nature
of it to me. It was black at the root, but with a milky

305 flower. The gods call it moly. It is hard for mortal
men to dig up, but the gods have power to do all things.
  'Then Hermes went away, passing over the wooded island,
toward tall Olympos, and I meanwhile made my way to the house
of Circe, but my heart was a storm in me as I went. Now

310 I stood outside at the doors of the goddess with the glorious
hair, and standing I shouted aloud; and the goddess heard me,
and at once she opened the shining doors and came out and invited
me in; and I, deeply troubled in my heart, went in with her.
She made me sit down in a chair that was wrought elaborately

315 and splendid with silver nails, and under my feet was a footstool.
She made a potion for me to drink and gave it in a golden
cup, and with evil thoughts in her heart added the drug to it.
Then when she had given it and I drank it off, without being
enchanted, she struck me with her wand and spoke and named me:

320 "Go to your sty now and lie down with your other friends there."
  'So she spoke, but I, drawing from beside my thigh the sharp sword,
rushed forward against Circe as if I were raging to kill her,
but she screamed aloud and ran under my guard, and clasping both knees
in loud lamentation spoke to me and addressed me in winged words:

325 "What man are you and whence? Where are your city and parents?
The wonder is on me that you drank my drugs and have not been
enchanted, for no other man beside could have stood up
under my drugs, once he drank and they passed the barrier
of his teeth. There is a mind in you no magic will work on.

330 You are then resourceful Odysseus. Argeïphontes
of the golden staff was forever telling me you would come
to me, on your way back from Troy with your fast black ship.
Come then, put away your sword in its sheath, and let us
two go up into my bed so that, lying together

335 in the bed of love, we may then have faith and trust in each other."
  'So she spoke, and I answered her again and said to her:
"Circe, how can you ask me to be gentle with you, when it
is you who turned my companions into pigs in your palace?
And now you have me here myself, you treacherously

340 ask me to go into your chamber, and go to bed with you,
so that when I am naked you can make me a weakling, unmanned.
I would not be willing to go to bed with you unless

you can bring yourself, O goddess, to swear me a great oath
that there is no other evil hurt you devise against me."

345   'So I spoke, and she at once swore me the oath, as I asked her,
But after she had sworn me the oath, and made an end of it,
I mounted the surpassingly beautiful bed of Circe.
      'Meanwhile, the four maidservants, who wait on Circe
in her house, were busy at their work, all through the palace.
350 These are daughters born of the springs and from the coppices
and the sacred rivers which flow down to the sea. Of these
one laid the coverlets, splendid and stained in purple, over
the backs of the chairs, and spread on the seats the cloths to sit on.
The second drew up the silver tables and placed them in front of
355 the chairs, and laid out the golden serving baskets upon them.
The third mixed wine, kindly sweet and fragrant, in the silver
mixing bowl, and set out the golden goblets. The fourth one
brought in water, then set about building up an abundant
fire, underneath the great caldron, and the water heated.
360 But when the water had come to a boil in the shining bronze, then
she sat me down in the bathtub and washed me from the great caldron,
mixing hot and cold just as I wanted, and pouring it
over shoulders and head, to take the heart-wasting weariness
from my limbs. When she had bathed me and anointed me with olive oil,
365 she put a splendid mantle and a tunic upon me,
and made me sit down in a chair that was wrought elaborately
and splendid with silver nails, and under my feet was a footstool.
A maidservant brought water for us and poured it from a splendid
and golden pitcher, holding it above a silver basin,
370 for us to wash, and she pulled a polished table before us.
A grave housekeeper brought in the bread and served it to us,
adding many good things to it, generous with her provisions,
and told us to eat, but nothing pleased my mind, and I sat there
thinking of something else, mind full of evil imaginings.
375   'When Circe noticed how I sat there without ever putting
my hands out to the food, and with the strong sorrow upon me,
she came close, and stood beside me and addressed me in winged words:
"Why, Odysseus, do you sit so, like a man who has lost his
voice, eating your heart out, but touch neither food nor drink. Is it
380 that you suspect me of more treachery? But you have nothing
to fear, since I have already sworn my strong oath to you."
      'So she spoke, but I answered her again and said to her:
"Oh, Circe, how could any man right in his mind ever
endure to taste of the food and drink that are set before him,

385 until with his eyes he saw his companions set free? So then,
if you are sincerely telling me to eat and drink, set them
free, so my eyes can again behold my eager companions."
'So I spoke, and Circe walked on out through the palace,
holding her wand in her hand, and opened the doors of the pigsty,
390 and drove them out. They looked like nine-year-old porkers. They stood
ranged and facing her, and she, making her way through their
ranks, anointed each of them with some other medicine,
and the bristles, grown upon them by the evil medicine Circe
had bestowed upon them before, now fell away from them,
395 and they turned back once more into men, younger than they had been
and taller for the eye to behold and handsomer by far.
They recognized me, and each of them clung to my hand. The lovely
longing for lamentation came over us, and the house echoed
terribly to the sound, and even the goddess took pity,
400 and she, shining among goddesses, came close and said to me:
"Son of Laertes and seed of Zeus, resourceful Odysseus,
go back down now to your fast ship and the sand of the seashore,
and first of all, drag your ship up on the land, stowing
your possessions and all the ship's running gear away in the sea caves,
405 and then come back, and bring with you your eager companions."
'So she spoke, and the proud heart in me was persuaded,
and I went back down to my fast ship and the sand of the seashore,
and there I found beside the fast ship my eager companions
pitiful in their lamentation and weeping big tears.
410 And as, in the country, the calves, around the cows returning
from pasture back to the dung of the farmyard, well filled with grazing,
come gamboling together to meet them, and the pens no longer
can hold them in, but lowing incessantly they come running
around their mothers, so these men, once their eyes saw me,
415 came streaming around me, in tears, and the spirit in them made them
feel as if they were back in their own country, the very
city of rugged Ithaka, where they were born and raised up.
So they came in tears about me, and cried in winged words:
'O great Odysseus, we are as happy to see you returning
420 as if we had come back to our own Ithakan country.
But come, tell us about the death of our other companions."
'So they spoke, but I answered in soft words and told them:
"First of all, let us drag our ship up on the land, stowing
our possessions and all the ship's running gear away in the sea caves,
425 and then make haste, all of you, to come along with me,
so that you can see your companions, in the sacred dwelling

of Circe, eating and drinking, for they have all in abundance."

     'So I spoke, and at once they did as I told them. Only
Eurylochos was trying to hold back all my other
430   companions, and he spoke to them and addressed them in winged words:
"Ah, poor wretches. Where are we going? Why do you long for
the evils of going down into Circe's palace, for she will
transform the lot of us into pigs or wolves or lions,
and so we shall guard her great house for her, under compulsion.
435   So too it happened with the Cyclops, when our companions
went into his yard, and the bold Odysseus was of their company;
for it was by this man's recklessness that these too perished."

     'So he spoke, and I considered in my mind whether
to draw out the long-edged sword from beside my big thigh,
440   and cut off his head and throw it on the ground, even though
he was nearly related to me by marriage; but my companions
checked me, first one then another speaking, trying to soothe me:
"Zeus-sprung Odysseus, if you ask us to, we will leave
this man here to stay where he is and keep watch over
445   the ship. You show us the way to the sacred dwelling of Circe."

     'So they spoke, and started up from the ship and the seashore;
nor would Eurylochos be left alone by the hollow
ship, but followed along in fear of my fierce reproaches.

     'Meanwhile, inside the house, Circe with loving care bathed
450   the rest of my companions, and anointed them well with olive oil,
and put about them mantles of fleece and tunics. We found them
all together, feasting well in the halls. When my men
looked each other in the face and knew one another,
they burst into an outcry of tears, and the whole house echoed,
455   But she, shining among goddesses, came close and said to us:
"Son of Laertes and seed of Zeus, resourceful Odysseus,
no longer raise the swell of your lamentation. I too
know all the pains you have suffered on the sea where the fish swarm,
and all the damage done you on the dry land by hostile
460   men. But come now, eat your food and drink your wine, until
you gather back again into your chests that kind of spirit
you had in you when first you left the land of your fathers
on rugged Ithaka. Now you are all dried out, dispirited
from the constant thought of your hard wandering, nor is there any
465   spirit in your festivity, because of so much suffering."

     'So she spoke, and the proud heart in us was persuaded.
There for all our days until a year was completed
we sat there feasting on unlimited meat and sweet wine.

But when it was the end of a year, and the months wasted
470 away, and the seasons changed, and the long days were accomplished,
then my eager companions called me aside and said to me:
"What ails you now? It is time to think about our own country,
if truly it is ordained that you shall survive and come back
to your strong-founded house and to the land of your fathers."
475 'So they spoke, and the proud heart in me was persuaded.
So for the whole length of the day until the sun's setting
we sat there feasting on unlimited meat and sweet wine.
But when the sun went down and the sacred darkness came over,
they lay down to sleep all about the shadowy chambers,
480 but I, mounting the surpassingly beautiful bed of Circe,
clasped her by the knees and entreated her, and the goddess
listened to me, and I spoke to her and addressed her in winged words:
"O Circe, accomplish now the promise you gave, that you
would see me on my way home. The spirit within me is urgent
485 now, as also in the rest of my friends, who are wasting
my heart away, lamenting around me, when you are elsewhere."
'So I spoke, and she, shining among goddesses, answered:
"Son of Laertes and seed of Zeus, resourceful Odysseus,
you shall no longer stay in my house when none of you wish to;
490 but first there is another journey you must accomplish
and reach the house of Hades and of revered Persephone,
there to consult with the soul of Teiresias the Theban,
the blind prophet, whose senses stay unshaken within him,
to whom alone Persephone has granted intelligence
495 even after death, but the rest of them are flittering shadows."
'So she spoke, and the inward heart in me was broken,
and I sat down on the bed and cried, nor did the heart in me
wish to go on living any longer, nor to look on the sunlight.
But when I had glutted myself with rolling about and weeping,
500 then at last I spoke aloud and answered the goddess:
"Circe, who will be our guide on that journey? No one
has ever yet in a black ship gone all the way to Hades'."
'So I spoke, and she, shining among goddesses, answered:
"Son of Laertes and seed of Zeus, resourceful Odysseus,
505 let no need for a guide on your ship trouble you; only
set up your mast pole and spread the white sails upon it,
and sit still, and let the blast of the North Wind carry you.
But when you have crossed with your ship the stream of the Ocean, you will
find there a thickly wooded shore, and the groves of Persephone,
510 and tall black poplars growing, and fruit-perishing willows;

then beach your ship on the shore of the deep-eddying Ocean
and yourself go forward into the moldering home of Hades.
There Pyriphlegethon and Kokytos, which is an off-break
from the water of the Styx, flow into Acheron. There is
515 a rock there, and the junction of two thunderous rivers.
There, hero, you must go close in and do as I tell you.
Dig a pit of about a cubit in each direction,
and pour it full of drink offerings for all the dead, first
honey mixed with milk, then a second pouring of sweet wine,
520 and the third, water, and over all then sprinkle white barley,
and promise many times to the strengthless heads of the perished
dead that, returning to Ithaka, you will slaughter a barren
cow, your best, in your palace and pile the pyre with treasures,
and to Teiresias apart dedicate an all-black
525 ram, the one conspicuous in all your sheepflocks.
But when with prayers you have entreated the glorious hordes
of the dead, then sacrifice one ram and one black female,
turning them toward Erebos, but yourself turn away from them
and make for where the river runs, and there the numerous
530 souls of the perished dead will come and gather about you.
Then encourage your companions and tell them, taking
the sheep that are lying by, slaughtered with the pitiless
bronze, to skin these, and burn them, and pray to the divinities,
to Hades the powerful, and to revered Persephone,
535 while you yourself, drawing from beside your thigh the sharp sword,
crouch there, and do not let the strengthless heads of the perished
dead draw nearer to the blood until you have questioned Teiresias.
Then, leader of the host, the prophet will soon come to you,
and he will tell you the way to go, the stages of your journey,
540 and tell you how to make your way home on the sea where the fish swarm."
       'So she spoke, and Dawn of the golden throne came on us,
and she put clothing upon me, an outer cloak and a tunic,
while she, the nymph, mantled herself in a gleaming white robe
fine-woven and delightful, and around her waist she fastened
545 a handsome belt of gold, and on her head was a wimple;
while I walked all about the house and roused my companions,
standing beside each man and speaking to him in kind words:
"No longer lie abed and dreaming away in sweet sleep.
The queenly Circe has shown me the way. So let us go now."
550   'So I spoke, and the proud heart in them was persuaded.
Yet I did not lead away my companions without some
loss. There was one, Elpenor, the youngest man, not terribly
powerful in fighting nor sound in his thoughts. This man,

apart from the rest of his friends, in search of cool air, had lain
555 down drunkenly to sleep on the roof of Circe's palace,
and when his companions stirred to go he, hearing their tumult
and noise of talking, started suddenly up, and never thought,
when he went down, to go by way of the long ladder,
but blundered straight off the edge of the roof, so that his neck bone
560 was broken out of its sockets, and his soul went down to Hades'.
    'Now as my men were on their way I said a word to them:
"You think you are on your way back now to your own beloved
country, but Circe has indicated another journey
for us, to the house of Hades and of revered Persephone
565 there to consult with the soul of Teiresias the Theban."
    'So I spoke, and the inward heart in them was broken.
They sat down on the ground and lamented and tore their hair out,
but there came no advantage to them for all their sorrowing.
    'When we came down to our fast ship and the sand of the seashore,
565 we sat down, sorrowful, and weeping big tears. Circe
meanwhile had gone down herself to the side of the black ship,
and tethered aboard it a ram and one black female, easily
passing by us unseen. Whose eyes can follow the movement
of a god passing from place to place, unless the god wishes?

Questions for Review and Discussion

1. Why does Circe transform Odysseus's men into swine? What is the significance of transforming them into swine as opposed to some other animal?

2. Circe attempts to subjugate Odysseus, but he is able to meet the challenge with the assistance of the moly—a white flower with black roots given to him by Hermes. What does the moly flower represent?

3. Circe's initial encounter with Odysseus is based on mutual hostility and distrust. But after he has successfully thwarted her challenge, her powers become benevolent. Why does her attitude and conduct towards Odysseus change?

4. What role does Circe play in Odysseus's journey as he makes his way home?

5. What does Odysseus learn from his interaction with Circe?

6. What are the gender dynamics in the confrontation and later reconciliation between Circe and Odysseus?

7. In the opening book of the *Odyssey*, Odysseus is on Kalypso's island where he has been held captive for several years. When Kalypso is ordered to release Odysseus, she attempts to extend his stay by bribing him. In contrast to Kalypso, Circe makes no attempt to bribe or coerce Odysseus into staying with her when he solicits her assistance in resuming his journey homeward. Instead, she gives him the necessary provisions, directions, and points the way out. What does Circe's conduct indicate about her character and self-image?

8. Circe lives on an island, a geographically and culturally isolated space outside of the confines of civilized society. Is there a connection between her geographical and cultural isolation and her independence from male validation and/or authority? Explain.

9. In what ways might Circe be considered a positive role model for women today?

Chapter 6

Medea

GLOSSARY OF NAMES

AEGEUS King of Athens; promises Medea safe haven if she can cure him and his wife of their barrenness

CHORUS Corinthian women who comment on the action and in whom Medea confides

CIRCE Medea's aunt; daughter of sun god Helios and Perse, a sea nymph; enchantress who turned Odysseus's men to swine (see Chapter 5: Circe)

CREON King of Corinth; banishes Medea and her children

EURIPIDES Prominent Greek playwright; author of *Medea*

GLAUCE Princess of Corinth; daughter of Creon; murdered by Medea

HELIOS Sun god; grandfather of Medea

JASON Hero who obtained the Golden Fleece; son of King Aeson of Iolcus; married Medea; angered her by marrying the princess of Corinth

MEDEA Princess of Colchis; skilled sorceress; granddaughter of Helios; niece of Circe; wife of Jason

NURSE Nurse to the children

PELIAS Jason's uncle who sent him in search of the Golden Fleece; killed by his daughters who had been tricked into doing so by Medea

TUTOR Tutor to children

Medea is the granddaughter of the sun god, Helios, and the niece of Circe. Skilled in witchcraft, she has powers beyond ordinary mortals. She uses these considerable powers to help Jason obtain the Golden Fleece. She betrays her own family and tricks Pelias's daughters into murdering their own father. And she does it all for the love of Jason. Apparently unappreciative of her contribution to his success, Jason rewards Medea by rejecting her in favor of a younger woman, the princess of Corinth. The prominent Greek playwright, Euripides, tells the story of Medea's revenge. In the process of interpreting the myth, Euripides adds some unique features, most notably, Medea's murder of her own children.

Euripides was born in 480 B.C.E. in a city outside of Athens. We have little biographical information about him. He seems to have suffered the consequence of his unorthodoxy in that he didn't garner the same respect as the two leading dramatists of his day, Aeschylus and Sophocles. In his attempt to explore the social, cultural, and psychological dilemmas of real people in real life situations, Euripides is remarkably modern. Consequently, he was misunderstood and rejected by his contemporaries. His work went largely unheralded until long after his death, at which time he became one of the best-loved and most frequently performed dramatists.

Euripides's unorthodox tendencies in his plays can be evidenced in a number of ways. Critical of the gods, he diminishes their stature, reducing them to petty, cruel tyrants who engage in egotistical behaviors. He boldly challenges traditional values and the socially accepted mores of his time. He articulates a staunch antimilitaristic position by showing the devastating impact and extent of human suffering inflicted on the lives of ordinary people as a consequence of war. He exhibits egalitarian tendencies by elevating traditionally minor or supporting characters (women, children, and servants) to more prominent positions. His characters are unusual in that they speak openly of mundane concerns and complaints that are common to all humanity. He blurs the separation between the public sphere and the private sphere so that the two realms become inextricably interlinked, with each having ramifications on the opposing realm. He challenges gender stereotyping and socially constructed ideals of feminine and masculine behavior. And, finally, he provides a forceful critique of the gender inequity and ethnocentrism of Greek society and anticipates the disastrous consequences that can ensue if a society continues to marginalize and oppress its female half and its ethnic minorities. He warns us that if the oppressed continue to be denied access, voice, and power, they may resort to acts of unspeakable violence as a means of revenge. More than other tragedians, Euripides shows the potential for monstrosity of an oppressed group if it situates itself in the role of the oppressor in a hierarchy of power.

Euripides's *Medea*, produced in 431 B.C.E., dramatizes the story of Medea and her husband, Jason. The opening scene plunges us in the middle of the dilemma. Against Medea's wishes, Jason has decided to take on a new wife—the young daughter of Creon, the ruler of Corinth. Medea, who had saved Jason's life, helped him attain the Golden Fleece, and bore his two sons, confronts him with his ingratitude and betrayal. Jason responds by minimizing—if not negating entirely—her role in his success. In spite of Jason's reassurances, Medea remains unconvinced, angry, and determined to seek revenge. She hatches a diabolical plan that will satiate her appetite for vengeance, manipulating Creon, Aegeus, and Jason in order to achieve her goal. Meanwhile, she reveals her plan to the Chorus. The Chorus does not divulge her secret, possibly because it is composed of women who sympathize with Medea's plight and endorse her assessment of the degrading and pitiful status of women in Greek society.

The events unfold according to Medea's plan. The princess dies a painful death; Creon dies while attempting to rescue her; and Medea murders her own children in order to punish Jason and deny him his progeny. The play concludes with Medea confronting Jason while on the chariot that will whisk her to the safe haven of Athens as promised to her by Aegeus. She carries the bodies of her two sons, and, in a final gesture of defiance, she refuses to release the bodies to Jason for burial.

One of the most compelling aspects of the play is Medea's violation of the traditional roles and values that are expected of her as a female and as a mother. The mother-child bond is the primary connection between any two human beings. Mothers are expected to be nurturing and loving toward their children, willing to sacrifice even themselves for the sake of their offspring. Medea, however, turns this gender-prescribed role on its head: she murders her own children. By doing this, she usurps a privilege traditionally assigned to men in Greek society: the patriarchal axiom that endows them with the right to dispose of wives and children as they see fit and with apparent impunity. Zeus, for example, sanctions the abduction and rape of his daughter, Persephone; Agamemnon orchestrates the sacrifice of his daughter, Iphigenia. These behaviors are barbaric and reveal a society that is bereft of a moral code of conduct. Medea implicitly exposes the barbarism of these acts by challenging male hegemony and refusing to adhere to a sexist double standard. Her conduct suggests that if it is acceptable for men to engage in such monstrous behaviors, then it should also be acceptable for women to do the same.

As a foreigner and a sorceress, but primarily as a woman, Medea challenges the traditional roles assigned to women. In her opening speech, she bemoans the fate of foreigners, women in general, the patriarchal institution of marriage, and the institution of motherhood on the grounds that all are oppressive and circumscribe a subordinate status for those designated as 'Other' by male-dominated Greek society. She declares emphatically that she would rather be a warrior in battle than bear a single child. She vilifies a system that denies women legitimate means or opportunity to protest or seek redress for injustices. She elicits sympathy from the Chorus in her declaration that a woman's fate consists of being used and abused, only to be relegated to the margins once her services are no longer needed. Her words express the collective resentment of the women of her time who propagate the species to supply the human fodder that fuels a system which begrudges their contribution and their very existence. But her boldest challenge to systemic racism and sexism comes not simply through her vocal condemnation of an oppressive system. It comes through her actions. Medea does the unthinkable for a woman living in Greek society: she formulates and implements a plan for revenge—and she gets away with it. With a final stroke of diabolical genius, she uses none other than the city of Athens against Greek society by securing a safe refuge for herself there, under the protection of King Aegeus.

Medea further violates gender norms in that she demonstrates an intellectual acumen above and beyond any other character in the play. Although she is a skilled sorceress and a descendent of the sun god Helios, it is her human attributes that predominate. Medea is a brilliant strategist, wielding her femininity and irresistible charm as lethal weapons of war. She hypocritically assumes the supplicant's gesture by dropping to her knees for Creon and Aegeus respectively, as if to reassure each that she acknowledges her subordinate status. She plots her course of action with the ruthless efficiency, cunning, and determination of a military planner. She even has the foresight to secure a safe haven for herself and a chariot to get her there unimpeded. She is a woman operating in the masculine arena in a society in which the lines separating masculine/public realm and feminine/private realm are clearly delineated. Medea uses patriarchal ideology to her advantage: she successfully exploits socially constructed gender stereotypes to vanquish her enemies.

All the men fall captive to Medea's duplicity. Remarkably adept at manipulation, she exploits Creon's concern for the welfare of his daughter by asking him for a 24-hour reprieve so she can supposedly secure a home for her own children. She exploits Aegeus's desire to have children by extracting from him a promise to grant her a safe haven in Athens, in exchange for which she will provide him with drugs that will cure him and his wife of their barrenness. She fuels Jason's ego by feigning a woman's ostensible weakness and lack of foresight. She is an imposing figure who towers above all the other characters in the play. The males diminish in stature and cannot compete with this formidable female adversary. By using their own tools against them, Medea challenges their masculine sense of identity and undermines the artificial boundaries created to reinforce and perpetuate a gender hierarchy. Compared to her, Jason emerges as a sniveling, weak, and gullible fool.

Euripides's use of children was innovative for the Athenian stage. Unlike his contemporaries for whom children hardly make an appearance, Euripides negotiates a prominent space for the child. Medea's children appear intermittently throughout the play, but even when they are absent from the stage, Euripides never lets us forget them or forget that the outcome of the tragedy hinges on their fate. Although they are largely silent (with the exception of the few words they utter behind the scene as their mother is about to murder them), their fate constitutes the focal point of the tragedy.

Medea commits the unconscionable, nefarious act of child murder. What is remarkable about the play is not simply that it dramatizes a mother willfully murdering her own children, but doing so with apparent impunity. Medea does not seem to be alone in harboring resentment toward children whose very existence appears to exert a burden on the adults around them. The climate of the play is laced with anti child sentiments. The adults fluctuate between viewing the children as an inconvenience to viewing them with outright animosity. The dialogue expresses this hostility and prepares the way for their murder. We are told that Medea hates her children; that they should be hidden from view; that it would have been better for them had they not been born; that Jason does not love them and has failed to fulfill his parental responsibilities; that Jason's conduct is typical of Greek males; and that their presence initially elicits disgust from Jason's new bride. The Chorus seems to endorse a preference for the childless state by declaring those who do not have children experience greater fortune and lead easier lives than those who have children. Fully aware of Medea's intention to murder her children, the Chorus harbors her secret and stands by, deliberating whether to rescue them while overhearing their plaintive cries for help. Medea curses the children, and after stifling her maternal voice, follows through with her decision to murder them.

Jason and Medea use their children as tools to advance their different agendas. Jason claims to act on his children's behalf, but he makes no prior attempt to advocate for them or to challenge their banishment until Medea convinces him to intercede on their behalf with his young bride. With twisted logic, Medea justifies murdering her children on the grounds that no one will give them sanctuary. In other words, like Jason, she purports to be acting in their best interest. As is the case with Jason whose political ambition takes precedence over the welfare of his children, Medea's ambition for revenge takes precedence over the welfare of her children. She conveniently fails to acknowledge that her children will be denied a safe refuge because she has chosen them as the vehicle to deliver the poisoned gifts to the princess. Through her actions, Medea seals their fate. In the final confrontation with Jason, Medea reveals the real motives for her barbarous act: to inflict pain on Jason and deny him his progeny. The children function as means to an end. By articulating the treatment of and attitudes towards Medea's children, Euripides exposes the hypocrisy underlying Greek society, a society which claims to nurture children and yet treats them as nuisances, inconveniences, and helpless pawns in adult conflicts and power plays.

Medea's murder of her children, however, constitutes a logical consequence of the view of motherhood promulgated by Aristotle and reinforced by Greek male-dominated society, namely, that the woman is not the true parent of the child. She acts merely as the fertile soil that incubates the seed. Jason's seed, planted in the fertile soil of a woman's womb, is perceived as a temporary occupant of female space. The mother serves as a necessary agent for bringing that seed to maturity, but, according to the Greek worldview, she cannot claim parenthood. The male claims sole authority of even her most intimate space as well as its production. Medea's body, therefore, has been turned into a commodity over which she has no ownership. Accordingly, Medea's act of infanticide can be seen as a revolt against a colonial authority—a retaliation against Jason and Greek society for occupying her space and appropriating her labor.

The use of the deus ex machina (god on a machine) to provide for Medea's escape generated a great deal of debate among Euripides's audience and contemporaries. Aristotle was critical of its use in this play because he felt it did not arise organically from the plot. However, it is precisely because the chariot is such an artificial means of concluding the drama that it serves Euripides's vision well. By imposing a magical and unnatural solution on what has otherwise been a very prosaic marital conflict situated in the domestic arena, Euripides is able to do a number of things. He demonstrates that the gods are not particularly concerned with morality and justice in so far as the sun god Helios sends the chariot to rescue his granddaughter, while flagrantly disregarding the fact that she has just murdered her own children. Furthermore, through his use of this device, Euripides reinforces his central message—that when an oppressed group has no legitimate means to redress an injustice, it will resort to whatever means necessary, natural or otherwise, to avenge itself. Euripides suggests that if the anger of the oppressed is pent up indefinitely, when it finally does manifest itself, it may do so through acts of unnatural, unspeakable, and uncontrollable violence.

Euripides's *Medea* acts as a cautionary tale. Its continued relevance lies not only in the depiction of a scorned woman seeking revenge. It explores many of the issues we are still grappling with today: gender stereotyping, gender socialization, and gender stratification; the power dynamics between men and women; oppressive systems that continue to deny access, power, and voice to those designated as Other; and the dangers that lie ahead for a society if it does not provide a legitimate means to its diverse populations for redressing injustices. Finally, Euripides's dramatization of a woman who has been scorned by her husband in favor of a younger and more prestigious female resonates with the experiences of many women today.

The *Medea* translation below is by Rex Warner.

REFERENCES

Bates, William Nickerson. *Euripides: A Student of Human Nature.* Philadelphia: U of Pennsylvania P, 1930.

Blundell, Sue. "The Play Explores Social Conflict Between Men and Women." *Readings on Medea: The Greenhaven Press Literary Companion to World Literature.* Ed. Don Nardo. San Diego: Greenhaven, 2001. 68–75.

Clauss, James J., and Sarah Iles Johnston, eds. *Medea: Essays on Medea in Myth, Literature, Philosophy, and Art.* Princeton: Princeton UP, 1997.

Corti, Lillian. *The Myth of Medea and the Murder of Her Children.* Connecticut: Greenwood, 1998.

Decharme, Paul. *Euripides and The Spirit of His Dramas.* Trans. James Loeb. New York: Macmillan, 1906.

Kerenyi, Karl. *Goddesses of Sun and Moon.* Trans. Murray Stein. Dallas: Spring, 1979.

Kitto, H.D.F. "The *Medea* of Euripides." *Medea: Myth and Dramatic Form.* Eds. James L. Sanderson and Everett Zimmerman. Boston: Houghton Mifflin, 1967. 286–297.

Knox, Bernard. "Euripides Prophecies a World of Violence and Disorder." *Readings on Medea: The Greenhaven Press Literary Companion to World Literature.* Ed. Don Nardo. San Diego: Greenhaven, 2001. 59–63.

McDonald, Marianne. "Medea as Politician and Diva: Riding the Dragon Into the Future." *Medea: Essays in Medea in Myth, Literature, Philosophy, and Art.* Eds. James L. Clauss and Sarah Iles Johnston. Princeton: Princeton UP, 1997. 297–323.

Nardo, Don, ed. *Readings on Medea: The Greenhaven Press Literary Companion to World Literature.* San Diego: Greenhaven, 2001.

Pomeroy, Sarah B. *Goddesses, Whores, Wives, and Slaves: Women in Classical Antiquity.* New York: Schocken, 1975.

Warner, Rex, trans. "The Medea." *The Complete Greek Tragedies: Euripides 1.* Eds. David Grene and Richmond Lattimore. Chicago: U of Chicago P, 1955. 56–108.
Wilkinson, Tanya. *Medea's Folly: Women, Relationships, and the Search For Identity.* Berkeley: Pagemill, 1998.

The Medea

SCENE: *In front of Medea's house in Corinth. Enter from the house Medea's nurse.*

Nurse How I wish the Argo never had reached the land
Of Colchis, skimming through the blue Symplegades,
Nor ever had fallen in the glades of Pelion
The smitten fir-tree to furnish oars for the hands
5 Of heroes who in Pelias' name attempted
The Golden Fleece! For then my mistress Medea
Would not have sailed for the towers of the land of Iolcus,
Her heart on fire with passionate love for Jason;
Nor would she have persuaded the daughters of Pelias
10 To kill their father, and now be living here
In Corinth with her husband and children. She gave
Pleasure to the people of her land of exile,
And she herself helped Jason in every way.
This is indeed the greatest salvation of all—
15 For the wife not to stand apart from the husband.
But now there's hatred everywhere, Love is diseased.
For, deserting his own children and my mistress,
Jason has taken a royal wife to his bed,
The daughter of the ruler of this land, Creon.
20 And poor Medea is slighted, and cries aloud on the
Vows they made to each other, the right hands clasped
In eternal promise. She calls upon the gods to witness
What sort of return Jason has made to her love.
She lies without food and gives herself up to suffering,
25 Wasting away every moment of the day in tears.
So it has gone since she knew herself slighted by him.
Not stirring an eye, not moving her face from the ground,
No more than either a rock or surging sea water
She listens when she is given friendly advice.
30 Except that sometimes she twists back her white neck and

Moans to herself, calling out on her father's name,
And her land, and her home betrayed when she came away with
A man who now is determined to dishonor her.
Poor creature, she has discovered by her sufferings
35   What it means to one not to have lost one's own country.
She has turned from the children and does not like to see them.
I am afraid she may think of some dreadful thing,
For her heart is violent. She will never put up with
The treatment she is getting. I know and fear her
40   Lest she may sharpen a sword and thrust to the heart,
Stealing into the palace where the bed is made,
Or even kill the king and the new-wedded groom,
And thus bring a greater misfortune on herself.
She's a strange woman. I know it won't be easy
45   To make an enemy of her and come off best.
But here the children come. They have finished playing.
They have no thought at all of their mother's trouble.
Indeed it is not usual for the young to grieve.

*(Enter from the right the slave who is the tutor to Medea's
two small children. The children follow him.)*

Tutor You old retainer of my mistress' household,
50   Why are you standing here all alone in front of the
Gates and moaning to yourself over your misfortune?
Medea could not wish you to leave her alone.
Nurse Old man, and guardian of the children of Jason,
If one is a good servant, it's a terrible thing
55   When one's master's luck is out; it goes to one's heart.
So I myself have got into such a state of grief
That a longing stole over me to come outside here
And tell the earth and air of my mistress' sorrows.
Tutor Has the poor lady not yet given up her crying?
60   *Nurse* Given up? She's at the start, not halfway through her tears.
Tutor Poor fool—if I may call my mistress such a name—
How ignorant she is of trouble more to come.
Nurse What do you mean, old man? You needn't fear to speak.
Tutor Nothing. I take back the words which I used just now.
65   *Nurse* Don't, by your beard, hide this from me, your fellow-servant.
If need be, I'll keep quiet about what you tell me.
Tutor I heard a person saying, while I myself seemed

Not to be paying attention, when I was at the place
Where the old draught-players sit, by the holy fountain,
70   That Creon, ruler of the land, intends to drive
These children and their mother in exile from Corinth.
But whether what he said is really true or not
I do not know. I pray that it may not be true.
Nurse And will Jason put up with it that his children
75   Should suffer so, though he's no friend to their mother?
Tutor Old ties give place to new ones. As for Jason, he
No longer has a feeling for this house of ours.
Nurse It's black indeed for us, when we add new to old
Sorrows before even the present sky has cleared.
80 *Tutor* But you be silent, and keep all this to yourself.
It is not the right time to tell our mistress of it.
Nurse Do you hear, children, what a father he is to you?
I wish he were dead—but no, he is still my master.
Yet certainly he has proved unkind to his dear ones.
85 *Tutor* What's strange in that? Have you only just discovered
That everyone loves himself more than his neighbor?
Some have good reason, others get something out of it.
So Jason neglects his children for the new bride.
Nurse Go indoors, children. That will be the best thing.
90   And you, keep them to themselves as much as possible.
Don't bring them near their mother in her angry mood.
For I've seen her already blazing her eyes at them
As though she meant some mischief and I am sure that
She'll not stop raging until she has struck at someone.
95   May it be an enemy and not a friend she hurts!

(*Medea is heard inside the house.*)

Medea Ah, wretch! Ah, lost in my sufferings,
I wish, I wish I might die.
Nurse What did I say, dear children? Your mother
Frets her heart and frets it to anger.
100   Run away quickly into the house,
And keep well out of her sight.
Don't go anywhere near, but be careful
Of the wildness and bitter nature
Of that proud mind.
105   Go now! Run quickly indoors.

It is clear that she soon will put lightning
In that cloud of her cries that is rising
With a passion increasing. O, what will she do,
Proud-hearted and not to be checked on her course,
110   A soul bitten into with wrong?

(The Tutor takes the children into the house.)

Medea   Ah, I have suffered
What should be wept for bitterly. I hate you,
Children of a hateful mother. I curse you
And your father. Let the whole house crash.
115   *Nurse*   Ah, I pity you, you poor creature.
How can your children share in their father's
Wickedness? Why do you hate them? Oh children,
How much I fear that something may happen!
Great people's tempers are terrible, always
120   Having their own way, seldom checked,
Dangerous they shift from mood to mood.
How much better to have been accustomed
To live on equal terms with one's neighbors.
I would like to be safe and grow old in a
125   Humble way. What is moderate sounds best,
Also in practice *is* best for everyone.
Greatness brings no profit to people.
God indeed, when in anger, brings
Greater ruin to great men's houses.

*(Enter, on the right, a Chorus of Corinthian women. They have come to
inquire about Medea and to attempt to console her.)*

130   *Chorus*   I heard the voice, I heard the cry
Of Colchis' wretched daughter.
Tell me, mother, is she not yet
At rest? Within the double gates
Of the court I heard her cry. I am sorry
135   For the sorrow of this home. O, say, what has happened?
Nurse   There is no home. It's over and done with.
Her husband holds fast to his royal wedding,
While she, my mistress, cries out her eyes
There in her room, and takes no warmth from
140   Any word of any friend.

Medea Oh, I wish
   That lightning from heaven would split my head open.
   Oh, what use have I now for life?
   I would find my release in death
145   And leave hateful existence behind me.
Chorus O God and Earth and Heaven!
   Did you hear what a cry was that
   Which the sad wife sings?
   Poor foolish one, why should you long.
150   For that appalling rest?
   The final end of death comes fast.
   No need to pray for that.
   Suppose your man gives honor
   To another woman's bed.
155   It often happens. Don't be hurt.
   God will be your friend in this.
   You must not waste away
   Grieving too much for him who shared your bed.
Medea Great Themis, lady Artemis, behold
160   The things I suffer, though I made him promise,
   My hateful husband. I pray that I may see him,
   Him and his bride and all their palace shattered
   For the wrong they dare to do me without cause.
   Oh, my father! Oh, my country! In what dishonor
165   I left you, killing my own brother for it.
Nurse Do you hear what she says, and how she cries
   On Themis, the goddess of Promises, and on Zeus,
   Whom we believe to be the Keeper of Oaths?
   Of this I am sure, that no small thing
170   Will appease my mistress' anger.
Chorus Will she come into our presence?
   Will she listen when we are speaking
   To the words we say?
   I wish she might relax her rage
175   And temper of her heart.
   My willingness to help will never
   Be wanting to my friends.
   But go inside and bring her
   Out of the house to us,
180   And speak kindly to her: hurry,

Before she wrongs her own.
This passion of hers moves to something great.

Nurse I will, but I doubt if I'll manage
To win my mistress over.

185 But still I'll attempt it to please you.
Such a look she will flash on her servants
If any comes near with a message,
Like a lioness guarding her cubs.
It is right, I think, to consider

190 Both stupid and lacking in foresight
Those poets of old who wrote songs
For revels and dinners and banquets,
Pleasant sounds for men living at ease;
But none of them all has discovered

195 How to put to an end with their singing
Or musical instruments grief,
Bitter grief, from which death and disaster
Cheat the hopes of a house. Yet how good
If music could cure men of this! But why raise

200 To no purpose the voice at a banquet? For *there* is
Already abundance of pleasure for men
With a joy of its own.

(*The Nurse goes into the house.*)

Chorus I heard a shriek that is laden with sorrow.
Shrilling out her hard grief she cries out

205 Upon him who betrayed both her bed and her marriage.
Wronged, she calls on the gods,
On the justice of Zeus, the oath sworn,
Which brought her away
To the opposite shore of the Greeks

210 Through the gloomy salt straits to the gateway
Of the salty unlimited sea.

(*Medea, attended by servants, comes out of the house.*)

Medea Women of Corinth, I have come outside to you
Lest you should be indignant with me; for I know
That many people are overproud, some when alone,

215 And others when in company. And those who live
Quietly, as I do, get a bad reputation.

For a just judgment is not evident in the eyes
When a man at first sight hates another, before
Learning his character, being in no way injured;
220   And a foreigner especially must adapt himself.
I'd not approve of even a fellow-countryman
Who by pride and want of manners offends his neighbors.
But on me this thing has fallen so unexpectedly,
It has broken my heart. I am finished. I let go
225   All my life's joy. My friends, I only want to die.
It was everything to me to think well of one man,
And he, my own husband, has turned out wholly vile.
Of all things which are living and can form a judgment
We women are the most unfortunate creatures.
230   Firstly, with an excess of wealth it is required
For us to buy a husband and take for our bodies
A master; for not to take one is even worse.
And now the question is serious whether we take
A good or bad one; for there is no easy escape
235   For a woman, nor can she say no to her marriage.
She arrives among new modes of behavior and manners,
And needs prophetic power, unless she has learned at home,
How best to manage him who shares the bed with her.
And if we work out all this well and carefully,
240   And the husband lives with us and lightly bears his yoke,
Then life is enviable. If not, I'd rather die.
A man, when he's tired of the company in his home,
Goes out of the house and puts an end to his boredom
And turns to a friend or companion of his own age.
245   But we are forced to keep our eyes on one alone.
What they say of us is that we have a peaceful time
Living at home, while they do the fighting in war.
How wrong they are! I would very much rather stand
Three times in the front of battle than bear one child.
250   Yet what applies to me does not apply to you.
You have a country. Your family home is here.
You enjoy life and the company of your friends.
But I am deserted, a refugee, thought nothing of
By my husband—something he won in a foreign land.
255   I have no mother or brother, nor any relation
With whom I can take refuge in this sea of woe.

This much then is the service I would beg from you:
If I can find the means or devise any scheme
To pay my husband back for what he has done to me—
260   Him and his father-in-law and the girl who married him—
Just to keep silent. For in other ways a woman
Is full of fear, defenseless, dreads the sight of cold
Steel; but, when once she is wronged in the matter of love,
No other soul can hold so many thoughts of blood.
265 *Chorus* This I will promise. You are in the right, Medea,
In paying your husband back. I am not surprised at you
For being sad.

              But look! I see our King Creon
Approaching. He will tell us of some new plan.

(Enter, from the right, Creon, with attendants.)

270 *Creon* You, with that angry look, so set against your husband,
Medea, I order you to leave my territories
An exile, and take along with you your two children,
And not to waste time doing it. It is my decree,
And I will see it done. I will not return home
275   Until you are cast from the boundaries of my land.
Medea Oh, this is the end for me. I am utterly lost.
Now I am in the full force of the storm of hate
And have no harbor from ruin to reach easily.
Yet still, in spite of it all, I'll ask the question:
280   What is your reason, Creon, for banishing me?
Creon I am afraid of you—why should I dissemble it?—
Afraid that you may injure my daughter mortally.
Many things accumulate to support my feeling.
You are a clever woman, versed in evil arts,
285   And are angry at having lost your husband's love.
I hear that you are threatening, so they tell me,
To do something against my daughter and Jason
And me, too. I shall take my precautions first.
I tell you, I prefer to earn your hatred now
290   Than to be soft-hearted and afterward regret it.
Medea This is not the first time, Creon. Often previously
Through being considered clever I have suffered much.
A person of sense ought never to have his children
Brought up to be more clever than the average.

295   For, apart from cleverness bringing them no profit,
       It will make them objects of envy and ill-will.
       If you put new ideas before the eyes of fools
       They'll think you foolish and worthless into the bargain;
       And if you are thought superior to those who have
300   Some reputation for learning, you will become hated.
       I have some knowledge myself of how this happens;
       For being clever, I find that some will envy me,
       Others object to me. Yet all my cleverness
       Is not so much.
305   Well, then, are you frightened, Creon,
       That I should harm you? There is no need. It is not
       My way to transgress the authority of a king.
       How have you injured me? You gave your daughter away
       To the man you wanted. Oh, certainly I hate
310   My husband, but you, I think, have acted wisely;
       Nor do I grudge it you that your affairs go well.
       May the marriage be a lucky one! Only let me
       Live in this land. For even though I have been wronged,
       I will not raise my voice, but submit to my betters.
315 *Creon* What you say sounds gentle enough. Still in my heart
       I greatly dread that you are plotting some evil,
       And therefore I trust you even less than before.
       A sharp-tempered woman, or, for that matter, a man,
       Is easier to deal with than the clever type
320   Who holds her tongue. No. You must go. No need for more
       Speeches. The thing is fixed. By no manner of means
       Shall you, an enemy of mine, stay in my country.
     Medea I beg you. By your knees, by your new-wedded girl.
     Creon Your words are wasted. You will never persuade me.
325 *Medea* Will you drive me out, and give no heed to my prayers?
     Creon I will, for I love my family more than you.
     Medea O my country! How bitterly now I remember you!
     Creon I love my country too—next after my children.
     Medea Oh what an evil to men is passionate love!
330 *Creon* That would depend on the luck that goes along with it.
     Medea O God, do not forget who is the cause of this!
     Creon Go. It is no use. Spare me the pain of forcing you.
     Medea I'm spared no pain. I lack no pain to be spared me.
     Creon Then you'll be removed by force by one of my men.

335   *Medea* No, Creon, not that! But do listen, I beg you.

    Creon Woman, you seem to want to create a disturbance.

    Medea I *will* go into exile. *This* is not what I beg for.

    Creon Why then this violence and clinging to my hand?

    Medea Allow me to remain here just for this one day,

340   So I may consider where to live in my exile,

    And look for support for my children, since their father

    Chooses to make no kind of provision for them.

    Have pity on them! You have children of your own.

    It is natural for you to look kindly on them.

345   For myself I do not mind if I go into exile.

    It is the children being in trouble that I mind.

    Creon There is nothing tyrannical about my nature,

    And by showing mercy I have often been the loser.

    Even now I know that I am making a mistake.

350   All the same you shall have your will. But this I tell you,

    That if the light of heaven tomorrow shall see you,

    You and your children in the confines of my land,

    You die. This word I have spoken is firmly fixed.

    But now, if you must stay, stay for this day alone.

355   For in it you can do none of the things I fear.

(Exit Creon with his attendants.)

    Chorus Oh, unfortunate one! Oh, cruel!

    Where will you turn? Who will help you?

    What house or what land to preserve you

    From ill can you find?

360   Medea, a god has thrown suffering

    Upon you in waves of despair.

    Medea Things have gone badly every way. No doubt of that

    But not these things this far, and don't imagine so.

    There are still trials to come for the new-wedded pair,

365   And for their relations pain that will mean something.

    Do you think that I would ever have fawned on that man

    Unless I had some end to gain or profit in it?

    I would not even have spoken or touched him with my hands.

    But he has got to such a pitch of foolishness

370   That, though he could have made nothing of all my plans

    By exiling me, he has given me this one day

    To stay here, and in this I will make dead bodies

Of three of my enemies—father, the girl, and my husband.
I have many ways of death which I might suit to them,
375   And do not know, friends, which one to take in hand;
Whether to set fire underneath their bridal mansion,
Or sharpen a sword and thrust it to the heart,
Stealing into the palace where the bed is made.
There is just one obstacle to this. If I am caught
380   Breaking into the house and scheming against it,
I shall die, and give my enemies cause for laughter.
It is best to go by the straight road, the one in which
I am most skilled, and make away with them by poison.
So be it then.
385   And now suppose them dead. What town will receive me?
What friend will offer me a refuge in his land,
Or the guaranty of his house and save my own life?
There is none. So I must wait a little time yet,
And if some sure defense should then appear for me,
390   In craft and silence I will set about this murder.
But if my fate should drive me on without help,
Even though death is certain, I will take the sword
Myself and kill, and steadfastly advance to crime.
It shall not be—I swear it by her, my mistress,
395   Whom most I honor and have chosen as partner,
Hecate, who dwells in the recesses of my hearth—
That any man shall be glad to have injured me.
Bitter I will make their marriage for them and mournful,
Bitter the alliance and the driving me out of the land.
400   Ah, come, Medea, in your plotting and scheming
Leave nothing untried of all those things which you know.
Go forward to the dreadful act. The test has come
For resolution. You see how you are treated. Never
Shall you be mocked by Jason's Corinthian wedding,
405   Whose father was noble, whose grandfather Helius.
You have the skill. What is more, you were born a woman,
And women, though most helpless in doing good deeds,
Are of every evil the cleverest of contrivers.
Chorus Flow backward to your sources, sacred rivers,
410   And let the world's great order be reversed.
It is the thoughts of *men* that are deceitful,
Their pledges that are loose.

Story shall now turn my condition to a fair one,
Women are paid their due.
415   No more shall evil-sounding fame be theirs.

Cease now, you muses of the ancient singers,
To tell the tale of my unfaithfulness;
For not on us did Phoebus, lord of music,
Bestow the lyre's divine
420   Power, for otherwise I should have sung an answer
To the other sex. Long time
Has much to tell of us, and much of them.

You sailed away from your father's home,
With a heart on fire you passed
425   The double rocks of the sea.
And now in a foreign country
You have lost your rest in a widowed bed,
And are driven forth, a refugee
In dishonor from the land.

430   Good faith has gone, and no more remains
In great Greece a sense of shame.
It has flown away to the sky.
No father's house for a haven
Is at hand for you now, and another queen
435   Of your bed has dispossessed you and
Is mistress of your home.

(Enter Jason, with attendants.)

Jason   This is not the first occasion that I have noticed
How hopeless it is to deal with a stubborn temper.
For, with reasonable submission to our ruler's will,
440   You might have lived in this land and kept your home.
As it is you are going to be exiled for your loose speaking.
Not that I mind myself. You are free to continue
Telling everyone that Jason is a worthless man.
But as to your talk about the king, consider
445   Yourself most lucky that exile is your punishment.
I, for my part, have always tried to calm down
The anger of the king, and wished you to remain.
But you will not give up your folly, continually

Speaking ill of him, and so you are going to be banished.
450   All the same, and in spite of your conduct, I'll not desert
My friends, but have come to make some provision for you,
So that you and the children may not be penniless
Or in need of anything in exile. Certainly
Exile brings many troubles with it. And even
455   If you hate me, I cannot think badly of you.
Medea O coward in every way—that is what I call you,
With bitterest reproach for your lack of manliness,
You have come, you, my worst enemy, have come to me!
It is not an example of overconfidence
460   Or of boldness thus to look your friends in the face,
Friends you have injured—no, it is the worst of all
Human diseases, shamelessness. But you did well
To come, for I can speak ill of you and lighten
My heart, and you will suffer while you are listening.
465   And first I will begin from what happened first.
I saved your life, and every Greek knows I saved it,
Who was a shipmate of yours aboard the Argo,
When you were sent to control the bulls that breathed fire
And yoke them, and when you would sow that deadly field.
470   Also that snake, who encircled with his many folds
The Golden Fleece and guarded it and never slept,
I killed, and so gave you the safety of the light.
And I myself betrayed my father and my home,
And came with you to Pelias' land of Iolcus.
475   And then, showing more willingness to help than wisdom,
I killed him, Pelias, with a most dreadful death
At his own daughters' hands, and took away your fear.
This is how I behaved to you, you wretched man,
And you forsook me, took another bride to bed,
480   Though you had children; for, if that had not been,
You would have had an excuse for another wedding.
Faith in your word has gone. Indeed, I cannot tell
Whether you think the gods whose names you swore by then
Have ceased to rule and that new standards are set up,
485   Since you must know you have broken your word to me.
O my right hand, and the knees which you often clasped
In supplication, how senselessly I am treated

By this bad man, and how my hopes have missed their mark!
Come, I will share my thoughts as though you were a friend—
490   You! Can I think that you would ever treat me well?
But I will do it, and these questions will make you
Appear the baser. Where am I to go? To my father's?
Him I betrayed and his land when I came with you.
To Pelias' wretched daughters? What a fine welcome
495   They would prepare for me who murdered their father!
For this is my position—hated by my friends
At home, I have, in kindness to you, made enemies
Of others whom there was no need to have injured.
And how happy among Greek women you have made me
500   On your side for all this! A distinguished husband
I have—for breaking promises. When in misery
I am cast out of the land and go into exile,
Quite without friends and all alone with my children,
That will be a fine shame for the new-wedded groom,
505   For his children to wander as beggars and she who saved him.
O God, you have given to mortals a sure method
Of telling the gold that is pure from the counterfeit;
Why is there no mark engraved upon men's bodies,
By which we could know the true ones from the false ones?
510   *Chorus* It is a strange form of anger, difficult to cure,
When two friends turn upon each other in hatred.
Jason As for me, it seems I must be no bad speaker.
But, like a man who has a good grip of the tiller,
Reef up his sail, and so run away from under
515   This mouthing tempest, woman, of your bitter tongue.
Since you insist on building up your kindness to me,
My view is that Cypris was alone responsible
Of men and gods for the preserving of my life.
You are clever enough—but really I need not enter
520   Into the story of how it was love's inescapable
Power that compelled you to keep my person safe.
On this I will not go into too much detail.
In so far as you helped me, you did well enough.
But on this question of saving me, I can prove
525   You have certainly got from me more than you gave.
Firstly, instead of living among barbarians,

You inhabit a Greek land and understand our ways,
How to live by law instead of the sweet will of force.
And all the Greeks considered you a clever woman.
530   You were honored for it; while, if you were living at
The ends of the earth, nobody would have heard of you.
For my part, rather than stores of gold in my house
Or power to sing even sweeter songs than Orpheus,
I'd choose the fate that made me a distinguished man.
535   There is my reply to your story of my labors.
Remember it was you who started the argument.
Next for your attack on my wedding with the princess:
Here I will prove that, first, it was a clever move,
Secondly, a wise one, and, finally, that I made it
540   In your best interests and the children's. Please keep calm.
When I arrived here from the land of Iolcus,
Involved, as I was, in every kind of difficulty,
What luckier chance could I have come across than this,
An exile to marry the daughter of the king?
545   It was not—the point that seems to upset you—that I
Grew tired of your bed and felt the need of a new bride;
Nor with any wish to outdo your number of children.
We have enough already. I am quite content.
But—this was the main reason—that we might live well,
550   And not be short of anything. I know that all
A man's friends leave him stone-cold if he becomes poor.
Also that I might bring my children up worthily
Of my position, and, by producing more of them
To be brothers of yours, we would draw the families
555   Together and all be happy. You need no children.
And it pays me to do good to those I have now
By having others. Do you think this a bad plan?
You wouldn't if the love question hadn't upset you.
But you women have got into such a state of mind
560   That, if your life at night is good, you think you have
Everything; but, if in that quarter things go wrong,
You will consider your best and truest interests
Most hateful. It would have been better far for men
To have got their children in some other way, and women
565   Not to have existed. Then life would have been good.

Chorus Jason, though you have made this speech of yours look well,
    Still I think, even though others do not agree,
    You have betrayed your wife and are acting badly.

Medea Surely in many ways I hold different views
570   From others, for I think that the plausible speaker
    Who is a villain deserves the greatest punishment.
    Confident in his tongue's power to adorn evil,
    He stops at nothing. Yet he is not really wise.
    As in your case. There is no need to put on the airs
575   Of a clever speaker, for one word will lay you flat.
    If you were not a coward, you would not have married
    Behind my back, but discussed it with me first.

Jason And you, no doubt, would have furthered the proposal,
    If I had told you of it, you who even now
580   Are incapable of controlling your bitter temper.

Medea It was not that. No, you thought it was not respectable
    As you got on in years to have a foreign wife.

Jason Make sure of this: it was not because of a woman
    I made the royal alliance in which I now live,
585   But, as I said before, I wished to preserve you
    And breed a royal progeny to be brothers
    To the children I have now, a sure defense to us.

Medea Let me have no happy fortune that brings pain with it,
    Or prosperity which is upsetting to the mind!

590 *Jason* Change your ideas of what you want, and show more sense.
    Do not consider painful what is good for you,
    Nor, when you are lucky, think yourself unfortunate.

Medea You can insult me. You have somewhere to turn to.
    But I shall go from this land into exile, friendless.

595 *Jason* It was what you chose yourself. Don't blame others for it.

Medea And how did I choose it? Did I betray my husband?

Jason You called down wicked curses on the king's family.

Medea A curse, that is what I am become to your house too.

Jason I do not propose to go into all the rest of it;
600   But, if you wish for the children or for yourself
    In exile to have some of my money to help you,
    Say so, for I am prepared to give with open hand,
    Or to provide you with introductions to my friends
    Who will treat you well. You are a fool if you do not
605   Accept this. Cease your anger and you will profit.

Medea I shall never accept the favors of friends of yours,
      Nor take a thing from you, so you need not offer it.
      There is no benefit in the gifts of a bad man.
Jason Then, in any case, I call the gods to witness that
610   I wish to help you and the children in every way,
      But you refuse what is good for you. Obstinately
      You push away your friends. You are sure to suffer for it.
Medea Go! No doubt you hanker for your virginal bride,
      And are guilty of lingering too long out of her house.
615   Enjoy your wedding. But perhaps—with the help of God—
      You will make the kind of marriage that you will regret.

                   (*Jason goes out with his attendants.*)

Chorus When love is in excess
      It brings a man no honor
      Nor any worthiness.
620   But if in moderation Cypris comes,
      There is no other power at all so gracious.
      O goddess, never on me let loose the unerring
      Shaft of your bow in the poison of desire.

      Let my heart be wise.
625   It is the gods' best gift.
      On me let mighty Cypris
      Inflict no wordy wars or restless anger
      To urge my passion to a different love.
      But with discernment may she guide women's weddings,
630   Honoring most what is peaceful in the bed.

      O country and home,
      Never, never may I be without you,
      Living the hopeless life,
      Hard to pass through and painful,
635   Most pitiable of all.
      Let death first lay me low and death
      Free me from this daylight.
      There is no sorrow above
      The loss of a native land.

640   I have seen it myself,
      Do not tell of a secondhand story.
      Neither city nor friend

Pitied you when you suffered
The worst of sufferings.
645 O let him die ungraced whose heart
Will not reward his friends,
Who cannot open an honest mind
No friend will he be of mine.

(*Enter Aegeus, king of Athens, an old friend of Medea.*)

Aegeus Medea, greeting! This is the best introduction
650   Of which men know for conversation between friends.
Medea Greeting to you too, Aegeus, son of King Pandion.
     Where have you come from to visit this country's soil?
Aegeus I have just left the ancient oracle of Phoebus.
Medea And why did you go to earth's prophetic center?
655 *Aegeus* I went to inquire how children might be born to me.
Medea Is it so? Your life still up to this point is childless?
Aegeus Yes. By the fate of some power we have no children.
Medea Have you a wife, or is there none to share your bed?
Aegeus There is. Yes, I am joined to my wife in marriage.
660 *Medea* And what did Phoebus say to you about children?
Aegeus Words too wise for a mere man to guess their meaning.
Medea It is proper for me to be told the god's reply?
Aegeus It is. For sure what is needed is cleverness.
Medea Then what was his message? Tell me, if I may hear.
665 *Aegeus* I am not to loosen the hanging foot of the wine-skin . . .
Medea Until you have done something, or reached some country?
Aegeus Until I return again to my hearth and house.
Medea And for what purpose have you journeyed to this land?
Aegeus There is a man called Pittheus, king of Troezen.
670 *Medea* A son of Pelops, they say, a most righteous man.
Aegeus With him I wish to discuss the reply of the god.
Medea Yes. He is wise and experienced in such matters.
Aegeus And to me also the dearest of all my spear-friends.
Medea Well, I hope you have good luck, and achieve your will.
675 *Aegeus* But why this downcast eye of yours, and this pale cheek?
Medea O Aegeus, my husband has been the worst of all to me.
Aegeus What do you mean? Say clearly what has caused this grief.
Medea Jason wrongs me, though I have never injured him.
Aegeus What has he done? Tell me about it in clearer words.

680 *Medea* He has taken a wife to his house, supplanting me.

Aegeus Surely he would not dare to do a thing like that.

Medea Be sure he has. Once dear, I now am slighted by him.

Aegeus Did he fall in love? Or is he tired of your love?

Medea He was greatly in love, this traitor to his friends.

685 *Aegeus* Then let him go, if, as you say, he is so bad.

Medea A passionate love—for an alliance with the king.

Aegeus And who gave him his wife? Tell me the rest of it.

Medea It was Creon, he who rules this land of Corinth.

Aegeus Indeed, Medea, your grief was understandable.

690 *Medea* I am ruined. And there is more to come: I am banished.

Aegeus Banished? By whom? Here you tell me of a new wrong.

Medea Creon drives me an exile from the land of Corinth.

Aegeus Does Jason consent? I cannot approve of this.

Medea He pretends not to, but he will put up with it.

695   Ah, Aegeus, I beg and beseech you, by your beard
         And by your knees I am making myself your suppliant,
         Have pity on me, have pity on your poor friend,
         And do not let me go into exile desolate,
         But receive me in your land and at your very hearth.

700   So may your love, with God's help, lead to the bearing
         Of children, and so may you yourself die happy.
         You do not know what a chance you have come on here.
         I will end your childlessness, and I will make you able
         To beget children. The drugs I know can do this.

705 *Aegeus* For many reasons, woman, I am anxious to do
         This favor for you. First, for the sake of the gods,
         And then for the birth of children which you promise,
         For in that respect I am entirely at my wits' end.
         But this is my position: if you reach my land,

710   I, being in my rights, will try to befriend you.
         But this much I must warn you of beforehand:
         I shall not agree to take you out of this country;
         But if you by yourself can reach my house, then you
         Shall stay there safely. To none will I give you up

715   But from this land you must make your escape yourself,
         For I do not wish to incur blame from my friends.

Medea It shall be so. But, if I might have a pledge from you
         For this, then I would have from you all I desire.

Aegeus Do you not trust me? What is it rankles with you?

720 *Medea* I trust you, yes. But the house of Pelias hates me,
         And so does Creon. If you are bound by this oath,
         When they try to drag me from your land, you will not
         Abandon me; but if our pact is only words,
         With no oath to the gods, you will be lightly armed,
725   Unable to resist their summons. I am weak,
         While they have wealth to help them and a royal house.

Aegeus You show much foresight for such negotiations.
         Well, if you will have it so, I will not refuse.
         For, both on my side this will be the safest way
730   To have some excuse to put forward to your enemies,
         And for you it is more certain. You may name the gods.

Medea Swear by the plain of Earth, and Helius, father
         Of my father, and name together all the gods . . .

Aegeus That I will act or not act in what way? Speak.

735 *Medea* That you yourself will never cast me from your land,
         Nor, if any of my enemies should demand me,
         Will you, in your life, willingly hand me over.

Aegeus I swear by the Earth, by the holy light of Helius,
         By all the gods, I will abide by this you say.

740 *Medea* Enough. And, if you fail, what shall happen to you?

Aegeus What comes to those who have no regard for heaven.

Medea Go on your way. Farewell. For I am satisfied.
         And I will reach your city as soon as I can,
         Having done the deed I have to do and gained my end.

(Aegeus goes out.)

745 *Chorus* May Hermes, god of travelers,
         Escort you, Aegeus, to your home!
         And may you have the things you wish
         So eagerly; for you
         Appear to me to be a generous man.

750 *Medea* God, and God's daughter, justice, and light of Helius!
         Now, friends, has come the time of my triumph over
         My enemies, and now my foot is on the road.
         Now I am confident they will pay the penalty.
         For this man, Aegeus, has been like a harbor to me
755   In all my plans just where I was most distressed.

To him I can fasten the cable of my safety
When I have reached the town and fortress of Pallas.
And now I shall tell to you the whole of my plan.
Listen to these words that are not spoken idly.
760 I shall send one of my servants to find Jason
And request him to come once more into my sight.
And when he comes, the words I'll say will be soft ones.
I'll say that I agree with him, that I approve
The royal wedding he has made, betraying me.
765 I'll say it was profitable, an excellent idea.
But I shall beg that my children may remain here:
Not that I would leave in a country that hates me
Children of mine to feel their enemies' insults,
But that by a trick I may kill the king's daughter.
770 For I will send the children with gifts in their hands
To carry to the bride, so as not to be banished—
A finely woven dress and a golden diadem.
And if she takes them and wears them upon her skin
She and all who touch the girl will die in agony;
775 Such poison will I lay upon the gifts I send.
But there, however, I must leave that account paid.
I weep to think of what a deed I have to do
Next after that; for I shall kill my own children.
My children, there is none who can give them safety.
780 And when I have ruined the whole of Jason's house,
I shall leave the land and flee from the murder of my
Dear children, and I shall have done a dreadful deed.
For it is not bearable to be mocked by enemies.
So it must happen. What profit have I in life?
785 I have no land, no home, no refuge from my pain.
My mistake was made the time I left behind me
My father's house, and trusted the words of a Greek,
Who, with heaven's help, will pay me the price for that.
For those children he had from me he will never
790 See alive again, nor will he on his new bride
Beget another child, for she is to be forced
To die a most terrible death by these my poisons.
Let no one think me a weak one, feeble-spirited,
A stay-at-home, but rather just the opposite,

795   One who can hurt my enemies and help my friends;
For the lives of such persons are most remembered.
Chorus Since you have shared the knowledge of your plan with us,
I both wish to help you and support the normal
Ways of mankind, and tell you not to do this thing.
800   *Medea* I can do no other thing. It is understandable
For you to speak thus. You have not suffered as I have.
Chorus But can you have the heart to kill your flesh and blood?
Medea Yes, for this is the best way to wound my husband.
Chorus And you, too. Of women you will be most unhappy.
805   *Medea* So it must be. No compromise is possible.

(She turns to the Nurse.)

Go, you, at once, and tell Jason to come to me.
You I employ on all affairs of greatest trust.
Say nothing of these decisions which I have made,
If you love your mistress, if you were born a woman.
810   *Chorus* From of old the children of Erechtheus are
Splendid, the sons of blessed gods. They dwell
In Athens' holy and unconquered land,
Where famous Wisdom feeds them and they pass gaily
Always through that most brilliant air where once, they say,
815   That golden Harmony gave birth to the nine
Pure Muses of Pieria.

And beside the sweet flow of Cephisus' stream,
Where Cypris sailed, they say, to draw the water,
And mild soft breezes breathed along her path,
820   And on her hair were flung the sweet-smelling garlands
Of flowers of roses by the Lovers, the companions
Of Wisdom, her escort, the helpers of men
In every kind of excellence.

How then can these holy rivers
825   Or this holy land love you,
Or the city find you a home,
You, who will kill your children,
You, not pure with the rest?
O think of the blow at your children
830   And think of the blood that you shed.

O, over and over I beg you,
By your knees I beg you do not
Be the murderess of your babes!

O where will you find the courage
835   Or the skill of hand and heart,
When you set yourself to attempt
A deed so dreadful to do?
How, when you look upon them,
Can you tearlessly hold the decision
840   For murder? You will not be able,
When your children fall down and implore you,
You will not be able to dip
Steadfast your hand in their blood.

(Enter Jason with attendants.)

Jason I have come at your request. Indeed, although you are
845   Bitter against me, this you shall have: I will listen
To what new thing you want, woman, to get from me.
Medea Jason, I beg you to be forgiving toward me
For what I said. It is natural for you to bear with
My temper, since we have had much love together.
850   I have talked with myself about this and I have
Reproached myself. "Fool" I said, "why am I so mad?
Why am I set against those who have planned wisely?
Why make myself an enemy of the authorities
And of my husband, who does the best thing for me
855   By marrying royalty and having children who
Will be as brothers to my own? What is wrong with me?
Let me give up anger, for the gods are kind to me.
Have I not children, and do I not know that we
In exile from our country must be short of friends?"
860   When I considered this I saw that I had shown
Great lack of sense, and that my anger was foolish.
Now I agree with you. I think that you are wise
In having this other wife as well as me, and I
Was mad. I should have helped you in these plans of yours,
865   Have joined in the wedding, stood by the marriage bed,
Have taken pleasure in attendance on your bride.
But we women are what we are—perhaps a little

Worthless; and you men must not be like us in this,
Nor be foolish in return when we are foolish.

870   Now, I give in, and admit that then I was wrong.
I have come to a better understanding now.

(She turns toward the house.)

Children, come here, my children, come outdoors to us!
Welcome your father with me, and say goodbye to him,
And with your mother, who just now was his enemy,

875   Join again in making friends with him who loves us.

(Enter the children, attended by the Tutor.)

We have made peace, and all our anger is over.
Take hold of his right hand—O God, I am thinking
Of something which may happen in the secret future.
O children, will you just so, after a long life,

880   Hold out your loving arms at the grave? O children,
How ready to cry I am, how full of foreboding!
I am ending at last this quarrel with your father,
And, look my soft eyes have suddenly filled with tears.
Chorus   And the pale tears have started also in my eyes.

885   O may the trouble not grow worse than now it is!
Jason   I approve of what you say. And I cannot blame you
Even for what you said before. It is natural
For a woman to be wild with her husband when he
Goes in for secret love. But now your mind has turned

890   To better reasoning. In the end you have come to
The right decision, like the clever woman you are.
And of you, children, your father is taking care.
He has made, with God's help, ample provision for you.
For I think that a time will come when you will be

895   The leading people in Corinth with your brothers.
You must grow up. As to the future, your father
And those of the gods who love him will deal with that.
I want to see you, when you have become young men,
Healthy and strong, better men than my enemies.

900   Medea, why are your eyes all wet with pale tears?
Why is your cheek so white and turned away from me?
Are not these words of mine pleasing for you to hear?
Medea   It is nothing. I was thinking about these children.

Jason You must be cheerful. I shall look after them well.

905 *Medea* I will be. It is not that I distrust your words,
But a woman is a frail thing, prone to crying.

Jason But why then should you grieve so much for these children?

Medea I am their mother. When you prayed that they might live
I felt unhappy to think that these things will be.

910 But come, I have said something of the things I meant
To say to you, and now I will tell you the rest.
Since it is the king's will to banish me from here—
And for me, too, I know that this is the best thing,
Not to be in your way by living here or in

915 The king's way, since they think me ill-disposed to them—
I then am going into exile from this land;
But do you, so that you may have the care of them,
Beg Creon that the children may not be banished.

Jason I doubt if I'll succeed, but still I'll attempt it.

920 *Medea* Then you must tell your wife to beg from her father
That the children may be reprieved from banishment.

Jason I will, and with her I shall certainly succeed.

Medea If she is like the rest of us women, you will.
And I, too, will take a hand with you in this business,

925 For I will send her some gifts which are far fairer,
I am sure of it, than those which now are in fashion,
A finely woven dress and a golden diadem,
And the children shall present them. Quick, let one of you
Servants bring here to me that beautiful dress.

(One of her attendants goes into the house.)

930 She will be happy not in one way, but in a hundred,
Having so fine a man as you to share her bed,
And with this beautiful dress which Helius of old,
My father's father, bestowed on his descendants.

(Enter attendant carrying the poisoned dress and diadem.)

935 There, children, take these wedding presents in your hands.
Take them to the royal princess, the happy bride,
And give them to her. She will not think little of them.

Jason No, don't be foolish, and empty your hands of these.
Do you think the palace is short of dresses to wear?

940 Do you think there is no gold there? Keep them, don't give them

Away. If my wife considers me of any value,
She will think more of me than money, I am sure of it.
Medea No, let me have my way. They say the gods themselves
Are moved by gifts, and gold does more with men than words.

945 Hers is the luck, her fortune that which god blesses;
She is young and a princess; but for my children's reprieve
I would give my very life, and not gold only.
Go children, go together to that rich palace,
Be suppliants to the new wife of your father,

950 My lady, beg her not to let you be banished.
And give her the dress—for this is of great importance,
That she should take the gift into her hand from yours.
Go, quick as you can. And bring your mother good news
By your success of those things which she longs to gain.

> *(Jason goes out with his attendants, followed by the Tutor
> and the children carrying the poisoned gifts.)*

955 *Chorus* Now there is no hope left for the children's lives.
Now there is none. They are walking already to murder.
The bride, poor bride, will accept the curse of the gold,
Will accept the bright diadem.
Around her yellow hair she will set that dress

960 Of death with her own hands.

The grace and the perfume and glow of the golden robe
Will charm her to put them upon her and wear the wreath,
And now her wedding will be with the dead below,
Into such a trap she will fall,

965 Poor thing, into such a fate of death and never
Escape from under that curse.

You, too, O wretched bridegroom, making your match with kings,
You do not see that you bring
Destruction on your children and on her,

970 Your wife, a fearful death.
Poor soul, what a fall is yours!

In your grief, too, I weep, mother of little children,
You who will murder your own,
In vengeance for the loss of married love

975 Which Jason has betrayed

As he lives with another wife.

(Enter the Tutor with the children.)

Tutor Mistress, I tell you that these children are reprieved,
And the royal bride has been pleased to take in her hands
Your gifts. In that quarter the children are secure.
980   But come,
Why do you stand confused when you are fortunate?
Why have you turned round with your cheek away from me?
Are not these words of mine pleasing for you to hear?
Medea Oh! I am lost!
985 *Tutor* That word is not in harmony with my tidings.
Medea I am lost, I am lost!
Tutor   Am I in ignorance telling you
Of some disaster, and not the good news I thought?
Medea You have told what you have told. I do not blame you.
990 *Tutor* Why then this downcast eye, and this weeping of tears?
Medea Oh, I am forced to weep, old man. The gods and I,
I in a kind of madness, have contrived all this.
Tutor Courage! You, too, will be brought home by your children.
Medea Ah, before that happens I shall bring others home.
995 *Tutor* Others before you have been parted from their children.
Mortals must bear in resignation their ill luck.
Medea That is what I shall do. But go inside the house,
And do for the children your usual daily work.

(The Tutor goes into the house. Medea turns to her children.)

1000   O children, O my children, you have a city,
You have a home, and you can leave me behind you,
And without your mother you may live there forever.
But I am going in exile to another land
Before I have seen you happy and taken pleasure in you,
1005   Before I have dressed your brides and made your marriage beds
And held up the torch at the ceremony of wedding.
Oh, what a wretch I am in this my self-willed thought!
What was the purpose, children, for which I reared you?
For all my travail and wearing myself away?
1010   They were sterile, those pains I had in the bearing of you.
Oh surely once the hopes in you I had, poor me,

Were high ones: you would look after me in old age,
And when I died would deck me well with your own hands;
A thing which all would have done. Oh but now it is gone,
1015   That lovely thought. For, once I am left without you,
Sad will be the life I'll lead and sorrowful for me.
And you will never see your mother again with
Your dear eyes, gone to another mode of living.
Why, children, do you look upon me with your eyes?
1020   Why do you smile so sweetly that last smile of all?
Oh, Oh, what can I do? My spirit has gone from me,
Friends, when I saw that bright look in the children's eyes.
I cannot bear to do it. I renounce my plans
I had before. I'll take my children away from
1025   This land. Why should I hurt their father with the pain
They feel, and suffer twice as much of pain myself?
No, no, I will not do it. I renounce my plans.
Ah, what is wrong with me? Do I want to let go
My enemies unhurt and be laughed at for it?
1030   I must face this thing. Oh, but what a weak woman
Even to admit to my mind these soft arguments.
Children, go into the house. And he whom law forbids
To stand in attendance at my sacrifices,
Let him see to it. I shall not mar my handiwork.
1035   Oh! Oh!
Do not, O my heart, you must not do these things!
Poor heart, let them go, have pity upon the children.
if they live with you in Athens they will cheer you.
No! By Hell's avenging furies it shall not be—
1040   This shall never be, that I should suffer my children
To be the prey of my enemies' insolence.
Every way is it fixed. The bride will not escape.
No, the diadem is now upon her head, and she,
The royal princess, is dying in the dress, I know it.
1045   But—for it is the most dreadful of roads for me
To tread, and them I shall send on a more dreadful still—
I wish to speak to the children.

(She calls the children to her.)

Come, children, give
Me your hands, give your mother your hands to kiss them.

1050   Oh the dear hands, and O how dear are these lips to me,
And the generous eyes and the bearing of my children!
I wish you happiness, but not here in this world.
What is here your father took. Oh how good to hold you!
How delicate the skin, how sweet the breath of children!
1055   Go, go! I am no longer able, no longer
To look upon you. I am overcome by sorrow.

(The children go into the house.)

I know indeed what evil I intend to do,
But stronger than all my afterthoughts is my fury,
Fury that brings upon mortals the greatest evils.

(She goes out to the right, toward the royal palace.)

1060   *Chorus* Often before
I have gone through more subtle reasons,
And have come upon questionings greater
Than a woman should strive to search out.
But we too have a goddess to help us
1065   And accompany us into wisdom,
Not all of us. Still you will find
Among many women a few,
And our sex is not without learning.
This I say, that those who have never
1070   Had children, who know nothing of it,
In happiness have the advantage
Over those who are parents.
The childless, who never discover
Whether children turn out as a good thing
1075   Or as something to cause pain, are spared
Many troubles in lacking this knowledge.
And those who have in their homes
The sweet presence of children, I see that their lives
Are all wasted away by their worries.
1080   First they must think how to bring them up well and
How to leave them something to live on.
And then after this whether all their toil
Is for those who will turn out good or bad,
Is still an unanswered question.
1085   And of one more trouble, the last of all,

That is common to mortals I tell.
For suppose you have found them enough for their living,
Suppose that the children have grown into youth
And have turned out good, still, if God so wills it,

1090   Death will away with your children's bodies,
And carry them off into Hades.
What is our profit, then, that for the sake of
Children the gods should pile upon mortals
After all else

1095   This most terrible grief of all?

(Enter Medea, from the spectators' right.)

Medea   Friends, I can tell you that for long I have waited
For the event. I stare toward the place from where
The news will come. And now, see one of Jason's servants
Is on his way here, and that labored breath of his

2000   Shows he has tidings for us, and evil tidings.

(Enter, also from the right, the Messenger.)

Messenger   Medea, you who have done such a dreadful thing,
So outrageous, run for your life, take what you can,
A ship to bear you hence or chariot on land.
Medea   And what is the reason deserves such flight as this?

2005   *Messenger*   She is dead, only just now, the royal princess,
And Creon dead, too, her father, by your poisons.
Medea   The finest words you have spoken. Now and hereafter
I shall count you among my benefactors and friends.
Messenger   What! Are you right in the mind? Are you not mad,

2010   Woman? The house of the king is outraged by you.
Do you enjoy it? Not afraid of such doings?
Medea   To what you say I on my side have something too
To say in answer. Do not be in a hurry, friend,
But speak. How did they die? You will delight me twice

2015   As much again if you say they died in agony.
Messenger   When those two children, born of you, had entered in,
Their father with them, and passed into the bride's house,
We were pleased, we slaves who were distressed by your wrongs.
All through the house we were talking of but one thing,

2020   How you and your husband had made up your quarrel.

Some kissed the children's hands and some their yellow hair,
And I myself was so full of my joy that I
Followed the children into the women's quarters.
Our mistress, whom we honor now instead of you,
2025 Before she noticed that your two children were there,
Was keeping her eye fixed eagerly on Jason.
Afterwards, however, she covered up her eyes,
Her cheek paled, and she turned herself away from him,
So disgusted was she at the children's coming there.
2030 But your husband tried to end the girl's bad temper,
And said "You must not look unkindly on your friends.
Cease to be angry. Turn your head to me again.
Have as your friends the same ones as your husband has.
And take these gifts, and beg your father to reprieve
2035 These children from their exile. Do it for my sake."
She, when she saw the dress, could not restrain herself.
She agreed with all her husband said, and before
He and the children had gone far from the palace,
She took the gorgeous robe and dressed herself in it,
2040 And put the golden crown around her curly locks,
And arranged the set of the hair in a shining mirror,
And smiled at the lifeless image of herself in it.
Then she rose from her chair and walked about the room,
With her gleaming feet stepping most soft and delicate,
2045 All overjoyed with the present. Often and often
She would stretch her foot out straight and look along it.
But after that it was a fearful thing to see.
The color of her face changed, and she staggered back,
She ran, and her legs trembled, and she only just
2050 Managed to reach a chair without falling flat down.
An aged woman servant who, I take it, thought
This was some seizure of Pan or another god,
Cried out "God bless us," but that was before she saw
The white foam breaking through her lips and her rolling
2055 The pupils of her eyes and her face all bloodless.
Then she raised a different cry from that "God bless us,"
A huge shriek, and the women ran, one to the king,
One to the newly wedded husband to tell him
What had happened to his bride; and with frequent sound

2060   The whole of the palace rang as they went running.
        One walking quickly round the course of a race-track
        Would now have turned the bend and be close to the goal,
        When she, poor girl, opened her shut and speechless eye,
        And with a terrible groan she came to herself.
2065   For a twofold pain was moving up against her.
        The wreath of gold that was resting around her head
        Let forth a fearful stream of all-devouring fire,
        And the finely woven dress-your children gave to her,
        Was fastening on the unhappy girl's fine flesh.
2070   She leapt up from the chair, and all on fire she ran,
        Shaking her hair now this way and now that, trying
        To hurl the diadem away; but fixedly
        The gold preserved its grip, and, when she shook her hair,
        Then more and twice as fiercely the fire blazed out.
2075   Till, beaten by her fate, she fell down to the ground,
        Hard to be recognized except by a parent.
        Neither the setting of her eyes was plain to see,
        Nor the shapeliness of her face. From the top of
        Her head there oozed out blood and fire mixed together.
2080   Like the drops on pine-bark, so the flesh from her bones
        Dropped away, torn by the hidden fang of the poison.
        It was a fearful sight; and terror held us all
        From touching the corpse. We had learned from what had happened.
        But her wretched father, knowing nothing of the event,
2085   Came suddenly to the house, and fell upon the corpse,
        And at once cried out and folded his arms about her,
        And kissed her and spoke to her, saying, "O my poor child,
        What heavenly power has so shamefully destroyed you?
        And who has set me here like an ancient sepulcher,
2090   Deprived of you? O let me die with you, my child!"
        And when he had made an end of his wailing and crying,
        Then the old man wished to raise himself to his feet;
        But, as the ivy clings to the twigs of the laurel,
        So he stuck to the fine dress, and he struggled fearfully.
2095   For he was trying to lift himself to his knee,
        And she was pulling him down, and when he tugged hard
        He would be ripping his aged flesh from his bones.
        At last his life was quenched, and the unhappy man

Gave up the ghost, no longer could hold up his head.
2100 There they lie close, the daughter and the old father,
Dead bodies, an event he prayed for in his tears.
As for your interests, I will say nothing of them,
For you will find your own escape from punishment.
Our human life I think and have thought a shadow,
2105 And I do not fear to say that those who are held
Wise among men and who search the reasons of things
Are those who bring the most sorrow on themselves.
For of mortals there is no one who is happy.
If wealth flows in upon one, one may be perhaps
2110 Luckier than one's neighbor, but still not happy.

(Exit.)

Chorus Heaven, it seems, on this day has fastened many
Evils on Jason, and Jason has deserved them.
Poor girl, the daughter of Creon, how I pity you
And your misfortunes, you who have gone quite away
2115 To the house of Hades because of marrying Jason.
Medea Women, my task is fixed: as quickly as I may
To kill my children, and start away from this land,
And not, by wasting time, to suffer my children
To be slain by another hand less kindly to them.
2120 Force every way will have it they must die, and since
This must be so, then I, their mother, shall kill them.
Oh, arm yourself in steel, my heart! Do not hang back
From doing this fearful and necessary wrong.
Oh, come, my hand, poor wretched hand, and take the sword,
2125 Take it, step forward to this bitter starting point,
And do not be a coward, do not think of them,
How sweet they are, and how you are their mother. Just for
This one short day be forgetful of your children,
Afterward weep; for even though you will kill them,
2130 They were very dear—Oh, I am an unhappy woman!

(With a cry she rushes into the house.)

Chorus O Earth, and the far shining
Ray of the Sun, look down, look down upon
This poor lost woman, look, before she raises

The hand of murder against her flesh and blood.
2135　Yours was the golden birth from which
She sprang, and now I fear divine
Blood may be shed by men.
O heavenly light, hold back her hand,
Check her, and drive from out the house
2140　The bloody Fury raised by fiends of Hell.

Vain waste, your care of children;
Was it in vain you bore the babes you loved,
After you passed the inhospitable strait
Between the dark blue rocks, Symplegades?
2145　O wretched one, how has it come,
This heavy anger on your heart,
This cruel bloody mind?
For God from mortals asks a stern
Price for the stain of kindred blood
2150　In like disaster falling on their homes.

(A cry from one of the children is heard.)

Chorus Do you hear the cry, do you hear the children's cry?
　O you hard heart, O woman fated for evil!
One of the children (from within) What can I do and how escape my mother's
　hands?
2155　*Another child (from within)* O my dear brother, I cannot tell. We are lost.
Chorus Shall I enter the house? Oh, surely I should
　Defend the children from murder.
A child (from within) O help us, in God's name, for now we need your help.
　Now, now we are close to it. We are trapped by the sword.
2160　*Chorus* O your heart must have been made of rock or steel,
　You who can kill
　With your own hand the fruit of your own womb.
　Of one alone I have heard, one woman alone
　Of those of old who laid her hands on her children,
2165　Ino, sent mad by heaven when the wife of Zeus
　Drove her out from her home and made her wander;
　And because of the wicked shedding of blood
　Of her own children she threw
　Herself, poor wretch, into the sea and stepped away
2170　Over the sea-cliff to die with her two children.

What horror more can be? O women's love,
So full of trouble,
How many evils have you caused already!

(*Enter Jason, with attendants.*)

Jason You women, standing close in front of this dwelling,
2175 Is she, Medea, she who did this dreadful deed,
Still in the house, or has she run away in flight?
For she will have to hide herself beneath the earth,
Or raise herself on wings into the height of air,
If she wishes to escape the royal vengeance,
2180 Does she imagine that, having killed our rulers,
She will herself escape uninjured from this house?
But I am thinking not so much of her as for
The children—her the king's friends will make to suffer
For what she did. So I have come to save the lives
2185 Of my boys, in case the royal house should harm them
While taking vengeance for their mother's wicked deed.
Chorus O Jason, if you but knew how deeply you are
Involved in sorrow, you would not have spoken so.
Jason What is it? That she is planning to kill me also?
2190 *Chorus* Your children are dead, and by their own mother's hand.
Jason What! That is it? O woman, you have destroyed me!
Chorus You must make up your mind your children are no more.
Jason Where did she kill them? Was it here or in the house?
Chorus Open the gates and there you will see them murdered.
2195 *Jason* Quick as you can unlock the doors, men, and undo
The fastenings and let me see this double evil,
My children dead and her—Oh her I will repay.

(*His attendants rush to the door. Medea appears above the house in a chariot
drawn by dragons. She has the dead bodies of the children with her.*)

Medea Why do you batter these gates and try to unbar them,
Seeking the corpses and for me who did the deed?
2200 You may cease your trouble, and, if you have need of me,
Speak, if you wish. You will never touch me with your hand,
Such a chariot has Helius, my father's father,
Given me to defend me from my enemies.
Jason You hateful thing, you woman most utterly loathed
2205 By the gods and me and by all the race of mankind,

You who have had the heart to raise a sword against
Your children, you, their mother, and left me childless—
You have done this, and do you still look at the sun
And at the earth, after these most fearful doings?

2210   I wish you dead. Now I see it plain, though at that time
I did not, when I took you from your foreign home
And brought you to a Greek house, you, an evil thing,
A traitress to your father and your native land.
The gods hurled the avenging curse of yours on me.

2215   For your own brother you slew at your own hearthside,
And then came aboard that beautiful ship, the Argo.
And that was your beginning. When you were married
To me, your husband, and had borne children to me,
For the sake of pleasure in the bed you killed them.

2220   There is no Greek woman who would have dared such deeds,
Out of all those whom I passed over and chose you
To marry instead, a bitter destructive match,
A monster, not a woman, having a nature
Wilder than that of Scylla in the Tuscan sea.

2225   Ah! no, not if I had ten thousand words of shame
Could I sting you. You are naturally so brazen.
Go, worker in evil, stained with your children's blood.
For me remains to cry aloud upon my fate,
Who will get no pleasure from my newly wedded love,

2230   And the boys whom I begot and brought up, never
Shall I speak to them alive. Oh, my life is over!

Medea Long would be the answer which I might have made to
These words of yours, if Zeus the father did not know
How I have treated you and what you did to me.

2235   No, it was not to be that you should scorn my love,
And pleasantly live your life through, laughing at me;
Nor would the princess, nor he who offered the match,
Creon, drive me away without paying for it,
So now you may call me a monster, if you wish,

2240   A Scylla housed in the caves of the Tuscan sea.
I too, as I had to, have taken hold of your heart.

Jason You feel the pain yourself. You share in my sorrow.

Medea Yes, and my grief is gain when you cannot mock it.

Jason O children, what a wicked mother she was to you!

2245 *Medea* They died from a disease they caught from their father.
Jason I tell you it was not my hand that destroyed them.
Medea But it was your insolence, and your virgin wedding.
Jason And just for the sake of that you chose to kill them.
Medea Is love so small a pain, do you think, for a woman?
2250 *Jason* For a wise one, certainly. But you are wholly evil.
Medea The children are dead. I say this to make you suffer.
Jason The children, I think, will bring down curses on you.
Medea The gods know who was the author of this sorrow.
Jason Yes, the gods know indeed, they know your loathsome heart.
2255 *Medea* Hate me. But I tire of your barking bitterness.
Jason And I of yours. It is easier to leave you.
Medea How then? What shall I do? I long to leave you too.
Jason Give me the bodies to bury and to mourn them.
Medea No, that I will not. I will bury them myself,
2260   Bearing them to Hera's temple on the promontory;
    So that no enemy may evilly treat them
    By tearing up their grave. In this land of Corinth
    I shall establish a holy feast and sacrifice
    Each year for ever to atone for the blood guilt.
2265   And I myself go to the land of Erechtheus
    To dwell in Aegeus' house, the son of Pandion.
    While you, as is right, will die without distinction,
    Struck on the head by a piece of the Argo's timber,
    And you will have seen the bitter end of my love.
2270 *Jason* May a Fury for the children's sake destroy you,
    And justice, Requitor of blood.
Medea What heavenly power lends an ear
    To a breaker of oaths, a deceiver?
Jason Oh, I hate you, murderess of children.
2275 *Medea* Go to your palace. Bury your bride.
Jason I go, with two children to mourn for.
Medea Not yet do you feel it. Wait for the future.
Jason Oh, children I loved!
Medea   I loved them, you did not.
2280 *Jason* You loved them, and killed them.
Medea   To make you feel pain.
Jason Oh, wretch that I am, how I long
    To kiss the dear lips of my children!

Medea Now you would speak to them, now you would kiss them.
2285   Then you rejected them.
Jason   Let me, I beg you,
       Touch my boys' delicate flesh.
Medea I will not. Your words are all wasted.
Jason O God, do you hear it, this persecution,
2290   These my sufferings from this hateful
       Woman, this monster, murderess of children?
       Still what I can do that I will do:
       I will lament and cry upon heaven,
       Calling the gods to bear me witness
2295   How you have killed my boys and prevent me from
       Touching their bodies or giving them burial.
       I wish I had never begot them to see them
       Afterward slaughtered by you.
Chorus Zeus in Olympus is the overseer
2300   Of many doings. Many things the gods
       Achieve beyond our judgment. What we thought
       Is not confirmed and what we thought not god
       Contrives. And so it happens in this story.

(Curtain.)

Questions for Review and Discussion

1. In her opening speech, Medea bemoans the fate of foreigners, women in general, and the institutions of marriage and motherhood. She elicits sympathy from the Chorus since her words apparently echo their collective resentment for the plight of women in Greek society. What are some of the traditional roles and values expected of Medea as a female, and how does she violate them?
2. Medea challenges sexism and sexist double standards through her words as well as her deeds. Which of her actions usurp the rights that had traditionally been assigned to males?
3. Medea successfully exploits socially constructed gender stereotypes to vanquish her enemies. How does she use traditional concepts of femininity to advance her agenda?
4. Jason, Creon, and Aegeus are manipulated by Medea to varying degrees. How is she able to exploit their concerns to further her goal?
5. What evidence is there in the play to indicate that Medea's choice to murder her own children was a difficult one for her to make?
6. Discuss the role of the children, the nurse, the tutor, and the Chorus. How does their presence contribute to the unfolding of Euripides's vision in the play?

7. Medea assumes that the sacrifices she has made will be acknowledged, rewarded, and reciprocated by Jason, the man she loves. What evidence can you find in the play to indicate that Medea is justified in making this assumption?

8. What are the gender dynamics in the play?

9. What arguments can be made to support the position that Medea represents marginalized groups who have been denied access, power, and voice?

10. Euripides's *Medea* can be interpreted as an exploration of the horrifying actions that can ensue when oppressive systems deny members of various groups legitimate access to power and legitimate means to seek redress for injustices. What are some of the issues that challenge us today which appear to reinforce the accuracy of Euripides's vision?

Chapter 7

Sita

Glossary of Names and Terms

AGNI God of Fire

AVATAR Incarnation of a god into another form; incarnation of Vishnu on earth is Rama; incarnation of Lakshmi on earth is Sita

AYODHYA Capital city of Kosala; ruled by King Dasarath, father of Rama

BRAHMA Creator god of Hindu triad of gods which includes Śiva and Vishnu

DASARATH King of Kosala; earthly father of Rama

DHARMA Righteous behavior; appropriate codes of conduct; laws, duties, and obligations; supersedes individual needs and desires

HANUMAN Monkey king who aids Rama in rescuing Sita

INDRA Warrior-god in Hindu tradition

JANAKA King of Mithila; Sita's father

KAIKEYI Dasarath's youngest queen and the mother of Bharata; responsible for Rama's exile

KUSA Son of Rama and Sita; twin brother of Lava

LAKSHMANA Rama's devoted half-brother; goes with him into exile in the forest; son of Queen Sumitra

LAVA Son of Rama and Sita; twin brother of Kusa

MOKSHA Final emancipation from endless cycles of death and rebirth

RAKSHASAS Warrior-demons

RAMA Hero of the *Ramayana;* incarnation of the god Vishnu

RAMAYANA One of the two greatest Hindu epics in Indian literature; narrates adventures of Rama before, during, and after his fourteen-year exile from Ayodhya

RAVANA Demon king of Lanka; kidnaps Sita from the forest; defeated by Rama

SAMSARA Endless cycles of death and rebirth

SHURPANAKHA Ravana's demon sister; falls in love with Rama

SITA Daughter of King Janaka; Rama's loyal wife; goes with him into exile in the forest; incarnation of goddess Lakshmi

SUGRIVA Monkey king of Kiskindha who aids Rama in rescuing Sita

VALMIKI Sage and poet; credited with authorship of *Ramayana;* helps Sita and her twin sons

VIBHISHANA Ravana's brother who leaves Lanka to help Rama

The story of Sita is told in the *Ramayana,* one of the two greatest Hindu epics in Indian literature. Although we cannot date the *Ramayana* with any precision, we can say that it assumed the form we know between the second century B.C.E. and the first century C.E. The work has traditionally been ascribed to the sage Valmiki. The original was written in Sanskrit and consists of 24,000 stanzas. Valmiki remains

Sita's Family Tree

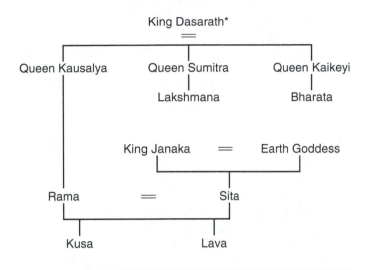

King Dasarath*

Queen Kausalya   Queen Sumitra   Queen Kaikeyi

Lakshmana   Bharata

King Janaka   =   Earth Goddess

Rama   =   Sita

Kusa   Lava

---

* According to the *Ramayana*, King Dasarath had 350 women in his harem. However, Queen Kausalya, Queen Sumitra, and Queen Kaikeyi were considered the chief queens.

a shadowy figure since little is known about his life, but scholars speculate that he probably had a close connection with the kings of Ayodhya. Valmiki collected stories, myths, songs, and legends about the god Vishnu in his incarnation as Rama, and he fashioned them into the *Ramayana,* a poetic narrative replete with gods and demons and magical happenings.

The *Ramayana* narrates the adventures of the god Rama, heir apparent to his father's kingdom of Ayodhya. Rama is unjustly exiled in the forest for fourteen years where he is joined by his wife, Sita, and his brother, Lakshmana. While in the forest, the three encounter Ravana's sister, the demoness Shurpanakha of the Rakshasis who falls in love with Rama. When Rama spurns her advances, Shurpanakha vents her jealous rage at Sita and vows revenge. Enticed by descriptions of Sita's unparalleled beauty, Ravana plots to capture Sita. He disguises himself as a wandering monk and abducts her from the forest, holding her hostage for one year. With the assistance of Hanuman, the monkey king, Rama and Lakshmana defeat Ravana's army and rescue Sita. Sita's joy at seeing Rama is not reciprocated, however. Despite her protestations of innocence, Rama doubts her chastity and is not mollified until she emerges unscathed from her ordeal by fire.

After Rama becomes king of Ayodhya, he continues to be haunted by questions of Sita's fidelity. He finally succumbs to public opinion by banishing her. Sita goes to live in the ashram of the sage Valmiki where she gives birth to Rama's twin sons,

Lava and Kusa. The couple is eventually reconciled, but Rama continues to doubt his wife's sexual fidelity. As final proof of her innocence, Sita calls upon the earth goddess which gave her birth to testify to her virtue by swallowing her up forever. The earth complies and Sita is swallowed up into its entrails. Rama is finally convinced of his wife's purity. However, it is too late. Sita may be vindicated, but she is also gone forever.

The *Ramayana* can be read on many different levels. It is at once an entertaining love story, full of intrigue and adventure, populated with magical creatures and supernatural happenings. It provides a graphic panorama of the culture and times of the ancient Hindus, imagined or real, when the world was ruled by warrior heroes, kings, and gods, waging battle against demons and monsters. It serves as an illustration of the forces of good triumphing over the forces of evil. It depicts an age when men and women understood their passage on earth as an opportunity to liberate themselves from the endless cycles of birth and death (*samsara*) through final emancipation (*moksha*). It is a didactic tale, populated with characters that serve as models for ideal Hindu behavior and interaction. It is a great work of literature. And, finally, the *Ramayana* is a spiritual treatise that tells the story of a god who assumes human form in order to destroy demons, who manifests a love for his devotees, and who serves as a model for ideal human behavior.

The characters of Sita and Rama can be problematic for some audiences steeped in Western values. Sita appears to be self-effacing, full of self-blame, and tolerant of the psychological and emotional abuse inflicted upon her by her spouse. Rama appears to be self-absorbed, demanding, guilty of victim-blaming, and willing to abandon his wife in order to preserve his reputation. However, an audience steeped in traditional Hindu values would interpret these characters in a far more positive light because Sita and Rama adhere strictly to the Hindu laws of *dharma*. According to Hindu tradition, every individual must be loyal to *dharma*, or righteous behavior. *Dharma* presupposes the existence of an appropriate code of conduct ascribed to each familial and social role in life. A person must adhere to *dharma* even if such adherence conflicts with one's personal desires or wishes. The needs of the individual are thus subsumed by socially constructed or divinely inspired (depending on one's perspective) codes of conduct that define appropriate behavior according to one's role. However, not everyone in India necessarily subscribes to this view. Research indicates that low caste Hindus are less likely to agree with traditional (high caste) visions of *dharma*. (For more information on Hinduism, please see Chapter 8 in this text.)

The conduct of both Sita and Rama is posited as the ideal since both demonstrate obedience to *dharma* regardless of the extent of personal sacrifice. Proponents of contemporary Hindu fundamentalism (Hindutva or "Hinduness") regard Rama as an example of manhood. He is considered a hero because as a man, as a future king, and as the avatar of Vishnu, he consistently places the needs of his community above his own personal needs; Sita is considered a heroine because as a female, as a wife, and as the avatar of Lakshmi, she consistently places her husband's welfare and wishes above her own. She epitomizes the wifely devotion that young Hindu females are encouraged to emulate.

Sita is the product of a miraculous birth. When her father, King Janaka is plowing the land in preparation for a sacrifice, Sita emerges from the earth, covered in dust. Commentators have speculated that the king was involved in some sort of ritual in which his plowing of the earth represents a symbolic coupling with the land in order to precipitate fertility. A product of Janaka's "union" with the earth, Sita manifests earthly abundance and growth. Her name means "furrow," a symbol for the female genitals in agrarian religions. Seed entering the furrow was analogous to the entrance of semen into the womb and its subsequent transformation and rebirth. Literally born from the womb of the earth, Sita is connected with the powers of earthly fertility and the land that has been cultivated in preparation for insemination. Her emergence from the plowed earth aligns her with other chthonic goddesses who are associated with the fecundity and fertility of the land.

Although her divinity is not stressed in Valmiki's *Ramayana,* in later traditions Sita comes to be revered as an incarnation of the goddess Lakshmi, the consort of the Hindu god Vishnu. When Vishnu assumes human manifestation as Rama, Lakshmi assumes human manifestation as Sita. Together, Sita and Rama represent the ideal married couple in human and divine form within the Hindu tradition.

Chapter 14 of the *Ramayana* is translated and retold by Krishna Dharma. It narrates the episode of Sita's ordeal by fire.

REFERENCES

Dharma, Krishna, trans. *Ramayana: India's Immortal Tale of Adventure, Love, and Wisdom.* California: Torchlight Publishing, Inc., 2000.

Fuller, C.J. *The Camphor Flame: Popular Hinduism and Society in India.* Princeton: Princeton UP, 1992.

Hawley, John Stratton, and Donna Marie Wulff, ed. *Devi: Goddesses of India.* Berkeley: U of California P, 1996.

Kinsley, David R. *Hindu Goddesses: Visions of the Divine Feminine in the Hindu Religious Tradition.* Berkeley: U of California P, 1966.

Menon, Ramesh, trans. *The Ramayana.* New York: North Point, 2001.

Narayan, R.K., trans. *The Ramayana: A Shortened Modern Prose Version of the Indian Epic.* New York: Viking, 1972.

Shulman, David. "Fire and Flood: The Testing of Sita in Kampan's *Iramavataram.*" Ed. Paula Rickman. *Many Ramayanas: The Diversity of a Narrative Tradition in South Asia.* Berkeley: U of California P, 1991. 89–113.

Young, Serenity, ed. *An Anthology of Sacred Texts By and About Women.* New York: Crossroad, 1999.

Ramayana

India's Immortal Tale Of Adventure, Love, and Wisdom

Sita's Ordeal

After witnessing Ravana's destruction, the gods and rishis departed joyfully for their various heavenly abodes. Matali bowed before Rama and received permission to return with his chariot to Indra. Rama watched as the celestial vehicle rose high into the sky and disappeared. His fury with the Rakshasas had completely subsided. He now thought of Vibhishana's installation as the new king of Lanka. As the city was upon the earth, it was within the jurisdiction of the earth's emperors, although inhabited by the Rakshasas. Thus Rama desired to install the pious Vibhishana as its righteous ruler so as to quickly reestablish order in the devastated city.

Rama asked Lakshmana to perform the ceremony of consecrating Vibhishana on Lanka's throne. Lakshmana immediately had the monkeys fetch seawater in large golden jars. With that water he duly consecrated Vibhishana, carefully following the directions given in the Vedas. Vibhishana sat upon the throne and blazed with regal splendor. The Rakshasas were joyful to see Ravana's brother assume the rulership of Lanka, and they brought him many gifts and offerings. Vibhishana offered all of these to Rama, who accepted them out of his love for the Rakshasa.

When the ceremony was complete, Rama asked Hanuman to go quickly to Sita. He was aching to see her again and he said to Hanuman, "Please inform the princess of the good news. I long to see her. Tell her to make herself ready so that very soon I may meet with her."

Hanuman at once left for the gardens. As he made his way through Lanka he was honored by the Rakshasas, who folded their palms as he passed by. Quickly reaching the ashoka grove, he saw Sita still lying at the foot of the simshapa tree. She was unaware of Rama's victory and appeared mournful. Upon seeing Hanuman, however, she quickly stood up in hope. Surely the monkey must be bearing good news. The princess listened expectantly as Hanuman told her all that had happened.

"O godly lady, your husband has come out victorious. The demon Ravana is no more and the virtuous Vibhishana is now the ruler of Lanka. Dear mother, your woes are ended. Please prepare yourself to see your Lord Rama."

Sita was stunned with joy. She could not make any reply and simply stood for some time gazing at Hanuman with tears flowing from her eyes. At last she said in a choked voice, "O good monkey, I cannot think of anything I can offer you in return for this news. Not gold nor silver nor gems nor even the sovereignty of all the worlds is equal to the value of this message."

Hanuman replied that hearing her joyful reply was itself more valuable than any gift. And, having seen Rama emerge victorious and happy, Hanuman desired nothing more.

Sita praised Hanuman again and again as the monkey stood with his head bowed and palms joined together. When the princess stopped speaking he said to her, "If you permit me, I shall punish these wicked Rakshasis who have made your life so miserable. I would like to give them a good thrashing. They surely deserve death for their evil conduct against you, O divine lady."

Sita pondered for some moments within herself. She looked at the Rakshasis who sat at a distance, no longer concerned with her now that Ravana was dead. Turning to Hanuman, Sita replied, "These Rakshasis were simply carrying out Ravana's order. No blame should be attached to them. Furthermore, any suffering I felt was surely the result of my own past misdeeds, for such is the universal law. Indeed, there is an ancient maxim which is always the code of the virtuous: 'A righteous man does not consider the offenses of others against him. At all costs he always observes the vow of not returning evil for evil, for the virtuous consider good conduct their ornament.'" Sita said that compassion should always be shown toward sinners, for no one was ever found to be free of sin.

Admonished in this way, Hanuman bowed to her and made no argument. Sita had spoken well, quite in accord with her noble character. After reflecting on her words for some moments the monkey then asked, "I wish to return now to Rama. Please give me a message for him."

Sita replied that she only wished to see him. Hanuman assured her that she would very soon see Rama. Bowing once again he left and made his way back to Vibhishana's palace, where Rama was waiting.

Hearing of Sita's condition, Rama asked Vibhishana to arrange that she be given celestial clothes and ornaments. "O king of the Rakshasas, please have that princess bathed with heavenly unguents and dressed in the finest silks. Then have her brought here. My heart is burning with desire to see her again."

Vibhishana personally went to Sita with Rama's instruction, but Sita, anxious to see Rama said, "I wish to see my husband immediately, without having bathed and dressed."

Sita had suffered through almost a year of torture. She had never stopped thinking of the day she would be reunited with Rama. Here it was at last. How could she possibly wait another moment?

Vibhishana replied gently that it was Rama's desire that she prepare herself. Sita, accepting Rama's word as her order, aquiesced, and Vibhishana immediately arranged for her bath and clothing. In a short while the princess was adorned in costly robes and jewels worthy of the consorts of the gods. She mounted a golden palanquin bedecked with celestial gems and was borne into Rama's presence.

Crowds of Rakshasas and monkeys filled the streets, all anxious for a glimpse of the princess. Seated on the palanquin behind a silk veil, Sita shone like the sun shrouded by a cloud. Rakshasas wearing dark jackets and turbans and carrying staffs fitted with bells cleared a path for her. The crowds of onlookers, who were roaring like the ocean, parted as the palanquin made its way slowly along the main highway.

Vibhishana went ahead and informed Rama that his wife was on her way. Hearing that she was on a palanquin, Rama said to Vibhishana, "The princess should be asked to dismount and proceed on foot. The people desire to see her and that is not condemned by scripture. A house, a veil or a costume are never the protection of a chaste woman. Her character alone is her shield."

Lakshmana, Sugriva and Hanuman looked at Rama with surprise. He appeared to be displeased with Sita. His expression was stern and thoughtful. As Vibhishana conducted Sita into his presence Rama looked at her without smiling.

Sita was overjoyed to see Rama again and her face shone like the moon, but she felt abashed when she saw his grave expression. Her limbs trembled and she stood before him with her head bowed and hands folded.

Rama's heart was torn. He deeply wanted to show his love for Sita and to take her back at once, but he feared public censure. As a king he wanted to set the highest example for the people. Sita had been in the house of another man for almost a year. Whatever the circumstances, that would surely be criticized by some of the people. Questions about her chastity might be raised. That would never be acceptable for the wife of an emperor.

Looking at Sita, whose face was bathed in tears, Rama said, "O blessed one, I have won you back today. After conquering my enemies in battle, I have avenged the insult given me through your abduction. You, too, are fully avenged, O princess. The evil Ravana is no more."

Rama stopped speaking, his heart balking at what he had to say next. Steadying his mind he continued to address the tremulous Sita. "Now that I have wiped off the stain of insult on my noble house and established my truthfulness and resolve, no further purpose remains for me in this matter. O gentle lady, I have not undergone this endeavor out of a desire to again have you as my wife. You have long dwelt in the house of another. How then can I take you back into my house? Your good character has become suspect. Ravana clasped you in his arms and looked upon you with a lustful eye. Therefore, my attachment for you has ended. Please go wherever you may desire. Perhaps you may now find shelter with Lakshmana or Bharata or Shatrughna, or even Vibhishana. As beautiful as you are, O Sita, how could Ravana have left you alone?"

Sita was shocked. She wept loudly and shook like a sapling caught in a storm. Greatly shamed by her husband's words, she shrank into herself. Rama's speech had pierced her like poisoned arrows and she cried in pain for a long time. Gradually gathering her senses she replied to Rama in faltering tones.

"Why do you address me with such unkind words, O hero, like a common man addressing some vulgar woman? You are judging all women by the standards of a degraded few. Give up your doubts in me for I am without blame. When Ravana snatched me I was helpless and dragged against my will. Although I could not control my limbs, my heart remained under my control and did not deviate from you even slightly. If, in spite of our living together in love for so long, you still do not trust me, then I am surely undone for good."

Angry, Sita admonished and taunted Rama. Why had he gone to such great endeavors? He could have sent a message with Hanuman telling her that he was rejecting her. Then she would have immediately given up her life and saved him all the effort of war. It seemed he had given way to anger alone, just like an ordinary man. Like a mean man, he had not considered her devotion and chastity toward him. He had forgotten her divine origins and taken her to be an ordinary woman.

Sita, still weeping, turned to Lakshmana. "O prince, please raise for me a pyre. This is my only recourse now. I no longer desire to live, being smitten with false reproaches. As my husband has renounced me in a public gathering, I shall enter fire and give up my life."

Lakshmana was indignant. How could Rama act in this way? He looked at his brother, but Rama remained impassive. He returned Lakshmana's glance with a slight nod. Lakshmana understood his desire and, feeling deeply pained and perplexed, constructed a pyre.

Rama stood like Yamaraja, the god of justice. No one dared approach him or say anything. Only Sita came near him. She walked around him in respect and approached the blazing fire. The princess then prayed with folded hands. "If I have never been unfaithful to Rama either in mind, words or body, may the fire-god protect me on all sides. As my heart ever abides in Rama, so may the fire-god save me now. As all the gods are witness to my chastity, let the fire-god protect me."

After uttering this prayer Sita walked around the fire and then fearlessly entered it before the vast assembly. Sita seemed like a golden altar with its sacred fire. Gods, rishis, Gandharvas, Siddhas and other divine beings observed Sita walking deep into the fire and all the women in the assembly sent up a great cry as they watched her ascend the pyre, like a goddess fallen from heaven and entering hell. A gasp of amazement and shock came from the crowd as she disappeared into the flames.

Rama was blinded by tears. He was afflicted to hear the cries of the people. With his mind set on virtue and his heart wracked with grief, he watched Sita walk into the fire. From the sky the gods, headed by Brahma, addressed

Rama. "How are you allowing this divine lady to enter fire? Do you not recall your actual identity? What is this play of yours, O Lord?"

Rama looked at the gods and folded his palms. He replied, "I take myself to be a human. My name is Rama, the son of Dasarath. Let Brahma tell me who I was in my former lives."

From the sky the four-headed Brahma, seated upon his swan carrier, replied, "O Rama, I know you as the original creator of the cosmos. You are Vishnu and Narayana, the one supreme person who is known by many names. All the gods come from you and the worlds rest upon your energy. You exist within and without all things and reside in the heart of every being. Your existence and actions are inconceivable. You have appeared as Rama for the destruction of Ravana and the deliverance of your devoted servants. Now that you have accomplished your purposes you should return to your own abode."

Rama bowed his head and said nothing. At that moment the fire-god emerged from the fire holding Sita in his arms. The princess was dressed in a red robe and she shone brightly like the rising sun. She wore a garland of celestial flowers and she was adorned with brilliant gems. Her dark, curly hair framed her face, which glowed with transcendent beauty.

Agni placed Sita before Rama and spoke in a voice that boomed out like thunder. "Here is your wife Sita. No sin exists in her. Neither by word, deed nor thought, not even by glance has she ever been unfaithful to you.

Ravana forcefully snatched her away while she was helpless and forlorn. Although kept captive by him, her mind and heart remained focused on you at every moment. She did not give a single thought to Ravana despite being tempted and threatened by him in many ways. Therefore, O Rama, accept her back with an open heart."

Rama experienced great joy upon hearing Agni's speech. His eyes flooded with tears as he replied to the fire-god: "Sita needed this purificatory ordeal. Otherwise the world would have condemned me as foolish and controlled by lust. She dwelt in Ravana's house for a long time and her chastity had to be proven to the world, although I know of her undivided love for me. Indeed, guarded as she is by her own moral power, Ravana could not have violated Sita any more than the sea could transgress its bounds."

Rama declared Sita to be as inseparable from him as sunlight from the sun. He could no more renounce her than a virtuous man could renounce righteousness.

Sita bloomed with happiness. She sat next to Rama on a golden throne. The gods and rishis appeared in the assembly offering praises to Rama. Shiva personally came before Rama and said, "You have killed the scourge and dread of the universe, O Rama. You should now depart for Ayodhya and comfort your relatives there. Then be pleased to rule over this world for a long time."

Shiva told Rama that his father Dasarath was present, seated in a celestial chariot in the sky. Rama looked up and saw the chariot descending slowly. His father, appearing in a body that shone with celestial splendor, gazed down at him. Leaving the chariot, he came down to earth and embraced Rama tightly. He sat next to his son and began to speak.

"Although I reside with Indra, I do not feel as much pleasure there as I do now upon seeing you again. The words uttered by Kaikeyi when sending you into exile are still impressed upon my heart, but today I am fully rid of my sorrow. I have been redeemed by you, dear Rama. Fourteen years have passed and your exile is ended. I long to see you return to Ayodhya and assume the throne, after pacifying Kaushalya and the mighty Bharata. O Rama, I now understand your identity. You are the Supreme Lord, born on earth for the good of the world."

Rama asked his father to retract the words he had uttered when he had disowned Kaikeyi and her son. They were both blameless in every respect. Dasarath assented to Rama's request. He embraced Lakshmana and praised him for his selfless service to Rama, asking him to continue that service when Rama became the emperor.

Dasarath then spoke to Sita. "O daughter, do not think ill of Rama for his repudiation of you. He only desired to prove your absolute purity. Your entering the fire was an act which will forever overshadow the renown of all virtuous ladies."

Sita folded her palms and bowed to her father-in-law, who rose again to his aerial chariot and left for the heavens. The other gods paid their respects to Rama and then left for their own abodes. Indra approach Rama and said, "A sight of the gods can never go in vain. O Rama, pray tell us what you desire and it shall be done at once."

Smiling, Rama asked Indra to return to life all the slain monkeys, even those whose bodies had been torn and devoured. He also asked that wherever the monkeys may live there should be abundant fruits and roots for their food.

Indra replied, "Although difficult to grant, your desire shall be fulfilled. Let all the monkeys rise again, even those whose heads and limbs have been severed. Let them be reunited with their families and let trees full of fruit even out of season, forever grow where they dwell."

The powerful god sprinkled celestial nectar from the sky. The monkeys who were killed then rose from the ground, amazed to see themselves healed and restored to life. They looked at one another and asked, "What miracle is this?" They leapt and shouted for joy, coming together like a great roaring ocean.

Indra bid farewell to Rama and departed along with all the other gods. As the gods' blazing chariots disappeared into the sky Rama ordered that the monkeys camp for the night, while he and Sita rested in Vibhishana's palace.

Questions for Review and Discussion

1. According to Hindu tradition, a wife is subordinate to her husband. She must be willing to assume a subservient role and remain pure, faithful, and devoted to her husband by consistently subordinating her needs to his. She must meet all

challenges, trials, and temptations with steadfast resolve, keeping his welfare and reputation foremost in her mind. How does Sita fulfill these expectations and requirements imposed on her by her society?

2. Sita represents the ideal wife within the Hindu tradition. She is unwavering in her devotion to her husband and accepts his decisions and actions without question, regardless of how unreasonable they may appear to be. What do you think of Sita as a wife? Defend your point of view.

3. Does Sita have a voice? Support your answer with concrete examples from the text.

4. Sita is required to give evidence of her virtue in a public setting through her ordeal by fire. But even her willingness to experience the ordeal by fire is not considered sufficient evidence of her sexual fidelity. Rama is not satisfied until Agni, the god of fire, emerges with Sita and corroborates her story. What does this say about the value attributed to a woman's testimony?

5. According to ancient Hindu tradition, Rama is justified in demanding a sign of Sita's virtue since a woman who has lived in the house of another man is impure. But according to alternative codes of behavior, Rama's conduct remains problematic since it appears that he is engaging in victim blaming. What is victim blaming? Do you think Rama engages in victim blaming? Defend your point of view.

6. When Sita successfully emerges from her ordeal by fire, her father-in-law, Dasarath, reassures her that her willingness to enter the fire to prove her virtue has won her unparalleled acclaim. What expectation is he reinforcing about the traditional role of wives in ancient Hindu society?

7. According to the laws of *dharma* which require complete devotion of the wife to her husband, Sita must demonstrate her fidelity to Rama—even if it means losing her own life to do so. In this instance, do you think the laws of *dharma* are compatible with a basic human need for self-preservation? What other examples exist in mythology or sacred texts of females who sacrifice their lives in obedience to a higher law?

8. Sita plays the role of intermediary since she is sometimes called upon to intercede with Rama on behalf of his devotees. Which of her qualities make her particularly suitable for this role?

9. The unusual manner of Sita's birth recalls Inanna's cry of "Who will plow my vulva? Who will plow my high field? Who will plow my wet ground?" What other parallels can you find between Sita and Inanna or between Sita and other figures in this collection?

10. In what ways might the marriage of Rama and Sita represent an ideal marriage? In what ways might it be far removed from an ideal marriage?

Chapter 8

Kali

GLOSSARY OF NAMES AND TERMS

AMBIKA Mother, Mother-dear; also known as Candika or Durga

ATHARVA VEDA One of the four collections of the *Vedas*

ATMAN Hidden Self; identified with Brahman

BRAHMAN Essence of reality; identified with Atman

CAMUNDA Composite of Canda and Munda; Kali's name in the *Devi-Mahatmya* after she has defeated demon generals, Canda and Munda

CANDA Demon general; in fierce battle with Ambika; defeated by Kali

CANDIKA The fierce one; another name for Ambika

DEVI Goddess

DEVI-MAHATMYA In the *Markandeya Purana;* includes depiction of Kali in her warrior aspect

DURGA She who deals with adversity; beyond reach; another name for Ambika

JÑANA-KANDA Universal part of each *Veda;* addresses perennial concerns of humanity; also known as the *Upanishads*

KALI Represents "Destroyer" aspect of goddess; also known as the Black One; Black Mother Time

KARMA-KANDA Most technical and least universal part of each *Veda*

MARKANDEYA PURANA Oldest of *Puranas;* fifth through sixth century C.E.

MUNDA Demon general; in fierce battle with Ambika; defeated by Kali

PURANAS Collection of stories that explicate the *Vedas;* designed for lay audience

RAKTABIJA Demon with ability to replicate himself; defeated by Kali

RIG VEDA One of the four collections of the *Vedas*

ŚAKTI Power; dynamic feminine life force; activates male

SAMA VEDA One of the four collections of the *Vedas*

SAMSARA Endless cycles of death and rebirth

ŚIVA Male deity; consort of Kali

ŚUMBHA Lord of demon army

TANTRISM Belief that ultimate reality finds deepest expression in union between male and female

UPANISHADS Universal part of each *Veda;* also known as Jñana-kanda

VEDAS Sacred writings; knowledge of the sacred

YAJUR VEDA One of the four collections of the *Vedas*

YOGA Disciplined activity that can free us from the potentially endless cycles of death and rebirth; can lead to ultimate illumination

From prehistoric times to the present, Hinduism has maintained an unbroken tradition of goddess-worship simultaneous with god-worship. Within the Hindu tradition, Kali remains a prominent goddess. Her considerable role attests to the fact that Hinduism is not inherently patriarchal in its orientation. However, that is not necessarily reflected in the culture since that continues to privilege the male. The abortion of female fetuses, outright infanticide, or systematic neglect of young girls has resulted in an imbalance in the number of males and females in India, with the former outnumbering the latter in some regions.

Although the goddess, or *Devi*, is frequently depicted as the consort of a male god, in some traditions she has been elevated to the rank of a supreme deity, most notably in Śaktism and Tantrism. Tantric ideology assumes that ultimate reality finds its deepest expression in the symbiotic relationship between male (Śiva) and female (Śakti). Śakti, which means power, is the dynamic, feminine life force that activates the male deities. Without Śakti, a male deity would remain inert—a significant factor in elevating the goddess's stature to that of at least an equal to her male counterpart.

Unlike other major religions, Hinduism does not trace its origins to a specific date in history; nor does it trace it to a specific authoritative text; nor does it consider a single scripture to be the source of its teachings. Rather, it derives its basic tenets from a large variety of sources, while simultaneously assimilating external influences, modifying and appropriating them to suit its purposes. Hinduism's fluidity enables it to embrace a diversity of Indian religious traditions. The mass of writings that constitute Hindu scripture far exceeds that of any other religion.

According to Hinduism, human beings have four sequential wants. The first two wants are pleasure and worldly success. They are known as the twin goals of the Path of Desire. The remaining two wants make up the Path of Renunciation: the desire to serve others (the religion of duty) and the desire to liberate oneself from the finite and limited. Hindus argue that the ultimate human desire for infinite being, infinite awareness, and infinite joy can be fulfilled. According to Hinduism, as expounded in the *Upanishads*, within every human life there is an infinite but hidden center, known as *Atman*. This *Atman*, or Hidden Self, is identical to *Brahman*, "the essence of reality." Human beings consist of body, personality, and *Atman-Brahman*. However, since *Atman* is buried under the distractions, noise, and impulses of superficial being, it is not easily discernible. Specifically, three qualities hinder our ability to achieve union with *Atman* and subsequent liberation: physical pain, psychological pain, and boredom with life. These obstacles can be overcome through engagement with a disciplined training known as *yoga*. Successful participation in yoga leads to the liberation that frees us from the potentially endless cycle of birth and death, known as *samsara*, thereby enabling us to achieve ultimate illumination.

While different Indian religious traditions claim divine revelation for different texts, the body of work known as the *Vedas* is considered sacred by all traditions. The term *veda*, derived from the root *vid* (to know) means knowledge of the sacred. Written in an archaic Sanskrit, the language of the *Vedas* was understood only by the Hindu elite and initially remained inaccessible to the people at large. Gradually, various movements arose within the Hindu traditions that translated the *Vedas* into a variety of local vernaculars, thereby increasing their accessibility.

The *Vedas* consist of four collections: Rig, Sama, Yajur, and Atharva. Each collection is divided into two parts: the *karma-kanda* and the *jñana-kanda*. The *karma-*

kanda, the most technical and least universal of the two parts, consists of hymns and philosophical interpretations of Hindu rituals. The *jñana-kanda* (also called the *Upanishads*) addresses the perennial concerns of humanity: the meaning of life and death; the role of the human being; the relationship of the human being to the rest of creation; the essence of reality; illumination; and the paths that lead to illumination. Such concerns, since they transcend racial, ethnic, spatial, and temporal boundaries, render the *jñana-kanda* with greater universal appeal.

The complex concepts in the *Vedas* have been explicated through the collection of short stories and narratives that comprise the *Puranas.* Designed for a lay audience, the *Puranas* are written in the form of a dialogue between a student and an illumined teacher. Their topics range from the creation of the universe, genealogies of patriarchs and kings, and mythologies of the deities. There are a total of 18 major *Puranas,* the oldest of which, the *Markandeya Purana,* was probably composed in the fifth or sixth century C.E. Each *Purana* is devoted to a particular deity. The selection below, depicting a manifestation of the goddess Kali, is known as the *Devi-Mahatmya* and is in the *Markandeya Purana.*

Kali's name literally means "the Black One." According to a less probable etymology, Kali is the feminine form of Kala, "time." She represents the aspect of the goddess that is commonly known as the "Destroyer." She is referred to as "Terrible Mother," "Black Mother Time," or "the Black One." She symbolizes the inexorable force of time, which devours and destroys everything in its path. Her black color, suggestive of the darkness that is at the beginning and at the end of life, reminds us of the inevitable confrontation with our own mortality. Instead of colorful jewels that adorn other goddesses, Kali adorns her otherwise naked body with skulls and limbs around her neck and waist. Kali's image, enhanced with trickles of blood emanating from her fanglike teeth, gaping mouth, and lolling tongue, is reinforced by disheveled hair, a bloodshot, penetrating stare, and a severed head that she dangles from one of her four hands. She is frequently depicted dancing on the corpse of her "spouse" Śiva in what some have interpreted as a sexually explicit gesture denoting—and promoting—female autonomy. Her usual habitat is the cremation ground where she receives those who come to her for refuge.

According to her devotees, Kali is the creatrix from which all life emerges. Containing the male principle within herself, Kali is parthenogenetic. As Black Mother Time, she gives birth to us from her unfathomable depths, nurtures us, feeds us, comforts us, amuses us, and, eventually, devours us. Kali serves to remind us that all of life is transitory: it runs through the process of growth, maturity, deterioration, death, and decay in a cycle in which life and death are inextricably woven together. Neither can be fully comprehended if perceived as isolated phenomenon. Kali's figure can thus simultaneously generate paradoxical feelings of terror and comfort.

Interest in Kali has recently grown among Westerners. Some contemporary readers perceive her as a powerful feminist role model, waging battle against patriarchy's oppressive strictures; as a symbol of female empowerment and liberation; as a fierce advocate for female sexual autonomy and sexual fulfillment; and as a dynamic celebrant for the release of suppressed violence and rage at perceived injustices. However, western interpretations of Kali are not necessarily embraced by her South Asian devotees. There are many Kalis and many ways of depicting and conceiving her. Some conceptions give prominence to certain of her qualities over others; some appear to contradict others; and some are replete with ambiguity. She remains a paradoxical figure with a fluid identity. But while her myths, rituals, and traditions may vary somewhat depending on the specific geographical and cultural location of worship, nevertheless, her devotees subscribe to many areas of commonalities.

Kali's most famous appearance in her warrior manifestation occurs in the *Devi-Mahatmya* of the *Markandeya Purana*. The *Devi-Mahatmya* is a complete poem, which projects the ultimate reality of the universe as being feminine in nature as Devi or the goddess. It is paradoxical in that its hymns are imbued with religious and spiritual outpourings while the description of the battle scenes abound with graphic detail of blood and carnage. In this work, Kali is described as emerging from the forehead of the goddess Ambika, also known as Candika or Durga, in much the same manner that the Greek goddess Athena emerges from the forehead of Zeus. Engaged in a furious battle with the demon generals Canda and Munda, Ambika's brow grows dark with anger. Suddenly, Kali springs from her forehead in full battle regalia: a necklace of skulls, a sword and noose, bloodshot eyes, and a gaping mouth with which she proceeds to smash and devour the demon warriors. She rages, howls, laughs, and slaughters her enemies, eventually seizing both Canda and Munda and decapitating them. She acts swiftly, effectively, and with a powerful force that obliterates all obstacles in her path. To signify her victory, Kali is renamed Camunda, a composite of Canda and Munda.

Kali successfully comes to the assistance of Candika again in the *Devi-Mahatmya* in her battle with Raktabija, the demon endowed with the ability to create an exact replica of himself from each drop of blood that falls from his body to the earth. To her delight, Kali is given the task of devouring Raktabija's blood before it touches the ground. Her frenzied activities on the battlefield seem to signify such an excessive relish in cannibalism and in the act of destruction as an end in itself that her actions frequently have to be curtailed and controlled by an outside agent, most notably Śiva.

In the selection below, Kali is depicted as the subordinate of Candika. Here, she is portrayed as lacking any maternal or nurturing instinct. Her furious—almost demonic—laughter in the midst of blood and carnage hardly conjures up an image of a warm, nurturing mother. So it is interesting that in later traditions, Kali assumes the mantle of the all-powerful mother of the universe who sustains and replenishes her creatures fatigued by the ravages of time and suffering. But her qualities of nurturer and destroyer are not as contradictory as they initially might appear. Just as time nurtures us and assists in our growth to vigor and strength, so time is also responsible for causing that vigor and strength to diminish. As commentators have observed, the benign aspect of time/Kali cannot be separated from the terror aspect.

Kali is an emanation of Durga, a name that means "beyond reach." By extension, therefore, Kali situates herself beyond the reach of anyone who attempts to circumscribe, define, or limit her image and actions. In her dual role of fierce warrior and a nurturing mother, Kali demonstrates that human activity cannot be neatly compartmentalized into masculine and feminine spheres. Furthermore, she repudiates any system that insists on such rigid compartmentalization. Kali can be viewed as representing ways of confronting and moving beyond limitations, whether those limitations are self-imposed or imposed by others. Comfortable in both masculine and feminine worlds, her uproarious laughter serves as a reminder of her indifference to societal conventions. Kali does not giggle and titter in a stereotypically feminine manner. Instead, she chortles and cackles unashamedly—even while in the midst of a bloody rampage. She exhibits an apparent disregard for whatever level of discomfort society may have toward her unconventional behavior. Finally, she repudiates all notions of gender-specific attributes.

The selection from Sections 7 and 8 of the *Devi-Mahatmya,* translated by Thomas B. Coburn, narrates Kali's victory over the forces of chaos, represented by the Asura army and led by Canda and Munda. It also includes her successful onslaught against Raktabija.

REFERENCES

Bhattacharyya, Narendra Nath. *Indian Mother Goddess.* Calcutta: Indian Studies, 1971.

———. *History of the Śakta Religion.* New Delhi: Munshiram Manoharlal, 1974.

Brown, C. Mackenzie. "Kali, The Mad Mother." *The Book of the Goddess, Past and Present: An Introduction to Her Religion.* Ed. Carl Olson. New York: Crossroad, 1990. 110–123.

Coburn, Thomas B. "Devi: The Great Goddess." *Devi: Goddesses of India.* Ed. John Stratton Hawley and Donna Mari Wulff. Berkeley: U of California P, 1996. 31–48.

———, trans. *Encountering the Goddess: A Translation of the Devi-Mahatmya and a Study of Its Interpretation.* New York: SUNY P, 1991.

Drèze, Jean and Amartya Sen. *India: Economic Development and Social Opportunity.* Oxford: Oxford UP, 1999.

Erndl, Kathleen M. *Victory to the Mother: The Hindu Goddess of Northwest India in Myth, Ritual, and Symbol.* New York: Oxford UP, 1993.

Gupta, Lina. "Kali, The Savior." *After Patriarchy: Feminist Transformations of World Religions.* Ed. Paula M. Cooey, William R. Eakin, and Joy B. Daniel. New York: Orbis, 1993. 15–38.

Hawley, John S., and Donna M. Wulff, eds. *Devi: Goddesses of India.* Berkeley: U of California P, 1996.

Kinsley, David R. *Hindu Goddesses: Visions of the Divine Feminine in the Hindu Religious Tradition.* Berkeley: U of California P, 1988.

———. "The Portrait of the Goddess in the *Devi-Mahatmya.*" *Journal of the American Academy of Religion* 46 (1978): 489–506.

Klostermaier, Klaus K. *Hindu Writings: A Short Introduction to the Major Sources.* Oxford: One World, 2000.

McDermott, Rachel Fell, and Jeffrey J. Kripal, eds. *Encountering Kali: In the Margins, At the Center, In the West.* Berkeley: U of California P, 2003.

Mookerjee, Ajit. *Kali: The Feminine Force.* Rochester: Destiny, 1988.

Pargiter, F. Eden, trans. *The Markandeya Purana.* The Asiatic Society of Bengal, 1904. Reissued by Delhi: Indological Book House, 1969.

Pintchman, Tracy. *The Rise of the Goddess in the Hindu Tradition.* Albany: SUNY P, 1994.

Preston, James J. *Cult of the Goddess: Social and Religious Change in a Hindu Temple.* Prospect Heights: Waveland P, 1985.

———, ed. *Mother Worship: Themes and Variations.* Chapel Hill: U of North Carolina P, 1982.

Devi-Mahatmya

The seer said:

Directed in this fashion by him, the demons, arranged as a fourfold army
With Caṇḍa and Muṇḍa at their head, went forth with upraised weapons.

Then they saw the Goddess, smiling slightly, mounted
On her lion on the great golden peak of the highest mountain.

Having seen her, they made ready in their efforts to abduct her,
While others approached her with swords drawn and bows bent.

Ambikā then uttered a great wrathful cry against them,
And her face became black as ink in anger.

From the knitted brows of her forehead's surface immediately
Came forth Kālī, with her dreadful face, carrying sword and noose.

She carried a strange skull-topped staff, and wore a garland of human heads;
She was shrouded in a tiger skin, and looked utterly gruesome with her emaciated skin,

Her widely gaping mouth, terrifying with its lolling tongue,
With sunken, reddened eyes and a mouth that filled the directions with roars.

She fell upon the great Asuras in that army, slaying them immediately.
She then devoured the forces of the enemies of the gods.

Attacking both the front and rear guard, having seized the elephants
Together with their riders and bells, she hurled them into her mouth with a single hand.

Likewise having flung the cavalry with its horses and the chariots with their charioteers
Into her mouth, she brutally pulverized them with her teeth.

She seized one by the hair, and another by the throat.
Having attacked one with her foot, she crushed another against her breast.

The weapons and missiles that were hurled by the demons
She seized with her mouth, and crunched them to bits with her teeth.

The army of all those mighty and distinguished demons
She destroyed: she devoured some, and thrashed the others.

Some were sliced by her sword, others pounded with her skull-topped staff.
Just in this way did the Asuras meet their destruction, ground up by the edges of her fangs.

Immediately upon seeing the entire army of the Asuras slain,
Caṇḍa rushed at the incredibly fearsome Kālī.

The great Asura enveloped the dread-eyed female with a horrendous great shower of arrows,
And Muṇḍa did the same with discuses hurled by the thousand.

This stream of discuses entering her mouth
Resembled a multitude of suns entering into the middle of a black cloud.

Then Kālī, her ugly teeth gleaming within her dreadful mouth,
Angrily cackled with terrible sounds.

Mounting her great lion, the Goddess ran at Caṇḍa,
And having seized him by the hair, she cut off his head with her sword.

On seeing Caṇḍa slain, Muṇḍa rushed at her.
She caused him to fall to the ground, wrathfully smitten with her sword.

On seeing Caṇḍa slain, and also the valorous Muṇḍa,
What was left of the assaulted army was overcome with fear, and fled in all directions.

Picking up the heads of Caṇḍa and Muṇḍa, Kālī
Approached Caṇḍikā and spoke words mixed with loud and cruel laughter:

"Here, as a present from me to you, are Caṇḍa and Muṇḍa, two beasts
Slain in the sacrifice of battle. Now you yourself can slay Śumbha and Niśumbha!"

The seer said:

Seeing the two great Asuras brought there,
The beautiful Caṇḍikā spoke these playful words to Kālī:

"Because you have seized Caṇḍa and Muṇḍa and brought them here,
You will henceforth be known in the world as the Goddess 'Cāmuṇḍā'."

The seer said:

When Caṇḍa had been killed and Muṇḍa slain,
And the extensive armies annihilated, the lord of demons

Śumbha became incensed, his mind deranged with anger.
He ordered the marshaling of all the Daitya armies.

"Now let the eighty-six Udāyudha demons with all their troops,
And the eighty-four Kambus surrounded with their own forces go forth.

May the fifty families of Koṭivīrya demons,
And the one hundred families of Dhūmra proceed at my command.

Similarly the Kālaka, Daurhṛda, Maurya, and Kālakeya demons
Should proceed quickly, prepared for battle, at my command."

Having issued these orders, Śumbha, lord of Asuras, whose directive is terrifying,
Sallied forth, surrounded by many thousands of magnificent troops.

On seeing him approach with his army in fearsome fashion, Caṇḍikā
Filled the space between earth and sky with the twanging of her bowstring.

Then her lion let loose a monstrous roar, O king,
And Ambikā elaborated this noise still further with the sound of her bell.

Kālī, her mouth agape and filling the directions with snarls,
Drowned out even the noise of the bowstring, lion, and bell with her gruesome sounds.

On hearing this din, the enraged Daitya armies
Surrounded the Goddess, her lion, and Kālī on all four sides.

At that very moment, O king, in order to destroy the enemies of the gods,
And for the sake of the well-being of the supreme gods, very valorous and powerful

Śaktis, having sprung forth from the bodies of Brahmā, Śiva, Skanda,
Viṣṇu, and Indra, and having the form of each, approached Caṇḍikā.

Whatever form, ornament, and mount a particular god possessed,
With that very form did his Śakti go forth to fight the Asuras.

In a heavenly conveyance drawn by swans, with rosary and waterpot,
Came forth the śakti of Brahmā: she is known as Brahmāṇī.

Māhesvarī sallied forth, mounted on a bull, bearing the best of tridents,
With great serpents for bracelets, adorned with the crescent of the moon.

Ambikā having the form of Guha (Skanda), as Kaumārī went forth to fight the demons,
With spear in hand, having the best of peacocks as her mount.

Then the *śakti* known as Vaiṣṇavī went forth, mounted on Garuda,
With conch, discus, club, bow and sword in hand.

The *śakti* of Hari who has the matchless form of a sacrificial boar
Then came forth, bearing the body of a sow.

Nārasiṃhī, having a form like the man-lion,
Then went forth, with many a constellation cast down by the tossing of her mane.

Then Aindrī, with thunderbolt in hand, mounted upon the lord of elephants,
Went forth; she had a thousand eyes, just like Indra.

Then Śiva, surrounded by these *śaktis* of the gods,
Said to Caṇḍikā: "May the demons now be quickly slain by you in order to please me."

Then from the body of the Goddess came forth the very frightening
Śakti of Caṇḍikā herself, gruesome and yelping like a hundred jackals.

And she, the invincible one, spoke to Śiva, of smokey, matted locks:
"You yourself become my messenger to Śumbha and Niśumbha.

Say to those two arrogant creatures
And to all the other demons who have assembled there for battle:

'If you wish to live, then Indra must get back the triple world,
The gods should have their proper portions of the sacrifice returned, and you should go back to the nether world.

If, on the other hand, you are desirous of battle because of ill-begotten arrogance about your strength,
Then come along: let my jackals satiate themselves on your flesh!'"

Since Śiva himself was sent by her as a messenger,
She has become known throughout the world as Śivadūtī ("She who has Śiva as messenger").

Upon hearing the words of the Goddess that were conveyed by Śiva, the great Asuras
Filled with pride went to where Kātyāyanī stood.

Then at the very beginning of the battle, the enemies of the gods,

Puffed up with pride, showered the Goddess with torrents of arrows,
lances, and spears.

She playfully broke the arrows, spears, lances, and axes that were hurled
With great arrows released from her twanging bow.

Then right in front of him (Śiva?) Kālī roamed about, ripping open some
with strokes of her spear,
   And crushing others with her skull-topped staff.

Wherever Brahmāṇī ran, she destroyed the prowess of the enemies,
Quenching their valor by dousing them with water from her waterpot.

Māheśvarī with her trident, Vaiṣṇavī with discus,
And Kaumārī with her most dreadful spear then slew the demons.

At the blow of Aindrī's thunderbolt, Daityas and Danavas fell
By the hundreds; torn open, they showered the ground with torrents of
blood.

Others fell ripped by the blow of Vārāhī's snout, their chests sundered
By the tips of her tusks, chopped up by her discus.

Nārasiṃhī devoured still other great demons; tearing them with her
claws,
   She roamed about the battlefield, filling the sky with her snorts.

The demons who were shattered by the cruel laughter of Śivadūtī
Fell broken to the ground, and she gobbled them up.

The leaders of the enemies of the gods, on seeing the great demons
Being pulverized by the band of Mothers with their respective weapons,
ran for their lives.

When he saw the demons fleeing, tormented by the band of Mothers,
The great cruel Raktabīja went forth to do battle.

Whenever a drop of blood fell from his body to the earth,
   Then out of it would rise up from the earth a great demon that was just like
him.

With club in hand, the great demon fought with Indra's *śakti,*
And Aindrī smote Raktabīja with her thunderbolt.

Blood immediately gushed forth from the one who was struck with the shaft.
From it there rose up mighty soldiers with the very same form.

However many drops of blood fell from his body,
So many men were born, comparable in valor, strength, and might.

And those men born of blood fought there

With the Mothers still more terribly, hurling their wicked weapons.

When his head was smashed again by a blow from her thunderbolt,
Blood flowed yet again, and from it men were born by the thousands.

Vaiṣṇavī assailed him with her discus in battle,
And Aindrī beat the lord of demons with her club.

The world was filled with great Asuras just like him,
Born by the thousands from the blood that flowed when he was cut by
Vaiṣṇavī's discus.

Kaumārī wounded him with her spear, and Vārāhī with her sword,
And Māheśvarī wounded the great demon Raktabīja with her trident.

The great demon Raktabīja, filled with rage, struck
Each and every one of the Mothers with his club.

From the flow of blood that fell in torrents to the earth
From the one who was wounded by the spear, lance, and so forth, demons
were born by the hundreds.

By those demons born from the blood of this one demon, the entire world
Was pervaded; then the gods became utterly terrified.

On seeing the gods quaking, Caṇḍikā immediately laughed aloud.
She spoke to Kālī: "O Cāmuṇḍā, open wide your mouth.

With this mouth of yours, quickly take in the drops of blood produced by
the fall of my weapons
And the great demons who are born from that blood.

Roam about on the battlefield, consuming the great demons who are born
from him.
Thus will this demon, his blood dried up, meet his destruction.

In this way, these terrible ones will be consumed by you, and no more will
be born."
Having spoken thus, the Goddess then gored him with her spear.

With her mouth Kālī seized upon the blood of Raktabīja.
The latter then struck Caṇḍikā with his club.

But the blow of the club did not cause her even the slightest pain,
While much blood flowed from his body when struck.

Cāmuṇḍā took it all into her mouth, from every direction,
And also into her mouth entered the great demons who were born from
his blood.

Cāmuṇḍā chewed them up, and drank his blood.

With spear, thunderbolt, arrows, swords, and lances the Goddess

Wounded Raktabīja, whose blood was being drunk by Cāmuṇḍā.
Mortally wounded by that constellation of weapons, the great demon Raktabīja

Fell to the earth bloodless, O king!
And then, O king, the gods entered into boundless joy.

When he was slain, the band of Mothers danced about, intoxicated by his blood.

Questions for Review and Discussion

1. Many men and women frequently wear jewelry to enhance their appearances. But what is deemed "appropriate" in terms of jewelry-wearing is determined by class, culture, race, age, gender, as well as other factors. Kali eschews the colorful jewels that traditionally adorn other goddesses. Instead, she adorns herself with skulls and limbs. Why? What possible statement might she be making about jewelry and other socially acceptable—or unacceptable—forms of adornment?

2. Kali is usually depicted naked. Why does she reject clothing and flaunt her nudity unashamedly? What are some possible interpretations for her nakedness?

3. Cremation grounds and cemeteries are places we go to cremate or bury our dead. They are associated with grief over the loss of a loved one and are not usually perceived as places which one frequents willingly or happily. Yet Kali chooses to inhabit cremation grounds. Why? What is the significance of her place of habitat?

4. Kali is described as having fanglike teeth with blood trickling from her mouth, disheveled hair, bloodshot eyes, and severed heads dangling from one of her hands. Why does Kali project such a menacing image?

5. Even though Kali has a terrifying image, she is perceived as a source of comfort. In what ways might it be possible to reconcile Kali's benign aspect with her terror aspect?

6. How can Kali be seen as a figure for disenfranchised and marginalized groups? Explain.

7. Everything about Kali seems to defy societal norms and assumptions. What are some of the ways in which she poses a challenge to humanity and threatens stability and order?

8. Through her appearance and conduct, Kali challenges socially constructed gender norms. Provide specific examples of Kali's appearance and conduct that defy stereotypical notions of femininity.

9. What do Kali and Medea have in common?

10. Discuss the ways in which Kali and what she embodies can have relevance for women today.

Chapter 9

Amaterasu

GLOSSARY OF NAMES AND TERMS

AMATERASU Full name is Amaterasu Opomikami; Japanese Sun Goddess; supreme kami of Shinto; emblem is the rising sun on the Japanese flag

AME NO MANA WI The heavenly well that assists in the birth of Amaterasu and Susanowo's offspring

IZANAGI Full name is Izanagi No Opomikami; male member of the divine couple that produced the Japanese Islands and other subsequent kami; brother/spouse of Izanami; father of Amaterasu and Susanowo

IZANAMI Female member of the divine couple that produced the Japanese Islands and other subsequent kami; sister/spouse of Izanagi

KAMI Natural powers or elements within nature

KOJIKI Oldest existing Japanese text; means "record of ancient things;" most important repository of Japanese myths, legends, and songs

OPO NO YASUMARO Compiled *Kojiki* in 712 C.E. from preexisting source documents

SHINTO Indigenous religion of Japan; the way of the gods; focused on the concerns of daily life

SUSANOWO Full mane is Paya Susanowo Nomikoto; brother of Amaterasu; son of Izanagi; ruler of the ocean; expelled by the deities after he insults Amaterasu

TAKAMA-NO-PARA Heavens; under jurisdiction of Amaterasu

UZUME Full name is Ame No Uzume No Mikoto; goddess who entices Amaterasu from her cave by soliciting laughter from the gods through her bawdy antics

The principal deity of Japanese Shinto is the sun goddess, Amaterasu. Shinto (the way of the gods) is a term encompassing a variety of beliefs and traditions that continue to permeate Japanese religious life. It combines a deep reverence for nature with a political ideology that is structured upon the belief that the royal family is directly descended from the goddess Amaterasu. Shinto teaches obedience to the group and submission to the higher authority. An individual is expected to act in accordance with the well-being of the community and to resist the urge to act in isolation by disregarding the welfare of others.

A basic tenet of Shinto religion is that all aspects of nature contain an element of divinity. From ancient times, the Japanese worshipped these elements or powers in natural phenomenon known as *kami*. Kami is immanent in nature, and through kami, one is connected with the divine realm and all its earthly manifestations. Existing in prodigious numbers, kami are worshipped in a number of loosely

Amaterasu's Family Tree

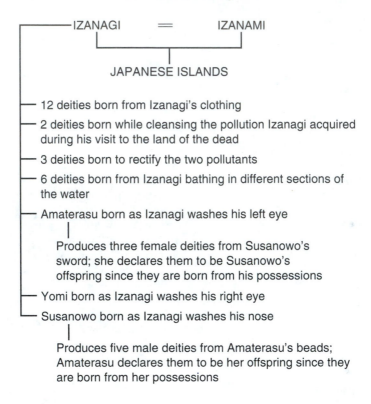

IZANAGI   ═   IZANAMI

JAPANESE ISLANDS

- 12 deities born from Izanagi's clothing
- 2 deities born while cleansing the pollution Izanagi acquired during his visit to the land of the dead
- 3 deities born to rectify the two pollutants
- 6 deities born from Izanagi bathing in different sections of the water
- Amaterasu born as Izanagi washes his left eye

  Produces three female deities from Susanowo's sword; she declares them to be Susanowo's offspring since they are born from his possessions

- Yomi born as Izanagi washes his right eye
- Susanowo born as Izanagi washes his nose

  Produces five male deities from Amaterasu's beads; Amaterasu declares them to be her offspring since they are born from her possessions

organized shrines dedicated to their honor. Shinto mythology promotes the belief that the Japanese islands are the progeny of two kami, Izanagi and Izanami. The divine couple then produced many other kami, culminating in the birth of the Japanese emperor, a direct descendent of Amaterasu. The emperor renounced his divine status after Japan's defeat in 1945. However, many right-wing groups in Japan are currently attempting to revive the old conceptions of kingship, patriotism, and honor.

Shinto is a malleable religion, able to accommodate, modify, and assimilate aspects from different cultural traditions. Consequently, it is quite feasible for a Japanese individual to embrace two religions simultaneously, with each religion enhancing and complementing the other. Shinto is perceived as focusing on the concerns of daily life, for example, while Buddhism is perceived as focusing on the concerns of the afterlife. The two traditions balance each other and are viewed as contributing to the creation of a harmonious whole. To further cement this relationship, many of the Buddhist deities are recognized as Shinto kami.

The supreme kami of Shinto is the female, Amaterasu, whose name means "Sacred Goddess Illuminating the Sky." Responsible for fertility, her myth reflects the Shinto interest in rituals designed to promote fertility. Amaterasu causes the plants to grow that feed humans and gods alike. Honored as the guardian of the Japanese people, her emblem is the rising sun on the Japanese flag. That the Japanese consider the sun to be a female deity and the moon to be a male deity is distinctive since most world mythologies usually designate the sun as masculine and the moon as feminine. It remains unclear why the Japanese feminized the sun, but the mythology suggests that the female has a luster and glory that is absent from the male. Amaterasu's story is told in the *Kojiki*.

Completed in 712 C.E., the *Kojiki* is the oldest extant book in Japanese. The title means "Record of Ancient Things." The work consists of an assortment of myths, legends, folk etymologies, songs, anecdotes, and genealogies, all of which are interspersed with historical and pseudo-historical narratives. Additionally, the *Kojiki* presents the statement of the imperial court concerning its own origins, the origin of the imperial clan and leading families, and an account of the development of Japan as a nation. Transmitted orally for many centuries, the *Kojiki* was subject to the vicissitudes and permutations of collective memory. By the time much of the content was committed to writing, it had become ancient history. A major contributing factor in the compilation of the *Kojiki* was the correction of errors, corruptions, and falsifications that had been allowed to seep in to the historical and genealogical documents kept by the leading families.

In 711 C.E., Opo no Yasumaro was commanded by the then Empress Gemmei to combine the two preexisting source documents (the "Imperial Sun-Lineage" and the "Ancient Dicta of Former Ages") that comprise the *Kojiki* into one work, and, in the process, to eliminate the existing fabrications and errors through the production of a single, historically "accurate" document. Yasumaro completed the work in 712 C.E.

The *Kojiki* consists primarily of material from the anecdotal source document containing myths, legends, songs, and folktales. It opens with the creation of the world, the origin of the gods, their subsequent progeny who constitute the imperial family, and it concludes with the death of the Emperor Suiko. It is in three books. Books II and III are in two discernibly different styles: genealogical information for each reign, written in a Chinese (*kambun*) style and a consistent format; songs, tales, and anecdotes, written in a Japanese style with no consistent format. Some chapters are self-contained narratives and can be construed as precursors to the Japanese short story; some songs are among the earliest recorded in the Japanese language and can be construed as the beginnings of early Japanese poetry.

The story of Amaterasu and her brother, Susanowo, is told in Book I of the *Kojiki*. Amaterasu, a sun deity, comes into being when Izanagi, a male deity, washes his left eye while he is in the process of purifying his body. Susanowo, Amaterasu's brother, comes into being when Izanagi washes his nose. Amaterasu is entrusted with Izanagi's necklace and given jurisdiction over Takama-No-Para (the heavens). Susanowo is entrusted with ruling the ocean.

The excerpt below begins with Chapter 11 in the *Kojiki*. It tells the story of Susanowo's overt dissatisfaction with the task he has been assigned; his ensuing expulsion by Izanagi; the contest with Amaterasu; Susanowo's victory rampage, which includes the destruction of the rice paddies and the desecration of Amaterasu's sacred hall of the harvest festival; Amaterasu's self-imposed seclusion; the deities' successful attempt to lure her out of hiding; and Susanowo's punishment.

The myth bears many similarities with the classical Greek myth of Demeter and Persephone. To begin with, Uzume in the story of Amaterasu and Iambe in the story of Demeter play comparable roles. Through bawdy antics, Uzume succeeds in eliciting the laughter of the gods that draws Amaterasu out of her cave and restores her to the community of the gods; through similar antics, Iambe succeeds in eliciting laughter from Demeter and draws her into the community of humans. Both Amaterasu and Demeter deprive the land of their life-generating qualities, thereby causing havoc on humans and gods alike. Both suffer an affront to their dignity. Both are outraged by the behaviors of their respective male siblings. Both retaliate. And both succeed in forcing others to respect them and accommodate their wishes.

The translation of Chapters 11 through 17 of the *Kojiki* is by Donald L. Philippi.

REFERENCES

Breen, John, and Mark Teeuwen, eds. *Shinto in History: Ways of the Kami.* Honolulu: U of Hawaii P, 2000.

Carmody, Denise Lardner. *Religious Woman: Contemporary Reflections on Eastern Texts.* New York: Crossroad, 1991.

Cleary, Thomas, and Sartaz Aziz. *Twilight Goddess: Spiritual Feminism and Feminine Spirituality.* Boston: Shambhala, 2000.

Hori, Ichiro, Alan L. Miller, and Joseph Mitsuo Kitagawa, eds. *Folk Religion in Japan: Continuity and Change.* Reissued edition. Chicago: U of Chicago P, 1994.

Kitagawa, Joseph M. *Religion in Japanese History.* New York: Columbia UP, 1966.
———, ed. *The Religious Traditions of Asia.* London: Macmillan, 1989.

Littleton, C. Scott. *Shinto: Origins, Rituals, Festivals, Spirits, Sacred Places.* New York: Oxford UP, 2002.

Nakamura, Kyoko Motomochi. "The Significance of Amaterasu in Japanese Religious History." *The Book of the Goddess Past and Present: An Introduction to Her Religion.* Ed. Carl Olson. New York: Crossroad, 1990. 176–189.

Ono, Sokyo. *Shinto: The Kami Way.* Boston: Charles E. Tuttle Co., 1994.

Philippi, Donald L., Trans. *Kojiki.* Princeton and Tokyo: Princeton UP and U of Tokyo P, 1968.

Reader, Ian. *Religion in Contemporary Japan.* Honolulu: U of Hawaii P, 1991.

Reid, D. "Japanese Religions." *Handbook of Living Religions.* Ed. John R. Hinnells. New York: Penguin, 1985. 365–391.

Rosenberg, Donna. *World Mythology: An Anthology of the Great Myths and Epics.* 2nd ed. Illinois: NTC Publishing Group, 1994.

Smyers, Karen A. "Women and Shinto: The Relation Between Purity and Pollution." *Women and World Religions.* Ed. Lucinda Joy Peach. New Jersey: Pearson Education, Inc., 2002. 117–125.

Kojiki

Izanagi Purifies Himself, Giving Birth to Many Deities Including Ama-Terasu-Opo-Mi-Kami and Susa-Nö-Wo

Hereupon, IZANAGI-NÖ-OPO-KAMÏ said:

"I have been to a most unpleasant land, a horrible, unclean land. Therefore I shall purify myself."

Arriving at [the plain] APAKI-PARA by the river-mouth of TATI-BANA in PIMUKA in TUKUSI, he purified and exorcised himself.

When he flung down his stick, there came into existence a deity named TUKI-TATU-PUNA-TO-NÖ-KAMÏ.

Next, when he flung down his sash, there came into existence a deity named MITI-NÖ-NAGA-TI-PA-NÖ-KAMÏ.

Next, when he flung down his bag, there came into existence a deity named TÖKI-PAKASI-NÖ-KAMÏ.

Next, when he flung down his cloak, there came into existence a deity named WADURAPI-NÖ-USI-NÖ-KAMÏ.

Next, when he flung down his trousers, there came into existence a deity named TI-MATA-NÖ-KAMÏ.

Next, when he flung down his headgear, there came into existence a deity named AKI-GUPI-NÖ-USI-NÖ-KAMÏ.

Next, when he flung down the arm-bands of his left arm, there came into existence a deity named OKI-ZAKARU-NÖ-KAMÏ; next, OKI-TU-NAGISA-BIKO-NÖ-KAMÏ; next, OKI-TU-KAPÏ-BERA-NÖ-KAMÏ.

Next, when he flung down the arm-bands of his right arm, there came into existence a deity named PE-ZAKARU-NÖ-KAMÏ; next, PE-TU-NAGISA-BIKO-NÖ-KAMÏ; next, PE-TU-KAPÏ-BERA-NÖ-KAMÏ.

The twelve deities in the above section, from PUNA-DO-NÖ-KAMÏ, through PE-TU-KAPÏ-BERA-NÖ-KAMÏ, all were born from his taking off the articles worn on his body.

Then he said:

"The current of the upper stream is a current too swift; the current of the lower stream is a current too weak."

Then, when he went down and dived into the middle stream and bathed, there came into existence a deity named YASO-MAGA-TU-PI-NŎ-KAMÏ; next, OPO-MAGA-TU-PI-NŎ-KAMÏ.

These two deities came into existence from the pollution which he took on when he went to that unclean land.

Next, in order to rectify these evils, there came into existence the deity KAMU-NAPOBI-NŎ-KAMÏ; next, OPO-NAPOBI-NŎ-KAMÏ; next, IDU-NŎ-ME-NŎ-KAMÏ. (Altogether three deities)

Next, when he bathed at the bottom of the water, there came into existence the deity named SŎKŎ-TU-WATA-TU-MI-NŎ-KAMÏ; next, SŎKŎ-DUTU-NŎ-WO-NŎ-MIKŎTŎ.

When he bathed in the middle [of the water], there came into existence the deity named NAKA-TU-WATA-TU-MI-NŎ-KAMÏ; next, NAKA-DUTU-NŎ-WO-NŎ-MIKŎTŎ.

When he bathed on the surface of the water, there came into existence the deity named UPA-TU-WATA-TU-MI-NŎ-MIKŎTŎ; next, UPA-DUTU-NŎ-WO-NŎ-MIKŎTŎ.

These three WATA-TU-MI deities are the deities worshipped by the MURAZI of the ADUMI as their ancestral deities. The MURAZI of the ADUMI are the descendants of UTUSI-PI-GANA-SAKU-NŎ-MIKŎTŎ, the child of these WATA-TU-MI deities.

The three deities SŎKŎ-DUTU-NŎ-WO-NŎ-MIKŎTŎ, NAKA-DUTU-NŎ-WO-NŎ-MIKŎTŎ, and UPA-DUTU-NŎ-WO-NŎ-MIKŎTŎ are the three great deities of SUMI-NŎ-YE.

Then when he washed his left eye, there came into existence a deity named AMA-TERASU-OPO-MI-KAMÏ.

Next, when he washed his right eye, there came into existence a deity named TUKU-YŎMI-NŎ-MIKŎTŎ.

Next, when he washed his nose, there came into existence a deity named TAKE-PAYA-SUSA-NŎ-WO-NŎ-MIKŎTŎ.

The fourteen deities in the above section, from YA-SO-MAGA-TU-PI-NŎ-KAMÏ through PAYA-SUSA-NŎ-WO-NŎ-MIKŎTŎ, are deities born from bathing his body.

Izanagi Entrusts Their Missions to the Three Noble Children

At this time IZANAGI-NŎ-MIKŎTŎ, rejoicing greatly, said:

"I have borne child after child, and finally in the last bearing I have obtained three noble children."

Then he removed his necklace, shaking the beads on the string so that they jingled, and, giving it to AMA-TERASU-OPO-MI-KAMÏ, he entrusted her with her mission, saying:

"You shall rule TAKAMA-NŎ-PARA."

The name of this necklace is MI-KURA-TANA-NÖ-KAMÏ.

Next he said to TUKU-YÖMI-NÖ-MIKÖTÖ, entrusting him with his mission: "You shall rule the realms of the night."

Next he said to TAKE-PAYA-SUSA-NÖ-WO-NÖ-MIKÖTÖ, entrusting him with his mission:

"You shall rule the ocean."

Susa-Nö-Wo Disobeys His Divine Trust and Is Expelled by Izanagi

While [the other deities] ruled [their realms] in obedience to the commands entrusted to them, PAYA-SUSA-NÖ-WO-NÖ-MIKÖTÖ did not rule the land entrusted to him. [Instead], he wept and howled [even] until his beard eight hands long extended down over his chest.

His weeping was such that it caused the verdant mountains to wither and all the rivers and seas to dry up. At this, the cries of malevolent deities were everywhere abundant like summer flies; and all sorts of calamities arose in all things.

Then IZANAGI-NÖ-OPO-MI-KAMÏ said to PAYA-SUSA-NÖ-WO-NÖ-MIKÖTÖ:

"Why is it you do not rule the land entrusted to you, but [instead] weep and howl?"

Then [Paya-susa-nö-wo-nö-mikötö] replied:

"I wish to go to the land of my mother, NE-NÖ-KATA-SU-KUNI. That is why I weep."

Then IZANAGI-NÖ-OPO-MI-KAMÏ, greatly enraged, said:

"In that case, you may not live in this land!"

Thus [saying], he expelled him with a divine expulsion.

This IZANAGI-NÖ-OPO-KAMÏ is enshrined in TAGA of APUMI.

Susa-Nö-Wo Ascends to Take His Leave of Ama-Terasu-Opo-Mi-Kami

At this time, PAYA-SUSA-NÖ-WO-NÖ-MIKÖTÖ said:

"In that case, before I go I will take my leave of AMA-TERASU-OPO-MI-KAMÏ."

When he ascended to the heavens, the mountains and rivers all roared, and the lands all shook.

Then AMA-TERASU-OPO-MI-KAMÏ heard this and was startled, saying:

"It is certainly not with any good intentions that my brother is coming up. He must wish to usurp my lands."

Then, undoing her hair, she wrapped it in hair-bunches. In the hair-bunches on the left and right [sides of her head], on the vine securing her hair, as well as on her left and right arms, she wrapped long strings of myriad MAGA-TAMA beads.

On her back she bore a thousand-arrow quiver; on the side of her chest she attached a five-hundred-arrow quiver.

Also she put on an awesome high arm-guard; and, shaking the upper tip of her bow, stamping her legs up to her very thighs into the hard earth, and kicking [the earth] about as if it were light snow, she shouted with an awesome fury, she shouted stamping her feet.

Thus waiting for him, she asked him:

"Why have you come?"

Then PAYA-SUSA-NÖ-WO-NÖ-MIKÖTÖ replied:

"I have no evil intentions. It is merely that the Great Deity divinely inquired about my weeping and howling. I said that I was weeping because I wished to go to the land of my mother. Then the Great Deity said: 'You may not live in this land,' and expelled me with a divine expulsion. Whereupon I came up intending to take leave upon my departure. I have no other intentions."

Then AMA-TERASU-OPO-MI-KAMÏ said:

"If that is so, how am I to know that your intentions are pure and bright?"

Then PAYA-SUSA-NÖ-WO-NÖ-MIKÖTÖ replied:

"Let us swear oaths and bear children."

Ama-Terasu-Opo-Mi-Kamï and Susa-Nö-Wo Bear Offspring to Test the Sincerity of the Latter's Motives. He Is Victorious

Whereupon they each stood on opposite sides of [the river] AMË-NÖ-YASU-NÖ-KAPA and swore their oaths.

At this time, AMA-TERASU-OPO-MI-KAMÏ, first asked for the sword ten hands long which TAKE-PAYA-SUSA-NÖ-WO-NÖ-MIKÖTÖ wore at his side. Breaking the sword in three pieces, she rinsed them, the jewels making a jingling sound, in [the heavenly well] AMË-NÖ-MANA-WI, chewed them to pieces, and spat them out.

In the misty spray there came into existence a deity named TAKÏRI-BIME-NÖ-MIKÖTÖ, also named OKI-TU-SIMA-PIME-NÖ-MIKÖTÖ; next, IKITI-SIMA-PIME-NÖ-MIKÖTÖ, also named SA-YÖRI-BIME-NÖ-MIKÖTÖ; and next, TAKITU-PIME-NÖ-MIKÖTÖ. (Three deities)

PAYA-SUSA-NÖ-WO-NÖ-MIKÖTÖ, asking for the long string of myriad MAGA-TAMA, beads wrapped on the left hair-bunch of AMA-TERASU-OPO-MI-KAMÏ, rinsed them, the jewels making a jingling sound, in [the heavenly well] AMË-NÖ-MANA-WI, chewed them to pieces, and spat them out.

In the misty spray there came into existence a deity named MASA-KATU-A-KATU-KATI-PAYA-PI-AMË-NÖ-OSI-PO-MIMI-NÖ-MIKÖTÖ.

Again, he asked for the beads wrapped on her right hair-bunch, chewed them to pieces, and spat them out.

In the misty spray there came into existence a deity named AMË-NÖ-PO-PI-NÖ-MIKÖTÖ.

Again, he asked for the beads wrapped on the vine securing her hair, chewed them to pieces, and spat them out.

In the misty spray there came into existence a deity named AMA-TU-PIKONE-NÖ-MIKÖTÖ.

Again, he asked for the beads wrapped on her left arm, chewed them to pieces, and spat them out.

In the misty spray there came into existence a deity named IKU-TU-PIKONE-NÖ-MIKÖTÖ.

Again, he asked for the beads wrapped on her right arm, chewed them to pieces, and spat them out.

In the misty spray there came into existence a deity named KUMANO-KUSUBI-NÖ-MIKÖTÖ.

At this time AMA-TERASU-OPO-MI-KAMĪ said to PAYA-SUSA-NÖ-WO-NÖ-MIKÖTÖ:

"The latter-born five male children came into existence from my possessions and are therefore naturally my children. The firstborn three female children came into existence from your possessions, and are therefore your children."

Thus saying, she distinguished [the offspring].

The first-born deity, TAKĪRI-BIME-NÖ-MIKÖTÖ, is enshrined in the OKI-TU-MIYA of MUNAKATA.

Next, ITIKI-SIMA-PIME-NÖ-MIKÖTÖ is enshrined in the NAKA-TU-MIYA of MUNAKATA.

Next, TAKITU-PIME-NÖ-MIKÖTÖ is enshrined in the PE-TU-MIYA of MUNAKATA.

These three deities are the three great deities worshipped by the KIMI of MUNAKATA.

Among the latter-born five deities, the child of AMË-NÖ-PO-PI-NÖ-MIKÖTÖ, TAKE-PIRA-TÖRI-NÖ-MIKÖTÖ is the ancestor of the KUNI-NÖ-MIYATUKO of IDUMO, of the KUNI-NÖ-MIYATUKO of MUZASI, of the KUNI-NÖ-MIYATUKO of KAMI-TU-UNAKAMI, of the KUNI-NÖ-MIYATUKO of SIMO-TU-UNA-KAMI, of the KUNI-NÖ-MIYATUKO of TÖPO-TU-APUMI.

Next, AMA-TU-PIKONE-NÖ-MIKÖTÖ is the ancestor of the KUNI-NÖ-MIYA-TUKO of OPUSI-KAPUTI, of the MURAZI of the NUKATA-BE-NÖ-YUWE, of the KUNI-NÖ-MIYATUKO of UBARAKĪ, of the ATAPË of TANAKA in YAMATÖ, of the KUNI-NÖ-MIYATUKO of YAMASIRÖ, of the KUNI-NÖ-MIYATUKO of UMAKUDA, of the KUNI-NÖ-MIYATUKO of KIPË in MITI-NÖ-SIRI, of the KUNI-NÖ-MIYATUKO of SUPAU, of the MIYATUKO of AMUTI in YAMATÖ, of the AGATA-NUSI of TAKËTI, of the INAKI of KAMAPU, and of the MIYATUKO of the SAKIKUSA-BE.

Susa-Nö-Wo Rages with Victory

Then PAYA-SUSA-NÖ-WO-NÖ-MIKÖTÖ said to AMA-TERASU-OPO-MI-KAMĪ:

"It was because my intentions were pure and bright that in the children I begot I obtained graceful maidens. By this it is obvious that I have won."

Thus saying, he raged with victory, breaking down the ridges between the rice paddies of AMA-TERASU-OPO-MI-KAMÏ and covering up the ditches.

Also he defecated and strewed the faeces about in the hall where the first fruits were tasted.

Even though he did this, AMA-TERASU-OPO-MI-KAMÏ did not reprove him, but said:

"That which appears to be faeces must be what my brother has vomited and strewn about while drunk. Also his breaking down the ridges of the paddies and covering up their ditches—my brother must have done this because he thought it was wasteful to use the land thus."

Even though she thus spoke with good intention, his misdeeds did not cease, but became even more flagrant.

When AMA-TERASU-OPO-MI-KAMÏ was inside the sacred weaving hall seeing to the weaving of the divine garments, he opened a hole in the roof of the sacred weaving hall and dropped down into it the heavenly dappled pony which he had skinned with a backwards skinning.

The heavenly weaving maiden, seeing this, was alarmed and struck her genitals against the shuttle and died.

Ama-Terasu-Opo-Mi-Kamï Conceals Herself. The Other Deities Lure Her Out. Susa-Nö-Wo Is Expelled

At this time, AMA-TERASU-OPO-MI-KAMÏ, seeing this, was afraid, and opening the heavenly rock-cave door, went in and shut herself inside.

Then TAKAMA-NÖ-PARA was completely dark, and the Central Land of the Reed Plains was entirely dark.

Because of this, constant night reigned, and the cries of the myriad deities were everywhere abundant, like summer flies; and all manner of calamities arose.

Then the eight-hundred myriad deities assembled in a divine assembly in the river-bed of the AMË-NÖ-YASU-NÖ-KAPA.

They caused the child of TAKA-MI-MUSUBI-NÖ-KAMÏ, OMÖPI-KANE-NÖ-KAMÏ, to ponder.

They gathered together the long-crying birds of TÖKÖ-YÖ and caused them to cry.

They took the heavenly hard rock from the upper stream of the river AMË-NÖ-YASU-NÖ-KAPA; they took iron from [the mountain] AMË-NÖ-KANA-YAMA. They sought the smith AMA-TU-MARA and commissioned ISI-KÖRI-DOME-NÖ-MIKÖTÖ to make a mirror.

They commissioned TAMA-NÖ-YA-NÖ-MIKÖTÖ to make long strings of myriad MAGA-TAMA beads.

They summoned AMË-NÖ-KO-YANE-NÖ-MIKÖTÖ and PUTO-TAMA-NÖ-MIKÖTÖ to remove the whole shoulder-bone of a male deer of the mountain

AMË-NÖ-KAGU-YAMA, and take heavenly PAPAKA wood from the mountain AMË-NÖ-KAGU-YAMA, and [with these] perform a divination.

They uprooted by the very roots the flourishing MA-SAKAKÏ trees of the mountain AMË-NÖ-KAGU-YAMA; to the upper branches they affixed long strings of myriad MAGA-TAMA beads; in the middle branches they hung a large-dimensioned mirror; in the lower branches they suspended white NIKITE cloth and blue NIKITE cloth.

These various objects were held in his hands by PUTO-TAMA-NÖ-MIKÖTÖ as solemn offerings, and AMË-NÖ-KO-YANE-NÖ-MIKÖTÖ intoned a solemn liturgy.

AMË-NÖ-TA-DIKARA-WO-NÖ-KAMÏ stood concealed beside the door, while AMË-NÖ-UZUME-NÖ-MIKÖTÖ bound up her sleeves with a cord of heavenly PI-KAGË vine, tied around her head a head-band of the heavenly MA-SAKI vine, bound together bundles of SASA leaves to hold in her hands, and overturning a bucket before the heavenly rock-cave door, stamped resoundingly upon it. Then she became divinely possessed, exposed her breasts, and pushed her skirt-band down to her genitals.

Then TAKAMA-NÖ-PARA shook as the eight-hundred myriad deities laughed at once.

Then AMA-TERASU-OPO-MI-KAMÏ, thinking this strange, opened a crack in the heavenly rock-cave door, and said from within:

"Because I have shut myself in, I thought that TAKAMA-NÖ-PARA would be dark, and that the Central Land of the Reed Plains would be completely dark. But why is it that AMË-NÖ-UZUME sings and dances, and all the eight-hundred myriad deities laugh?"

Then AMË-NÖ-UZUME said:

"We rejoice and dance because there is here a deity superior to you."

While she was saying this, AMË-NÖ-KO-YANE-NÖ-MIKÖTÖ and PUTO-TAMA-NÖ-MIKÖTÖ brought out the mirror and showed it to AMA-TERASU-OPO-MI-KAMÏ.

Then AMA-TERASU-OPO-MI-KAMÏ, thinking this more and more strange, gradually came out of the door and approached [the mirror.]

Then the hidden AMË-NÖ-TA-DIKARA-WO-NÖ-KAMÏ took her hand and pulled her out. Immediately PUTO-TAMA-NÖ-MIKÖTÖ extended a SIRI-KUMË rope behind her, and said:

"You may go back no further than this!"

When AMA-TERASU-OPO-MI-KAMÏ came forth, TAKAMA-NÖ-PARA and the Central Land of the Reed Plains of themselves became light.

At this time the eight-hundred myriad deities deliberated together, imposed upon PAYA-SUSA-NÖ-WO-NÖ-MIKÖTÖ a fine of a thousand tables of restitutive gifts, and also, cutting off his beard and the nails of his hands and feet, had him exorcised and expelled him with a divine expulsion.

Questions for Review and Discussion

1. Describe the process by which Amaterasu and Susanowo produce offspring.

2. After declaring himself the winner of his contest with Amaterasu, Susanowo engages in deliberately provocative acts. Why does he do so? What does his challenge to Amaterasu represent?

3. Although Susanowo engages in a series of abominable acts, Amaterasu initially makes excuses for him and attempts to justify his behavior. Why does she do this?

4. It is only after Susanowo has assaulted her sacred weaving hall that Amaterasu takes action. She withdraws into a cave, denying the land her presence. What arguments can be made in support of Amaterasu's course of action? What arguments can be made against it?

5. What are the consequences of Amaterasu's withdrawal into a cave?

6. Why do the deities align themselves with Amaterasu instead of with Susanowo?

7. How do the deities manage to entice Amaterasu out of her cave?

8. Is the fact that Amaterasu had never before seen the extent of her own beauty a significant factor in ending her self-imposed isolation? Explain.

9. What is the difference between being a victim and being a survivor? Does Amaterasu internalize the psychology of the victim or is she a survivor? Explain.

10. In what ways might Amaterasu be considered a good role model for women today? In what ways might she be considered problematic?

Chapter 10

Kuan Yin

GLOSSARY OF NAMES AND TERMS

AVALOKITEŚVARA Male Indian bodhisattva who later assumes the female identity of Kuan Yin

BODHI Perfected wisdom

BODHI TREE Also known as the Bo tree; tree under which the Buddha was sitting when he received enlightenment

BUDDHA Father of Buddhism; real name was Siddhartha Gautama

BODHISATTVA A being whose essence is perfected wisdom

CHÜEH-LIEN Authored the *Legend of Miao-Shan* in 1551

DUKKHA Suffering; part of the First Noble Truth: life consists of suffering

EIGHTFOLD PATH Rigorous, eight-step course that leads to enlightenment

HINAYANA BUDDHISM One of the major schools of thought within Buddhism; also known as the Small Vehicle or Theravada Buddhism

HSIANG-SHAN Located in the southwest region of kingdom of Miao-Chuang-Yen

HUI-CHEN Nun from the White Sparrow monastery

KUAN YIN A prominent bodhisattva in Mahayana Buddhism; possible composite of Avalokiteśvara, Tara, Sheng Mu, Matsu, and Miao-Shan

MAHAYANA BUDDHISM One of the major schools of thought within Buddhism; also known as the Large Vehicle

MARA The tempter who tries to lure the Buddha away from enlightenment

MATSU Goddess of the Sea; an indigenous Chinese goddess associated with Kuan Yin; has power to rescue those lost at sea

MIAO-CHUANG-YEN The king and father of Miao-Shan

MIAO-SHAN Youngest daughter of King Miao-Chuang-Yen; associated with Kuan Yin; defied her father by insisting on applying Buddhist principles to her life

MIAO-YEN Eldest daughter of King Miao-Chuang-Yen

MIAO-YIN Middle daughter of King Miao-Chuang-Yen

NAGA A spirit who carries Miao-Shan to a safe refuge in Hsiang-Shan

NIRVANA The permanent state of illumination/enlightenment

SAMADHI State of undifferentiated being; total absorption

SATTVA The essence of one's being

SHENG MU Holy Mother; an indigenous Chinese goddess associated with Kuan Yin; has the power to grant children

TANHA Desire; part of the Second Noble Truth: the desire to satisfy ourselves

TARA A Tibetan Buddhist goddess associated with Kuan Yin; emerged from Avalokiteśvara's tear

THERAVADA BUDDHISM The Way of the Elders; also known as Hinayana Buddhism (see above)

One of the most important bodhisattvas in Mahayana Buddhism is Kuan Yin. She is a composite figure that combines both Buddhist and Chinese virtues. Personifying the ideals of mercy and compassion, Kuan Yin is eager to answer the pleas of a suffering humanity. As the most famous bodhisattva in East Asia, Kuan Yin's primary focus is to address the concerns of women in all aspects of the domestic sphere, especially in matters of childbirth and child rearing. Her universal empathy with all sentient beings and her receptivity to their prayers distinguish her as a popular bodhisattva in Mahayana Buddhism.

The father of Buddhism, the Buddha, was born of royal lineage around 560 B.C.E. in northern India. However, according to some scholars, he may have been born a century later. His birth name was Siddhartha Gautama of the Shakyas. Blessed with a luxurious upbringing in which no expense was spared to anticipate and satisfy his every material want, the Buddha, nevertheless, became increasingly disenchanted with the fleeting nature of earthly pleasures. Accordingly, he abandoned his family, rejected the life of a prince, assumed the garb of an impoverished man, and set off into the forest in search of enlightenment. This is known as the Great Going Forth. His teachers were the Hindu masters and a band of ascetics.

Not entirely satisfied with the teachings of either ideology, the Buddha sat beneath a fig tree one day, vowing not to move until he had achieved enlightenment. The tree, which has since become known as the Bo tree, short for Bodhi, which means enlightenment, is also known as the Immovable Spot. It is while he is sitting under the Bodhi tree that the Buddha undergoes a series of tests placed before him by Mara, the tempter. He successfully thwarts each temptation and experiences the Great Awakening. Rooted in the same spot, he meditates for forty-nine days. As he emerges from this state, Mara attempts one last temptation: he urges him to abandon his ministry and enter Nirvana (the permanent and ultimate state of illumination) instead of wasting his time by trying to teach other humans who are presumably too inept to understand the profundity of his message. The Buddha's response is unequivocal: since there remains the possibility that some people will understand his message and will achieve enlightenment, his obligation is to delay Nirvana for himself while he spreads the word to others. This final rejection from the Buddha causes Mara to refrain from any further effort at temptation.

The Buddha began his public ministry of teaching, counseling, advising, and demonstrating by example. He founded, administered, and trained an order of monks—an order which was to grow dramatically during his lifetime. His ministry lasted forty-five years, coming to an end with his death around 480 B.C.E.—assuming his birth took place circa 560 B.C.E. While he was alive, the Buddha continuously rebuffed all attempts to turn him into a god, insisting that he was a human being. However, he seems not to have objected to the veneration of his relics.

The Buddha's message emerged largely as a reaction against the excesses of the Hinduism of his day. The Buddha preached a religion that was devoid of authority, of ritual, of metaphysical speculation, of tradition, and of conjecture on the supernatural. In their place, he advocated a religion of egalitarianism, self-reliance, and intense self-effort. Buddhism is a nontheistic religion in so far as it locates the cause of and cure for human suffering within the attitudes of human beings themselves instead of locating them in a supreme being. The word *buddha,* which comes from the Sanskrit root *budh,* meaning to wake up and to know, denotes the enlightened one or the awakened one.

The basic tenets of Buddhism are known as the Four Noble Truths.

1. The First Noble Truth is that life consists of suffering or *dukkha.* Life is saturated with pain at every level, causing disruption and dislocation. Pain and suffering are occasioned by the trauma of birth, sickness, decrepitude, fear of death, ties with the abhorrent, and separation from loved ones.

2. The Second Noble Truth locates the sources of pain and suffering in humanity's unenlightened pursuit for the unattainable and in the desire (*tanha*) to satisfy private inclinations by distinguishing ourselves from the rest of humanity in order to placate the ego.

3. The Third Noble Truth extends logically from the previous one. If the source of suffering is narrow self-interest and self-aggrandizement, we can overcome the dislocation that leads to suffering by denying our ego instead of fueling it, by abandoning our unattainable desires instead of trying to achieve them.

4. The Fourth Noble Truth promotes the Eightfold Path as the means for overcoming egotistical desires.

The Eightfold Path, consisting of treatment through rigorous training, charts the eight-step course that an individual should follow in order to achieve enlightenment. These steps consist of right knowledge (the knowledge articulated in the Four Noble Truths); right aspiration (the intention to seek illumination); right speech (control of the use of language by reflecting on why and how we use language); right behavior (control of behavior by reflecting on why and how we behave); right livelihood (pursuit of occupations that are conducive to spiritual advancement); right effort (the knowledge that illumination requires an enormous amount of effort); right mindfulness (a constant self-awareness and self-analysis of one's thoughts, words, actions, and surroundings); right absorption (the ultimate step that leads to illumination).

There exists a gap of about 150 years between the Buddha's spoken words and the first written records of his doctrine. This fact no doubt contributed to the split in direction that Buddhism experienced in later years. The two major schools of thought within Buddhism are the *Mahayana,* also known as the Large Vehicle, ("large" in this case implies superior) and the *Hinayana,* also known as the *Theravada* or Small Vehicle ("small" implying inferior). *Theravada* means the Way of the Elders. Both groups claim to represent the original spirit of Buddhism as taught and practiced by the Buddha.

Briefly, the differences between the two groups are the following: most Theravada Buddhists assume that in order to achieve Nirvana, one has to have been born a man. Theravada Buddhism argues that the human being should focus primarily on attaining Nirvana for himself and that emancipation is not contingent upon the salvation of others. Mahayana Buddhism, on the other hand, stresses that the fate of the individual is inextricably linked to the fate of all individuals and that enlightenment can only be achieved within the context of compassion for others. Theravada advocates a renunciation of the world in pursuit of illumination for oneself; Mahayana advocates a life dedicated to serving others and helping them to achieve illumination. Theravada posits the ideal as the disciple who embarks on the solitary journey to Nirvana with a commitment and an unwavering focus; Mahayana posits the ideal as the *bodhisattva,* one whose essential being (*sattva*) is perfected wisdom (*bodhi*). For Mahayana Buddhism, the bodhisattva is the being who, motivated by compassion for a suffering humanity, voluntarily renounces Nirvana in order to return to the world to help others achieve enlightenment. The bodhisattva plays a prominent role in Chinese and Japanese Buddhism where Mahayana Buddhism became very popular.

One of the most significant bodhisattvas in Mahayana Buddhism is Kuan Yin. She is known as a "celestial" bodhisattva—one who has transcended the stage of individual struggle and has attained the level of spiritual perfection, endowing her with miraculous and psychic powers to help those in distress. Celestial bodhisattvas eventually became deities in their own right.

Kuan Yin is the female Chinese Buddhist embodiment of the male Indian bodhisattva Avalokiteśvara. When and how the male Avalokiteśvara came to assume the female identity of Kuan Yin in China continues to be debated among scholars, but this female embodiment of a male bodhisattva seems to have been completed by around the tenth or eleventh century. Avalokiteśvara means, "Listening to the Cries of the World." The name Kuan Yin, which is usually translated as "She Who Listens to the World's Sounds," reflects her continuous attentiveness to the sounds of sorrow in order to alleviate suffering. She is frequently depicted with many arms, heads, and eyes in order to accentuate her access and receptivity to the cries of those in need. She continues to be a prominent deity in both China and Japan—where she is known as Kannon.

Three factors probably contributed to the sexual transformation of this bodhisattva: the association of Kuan Yin with Tara, a Tibetan Buddhist goddess; with two indigenous Chinese goddesses known as Sheng Mu and Matsu (Holy Mother and Goddess of the Sea, respectively); and the heroine, Princess Miao-Shan. The goddess Tara is said to have emerged from one of Avalokiteśvara's tears precipitated by witnessing the sufferings of humanity. Sheng Mu was said to have the power to grant children; the goddess Matsu, was known for rescuing those lost at sea. The Princess Miao-Shan defied her father by insisting on living her life in accordance with the Buddhist principles of piety, celibacy, and service to humankind. All of these qualities, reflecting compassion and mercy for the plight of a suffering humanity, merged in the figure of Kuan Yin.

Kuan Yin demonstrates compassion and mercy to the living, to the dying, and to those who have already made the transition from this world to the next. Her role as the comforter of the dead is told in the legend of the heroine Miao-Shan. In this legend, Kuan Yin is able to transform even the land of the dead into a paradise through her righteous and morally uplifting presence and through the recitation of Buddhist scriptures.

The legend tells the story of Kuan Yin in her manifestation as the Princess Miao-Shan, the youngest daughter of King Miao-Chuang. Blessed with intelligence and wisdom beyond her years, Miao-Shan/Kuan Yin leads a simple and pious life. She defies her father's repeated efforts to coerce her into marriage, preferring instead to lead a celibate, pious life. She miraculously survives her father's orders to execute her and takes refuge in a secluded hermitage where she devotes herself to a life of religious fulfillment. She soon learns of her father's sickness and impending death. Disguised as an aged monk, she cures her father of his illness by severing her own arms and eyes. Once cured, the king discovers that the holy elder is none other than his third daughter, Miao-Shan. The king prays for her recovery, and soon Miao-Shan becomes manifest as Kuan Yin in her thousand-armed and thousand-eyed form. Father and daughter are reconciled. Kuan Yin then enters paradise in the company of the Buddhas, where she keeps a constant vigil to answer the prayers of those who seek her assistance.

Several variations of the legend exist. For example, in one version, Kuan Yin is assisted in performing the difficult chores assigned to her in the monastery by supernatural beings. Another version describes Kuan Yin journeying to the land of the dead after her execution. The ruler of the underworld eventually evicts her from his domain because her compassion and virtue transform hell into a paradise. So Kuan Yin reenters the body of Miao-Shan and leads a pious, solitary life, only to have her solitude interrupted when she hears of her father's illness.

The story of Kuan Yin demonstrates the tensions between the Confucian ideal of participation in the social order, filial obedience, and fulfillment of obligations (including procreation) with the Buddhist ideal of renunciation of worldly gains and a life of celibacy. By defying her father in refusing to marry, Kuan Yin seems to be repudiating one of the most prominent Chinese virtues—that of obedience to one's parents. But she refrains from criticizing him for his abusive behavior; nor does she complain or attempt retaliation. She greets each persecution with equanimity and never succumbs to anger, hatred, or vengefulness. And as the story unfolds, Kuan Yin's love and respect for her father become readily apparent, to the degree that she willingly sacrifices her arms and eyes to heal him. The tension between Buddhist and Chinese ideals are resolved at the conclusion of the story when father and daughter are reunited and the father becomes a student of his daughter's teachings. Kuan Yin demonstrates that her compassion and mercy serve to enhance the love and reverence she has always felt for her father. In other words, Buddhist values do not subvert traditional Chinese values. Instead, they serve to complement and deepen them.

The story of Kuan Yin is told in the legend of Miao-Shan. The version below is narrated by Chüeh-lien in 1551 and is taken from Glen Dudbridge's study, *The Legend of Miao-Shan*.

REFERENCES

Blofeld, John. *The Bodhisattva of Compassion: The Mystical Tradition of Kuan Yin.* Boulder: Shambhala, 1978.

Carmody, Denise Lardner. *Religious Woman: Contemporary Reflections on Eastern Texts.* New York: Crossroad, 1991.

Chinnery, John. "China." *World Mythology.* Gen. Ed. Roy Willis. New York: Henry Holt and Co., 1993. 88–101.

Dudbridge, Glen. *The Legend of Miao-Shan.* London: Ithaca, 1978.

Gross, Rita M. "Buddhism." *Women in Religion.* Eds. Jean Holm and John Bowker. London: Pinter, 1999. 1–29.

Harvey, Andrew, and Anne Baring. *The Divine Feminine: Exploring the Feminine Face of God Throughout the World.* Berkeley: Conari, 1996.

Kinsley, David. *The Goddesses' Mirror: Visions of the Divine From East and West.* Albany: State U of New York P, 1989.

Paul, Diana Y. "Kuan-Yin: Savior and Savioress in Chinese Pure Land Buddhism." *The Book of the Goddess, Past and Present: An Introduction to her Religion.* Ed. Carl Olson. New York: Crossroad, 1990. 161–175.

———. *Women in Buddhism: Images of the Feminine in the Mahayana Tradition.* 2nd ed. Berkeley: U of California P, 1985.

Yü, Chün-fang. *Kuan-Yin: The Chinese Transformation of Avalokiteśvara.* New York: Columbia UP, 2000.

The Legend of Miao-shan

Chüeh-lien Miao-shan refused to take a husband, and most certainly achieved buddhahood.

Once in the past the Lü Master [Tao-] hsüan dwelt in the Ling-kan ssu in the Chung-nan mountains, practising religion. In a vision a *deva* attended him. The Master asked the *deva:* 'I have heard that the Mahāsattva Kuan-yin has many links and manifestations on Sahā, this earth. In what place are they most abundant?'

The *deva* replied: 'The Bodhisattva's appearances follow no fixed rule, but the pre-eminent site of his bodily manifestation is Hsiang-shan.'

The Master enquired: 'Where is this 'Hsiang-shan' now?'

The deva replied: 'Over two hundred *li* to the south of Mount Sung there are three hills in a row. The middle one is Hsiang-shan—that is the Bod-hisattva's place. To the north-east of the hill there was in the past a king whose name was King Miao-chuang-yen. His lady was named Pao-te. The king had no crown prince, only three daughters: the eldest Miao-yen, the second Miao-yin, the youngest Miao-shan. Of these three daughters two were already married.

Only the third, in conduct and appearance far transcending the ordinary, always wore dirty clothes and took but one meal a day, never eating strongly flavoured food, and pursued this life of abstention and religious discipline without faltering in her resolve.

The king said to Miao-shan: 'You are no longer a child now—you ought to take a husband.'

Miao-shan said: 'The river of desire has mighty waves, the sea of suffering has fathomless depths. I would never, for the sake of one lifetime of glory, plunge into aeons of misery. I earnestly desire to leave my home and pursue the way of religion.'

The king angrily cast her out into the flower garden at the rear of the palace, cut off her food and drink, and made her mother strongly urge her to take a husband.

Miao-shan said: 'Empty things come to an end—I desire what is infinite.'

Furious at hearing this, the king summoned Hui-chen, a nun of the White Sparrow monastery, to take her off to the monastery to grow vegetables, and to devise ways to induce her to return to the palace.

Miao-shan said: 'Surely you have heard that those who obstruct someone's monastic vocation will suffer torments for countless aeons? Do you dare oppose the best interests of the Buddhist religion and willingly accept the ret-ribution of hell?'

The nun answered: 'I am under the king's orders. This is nothing to do with me.'

Miao-shan would not consent. She remained firm in her desire to enter the order.

The nun reported it to the king, who in a great rage ordered troops to sur-round the monastery, behead the nuns and burn down their quarters.

Miao-shan was taken off by a *nāga* spirit to the foot of Hsiang-shan, not a hair of her injured.

She built a hut and lived there, clothed in grass and eating from the trees, unrecognised by anyone.

Three years had passed by when the king, in return for his crimes of destroying a monastery and killing the religious, contracted jaundice (*kāmalā*) and could find no rest.

Doctors could not cure him.

He advertised far and wide for someone to make him well.

At that point a strange monk appeared, saying: 'I have a divine remedy which can cure Your Majesty's sickness.'

The king asked: 'What medicine do you have?'

The monk said: 'If you use the arms and eyes of one free of anger to blend into a medicine and take it, then you will be cured.'

The king said: 'This medicine is hard to find.'

The monk said: 'No, it is not. There is a Hsiang-shan in the south-west of Your Majesty's dominion, and on the very peak of the hill is a holy one whose practice of religion has come to completion. This person has no anger. If you put your request to her she will certainly make the gift.'

The king ordered an equerry to take incense into the hills and bow to the holy one, saying: 'Our lord the king is sick. We venture to trouble you with a request for your arms and eyes in order to save the king's life. This will lead him to turn his mind to enlightenment.'

Hearing this, the holy one gouged out her two eyes and severed both arms with a knife, handing them over to the equerry.

At that moment, the whole earth shook. The equerry returned to the capital.

There they made the monk blend the medicine. The king took it and recovered from his sickness.

In solemn procession the king then went to Hsiang-shan, where he offered humble thanks and veneration.

He saw the holy one with no arms or eyes, physically defective. The king and his lady, looking from either side, were deeply moved to a painful thought: 'The holy one looks very like our daughter.'

The holy one said: 'I am indeed Miao-shan. Your daughter has offered her arms and eyes to repay her father's love.'

Hearing her words, the king embraced her with loud weeping. He said: 'I was so evil that I have made my daughter suffer terrible pain.'

The holy one said: 'I suffer no pain. Having yielded up my mortal eyes I shall receive diamond eyes; having given up my human arms I shall receive golden-coloured arms. If my vow is true these results will certainly follow.'

Heaven and earth then shook. And then the holy one was revealed as the All-merciful Bodhisattva Kuan-shih-yin of the Thousand Arms and Thousand Eyes, solemn and majestic in form, radiant with dazzling light, lofty and magnificent, like the moon amid the stars.

The king and his lady, together with the entire population of the land, conceived goodness in their hearts and committed themselves to the Three Treasures.

The Bodhisattva then entered *samādhi* and, perfectly upright, entered *nirvāṇa*.

Questions for Review and Discussion

1. Kuan Yin rejects a life of luxury and class privilege in favor of pursuing her own path for an authentic life. What does she lose and what does she gain by making this choice?

2. In her insistence upon celibacy, Kuan Yin follows the path of the virginal goddess. But virginity has been interpreted to mean something other than just a refusal to engage in sexual intercourse. It has also come to refer to females who refuse to submit to male domination through their insistence on exercising choice. In that sense of the word, how might Kuan Yin be considered a virgin?

3. In what ways might Kuan Yin's rejection of marriage amount to a repudiation of the patriarchal dictate that restricts a woman's role to that of wife and mother?

4. Why is Kuan Yin's father prepared to execute his daughter when she refuses to obey his demands that she marry? Is he just concerned with marrying her off, or does he recognize that her refusal to marry represents something much larger? Explain.

5. In what ways can Kuan Yin serve as an inspiration to women who seek an alternative to a traditional life of marriage and children?

6. Kuan Yin remains true to her goal of leading a celibate, spiritual life. But her example also holds out the possibility that tolerance of abuse can lead to redemption and vindication. What problems, if any, can such a position generate?

7. The figure of Kuan Yin is not without ambivalence. Even though her conduct represents the quintessence of mercy and compassion, it is also somewhat problematic. Her tolerance of abuse and persecution coupled with her willingness to forgive terrible injustices can lead to the conclusion that abuse and injustice should be tolerated in this life in the hope of attaining salvation in the next. What arguments can be made in support of the position that Kuan Yin goes too far in tolerating her father's abuse? Are there some actions that cannot and, perhaps, should not be tolerated or forgiven?

8. What arguments can be made in support of Kuan Yin's actions in coming to her father's aid and forgiving his past abuses?

9. What challenges does the story of Kuan Yin pose for an audience raised in a tradition of secular materialism?

10. In what ways might Kuan Yin be considered a positive role model for women? In what ways might she be considered a problematic one?

Chapter 11

Lilith

GLOSSARY OF NAMES AND TERMS

ALPHABET OF BEN SIRA   Composed between eighth and eleventh centuries; contains story of birth and education of Ben Sira and the stories he tells in the court of Nebuchadnezzar; includes story of Lilith

BABYLONIAN EXILE   Also called Babylonian Captivity (587–539 B.C.E.); deportation of Jews to Babylon by Nebuchadnezzar

BEN SIRA   "Prophet" and prodigy; conceived miraculously; may have been a fictional character

JEREMIAH   Ben Sira's father/grandfather

KABBALAH   Writings of Hebrew mystics of the Middle Ages; contributed to the subsequent demonization of Lilith

LILITH   Adam's first wife; demonized in Hebrew scripture

MIDRASH   Narrative that comments, interprets, and explores a question about or contradiction in biblical story

NEBUCHADNEZZAR   King of Babylonia from 605–562 B.C.E.; known for building the Gardens of Babylon, one of the seven wonders of the ancient world

SNVI, SNSVI, SMNGLOF   Three angels in charge of medicine; their names on an amulet protect infants from illnesses inflicted by Lilith

TALMUD   Two Hebrew texts written between 200 C.E. and 500 C.E.

TANAKH   Hebrew scripture

TORAH   Hebrew scripture; comprising of the first five books of the Old Testament

YAHWEH   Tansliteration from the Hebrew YHVH; one of the names for God in the Old Testament

ZOHAR   Kabbalist scripture

Judaism, a monotheistic religion founded by Abraham and Moses, was born in the Middle East approximately 3,700 years ago. Adherents of the religion are called Jews. They worship the one God, known as Yahweh. The sacred scripture of Jews, known as the Hebrew Bible or Tanakh, consists of a collection of books considered to be divinely inspired. The first five books of the Tanakh are called the Torah or the Five Books of Moses. The Tanakh contains descriptions of the early years of Jewish history, the trials and tribulations of the Jewish people, and the laws and rituals that are required of Jews.

Although the Hebrew scripture contains references to gods other than Yahweh, Judaism's basic contribution to religious thought was monotheism. Other gods mentioned in the scripture are portrayed as subordinates of Yahweh. Unlike those gods, the God of Israel claims righteousness, moral authority, justice, and a concern for the plight of His people while He simultaneously demands total, unequivocal obedience. Furthermore, unlike other gods, Yahweh was not confined to a particular locale—a quality that was to contribute to his power and ubiquitous influence. Yahweh was in all places at all times.

Jews believe that there is only one God and that they are His chosen people. As the descendents of Abraham, they claim a unique relationship with God, a relationship that was to be reflected in their ethical behavior and holiness, and one which was to be held up as an example for others to emulate. Jews believe that Yahweh intervened intermittently in Jewish history, guiding the Jewish people through many trials and tribulations, and providing them with a set of rules to live by, including the Ten Commandments. Yahweh's actions in history are perceived by the Jewish people as a reaffirmation of their unique status as His chosen people: they are punished when they transgress and rewarded when they are righteous and obedient. Their sacred text proclaims that Yahweh establishes a covenant with His chosen people whereby they keep God's laws and live their daily lives in accordance with those laws in exchange for the many privileges they have received and will continue to receive from Him.

Since the fall of the Israelite monarchy in Babylonia in 586 B.C.E. until the establishment of the state of Israel in 1948, Jews have been under the jurisdiction of non-Jews. Their forced exile for approximately 70 years in Babylonia during the sixth century B.C.E. constituted a formative event in Jewish consciousness. The expulsion of the Jewish people from Jerusalem by the Romans in 70 C.E. marked the beginning of their diaspora. Their traditions and customs survived through the efforts of their spiritual leaders known as rabbis.

Over the centuries, Judaism has evolved into many different traditions. These range from the ultra-orthodox Jews who strictly adhere to religious laws to reform Jews who interpret their faith and traditions in accordance with living in a modern society and who embrace gender equity in their beliefs and practices. Early Rabbinic Judaism, or the Judaism of the rabbis, was hostile toward women and perceived them as inferior creatures whose position was subordinate to that of men. Consequently, Jewish women were severely limited in their access to the different aspects of Jewish life. They were prohibited from studying the Torah and from participation in the public rituals of the synagogue, their place of worship. Evidence of early rabbinic attitudes toward women can be seen in the Hebrew figure of Lilith whom we encounter in Genesis, the first book of the Torah.

Genesis opens with the story of creation. But rather than presenting one consistent story, there are, in fact, two conflicting versions of creation in the first chapters of Genesis. The first version of creation in Genesis declares the following:

Then God said, "Let us make humankind in our image, according to our likeness; and let them have dominion over the fish of the sea, and over the birds of the air, and over the cattle, and over all the wild animals of the

*earth, and over every creeping thing that creeps upon the earth." So God
created humankind in his*
> *image,*
> *in the image of God he created*
> *them;*
> *male and female he created them. (1: 26–27).*

The second version of creation contradicts this not only in terms of the sequence of events but also in terms of the creation of the female. Genesis 1 clearly indicates that the animals were created before the first humans and that the first humans (man and woman) were created simultaneously. In Genesis 2, on the other hand, the sequence is reversed: the man is created first, followed by the animals, followed by the woman: "And the rib that the LORD God had taken from the man he made into a woman and brought her to the man" (Genesis 2:22).

As the subject of much debate, these conflicting versions of creation may be the result of a flawed intertwining of the earlier pre-Exile version of creation with the post-Exile Babylonian account. Early rabbinic commentary, beginning at approximately the tenth century C.E., contains attempts to reconcile the contradictions. Some biblical commentators have interpreted Genesis 1: 26–27 to mean that the first human being was androgynous. Others, however, most notably in Jewish folklore and rabbinic commentary, argue that this passage refers to Adam's first wife, Lilith.

References to Lilith as Eve's predecessor appear in the Talmud and are elaborated on in the midrash and the Kabbalah. The Talmud consists of two texts, written at approximately 200 C.E. and 500 C.E. respectively. Midrash is a narrative that often begins with a question, a crevice, a silence, or a contradiction in a biblical story and projects the story forward while interpreting and commenting on the scripture itself. Although midrash plays a contributing role in the perception of Lilith, the group primarily credited with her development and transformation appears many centuries after the Talmud. This group is the Kabbalistic mystics—literate, spiritual seekers of the Middle Ages. They transform Lilith from a female endowed with overpowering physical and intellectual abilities to a "scraggy-toothed hag." It is in the Zohar, the scripture of the Kabbalists, that Lilith becomes the harlot, the demon, the embodiment of darkness and evil.

Rabbinic and Kabbalistic sources present an image of Lilith designed to instill fear and loathing. As Adam's first wife, she is at once an evil, fiery spirit who seduces men in their sleep. Some sources describe her as frigid and childless while others claim that she is prodigiously fertile, giving birth to at least 100 demons a day. Blamed for the death of infants, her attributes are designed to reinforce her demonic qualities—a wild-haired and winged creature with an overtly voracious sexual appetite. As a complex figure, Lilith is frequently perceived in contradictory and conflicted ways. The body of literature surrounding her emphasizes her cosmic nature, the essential role she played in the creation process, her demonic qualities, and her strong association with sexuality and death.

A full-length retelling of the story of Lilith appears in the midrash *The Alphabet of Ben Sira,* an anonymous work of the medieval period. The approximate dates for the *Alphabet* range anywhere from the eighth to the eleventh centuries, C.E. An examination of internal textual evidence has led some scholars to conclude that the *Alphabet* was probably composed in a Muslim country.

The tone of the *Alphabet* is irreverent and much of the humor is scatological. References to animal behavior, human body parts, bodily functions, sexual activity, blatant vulgarities, obscenities, and absurdities have led commentators to conclude that the work may have been a form of an academic burlesque, a parody of sacred materials and commentary that served as an entertaining distraction for rabbinic scholars. However, in some circles, the *Alphabet* enjoyed respect and its contents were, and continue to be, taken seriously.

The *Alphabet* is generally preceded by a narrative of the extraordinary conception, birth, and early education of Ben Sira, "a prophet." Ben Sira's miraculous birth from a virgin signifies his exceptional status. The introduction to the *Alphabet* narrates the unusual manner of his conception. His mother, the virgin daughter of Jeremiah, is impregnated in the bathhouse by her own father's semen after the men of Ephraim threaten to sodomize him unless he masturbates. Because he is a righteous man, Jeremiah's spilled semen is preserved until it enters his daughter's vagina and impregnates her. She gives birth seven months later to Ben Sira: an exceptional infant endowed at birth with a full set of teeth and the power of speech.

While still in his infancy, Ben Sira dialogues with his mother. This may be evidence of an Islamic influence since an infant endowed with the power of speech echoes Surah 19 of the *Qur'an* in which the baby Jesus speaks from his cradle. Ben Sira cites passages from the Hebrew scripture, compares himself to his father, announces his prophethood, and predicts the composition of his alphabet book. During the first year of his life, his mother supports his penchant for "fatty meat and aged wine" by becoming a seamstress.

At the end of his first year, Ben Sira insists on learning the Torah at the synagogue. Met with initial opposition because of his young age, (the teacher cites a passage from the scripture that declares a child must be at least five years old to learn the Torah), Ben Sira counteracts by citing a different passage from the scripture that declares time is running short and there is still much to be done. After being challenged in this way, the teacher begins the lesson by asking Ben Sira to repeat the letters of the alphabet. Ben Sira's response to each letter with a brief aphorism constitutes the first part of the *Alphabet*. There are twenty-two aphorisms in all, arranged alphabetically and organized into a loose narrative framework.

In keeping with his extraordinary conception and birth, Ben Sira demonstrates prodigious learning abilities. By the age of seven, he has mastered a variety of sacred texts and their scholarly interpretations; the different languages spoken by palm trees, angels, and demons; and a wealth of knowledge in major and minor subjects. His fame quickly spreads throughout the world until King Nebuchadnezzar of Babylon invites him to live in his court as his advisor and guide.

The second part of the *Alphabet* takes place in the court of Nebuchadnezzar. It consists of a series of twenty-two episodes that narrate the experiences and stories of Ben Sira in the court. Nebuchadnezzar poses various questions and ordeals to test Ben Sira who responds to each challenge with a story. It is in this part of the *Alphabet,* in Ben Sira's fifth response to Nebuchadnezzar, that the story of Lilith appears.

Chapter 5 of the *Alphabet* tells us that the young son of Nebuchadnezzar becomes seriously ill. Nebuchadnezzar challenges Ben Sira to heal his child or suffer death. Ben Sira immediately proceeds to write an amulet with the names of the healing angels in order to cure the child. Although amulets originated in antiquity, their reputation as protective agents was so firmly entrenched in popular belief that the Hebrews unofficially adopted them. There were six types of amulets: those that were for general protective purposes; those that promote health; those that protect against the evil eye; those that prevent miscarriages; those that promote fertility; and those that protect mother and child in the childbed.

The story of Lilith comes as a response to Nebuchadnezzar's question to Ben Sira about the purpose and meaning of the amulet. Ben Sira's narrative describes Lilith's creation from the same earthy substance as her illustrious male counterpart, Adam. Lilith rejects Adam's command to lie beneath him in the position of submission during the act of sexual intercourse. Adam insists. Rather than submit to Adam's authority, Lilith pronounces the name of the Holy One and promptly flies away. Yahweh sends three angels to retrieve her with a promise that all will be forgiven if she returns. If, however, she refuses to return, one hundred of her offspring (demons) will die every day as punishment for her disobedience.

The angels pursue Lilith and overtake her in the middle of the Red Sea. She refuses Yahweh's offer but promises to refrain from inflicting illness and death on a child if the child wears a protective amulet with the angels' names. If, however, an infant does not have the protection of the amulet, Lilith will have dominion over the child for eight days if it is a male, and for twenty days if it is a female. The sequence of events suggests that Lilith's decision to become a child-slayer emerges as a form of angry retaliation at Yahweh's decree that one hundred of her own offspring be annihilated daily.

Lilith's repudiation of male authority and refusal to circumscribe her sexuality to patriarchal dictates has led to her rejection, degradation, vilification, and demonization by Jewish orthodoxy. Her refusal to lie beneath Adam constitutes a challenge to the prevailing sexual mores of the Hebrews. According to Jewish tradition, a woman who denies her spouse access to her body and/or who refuses to assume the subservient position in frontal copulation commits the heinous crime of abandonment. Hence, whatever positive attributes she may possess immediately convert to negative ones. Accordingly, Lilith is characterized as promiscuous, licentious, devious, and incorrigible. She is depicted as a fiery she-demon who is responsible for the seduction of wayward husbands, for the nocturnal emissions of men who sleep alone, for unbridled promiscuity, and for the killing of innocents.

It is important to note, however, that according to the *Alphabet,* Lilith is, indeed, created as Adam's equal. She is created simultaneously with Adam and is of the same earthy substance as he is. She interprets Adam's insistence that she lie beneath him as a form of tyranny. She is endowed with the power of voice and the power of agency. She is resourceful in that she flees Eden by pronouncing the Ineffable Name of God, indicating that she not only knows the Ineffable Name of God, but that she uses that knowledge to her advantage. She exercises choice by rejecting the offer to return to Eden—a choice that cements her repudiation of male authority. She refuses to compromise her autonomy. And she is prodigiously fertile.

The story of Lilith as told in the *Alphabet* has enjoyed a resurgence of interest in modern culture. Stripping her of the demonic aspects as promulgated in the Kabbalah and the Talmud, modern feminists embrace Lilith as a symbol of female empowerment. Lilith is reimaged as a sympathetic being who dares to challenge the patriarchal paradigm that systematically seeks to circumscribe her right—and the right of all women—to self-determination and autonomy. Because she is situated in a tradition that cannot or will not accommodate strong women, Lilith has been demonized by orthodoxy. She demands the freedom to move, to be herself, and to exercise her own choices. Lilith's position as Adam's first wife, her stubborn refusal to submit to male hegemony, her defiant struggle against oppression, and her unabashed sexuality contribute to perceptions of her as a role model for female autonomy, independence, equality, strength, and courage.

The selections of *The Alphabet of Ben Sira* are from *Rabbinic Fantasies: Imaginative Narratives From Classical Hebrew Literature,* edited by David Stern and Mark J. Mirsky.

REFERENCES

Cantor, Aviva. "Lilith, The Woman Who Would Be A Jew." *Which Lilith: Feminist Writers Re-Create The World's First Woman.* Eds. Enid Dame, Lilly Rivlin, and Henny Wenkart. New Jersey: Jason Aronson, Inc., 1998. 17–22.

Dame, Enid, Lilly Rivlin, and Henny Wenkart, eds. *Which Lilith? Feminist Writers Re-Create The World's First Woman.* New Jersey: Jason Aronson, Inc., 1998.

Koltuv, Barbara Black. *The Book of Lilith.* Maine: Nicolas-Hays, Inc., 1986.

Kvam, Kristen E., Linda Schearing, and Valarie H. Ziegler, eds. *Eve and Adam: Jewish, Christian, and Muslim Readings on Genesis and Gender.* Bloomington and Indianapolis: Indiana UP, 1999.

Myers, Carol, General Ed., and Toni Craven and Ross S. Kraemer, Associate Eds. *Women in Scripture: A Dictionary of Named and Unnamed Women in the*

Hebrew Bible, the Apocryphal/Deuterocanonical Books, and the New Testament. Boston and New York: Houghton Mifflin, 2000.

The New Oxford Annotated Bible With the Apocryphal/Deuterocanonical Books: New Revised Standard. 3rd ed. Ed. Michael D. Coogan. Oxford: Oxford UP, 2001.

Patai, Raphael. *The Hebrew Goddess.* New Jersey: KTAV Publishing House, Inc., 1967.

Pereira, Filomena Maria. *Lilith: The Edge of Forever.* Texas: Ide House, 1998.

Plaskow, Judith. "Lilith Revisited (1995 C.E.)." *Eve and Adam: Jewish, Christian, and Muslim Readings on Genesis and Gender.* Ed. Kristen E. Kvam, Linda S. Schearing, and Valarie H. Ziegler. Bloomington: Indiana UP, 1999. 425–430.

Rivlin, Lilly. "Lilith." *Which Lilith: Feminist Writers Re-Create The World's First Woman.* Eds. Enid Dame, Lilly Rivlin, and Henny Wenkart. New Jersey: Jason Aronson, Inc., 1998. 4–14.

Stern, David and Mark J. Mirsky, eds. *Rabbinic Fantasies: Imaginative Narratives From Classical Hebrew Literature.* New Haven: Yale UP, 1990.

The Alphabet of Ben Sira

V. Soon afterward the young son of the king took ill. Said Nebuchadnezzar, "Heal my son. If you don't, I will kill you." Ben Sira immediately sat down and wrote an amulet with the Holy Name, and he inscribed on it the angels in charge of medicine by their names, forms, and images, and by their wings, hands, and feet. Nebuchadnezzar looked at the amulet. "Who are these?"

"The angels who are in charge of medicine: Snvi, Snsvi, and Smnglof. After God created Adam, who was alone, He said, 'It is not good for man to be alone' (Genesis 2:18). He then created a woman for Adam, from the earth, as He had created Adam himself, and called her Lilith. Adam and Lilith immediately began to fight. She said, 'I will not lie below,' and he said, 'I will not lie beneath you, but only on top. For you are fit only to be in the bottom position, while I am to be in the superior one.' Lilith responded, 'We are equal to each other inasmuch as we were both created from the earth.' But they would not listen to one another. When Lilith saw this, she pronounced the Ineffable Name and flew away into the air. Adam stood in prayer before his Creator: 'Sovereign of the universe!' he said, 'the woman you gave me has run away.' At once, the Holy One, blessed be He, sent these three angels to bring her back.

"Said the Holy One to Adam, 'If she agrees to come back, fine. If not, she must permit one hundred of her children to die every day.' The angels left God and pursued Lilith, whom they overtook in the midst of the sea, in the mighty waters wherein the Egyptians were destined to drown. They told her God's word, but she did not wish to return. The angels said, 'We shall drown you in the sea.'

" 'Leave me!' she said. 'I was created only to cause sickness to infants. If the infant is male, I have dominion over him for eight days after his birth, and if female, for twenty days.'

"When the angels heard Lilith's words, they insisted she go back. But she swore to them by the name of the living and eternal God: 'Whenever I see you or your names or your forms in an amulet, I will have no power over that infant.' She also agreed to have one hundred of her children die every day. Accordingly, every day one hundred demons perish, and for the same reason, we write the angels' names on the amulets of young children. When Lilith sees their names, she remembers her oath, and the child recovers."

Questions for Review and Discussion

1. Ben Sira's miraculous conception identifies him with figures in other religious traditions who experience a similar miraculous conception. Can you identify any such figures? How is their conception similar to and different from the conception of Ben Sira?

2. According to the *Alphabet,* Lilith is created as Adam's equal and is made of the same earthy substance as he is. Why does Adam insist that she lie beneath him?

3. Why does Lilith take such issue with adopting the subordinate position during sexual intercourse? In what ways might her concern reflect something larger than just who assumes what position during copulation?

4. Why was Lilith rejected, demonized, and vilified by later rabbinic scholars? What is it about her that poses such a threat to their beliefs?

5. The image of Lilith as projected by rabbinic scholars fuels a climate of distrust against a certain type of woman. What type of woman is being censured through the condemnation of Lilith?

6. What can you derive about Lilith's attributes by analyzing her conduct? In what ways might she be perceived as a threat to women?

7. How might the demonic characterization of Lilith serve the interests of a male-dominant ideology whose goals are to keep women divided and subordinate to males?

8. What qualities does Lilith demonstrate that can lead to her reimaging as a role model for feminists?

9. Are you familiar with *Lilith Fair: A Celebration of Women in Music*? If so, why do you think the founders of *Lilith Fair* chose the name of Lilith for their festival?

Chapter 12

Eve

GLOSSARY OF NAMES AND TERMS

J SOURCE   Yahwist source; one of the authors (school of authors?) credited with writing sections of books 1–4 of the Old Testament; circa ninth century B.C.E.

HA-ADHAM   The first human being: either male, sexually undifferentiated, or androgynous

P SOURCE   Priestly source; one of the authors (school of authors?) credited with writing sections of books 1–4 of the Old Testament; circa sixth century B.C.E.

YAHWEH   Tansliteration from the Hebrew YHVH; one of the names for God in the Old Testament

Genesis 1 opens with an orderly version of creation in which God assumes center stage as the creator and sustainer of the universe. The act of creation follows a logical sequence that is neatly divided into six consecutive days and culminates with the simultaneous creation of "male and female" on day six. This version of creation is attributed to the Priestly School or the P source, dated approximately the sixth century B.C.E.

Although appearing subsequent to the Priestly version of creation, Genesis 2 contains an earlier version of creation. It is attributed to the J source of the ninth century B.C.E., and it contradicts the P source in a number of ways, not least of which is that it reverses the sequence of creation in the P source. In the J source, man is created before the animals, and woman is fashioned after the animals for the specific purpose of serving as man's ("ha-adham's") helpmate.

The meaning of "ha-adham," the first person created, is fraught with ambiguity and continues to provoke a diversity of responses. Some commentators maintain that the first creature formed is man and that woman is fashioned later from his rib; others maintain that "ha-adham" is a sexually undifferentiated earth creature; while still others maintain that "ha-adham" is actually a generic term for humankind: that the first creature is androgynous; that as such, both male and female hear the deity's admonition against eating the fruit from the tree of knowledge of good and evil; and that the subsequent fashioning of the female from the male's rib is, in effect, a separation and differentiation of the two distinct parts within the one, unified creature that had originally incorporated both sexes.

Man is situated in the garden and told to cultivate it but is prohibited from eating the fruit from the tree of the knowledge of good and evil. Observing the inappropriateness of man's solitary state, Yahweh decides to provide him with a helpmate. He creates animals, parading each in front of man so he can name them. The power to name holds a special significance. Naming delineates, categorizes, defines, and imposes meaning and order. But it also establishes hierarchy: the one being named is subordinate to the one doing the naming. Hence, man has authority over the animals, but this authority has been granted to him by God. Furthermore, by naming and classifying animals, the man emulates the divine action of using speech to designate purpose and place for the elements of creation.

The attempt to find a helpmate for man apparently proves futile: ". . . but for the man there was not found a helper as his partner" (2:20). So Yahweh causes man to fall into a deep sleep, removes one of his ribs, and fashions a female. This could refer to the differentiation of the sexes from the original androgyne, thus indicating that neither sex has priority over the other, that each sex finds fulfillment in the other, and that the two can become one flesh again through sexual intimacy and union. However, if one reads the text as affirmation that the male is created first, then the creation of the woman from the man's body constitutes an instance of a male giving birth—a deviation of the natural order of all living creatures since never before or since has a male been able to give birth. To reinforce this unprecedented and extraordinary relationship, when the man wakes up, he joyously embraces the female and declares: "This one shall be called Woman, for out of Man this one was taken" (2:23). Some commentators maintain that by "birthing" her and then by naming her, the man cements his privileged position in the gender hierarchy. His sovereignty is established; her subordination is augmented.

Genesis provides us with barely a few lines to witness this state before we are plummeted right into the conflict and turmoil of Genesis 3. The serpent appears and attempts to persuade the woman to eat the fruit from the tree of the knowledge of good and evil. The woman responds by relaying her version of the deity's admonition: ". . . but God said, 'You shall not eat of the fruit of the tree that is in the middle of the garden, nor shall you touch it, or you shall die'" (3:3). Unless one subscribes to the androgynous nature of the first creature, Genesis does not indicate that the woman heard the prohibition directly from God. Since God did not forbid the man from "touching" the tree, the woman's extension of an eating prohibition to include a touching prohibition can be attributed either to embellishment on her part or exaggeration on the man's part when he conveys God's prohibition to her. According to the J source, the deity does not engage in direct discourse with the woman exclusively until after the fall when punishment for her transgression is pronounced.

In allowing herself to be persuaded to eat the fruit, the woman experiences three consecutive stages that suggest a progressively higher level of thinking. First, she recognizes that the fruit will satisfy her physical appetite ("good for food"); second, she acknowledges that it will satisfy her aesthetic sensibility ("a delight to the eyes"); and third, that it will satisfy her thirst for knowledge ("that it was to be desired to make one wise"). Her reasoning, therefore, proceeds from a desire to satisfy her basic instinct to a human desire for higher intellect.

In addition, the woman demonstrates an ability to conceptualize and project attributes to the tree not available through sensory observation alone. This suggests that the woman is intelligent, capable of independent decision making, and endowed with the potential for greater complexity in thinking than man. By way of contrast, the man reveals an unsophisticated, unquestioning, and simplistic thought pattern when he later attempts to exonerate himself for his action.

After eating the fruit, the woman gives some to her husband. Both man and woman experience instantaneous transformation: ". . . the eyes of both were opened" (3:7). The impact is immediate. They become aware of their sexual differences and cover their nakedness. Their knowledge of difference rapidly increases and deepens their estrangement from each other and from God. Their interactions become fraught with a dualistic, male/female opposition. When confronted by God for his act of disobedience, the man explains what happened, not why it happened. He provides chronology but not causality. Rather than continuing to perceive her as a complement and source of union, the man proceeds to distance himself from her. Furthermore, in his attempt to exonerate himself, he appears to implicate God: "The woman whom you gave to be with me, she gave me from the tree, and I ate" (3:12). He blames the female first, then God, then himself.

The woman, on the other hand, provides chronology as well as causality: "The serpent tricked me, and I ate" (3:13). Unlike the man, she engages in internal reflection and articulates motivation: she was tricked; she succumbed to the trickery; she acted on it. Like the man, she begins by blaming an "other" (in her case, the serpent) for her action, but unlike him, she does not implicate her partner or the deity in her transgression. Furthermore, she is quicker at accepting responsibility for her action than her male counterpart.

Yahweh then curses the serpent above all animals and decrees that it shall crawl on its belly and eat dust. The serpent is cursed directly and punished; the man and woman are not cursed directly, but they are punished with a gender-specific punishment. The woman's punishment is twofold: she will be punished through her sexuality by experiencing hardship in childbirth: "I will greatly increase your pangs in childbearing; in pain you shall bring forth children" (3:16); and she is punished through a reinforcement of her subordinate position to the male: "Yet your desire shall be for your husband, and he shall rule over you" (3:16). The man, on the other hand, is punished through his labor, which now becomes alienated and fraught with sorrow and hardship. Henceforth, he must struggle to obtain food. Although the man is not cursed directly, his action has an indirect consequence on the earth: ". . . cursed is the ground because of you; in toil you shall eat of it all the days of your life" (3:17). The serpent is cursed directly and punished through the nature of its mobility; the woman is punished through sexuality and gender subservience; the man is punished through labor; the earth is cursed.

The man then renames his wife Eve because "she was the mother of all living" (3:20). The act of renaming signifies a change in the woman's status. No longer

identified exclusively as emerging from the man ("woman"), she will now be identified as the mother of all. The nature of both the naming and renaming suggest that
the female is denied an autonomous identity since she is defined exclusively in
terms of her relationship with others—her "mother"/spouse or her offspring.

The J source then concludes the narrative with the expulsion of Adam and Eve
from the garden. But before expelling them, the deity moderates his action by
clothing them. To deny them access to the tree of life and to ensure that no one
enters the garden unlawfully, the deity places cherubs with flaming swords to guard
its entrance.

The selection below comes from *The New Oxford Annotated Bible With the
Apocryphal/Deuterocanonical Books: New Revised Standard Version.*

REFERENCES

Armstrong, Karen. *In the Beginning: A New Interpretation of Genesis.* New York:
Ballantine, 1996.

Aschkenasy, Nehama. *Woman At the Window: Biblical Tales of Oppression and
Escape.* Detroit: Wayne State UP, 1998.

Bach, Alice, ed. *Women in the Hebrew Bible: A Reader.* New York: Routledge, 1999.

Eisler, Riane. *The Chalice and the Blade: Our History, Our Future.* San Francisco:
Harper, 1989.

Friedman, Richard Elliott. *Who Wrote The Bible?* New York: Harper, 1987.

Frymer-Kensky, Tikva. *In the Wake of the Goddesses: Women, Culture, and the Biblical Transformation of Pagan Myth.* New York: Fawcett Columbine, 1992.

Gadon, Elinor W. *The Once and Future Goddess: A Symbol For Our Time.* San
Francisco: Harper, 1989.

Harris, Kevin. *Sex, Ideology, and Religion: The Representation of Women in the
Bible.* New Jersey: Barnes and Noble, 1984.

Jones, Alexander, Gen. Ed. *The Jerusalem Bible: Reader's Edition.* New York: Doubleday and Co., Inc., 1968.

Kimelman, Reuven. "The Seduction of Eve and the Exegetical Politics of Gender."
Women in the Hebrew Bible: A Reader. Ed. Alice Bach. New York: Routledge,
1999. 241–269.

Kvam, Kristen E, Linda S. Schearing, and Valarie H. Ziegler, eds. *Eve and Adam:
Jewish, Christian, and Muslim Readings on Genesis and Gender.* Bloomington:
Indiana UP, 1999.

Lerner, Gerda. *The Creation of Patriarchy.* New York: Oxford UP, 1986.

Miles, Jack. *God: A Biography.* New York: Vintage, 1996.

*The New Oxford Annotated Bible With the Apocryphal/Deuterocanonical Books:
New Revised Standard.* 3rd ed. Ed. Michael D. Coogan. Oxford: Oxford UP,
2001.

Pagels, Elaine. *Adam, Eve, and the Serpent.* New York: Random House, 1988.

Phipps, William E. *Assertive Biblical Women.* Connecticut: Greenwood P, 1992.

Stone, Merlin. *When God Was a Woman.* San Diego: Harcourt Brace Jovanovich, 1976.

Trible, Phyllis. *God and the Rhetoric of Sexuality.* Philadelphia: Fortress, 1978.

———. "Eve and Adam: Genesis 2–3 Reread [1993 C.E.]." *Eve and Adam: Jewish, Christian, and Muslim Readings on Genesis and Gender.* Ed. Kristen E. Kvam, Linda S. Schearing, and Valarie H. Ziegler. Bloomington: Indiana UP, 1999. 430–438.

———. "Not a Jot, Not a Tittle: Genesis 2–3 After Twenty Years [1995 C.E.]." *Eve and Adam: Jewish, Christian, and Muslim Readings on Genesis and Gender.* Ed. Kristen E. Kvam, Linda S. Schearing, and Valarie H. Ziegler. Bloomington: Indiana UP, 1999. 439–444.

Genesis

1 In the beginning when God created[a] the heavens and the earth, [2]the earth was a formless void and darkness covered the face of the deep, while a wind from God[b] swept over the face of the waters. [3]Then God said, "Let there be light"; and there was light. [4]And God saw that the light was good; and God separated the light from the darkness. [5]God called the light Day, and the darkness he called Night. And there was evening and there was morning, the first day.

6 And God said, "Let there be a dome in the midst of the waters, and let it separate the waters from the waters." [7]So God made the dome and separated the waters that were under the dome from the waters that were above the dome. And it was so. [8]God called the dome Sky. And there was evening and there was morning, the second day.

9 And God said, "Let the waters under the sky be gathered together into one place, and let the dry land appear." And it was so. [10]God called the dry land Earth, and the waters that were gathered together he called Seas. And God saw that it was good. [11]Then God said, "Let the earth put forth vegetation: plants yielding seed, and fruit trees of every kind on earth that bear fruit with the seed in it." And it was so. [12]The earth brought forth vegetation: plants yielding seed of every kind, and trees of every kind bearing fruit with the seed in it. And God saw that it was good. [13]And there was evening and there was morning, the third day.

14 And God said, "Let there be lights in the dome of the sky to separate the day from the night; and let them be for signs and for seasons and for days and years, [15]and let them be lights in the dome of the sky to give light upon the earth." And it was so. [16]God made the two great lights—the greater light to rule

[a]Or *when God began to create* or *In the beginning God created*
[b]Or *while the spirit of God* or *while a mighty wind*

the day and the lesser light to rule the night—and the stars. [17]God set them in the dome of the sky to give light upon the earth, [18]to rule over the day and over the night, and to separate the light from the darkness. And God saw that it was good. [19]And there was evening and there was morning, the fourth day.

20 And God said, "Let the waters bring forth swarms of living creatures, and let birds fly above the earth across the dome of the sky." [21]So God created the great sea monsters and every living creature that moves, of every kind, with which the waters swarm, and every winged bird of every kind. And God saw that it was good. [22]God blessed them, saying, "Be fruitful and multiply and fill the waters in the seas, and let birds multiply on the earth." [23]And there was evening and there was morning, the fifth day.

24 And God said, "Let the earth bring forth living creatures of every kind: cattle and creeping things and wild animals of the earth of every kind." And it was so. [25]God made the wild animals of the earth of every kind, and the cattle of every kind, and everything that creeps upon the ground of every kind. And God saw that it was good.

26 Then God said, "Let us make humankind[a] in our image, according to our likeness; and let them have dominion over the fish of the sea, and over the birds of the air, and over the cattle, and over all the wild animals of the earth,[b] and over every creeping thing that creeps upon the earth."
[27]So God created humankind in his
>   image,
> in the image of God he created
>   them;[c]
> male and female he created them.

[28]God blessed them, and God said to them, "Be fruitful and multiply, and fill the earth and subdue it; and have dominion over the fish of the sea and over the birds of the air and over every living thing that moves upon the earth." [29]God said, "See, I have given you every plant yielding seed that is upon the face of all the earth, and every tree with seed in its fruit; you shall have them for food. [30]And to every beast of the earth, and to every bird of the air, and to everything that creeps on the earth, everything that has the breath of life, I have given every green plant for food." And it was so. [31]God saw everything that he had made, and indeed, it was very good. And there was evening and there was morning, the sixth day.

2 Thus the heavens and the earth were finished, and all their multitude. [2]And on the seventh day God finished the work that he had done, and he rested on the seventh day from all the work that he had done. [3]So God blessed

[a]Heb *adam*
[b]Syr: Heb *and over all the earth*
[c]Heb *him*

the seventh day and hallowed it, because on it God rested from all the work that he had done in creation.

4 These are the generations of the heavens and the earth when they were created.

In the day that the LORD[a] God made the earth and the heavens, [5]when no plant of the field was yet in the earth and no herb of the field was yet in the earth and no herb of the field had yet sprung up—for the LORD God had not caused it to rain upon the earth, and there was no one to till the ground; [6]but a stream would rise from the earth, and water the whole face of the ground—[7]then the LORD God formed man from the dust of the ground,[b] and breathed into his nostrils the breath of life; and the man became a living being. [8]And the LORD God planted a garden in Eden, in the east; and there he put the man whom he had formed. [9]Out of the ground the LORD God made to grow every tree that is pleasant to the sight and good for food, the tree of life also in the midst of the garden, and the tree of the knowledge of good and evil.

10 A river flows out of Eden to water the garden, and from there it divides and becomes four branches. [11]The name of the first is Pishon; it is the one that flows around the whole land of Havilah, where there is gold; [12]and the gold of that land is good; bdellium and onyx stone are there. [13]The name of the second river is Gihon; it is the one that flows around the whole land of Cush. [14]The name of the third river is Tigris, which flows east of Assyria. And the fourth river is the Euphrates.

15 The LORD God took the man and put him in the garden of Eden to till it and keep it. [16]And the LORD God commanded the man, "You may freely eat of every tree of the garden; [17]but of the tree of the knowledge of good and evil you shall not eat, for in the day that you eat of it you shall die."

18 Then the LORD God said; "It is not good that the man should be alone; I will make him a helper as his partner." [19]So out of the ground the LORD God formed every animal of the field and every bird of the air, and brought them to the man to see what he would call them; and whatever the man called every living creature, that was its name. [20]The man gave names to all cattle, and to the birds of the air, and to every animal of the field; but for the man[c] there was not found a helper as his partner. [21]So the LORD God caused a deep sleep to fall upon the man, and he slept; then he took one of his ribs and closed up its place with flesh. [22]And the rib that the LORD God had taken from the man he made into a woman and brought her to the man. [23]Then the man said,

---

[a]Heb YHWH, as in other places where "LORD" is spelled with capital letters (see also Exod 3.14–15 with notes).
[b]Or *formed a man* (Heb *adam*) *of dust from the ground* (Heb *adamah*)
[c]Or *for Adam*

"This at last is bone of my bones
    and flesh of my flesh;
    this one shall be called Woman,[a]
      for out of Man[b] this one was
        taken."

[24]Therefore a man leaves his father and his mother and clings to his wife, and they become one flesh. [25]And the man and his wife were both naked, and were not ashamed.

3 Now the serpent was more crafty than any other wild animal that the Lord God had made. He said to the woman, "Did God say, 'You shall not eat from any tree in the garden'?" [2]The woman said to the serpent, "We may eat of the fruit of the trees in the garden; [3]but God said, 'You shall not eat of the fruit of the tree that is in the middle of the garden, nor shall you touch it, or you shall die.'" [4]But the serpent said to the woman, "You will not die; [5]for God knows that when you eat of it your eyes will be opened, and you will be like God,[c] knowing good and evil." [6]So when the woman saw that the tree was good for food, and that it was a delight to the eyes, and that the tree was to be desired to make one wise, she took of its fruit and ate; and she also gave some to her husband, who was with her, and he ate. [7]Then the eyes of both were opened, and they knew that they were naked; and they sewed fig leaves together and made loincloths for themselves.

8 They heard the sound of the Lord God walking in the garden at the time of the evening breeze, and the man and his wife hid themselves from the presence of the Lord God among the trees of the garden. [9]But the Lord God called to the man, and said to him, "Where are you?" [10]He said, "I heard the sound of you in the garden, and I was afraid, because I was naked; and I hid myself." [11]He said, "Who told you that you were naked? Have you eaten from the tree of which I commanded you not to eat?" [12]The man said, "The woman whom you gave to be with me, she gave me fruit from the tree, and I ate." [13]Then the Lord God said to the woman, "What is this that you have done?" The woman said, "The serpent tricked me, and I ate." [14]The Lord God said to the serpent,

"Because you have done this,
    cursed are you among all animals
    and among all wild creatures;
upon your belly you shall go,
    and dust you shall eat
    all the days of your life.

[a]Heb *ishshah*
[b]Heb *ish*
[c]Or *gods*

[15]I will put enmity between you and the woman,
    and between your offspring and hers;
he will strike your head,
    and you will strike his heel."
[16]To the woman he said,
  "I will greatly increase your pangs in childbearing;
    in pain you shall bring forth children,
yet your desire shall be for your husband,
    and he shall rule over you."
[17]And to the man[a] he said,
  "Because you have listened to the voice of your wife,
    and have eaten of the tree
about which I commanded you,
  'You shall not eat of it,'
cursed is the ground because of you;
    in toil you shall eat of it all the days of your life;
[18]thorns and thistles it shall bring forth for you;
    and you shall eat the plants of the field.
[19]By the sweat of your face
    you shall eat bread
until you return to the ground,
    for out of it you were taken;
you are dust,
    and to dust you shall return."

20 The man named his wife Eve,[b] because she was the mother of all living. [21]And the LORD God made garments of skins for the man[c] and for his wife, and clothed them.

22 Then the LORD God said, "See, the man has become like one of us, knowing good and evil; and now, he might reach out his hand and take also from the tree of life, and eat, and live forever"—[23]therefore the LORD God sent him forth from the garden of Eden, to till the ground from which he was taken. [24]He drove out the man; and at the east of the garden of Eden he placed the cherubim, and a sword flaming and turning to guard the way to the tree of life.

Questions for Review and Discussion

1. The gender of the first creature continues to be debated. Was the first human an androgynous being ("humankind")? Or was it exclusively male from whose rib

[a]Or to Adam
[b]In Heb Eve resembles the word for living
[c]Or for Adam

the female was later created? If the latter interpretation is correct, what is the significance of Yahweh breathing directly into man's nostrils but apparently not doing the same to the woman when she was fashioned from man's rib?

2. Even if the text indicates that the female is a later creation from man's rib, what arguments can be made to support the position that the sequence of her creation does not disparage the female?

3. The text tells us that after creating the animals, the deity brings them to man to name. However, after fashioning woman, Yahweh takes her to man but does not give him a similar directive to name her. Even without such a directive, man declares, "This one shall be called Woman." Why is it significant that man does not receive a naming directive for woman?

4. What conclusions can you draw about the nature of the woman and the man based on their rationale and later explanations for eating the forbidden fruit?

5. The story of Adam and Eve has been interpreted as a metaphor for humanity rising from a state of childhood innocence to a state of adulthood—a transformation precipitated by their eating from the tree of the knowledge of good and evil. What arguments can be made to support this position? What arguments can be made to support the opposing position, namely, that the conduct of the human pair after their disobedience reflects less maturity and further regression?

6. Why does the serpent speak to the woman and not to the man? By contrast, in the Islamic tradition, the serpent speaks either to Adam or to Adam and Hawwa (Eve) simultaneously, but never to Hawwa alone. How might this significant difference lead to a difference in interpreting the nature and role of the female in the original transgression?

7. Also, in the Islamic tradition, Adam and Hawwa receive the identical punishment: expulsion from the garden. There is no mention of a gender-specific punishment for the first human couple in the *Qur'an*. How might this lead to a difference in interpretation from the Hebrew text concerning the consequences for the transgression?

8. When confronted by God for his transgression, the man immediately blames the woman. Similarly, when the woman is confronted, she blames the serpent. Neither appears willing to accept moral culpability for his/her actions. Instead, each finds an "other" to blame. What does this shifting of blame indicate about the nature of the relationship between the man and the woman and between them and God? How have these relationships changed since the human pair was first created?

9. How might the story of Adam and Eve legitimize and reinforce patriarchy? How might it critique and subvert patriarchal ideology?

Chapter 13

Virgin Mary

GLOSSARY OF NAMES AND TERMS

ANNA Prophetess in temple in Jerusalem who acknowledges Jesus as Messiah

BLACK MADONNA Also known as Black Virgin; statues of Virgin Mary with black face and hands

ELIZABETH Cousin of Virgin Mary; mother of John the Baptist; married to Zechariah

GOSPEL OF JOHN Written circa 90 C.E.; definitive identity of author is unknown

GOSPEL OF LUKE Written circa 80–85 C.E.; definitive identity of author is unknown

GOSPEL OF MARK Written circa 30 C.E.; definitive identity of author is unknown

GOSPEL OF MATTHEW Written circa 80–85 C.E.; definitive identity of author is unknown

JOSEPH Spouse of the Virgin Mary

MAGNIFICAT The Virgin Mary's longest speech; a response to Elizabeth's words of

praise in which she thanks God for selecting her to receive His blessings

MATER DOLOROSA Also known as Mother of Sorrows; weeps because of the immolation of her son

SIMEON Prophet in temple in Jerusalem who acknowledges Jesus as Messiah

SYNOPTIC GOSPELS Reference to the gospels of Matthew, Mark, and Luke because they can be situated alongside each other

THEOPHILUS Identity unknown; may have been a Roman administrator or official; Gospel of Luke is dedicated to him

VIRGIN MARY Also referred to as Miriam or Maria; virgin mother of Jesus

ZECHARIAH Father of John the Baptist; married to Mary's cousin, Elizabeth

Christianity, which began in the Middle East 2,000 years ago, was founded by the followers of Jesus Christ of Nazareth. Adherents of Christianity, known as Christians, believe that there is only one God, but unlike their Jewish and Muslim counterparts, they believe that this one God consists of three "persons" or entities, known as the Trinity: God the Father, God the Son, and God the Holy Spirit. Their holy book consists of the Old and New Testament of the Bible. They worship in churches and their spiritual leaders are called priests or ministers.

Christians believe that Jesus Christ is the son of God, sent to earth to redeem humanity from the consequences of its sins and to open the path to salvation. Conceived miraculously of the Virgin Mary, Jesus lived his life as a human being. Little is known about his early life until he began his ministry at about the age of thirty. He healed the sick, performed miracles, and preached a message of equality, love, compassion, and forgiveness. He sought out the disenfranchised, the poor, the disabled, the weak, the elderly, and women, embracing them as equals worthy of love and respect. Christians believe that Jesus was tortured and died on the cross for the sins of humanity and that he rose from the dead on the third day after his crucifixion. He is perceived as the Messiah ("the anointed one") promised in the Old Testament. Through his life, death, and resurrection, Jesus was able to restore human beings to their correct relationship with God.

Christians seek to live their lives according to the example set by Jesus: loving God, loving their fellow human beings, and treating them as equals in the sight of God. They believe in the Day of Judgment, a day when all souls will be judged according to the way each has lived. Eternal damnation in hell awaits those souls which have deviated from the path of God; eternal happiness in paradise awaits those souls which have adhered faithfully to the path of God. Currently, there are many denominations within the Christian faith, all of which agree on the basic tenets of Christianity, but each of which adheres to a different set of traditions and customs based on unique interpretations of the Bible that are deemed closer to Jesus' original intentions and message.

Little was known about the early Christian movement after the death of Christ until the 1940s when a discovery was made in the town of Nag Hammadi in Egypt. It was here that a Bedouin accidentally stumbled upon a jar containing religious manuscripts from approximately the second century C.E. Textual analysis of these manuscripts, consisting of gospels, epistles, teachings, and apocalypses, reveals a wide divergence of traditions. This led scholars to conclude that the early Christian movement that emerged following the death of Jesus in 30 C.E. consisted of a multiplicity of groups embracing conflicting views on many issues.

Scholars have been aware for some time that the body of texts comprising the New Testament canon emerged out of a series of internal conflicts and debates. With the domination of the orthodox tradition, alternative texts that contradicted or did not adhere to the orthodox agenda were systematically rejected, destroyed, or suppressed. The New Testament canon as we know it, therefore, consists of a particular strand of Christianity whose writings have survived because of consensus on authorship and because of shared political and religious ideology. Orthodoxy deemed certain texts worthy of inclusion into the canon while it rejected other early Christian writings that did not promote the same ideology. These debates and discussions about what to include and what to exclude continued for many years, and it wasn't until 367 C.E. that the New Testament canon emerged in the definitive form it has today. However, what constitutes canon continues to differ within several branches of Christianity, and what Catholics accept as canonical texts are perceived as apocryphal by several Protestant churches.

Composed approximately between the years 50–120 C.E., the New Testament consists of four sections: the Gospels, Acts, the Epistles, and the Book of Revelation. The Gospels ("good news") proclaim the good news through narratives about the life, death, and resurrection of Jesus; Acts address the early history of Christianity after Jesus' death; the Epistles are a series of letters written by Christian leaders to their communities in which they address matters of theology and praxis; and the Book of Revelation describes events culminating in the destruction of this world and the arrival of the next.

Definitive authorship of the four gospels continues to be debated. Orthodox claims that the gospels of Matthew and John were written by two of the disciples of Jesus and that the gospels of Mark and Luke were written by two associates of the apostles Peter and Paul have been called into question. The gospels themselves make no such claim about authorship, choosing instead to keep their authors' identities anonymous. The Gospel of Mark was written over 30 years after the death of Jesus, while the Gospel of John was written well over 60 years after the death of Jesus. Situated between the two are the gospels of Luke and Matthew, written between 80–85 C.E., over fifty years after Jesus' death. Textual evidence suggests that the authors of the gospels constructed their narratives by relying heavily on written and oral sources that had been circulating among several Christian communities for many years.

The gospels of Matthew, Mark, and Luke are called the "Synoptic Gospels" because they share common narratives, which can be placed alongside each other (synoptic means "seen together"). These three gospels not only share the same stories, but they occasionally tell the story verbatim. A comparative analysis of the synoptic gospels has led scholars to hypothesize that Matthew and Luke used Mark and one other source to construct their narratives. Additionally, Matthew and Luke each relied on at least one other source that is not shared by any other gospel.

The Virgin Mary rarely appears in the New Testament, and when she does appear, she is not always mentioned by name. Sometimes a reference is made to her presence. Occasionally, she is referred to as Miriam or Maria. She appears in Luke more frequently than in any of the other gospels, which is not surprising since Luke includes more passages dealing with women than do his counterparts. Matthew mentions the Virgin Mary only once after he provides the account of Jesus' birth, but he does not give her voice nor address her directly. Mark mentions her for a total of four lines, and John never mentions her by name but by her role as mother.

The selection below from the Gospel of Luke 1–2 is known as the infancy narrative. Unlike the other gospels, Luke provides a story of the annunciation of the birth of Jesus to the Virgin Mary and her reaction to the announcement (1:28–38). His account of the Virgin birth is presented through Mary's point of view, unlike the account in Matthew which privileges Joseph's point of view. Luke tells us twice that Mary pondered things in her heart (2:19, 51), indicating that Mary reflects on events. And, finally, Luke gives Mary voice: she speaks to the angel Gabriel; she sings praises to God in the Magnificat; and she chastises Jesus in the temple in Jerusalem for causing his parents such anxiety.

Luke begins his gospel by acknowledging that his narratives are based on materials that have been transmitted by "eyewitnesses and servants of the word." Although Luke dedicates the work to a "most excellent Theophilus," he never reveals the specific identity of this individual. Scholars have speculated that Theophilus may have been a Roman administrator or government official; others have argued that the text was written for a Christian audience and that since the name Theophilus literally means "beloved of God," Luke was utilizing the name as code for his Christian audience.

Luke opens his narrative with the angel's announcement to Zechariah that his wife, Elizabeth, will conceive a child named John; a subsequent announcement to Elizabeth's cousin, the Virgin Mary, about her forthcoming conception; Mary's visit to Elizabeth; Elizabeth's greeting, acknowledging Mary as the "mother of my lord;" Mary's response, known as the Magnificat (1:46–55); her return to Nazareth; the birth of John; and Zechariah's prophecy concerning the coming of Jesus. In this manner, the narratives of the dual conceptions and births are intertwined, with Mary and Elizabeth emerging as prominent figures who articulate God's plan and who serve as vehicles for its implementation.

In his description of the annunciation, Luke emphasizes that although Mary was well aware of the social humiliation and stigmatization associated with being pregnant and unwed, she accepts her fate with equanimity. Like Zechariah who had earlier questioned the angel about his aging wife's ability to conceive, Mary, too, questions her ability to conceive since she is a virgin. When the angel reassures her that the Holy Spirit will descend upon her and she will give birth to a holy child who will be called, "the Son of the most high," her response is unequivocal submission to the will of God. The same unequivocal submission is reiterated in the Magnificat, which she recites when responding to Elizabeth's words of praise for her. The Magnificat, Mary's longest speech in the Bible, reverberates with words from the Old Testament. In it, she praises God for selecting her as the recipient of His blessings, and she situates God's action as part of a larger context.

Luke 2 opens with Joseph and Mary leaving Nazareth for Bethlehem in order to register with the census; the birth of Jesus in a manger; the reference to Jesus as Mary's "firstborn son," leaving open the possibility that Mary had other children; the visit of the three shepherds; Jesus' circumcision; the visit to the temple in Jerusalem where Jesus is acknowledged by the prophets Simeon and Anna as the long awaited Messiah; and the return to Nazareth. It concludes with the story of the now twelve-year-old Jesus wandering off in the temple in Jerusalem to engage in religious dialogue with Jewish elders, his mother's subsequent reprimand for causing them such concern, and his return to Nazareth with his parents.

Mary's chastisement of Jesus for his behavior has raised problems and generated much debate among Christians. Interpretations for her actions vary and cover a broad spectrum of views: that it is culturally inappropriate for a mother to chastise her child since she appears to be usurping the father's role; that Mary should understand her subordinate position in relationship to her son; that her rebuke is perfectly legitimate when situated in the context of a mother's sheer terror at discovering she does not know the current whereabouts of her child; and that there has been some evidence to suggest that the entire episode of Jesus in the temple was not originally part of the Lukan narrative but attached to it later. Jesus' response that he must be in his father's house not only fails to address Mary's concern but appears to some commentators as a perfunctory dismissal of it. Luke 2 concludes with Jesus' return to Nazareth with his parents where, we are told, he was "obedient to them." This additional piece of information perhaps serves to mitigate the harshness of Jesus' earlier remark to his mother.

The Roman Catholic Church has articulated four mandatory articles of faith concerning the Virgin: she is the mother of God, as declared in the Council of Ephesus in 431 C.E.; she conceived Jesus with her virginity intact (her state as a perpetual virgin being declared by Christian leaders in the Lateran Council of 649 C.E.); she was conceived through Immaculate Conception which exempted her from the taint of original sin, making her worthy of carrying the Christ child in her womb (declared dogma in 1854); and she was assumed into heaven in both body and soul (declared dogma in 1950).

As the Mother of God, Mary continues a long tradition that goes back for centuries. Her qualities parallel many of the qualities of the Great Goddess of prepatriarchal times. The Great Goddess, worshipped for thousands of years before the onset of patriarchy, gave birth to a divine child who was both her son and her consort. Similarly, Mary gives birth to a divine child. Like the Great Goddess, Mary conceives parthenogenetically, that is to say, without male insemination. By doing so, she incarnates the divine rather than the human. She is associated with fertility and purportedly bestows fecundity to her devotees through her shrines and relics. She gives birth to Jesus on December 25, a date that was chosen to displace the older celebrations and a day that falls within the winter solstice (between December 21 and 26) when our ancient ancestors traditionally celebrated the Goddess's birthing of the sun. Just as the Goddess's son/consort dies and is resurrected annually to assure earthly fertility and renewal, the son of Mary dies and is resurrected, but in his case, the goal is to assure spiritual renewal. Mary has been referred to as the divine feminine and the feminine face of God. In her capacity as the Mater Dolorosa or Mother of Sorrows, she weeps because of her son's suffering and sacrifice, which recalls the Goddess in her different cultural manifestations as the bereaved mother who has lost her beloved child/consort. Images of Mary nursing her son are adopted from ancient Egyptian images of Isis nursing her son Horus. And as is the case with Isis, Mary's milk assumes sacred, life-nourishing qualities. Finally, Mary is known as the Queen of Heaven, a title that once belonged to Inanna of ancient Sumer, among others.

However, in spite of these parallels, there is one fundamental difference: the monotheistic vision of Christianity has no room for a goddess. The Virgin Mary is not divine. She is an exceptional mortal who undoubtedly plays a pivotal role in the birth of a god, but she is a mortal, nevertheless. The Goddess is grounded in earth and nature; the Virgin Mary, through her Immaculate Conception and Virgin

Birth, transcends nature. Images of the Great Goddess with her child serve as potent symbols of her sexuality, autonomy, and procreativity; images of the Virgin Mary with her child, on the other hand, serve as potent symbols of her chastity, purity, and submission to the will of a higher power. It has been argued that unlike the Great Goddess, who was worshipped as the all-powerful, all-embracing, all-sustaining creatrix, some traditions within Christianity have stripped the Virgin Mary of her sacred powers and relegated her to the margins as a subordinate figure in a drama that privileges a male deity. Attitudes toward the Virgin run the full spectrum from attempts to minimize her role to so high an exaltation of her stature and powers that she blurs the delineation between the human and the divine.

Goddess worship, although it was severely suppressed for many centuries, never entirely disappeared from view. Instead, it persisted, surfacing periodically in a variety of guises throughout history. It is openly practiced today, and some adherents argue that the ubiquitous and ongoing cult of the Virgin Mary attests to the strength of the movement. The belief that Mary is situated in the realm of the divine has been perpetuated and sustained by a popular tradition that conflicts with official Church teachings that attempt to dilute her power and subordinate it to that of her son.

An example of the possible convergence of goddess worship with the Virgin Mary can be seen in the phenomenon of the Black Virgin or Black Madonna, several hundred images and statues of the Virgin Mary portrayed with a black face and hands, most of which have been located in Western Europe (especially Spain, the most famous being Montserrat), and South America. Many of these statues occupy locations that were once used for prepatriarchal goddess worship. Although the Church attributes the blackness of these images to smoke pollution or exposure to the elements, this explanation is not entirely satisfactory since clothing of these statues has not undergone similar discoloration. The origin of the Black Virgin and the extent of her cult and influence have yet to be determined, but she has been hailed as visual evidence of the survival of goddess worship, her blackness denoting her earlier association with the dark, rich, fertile soil; earthly regeneration and replenishment; and the mysterious forces of life, death, and cosmic renewal.

The continued veneration of the Virgin Mary outside some circles of Christian orthodoxy has been cited as a reemergence of goddess worship. Even among official voices of the Church, there is a clamor to make Mary "Medatrix of all grace," a position that would place her equal with her son. Orthodoxy's fierce resistance to the deification of Mary is perceived as testament to the lingering power of an earlier tradition of goddess worship that refuses to be suppressed or silenced. According to this view, the tenacity with which both men and women have clung to an image of a compassionate and merciful feminine deity throughout history and throughout her many cultural manifestations satisfies a human hunger for a reassuring, nurturing, encompassing, mother-of-all figure—a hunger that refuses to be satiated.

The selection below from the Gospel according to Luke 1–2 is from *The New Oxford Annotated Bible With the Apocryphal/Deuterocanonical Books: New Revised Standard Verision.*

REFERENCES

Armstrong, Karen. *The Gospel According to Woman.* New York: Anchor, 1986.

Ashe, Geoffrey. *The Virgin.* London: Routledge and Kegan Paul, 1976.

Brown, Raymond E., Karl P. Donfried, Joseph A. Fitzmyer, and John Reumann, eds. *Mary in the New Testament: A Collaborative Assessment by Protestant and Roman Catholic Scholars.* Philadelphia: Fortress P, 1978.

Christ, Carol P. *Laughter of Aphrodite: Reflections on the Journey to the Goddess.* San Francisco: Harper and Row, 1987.

Drury, Clare. "Christianity." *Women in Religion.* Ed. Jean Holm and John Bowker. London: Pinter, 1999. 30–58.

Ehrman, Bart D. *The New Testament: A Historical Introduction to the Early Christian Writings.* 2nd ed. New York: Oxford UP, 2000.

———. *The New Testament and Other Early Christian Writings: A Reader.* New York: Oxford UP, 1998.

Eisler, Riane. *The Chalice and the Blade: Our History, Our Future.* San Francisco: HarperCollins, 1988.

Fiorenza, Elisabeth Schussler. *In Memory of Her: A Feminist Theological Reconstruction of Christian Origins.* New York: Crossroad, 1992.

Gadon, Elinor W. *The Once and Future Goddess: A Symbol for Our Time.* San Francisco: Harper, 1989.

Gardini, Walter. "The Feminine Aspect of God in Christianity." *Women in the World's Religions, Past and Present.* Ed. Ursula King. New York: Paragon House, 1987. 56–67.

Gaventa, Beverly Roberts. *Mary: Glimpses of the Mother of Jesus.* Minneapolis: Fortress P, 1999.

Harvey, Andrew, and Anne Baring. *The Divine Feminine: Exploring the Feminine Face of God Throughout the World.* Berkeley: Conari P, 1996.

Johnson, Elizabeth A. *Truly Our Sister: A Theology of Mary in the Communion of Saints.* New York: Continuum, 2003.

Kinsley, David. *The Goddess' Mirror: Visions of the Divine From East and West.* Albany: State U of New York P, 1989.

Long, Asphodel P. *In a Chariot Drawn by Lions: The Search for the Female in Deity.* Freedom: Crossing P, 1993.

Matter, E. Ann. "The Virgin Mary: A Goddess?" *The Book of the Goddess Past and Present: An Introduction to Her Religion.* Ed. Carl Olson. New York: Crossroad, 1990. 80–96.

The New Oxford Annotated Bible: New Revised Standard Version With Apocrypha. 3rd ed. Oxford: Oxford UP, 2001.

Nunnally-Cox, Janice. *Foremothers: Women of the Bible.* New York: Seabury, 1981.

Pagels, Elaine. *The Gnostic Gospels.* New York: Vintage, 1989.

Schaberg, Jane. *The Illegitimacy of Jesus: A Feminist Theological Interpretation of the Infancy Narratives.* San Francisco: Harper and Row, 1987.

Schotroff, Luise. *Let the Oppressed Go Free: Feminist Perspectives on the New Testament.* Trans. Annemarie S. Kidder. Louisville: Westminster/John Knox P, 1993.

Via, E. Jane. "Women in the Gospel of Luke." *Women in the World's Religions, Past and Present.* Ed. Ursula King. New York: Paragon House, 1987. 38–55.

Warner, Marina. *Alone of All Her Sex: The Myth and The Cult of the Virgin Mary.* New York: Alfred A. Knopf, 1976.

Luke 1–2

1 Since many have undertaken to set down an orderly account of the events that have been fulfilled among us, [2]just as they were handed on to us by those who from the beginning were eyewitnesses and servants of the word, [3]I too decided, after investigating everything carefully from the very first,[a] to write an orderly account for you, most excellent Theophilus, [4]so that you may know the truth concerning the things about which you have been instructed.

5 In the days of King Herod of Judea, there was a priest named Zechariah, who belonged to the priestly order of Abijah. His wife was a descendant of Aaron, and her name was Elizabeth. [6]Both of them were righteous before God, living blamelessly according to all the commandments and regulations of the Lord. [7]But they had no children, because Elizabeth was barren, and both were getting on in years.

8 Once when he was serving as priest before God and his section was on duty, [9]he was chosen by lot, according to the custom of the priesthood, to enter the sanctuary of the Lord and offer incense. [10]Now at the time of the incense offering, the whole assembly of the people was praying outside. [11]Then there appeared to him an angel of the Lord, standing at the right side of the altar of incense. [12]When Zechariah saw him, he was terrified; and fear overwhelmed him. [13]But the angel said to him, "Do not be afraid, Zechariah, for your prayer has been heard. Your wife Elizabeth will bear you a son, and you will name him John. [14]You will have joy and gladness, and many will rejoice at his birth, [15]for he will be great in the sight of the Lord. He must never drink wine or strong drink; even before his birth he will be filled with the Holy Spirit. [16]He will turn many of the people of Israel to the Lord their God. [17]With the spirit and power of Elijah he will go before him, to turn the hearts of parents to their children, and the disobedient to the wisdom of the righteous, to make ready a people

[a]*Or for a long time*

prepared for the Lord. [18]Zechariah said to the angel, "How will I know that this is so? For I am an old man, and my wife is getting on in years." [19]The angel replied, "I am Gabriel. I stand in the presence of God, and I have been sent to speak to you and to bring you this good news. [20]But now, because you did not believe my words, which will be fulfilled in their time, you will become mute, unable to speak, until the day these things occur."

21 Meanwhile the people were waiting for Zechariah, and wondered at his delay in the sanctuary. [22]When he did come out he could not speak to them, and they realized that he had seen a vision in the sanctuary. He kept motioning to them and remained unable to speak. [23]When his time of service was ended, he went to his home.

24 After those days his wife Elizabeth conceived, and for five months she remained in seclusion. She said, [25]"This is what the Lord has done for me when he looked favorably on me and took away the disgrace I have endured among my people."

26 In the sixth month the angel Gabriel was sent by God to a town in Galilee called Nazareth, [27]to a virgin engaged to a man whose name was Joseph, of the house of David. The virgin's name was Mary. [28]And he came to her and said, "Greetings, favored one! The Lord is with you."[b] [29]But, he was much perplexed by his words and wondered what sort of greeting this might be. [30]The angel said to her, "Do not be afraid, Mary, for you have found favor with God. [31]And now, you will conceive in your womb and bear a son, and you will name him Jesus. [32]He will be great, and will be called the Son of the Most High, and the Lord God will give to him the throne of his ancestor David. [33]He will reign over the house of Jacob forever, and of his kingdom there will be no end." [34]Mary said to the angel, "How can this be since I am a virgin?"[c] [35]The angel said to her, "The Holy Spirit will come upon you, and the power of the Most High will overshadow you; therefore the child to be born[d] will be holy; he will be called Son of God. [36]And now, your relative Elizabeth in old age has also conceived a son; and this is the sixth month for her who was said to be barren. [37]For nothing will be impossible with God." [38]Then Mary said, "Here am I, the servant of the Lord; let it be with me according to your word." Then the angel departed from her.

In those days Mary set out and went with haste to a Judean town in the hill country, [40]where she entered the house of Zechariah and greeted Elizabeth.[41]When Elizabeth heard Mary's greeting, the child leaped in her womb. And Elizabeth was filled with the Holy Spirit [42]and exclaimed with a loud cry, "Blessed are you among women, and blessed is the fruit of your womb. [43]And why has this happened to me that the mother of my Lord comes

[b]Other ancient authorities add *Blessed are you among women*
[c]Gk *I do not know a man*
[d]Other ancient authorities add *of you*

to me? [44]For as soon as I heard the sound of your greeting, the child in my womb leaped for joy. [45]And blessed is she who believed that there would be[e] a fulfillment of what was spoken to her by the Lord."

46 And Mary[f] said,

> "My soul magnifies the Lord,
47   and my spirit rejoices in God
>   my Savior,
48   for he has looked with favor on
>   the lowliness of his servant.
>   Surely, from now on all
>   generations will call me
>   blessed;
49   for the Mighty One has done
>   great things for me,
>   and holy is his name.
50   His mercy is for those who fear
>   him
>   from generation to generation.
51   He has shown strength with his
>   arm;
>   he has scattered the proud in the
>   thoughts of their hearts.
52   He has brought down the powerful
>   from their
>   thrones,
>   and lifted up the lowly;
53   he has filled the hungry with good
>   things,
>   and sent the rich away empty.
54   He has helped his servant Israel,
>   in remembrance of his mercy,
55   according to the promise he made
>   to our ancestors,
>   to Abraham and to his
>   descendants forever."

56 And Mary remained with her about three months and then returned to her home.

57 Now the time came for Elizabeth to give birth, and she bore a son. [58]Her neighbors and relatives heard that the Lord had shown his great mercy to her, and they rejoiced with her.

---

[e]Or *believed, for there will be*
[f]Other ancient authorities read *Elizabeth*

59 On the eighth day they came to circumcise the child, and they were going to name him Zechariah after his father. ⁶⁰But his mother said, "No; he is to be called John." ⁶¹They said to her, "None of your relatives has this name." ⁶²Then they began motioning to his father to find out what name he wanted to give him. ⁶³He asked for a writing tablet and wrote, "His name is John." And all of them were amazed. ⁶⁴Immediately his mouth was opened and his tongue freed, and he began to speak, praising God. ⁶⁵Fear came over all their neighbors, and all these things were talked about throughout the entire hill country of Judea. ⁶⁶All who heard them pondered them and said, "What then will this child become?" For, indeed, the hand of the Lord was with him.

67 Then his father Zechariah was filled with the Holy Spirit and spoke this prophecy:

68   "Blessed be the Lord God of
                Israel,
             for he has looked favorably on
             his people and redeemed
                them.

69   He has raised up a mighty savior[g]
                for us
             in the house of his servant
                David,

70   as he spoke through the mouth of
             his holy prophets from of
             old,

71   that we would be saved
                from our enemies and from the
                hand of all who hate us.

72   Thus he has shown the mercy
                promised to our ancestors,
             and has remembered his holy
                covenant,

73   the oath that he swore to our
                ancestor Abraham,
             to grant us 74 that we, being
                rescued from the hands of
                our enemies,
             might serve him without fear, 75 in
                holiness and righteousness
             before him all our days.

76   And you, child, will be called the
                prophet of the Most High;

---

[g]Gk *a horn of salvation*

for you will go before the Lord
to prepare his ways,

77　　　to give knowledge of salvation to
his people
by the forgiveness of their sins.

78　　　By the tender mercy of our God,
the dawn from on high will
break upon[h] us,

79　　　to give light to those who sit in
darkness and in the shadow
of death,
to guide our feet into the way
of peace."

80 The child grew and became strong in spirit, and he was in the wilderness until the day he appeared publicly to Israel.

2 In those days a decree went out from Emperor Augustus that all the world should be registered. [2]This was the first registration and was taken while Quinirius was governor of Syria. [3]All went to their own towns to be registered. [4]Joseph also went from the town of Nazareth in Galilee to Judea, to the city of David called Bethlehem, because he was descended from the house and family of David. [5]He went to be registered with Mary, to whom he was engaged and who was expecting a child. [6]While they were there, the time came for her to deliver her child. [7]And she gave birth to her firstborn son and wrapped him in bands of cloth, and laid him in a manger, because there was no place for them in the inn.

8 In that region there were shepherds living in the fields, keeping watch over their flock by night. [9]Then an angel of the Lord stood before them, and the glory of the Lord shone around them, and they were terrified. [10]But the angel said to them, "Do not be afraid; for see—I am bringing you good news of great joy for all the people: [11]to you is born this day in the city of David a Savior, who is the Messiah,[i] the Lord. [12]This will be a sign for you: you will find a child wrapped in bands of cloth and lying in a manger." [13]And suddenly there was with the angel a multitude of the heavenly host,[j] praising God and saying,

14　　　"Glory to God in the highest
heaven,
and on earth peace among those
whom he favors!"[k]

15 When the angels had left them and gone into heaven, the shepherds said to one another, "Let us go now to Bethlehem and see this thing that has

[h]Other ancient authorities read *has broken upon*
[i]Or *the Christ*
[j]Gk *army*
[k]Other ancient authorities read *peace, goodwill among people*

taken place, which the Lord has made known to us." [16]So they went with haste and found Mary and Joseph, and the child lying in the manger. [17]When they saw this, they made known what had been told them about this child; [18]and all who heard it were amazed at what the shepherds told them. [19]But Mary treasured all these words and pondered them in her heart. [20]The shepherds returned, glorifying and praising God for all they had heard and seen, as it had been told them.

21 After eight days had passed, it was time to circumcise the child; and he was called Jesus, the name given by the angel before he was conceived in the womb.

22 When the time came for their purification according to the law of Moses, they brought him up to Jerusalem to present him to the Lord [23](as it is written in the law of the Lord, "Every firstborn male shall be designated as holy to the Lord"), [24]and they offered a sacrifice according to what is stated in the law of the Lord, "a pair of turtledoves or two young pigeons."

25 Now there was a man in Jerusalem whose name was Simeon;[l] this man was righteous and devout, looking forward to the consolation of Israel, and the Holy Spirit rested on him. [26]It had been revealed to him by the Holy Spirit that he would not see death before he had seen the Lord's Messiah.[m] [27]Guided by the Spirit, Simeon[n] came into the temple; and when the parents brought in the child Jesus, to do for him what was customary under the law, [28]Simeon[o] took him in his arms and praised God, saying,

29	"Master, now you are dismissing
	your servant[p] in peace,
	according to your word;
30	for my eyes have seen your
	salvation,
31	which you have prepared in the
	presence of all peoples,
32	a light for revelation to the
	Gentiles
	and for glory to your people
	Israel."

33 And the child's father and mother were amazed at what was being said about him. [34]Then Simeon[q] blessed them and said to his mother Mary, "This child is destined for the falling and the rising of many in Israel, and to be a sign

[l]Gk *Symeon*
[m]Or *the Lord's Christ*
[n]Gk *In the Spirit, he*
[o]Gk *he*
[p]Gk *slave*
[q]Gk *Symeon*

that will be opposed [35]so that the inner thoughts of many will be revealed—and a sword will pierce your own soul too."

36 There was also a prophet, Anna[r] the daughter of Phanuel, of the tribe of Asher. She was of a great age, having lived with her husband seven years after her marriage, [37]then as a widow to the age of eighty-four. She never left the temple but worshiped there with fasting and prayer night and day. [38]At that moment she came, and began to praise God and to speak about the child[s] to all who were looking for the redemption of Jerusalem.

39 When they had finished everything required by the law of the Lord, they returned to Galilee, to their own town of Nazareth. [40]The child grew and became strong, filled with wisdom; and the favor of God was upon him.

41 Now every year his parents went to Jerusalem for the festival of the Passover. [42]And when he was twelve years old, they went up as usual for the festival. [43]When the festival was ended and they started to return, the boy Jesus stayed behind in Jerusalem, but his parents did not know it. [44]Assuming that he was in the group of travelers, they went a day's journey. Then they started to look for him among their relatives and friends. [45]When they did not find him, they returned to Jerusalem to search for him. [46]After three days they found him in the temple, sitting among the teachers, listening to them and asking them questions. [47]And all who heard him were amazed at his understanding and his answers. [48]When his parents[t] saw him they were astonished; and his mother said to him, "Child, why have you treated us like this? Look, your father and I have been searching for you in great anxiety." [49]He said to them, "Why were you searching for me? Did you not know that I must be in my Father's house?"[u] [50]But they did not understand what he said to them. [51]Then he went down with them and came to Nazareth, and was obedient to them. His mother treasured all these things in her heart.

52 And Jesus increased in wisdom and in years,[v] and in divine and human favor.

Questions for Review and Discussion

1. Describe Mary's demeanor and behavior in Luke 1–2. What evidence can you find to support the claim that she has voice and agency?
2. Greco-Roman mythology is littered with illustrations of male deities impregnating mortal females as a means of legitimizing and deifying the offspring of such unions. Luke was writing to an audience which would have been familiar with such stories

[r]Gk *Hanna*
[s]Gk *him*
[t]Gk *they*
[u]Or *be about my Father's interests?*
[v]Or *in stature*

concerning the origin of divine offspring. How does his story of the origin of Jesus differ from some similar stories we find in Greco-Roman mythology?

3. Many goddesses in Near East and classical mythology are referred to as "virgin" goddesses. However, in their case, virginity was not connected with chastity since many of them had lovers. In those instances, a virgin meant someone who is one unto herself, that is to say, an autonomous, independent being who had agency, self-expression, sexual autonomy, and was free of male domination. Using that definition of the word, what arguments can be made for or against Mary's status as a virgin?

4. What evidence can you find to support the claim that the role and qualities of the Great Goddess have been co-opted by Christianity and transformed to serve the interests of a patriarchal theology?

5. Through their characterization of the Virgin Mary as a pure, chaste, sexually abstinent mother, early orthodox Christians used her example to advocate a means by which ordinary women could control their "natural" proclivity for sin and transcend the "impurities" intrinsic to their female flesh. What ramifications does such thinking have on the lives of ordinary women?

6. Is the Virgin Mary a realistic role model for women? In what ways might her projected image inhibit or enhance a woman's self-actualization?

7. How does the Virgin Mary blur the line of demarcation that separates the human from the divine?

8. It has been argued that the Roman Catholic Church has had to accommodate popular beliefs about the Virgin Mary and officially sanction much of what it had vehemently opposed for many centuries. If this is so, what future accommodations do you think the Church may have to make if it wishes to incorporate the multifaceted and ubiquitous devotion to the Virgin Mary?

9. What claims, if any, can be made for the Virgin Mary as reversing or undoing the actions of Eve?

Chapter 14

Hawwa

GLOSSARY OF NAMES AND TERMS

AHADITH   Plural of hadith (see below)

ALLAH   The Arabic word for "The God"

ANGEL JIBRIL   Angel Gabriel

FATIHA   Opening chapter of the *Qur'an*; recited during each of the five daily prayers

HADITH   Collection of the words and deeds of the Prophet Muhammad

HAJJ   Pilgrimage to Mecca; required of all Muslims at least once in their lifetime

HAWWA   The Arabic name for Eve and from which the name Eve is derived

IBLIS   Arabic name for Satan

'ISA   The Arabic name for Jesus and from which the name Jesus is derived

ISLAM   Belief in one God and the Prophet Muhammad as His Messenger; shares many of the same prophets and stories as those found in Hebrew and Christian scriptures; Arabic for submission to the will of Allah

MECCA   City in Saudi Arabia; birthplace of Islam

MUHAMMAD   Prophet of Islam

MUSLIMS   Adherents of the religion of Islam; Arabic for those who submit to the will of Allah

NAFS   Arabic word for soul; a feminine noun

QUR'AN   The sacred text of Islam; revealed to the Prophet Muhammad

RAMADAN   Islam's holy month when the revelations to the Prophet Muhammad began

SALAAM   Arabic word for "peace"

SHEHADEH   One of the tenets of Islam; declaration of faith in the one God and in the Prophet Muhammad as His Messenger

SALAT   Five daily prayers required of all Muslims

SAWM   Obligatory fasting during the month of Ramadan

SURAH   Chapters in the *Qur'an*

ZAKAT   Charitable contributions to the needy; required of all Muslims

Hawwa (the Arabic name for Eve and from which the name of Eve is derived), is Adam's spouse, and her story is told in the *Qur'an*, the sacred text of Islam.

As one of the world's major monotheistic religions, Islam came into being over 1,300 years ago in the same part of the world that gave birth to Judaism and Christianity. Muslims (adherents of Islam) believe that Allah, the Arabic word for God, is the same God who revealed Himself to the Jews and Christians. They therefore believe in all the prophets referred to in the Hebrew and Christian scriptures. Muslims claim that Islam is a continuation of Judaism and Christianity and describe it as a natural progression of its monotheistic predecessors. Many of the stories that appear in the *Qur'an* will be familiar to readers of the Bible even though the details of the narrative may vary.

While having much in common with its monotheistic predecessors, Islam also differs in a number of ways. The fundamental tenet of Islam is the belief in the existence of the one and only God, ("I declare that nothing deserves to be worshipped except Allah") and in the Prophet Muhammad as His Messenger. Uncompromising in its monotheism, Islam bears a closer resemblance to Judaism than to Christianity since it rejects the concept of a three-in-one God (the Father, the Son, and the Holy Ghost) that Christianity embraces. The *Qur'an* tells us repeatedly that Allah has no offspring. The many references to 'Isa (Jesus) throughout the *Qur'an* identify him as a prophet of God, not His son. According to Islam, only Allah should be worshipped, and to worship anything or anyone other than Allah (including Jesus or Muhammad) is to commit a great sacrilege, the only unforgivable sin.

Unlike Judaism, however, Islam also does not subscribe to the concept of a "chosen people." Adamant in its egalitarianism, Islam claims all people are chosen people. In theory, Muslims believe that all humans are born equal in the sight of Allah, that all are born Muslims (believers in the one God), and that all are born free from the taint of original sin. The word *Islam* is derived from *salaam,* which means peace, and a *Muslim* is one who finds peace through submission to the will of God.

Islam is comprised of five basic tenets. Known as the five pillars of Islam, they are the following: *shehadah* (declaration of faith in the one God and in Muhammad as His prophet); *salat* (offering of prayers five times a day); *zakat* (contributions to the needy); *sawm* (fasting during the month of Ramadan); and *hajj* (making a pilgrimage to Mecca at least once in one's lifetime if physically and financially possible).

Muhammad, the Prophet of Islam, was born in 571 C.E. in Mecca. Although there were many prophets before him, he is regarded by Muslims as "The Seal of the Prophets," the final prophet, because there will be no more prophets after him. He received his first revelation during the month of Ramadan in 610 C.E. While meditating in a cave in the mountains near Mecca, he heard a voice declaring his status as a messenger of Allah and ordering him to recite. Later, the voice was revealed to be that of the Angel Jibril (the Arabic name for Gabriel).

Beginning in 610 C.E., the revelations were to continue for approximately 20 years until the prophet's death in 632 C.E. Muslims are unshaken in their belief that the revelations were not authored by Muhammad but transmitted to him from God. Muhammad, who was illiterate, recited the revelations to his disciples who then committed them to memory and subsequently wrote them down. The revelations were collected into a single text, the *Qur'an,* a word that means *recitation* as well as *reading* in Arabic and refers specifically to the revelations in oral and aural form. As Muslims explain it, the revelation begins with God and culminates in the *Qur'an.*

Although the *Qur'an* has been translated into many languages, Muslims regard these translations as interpretations. Only the original Arabic version is considered to be the Word of God, and no "translation" can capture the essence and spirit of the text in its entirety as does the Arabic original. The text is revered to such a degree that Muslims consider it a sin to tamper with the original Arabic in any way. Composed of rhymed prose, it is the most frequently memorized book in the world and serves to unify Arabic speaking and non-Arabic speaking Muslims throughout the world.

The *Qur'an* consists of 114 chapters called *surahs*. The first, the *Fatiha*, meaning the Opening, constitutes an essential part of the five daily prayers. The remaining surahs are organized by length, beginning with the longest and gradually decreasing in length until we encounter a series of very short, poetic surahs at the end. The *Qur'an* is approximately as long as the New Testament.

The *Qur'an* does not proceed chronologically like the Hebrew Scripture. Instead, its organization is much like a tapestry: a story weaves its way intermittently throughout the text in a series of threads. Collectively, the threads are woven together to form the whole. If one thread is removed, the whole infrastructure may unravel. For example, Surah 4:1 contains a reference to the creation of the first humans. That same thread is picked up again in Surah 7:189–190. Occasionally, a thread may appear as a reference in one or two verses. At other times, the same thread is presented sequentially in several consecutive verses. When each thread is in place, one can understand the message and appreciate the aesthetic value of the rhymed prose. Only by reading the entire *Qur'an* can one piece together the narrative into a complete story or thread.

The focus of this selection is on the creation of the first humans, Adam and Hawwa, and the temptation story. The Qur'anic version of creation conforms closely to the first version of creation presented in Genesis 1:26–27. However, it differs from the second version of creation in Genesis 2:18–25 since there is no mention in the *Qur'an* of an Eve being created from Adam's rib to serve as his subordinate and helpmate. Instead, this latter version entered the Islamic tradition through the *hadith* literature (a collection of reports of words and deeds attributed to the Prophet Muhammad) and not through the *Qur'an*.

Over the years, many *ahadith* (plural form of *hadith*) that were attributed to the prophet turned out to be false; others turned out to be true or partially true. Like the verses of the *Qur'an*, *ahadith* were initially collected orally and transmitted. A precise methodology was later developed to determine the authenticity of those chosen to be included in the vast body of written compilations. The chronological and geographical feasibility of the sequence of transmitters and their integrity, based on biographical dictionaries written about them, were used to separate true from false *ahadith*. In spite of this, the authenticity of some *ahadith* continues to be contested by various Islamic schools of thought. However, Muslim scholars generally agree that when a *hadith* appears to contradict or demonstrate inconsistencies with what is stated in the *Qur'an*, the latter always takes precedence because it is considered to be the primary source of Islam. The woman-as-Adam's-rib version of creation appears only in the *ahadith* and not in the *Qur'an*. It appears to contradict the letter and spirit of the creation of the first humans as presented in the *Qur'an* and probably found its way to Islam as a result of external influences and the assimilation of an ideology that is at variance with the Qur'anic version.

The examination of the Qur'anic verses pertaining to the creation of the first humans in translated versions presents a major challenge to non-Arabic speaking peoples because of the problems associated with the translation of a text from one language to another. In many of the English translations, the gender of the first human created is specified as "He." Although the Arabic word for *soul* (*nafs*) is a feminine noun, no gender is stipulated for the first human by the Arabic text. Many English translations violate the spirit and wording of the Arabic original by ascribing a masculine gender to the word *nafs* and translating the passage as ". . . created *his* mate from *him* . . ." Since the Arabic language does not have the neuter gender, a more accurate translation of the phrase would be the following: "Mankind, heed your Lord Who has created you from a single soul [nafs], and created her mate from her . . ." The English translation that comes close to the Arabic original is the one presented below. It attempts to approximate the original by denying the primacy of the masculine gender through its use of an ungendered pronoun.

The Qur'anic version of the creation of the first humans, therefore, opens up the distinct possibility that the first entity created may have been female. According to Surah 7:189–190, a single entity or soul was created first; this was followed by the creation of 'its' mate. The purpose of the creation of "the mate" was to enable it to "take rest in her [it]" in order to propagate the species ("it" referring to the soul). In other words, the Qur'anic version of creation does not specify the gender of the first and second beings to be created. It is possible to interpret Surahs 4: 1 and 7: 189–190 as referring not only to the creation of the first humans, Adam and Hawwa, but also to the sequence of creation that they share with their progeny.

Surah 7: 189–190 illustrates an egalitarian exchange between the woman and the man, an exchange that is unencumbered by divisive bickering or self-serving agendas. The surah tells us that once the female begins to feel heavy with her burden late in the pregnancy, both male and female make a genuinely touching appeal to Allah for a healthy child. They speak in unison and are motivated by a shared concern for their offspring. Furthermore, the lightness of the burden with which the female moves directly after conception is in stark contrast to Genesis 3 in which Yahweh inflicts a gender-specific curse on Eve to experience discomfort and pain during pregnancy, labor, and the birthing process.

As with the story of creation, segments of the temptation narrative appear intermittently throughout the *Qur'an*. The Qur'anic version of the story of Adam and Hawwa will be recognizable to readers of Genesis since it shares many of the same elements: Adam, Eve, a garden, a tree, a temptation, and the expulsion from the Garden of Eden. However, a close reading of the text reveals some substantial differences, most notably on the issue of culpability.

First of all, it should be noted that Hawwa is never mentioned by name in the *Qur'an*. Instead, she is referred to as Adam's spouse. Another major difference is that in Genesis 2 and 3, Adam names Eve: first as *woman* before the fall and later as Eve after the fall. Naming indicates power over the person or object being named. Genesis 2 and 3, therefore, suggest that the male has authority over the female and all other living things since he is endowed with the power of naming. This male prerogative of naming does not occur in the *Qur'an*. In fact, Surah 2:31 of the *Qur'an* explicitly states that Allah teaches Adam the names of everything—a clear indication that Allah, not Adam, has power over all living things. Adam's task is restricted to learning the names. It is significant, however, that it is Adam alone who is taught the names and is given the covenant, which he subsequently breaks. It is Adam alone who receives Allah's words of inspiration after asking for forgiveness (Surah 20:121). And it is before Adam alone that the angels are asked to prostrate themselves.

The temptation story itself differs significantly from its counterpart in Genesis. First of all, the *Qur'an* makes Adam and his spouse equally culpable in the temptation scene. With one exception, the *Qur'an* uses the Arabic dual form of nouns, verbs, and adjectives to indicate that *Iblis* (Satan) tempted both Adam and Hawwa and that both transgressed simultaneously. The one exception to the dual form occurs in Surah 20. Here Adam seems to be singled out for greater moral culpability. Surah 20: 115 tells us that Adam was weak in his resolve and had reneged on his pledge. And later, verse 120 of the same surah reinforces the point by declaring that Satan whispered specifically to Adam. There is no corresponding mention in the *Qur'an* of Satan engaging in exclusive dialogue with Hawwa or of approaching her separately. Therefore, the one exception to the dual form in the temptation scene singles out Adam—not Hawwa. Hawwa in the *Qur'an* is never singled out as either the initiator or the temptress who leads man astray. This marks a radical departure from her fate as it subsequently unfolds in the *ahadith* where it is made to correspond to the fate of Eve in Genesis in terms of her creation from Adam's rib, her role in the temptation scene, and her legacy.

The punishment inflicted on Adam and Hawwa in the *Qur'an* is identical, collective, and not gender-specific: they are both expelled from the Garden of Eden. Unlike what transpires in Genesis, Adam is not told that he will now have to work by the sweat of his brow; Hawwa is not cursed with pain in childbirth; and neither they nor their progeny have been cursed with original sin. And although the *Qur'an* declares that the seeds of enmity will be sown among some of them (". . . one of you a foe unto the other!"), there is no mention of one sex having power over the other.

Because the Qur'anic Hawwa is not singled out as the original source of temptation, and because her punishment is identical to that of Adam's, in purely moral terms, Hawwa is less culpable than her counterpart, Eve, in Genesis. However, she is also denied an individual voice: Hawwa does not speak either in the indirect or direct voice in the *Qur'an* except in unison with Adam. And since voice can be interpreted as an indication of agency, it is possible to argue that Hawwa is denied individual agency, and, by implication, she is also denied autonomy.

The Eve in Genesis is not only given a unique voice, she is given individual agency. The linguistic analysis of her dialogue indicates a sophisticated level of thinking and discernment, an autonomy, a volition as well as a willingness to accept responsibility for her actions—all of which are absent in the dialogue of Adam in Genesis. Hawwa's apparent lack of agency and absence of a separate identity is reinforced by the fact that she is referred to as Adam's spouse. In other words, she is not depicted as an autonomous being with a unique identity and a unique name. Instead, she is defined through her relationship with a male and her voice is united with his. Since the Qur'anic Hawwa is denied an individual voice, it can be argued that she is an undifferentiated being, one without the clear delineation, the voice, the agency, and the level of sophistication of her illustrious counterpart—all of which may make her a less interesting character than Eve when viewed from a purely literary perspective. However, although Hawwa is not as clearly articulated as Eve, she is also less morally culpable than Eve since, unlike Eve, she does not have to shoulder the primary burden of the act of disobedience that led to expulsion from the Garden of Eden.

The selections below are translated by M. M. Pickthall in *The Meaning of the Glorious Qur'an,* revised and edited in modern English by Arafat K. El-Ashi.

References

Ahmed, Leila. *Women and Gender in Islam: Historical Roots of a Modern Debate.* New Haven: Yale UP, 1992.

Al-Hibri, Azizah. "A Study of Islamic Herstory: Or How Did We Ever Get Into This Mess?" *Women and Islam.* Ed. Azizah Al-Hibri. Oxford: Pergamon, 1982. 207–219.

Ali, Abdullah Yusuf. Trans. *The Holy Qur'an: English Translation of the Meanings of The Qur'an with Notes.* Indianapolis: H&C International, 1992.

Ali, Al-Hajj Ta'lim (T.B. Irving). Trans. *The Qur'an: The First American Version.* Vermont: Amana, 1985.

Al-Khattab, Huda. *Bent Rib: A Journey Through Women's Issues in Islam.* London: Ta-Ha, 1997.

Badawi, Leila. "Islam." *Women in Religion.* Eds. Jean Holm and John Bowker. London: Pinter, 1999. 84–112.

Carmody, Denise Lardner. *Women and World Religions.* 2nd ed. Englewood Cliffs, NJ: Prentice Hall, 1989.

Hassan, Riffat. "The Issue of Woman-Man Equality in the Islamic Tradition (1993)." *Eve and Adam: Jewish, Christian, and Muslim Readings on Genesis and Gender.* Ed. Kristen E. Kvam, Linda S. Schearing, and Valarie H. Ziegler. Bloomington: Indiana UP, 1999. 464–476.

———. "Muslim Women and Post-Patriarchal Islam." *After Patriarchy: Feminist Transformations of the World Religions.* Faith Meets Faith Series. Eds. Paula M. Cooey, William R. Eakin, and Jay B. Daniel. New York: Orbis, 1994. 39–64.

————. "Muslim Feminist Hermeneutics." *In Our Own Voices: Four Centuries of American Women's Religious Writing.* Eds. Rosemary Skinner Keller and Rosemary Radford Ruether. San Francisco: Harper, 1994. 455–459.

Mernissi, Fatima. *The Veil and the Male Elite: A Feminist Interpretation of Women's Rights in Islam.* Trans. Mary Jo Lakeland. Massachusetts: Addison-Wesley, 1987.

Murata, Sachiko. *The Tao of Islam: A Sourcebook on Gender Relationships in Islamic Thought.* Albany: SUNY P, 1992.

Pickthall, M. M., trans. *The Meaning of the Glorious Qur'an: Explanatory Translation.* Ed. Arafat K. El-Ashi. Rev. ed. Maryland: Amana Publications, 2002.

Sells, Michael, trans. *Approaching The Qur'an: The Early Revelations.* Ashland, Oregon: White Clouds P, 1999.

Smith, Jane I. "Islam." *Women in World Religions.* Ed. Arvind Sharma. Albany: SUNY P, 1987. 235–250.

Smith, Jane I., and Yvonne Haddad. "Eve: Islamic Image of Woman." *Women and Islam.* Ed. Azizah Al-Hibri. Oxford: Pergamon, 1982. 135–144.

Stowasser, Barbara Freyer. *Women in The Qur'an, Traditions, and Interpretation.* New York: Oxford UP, 1994.

Wadud-Muhsin, Amina. *Qur'an and Woman.* Kuala Lumpur: Penerbit Fajar Bakti Sdn. *Bhd., 1992.*

Selections from the *Qur'an*

Surah 2: Al Baqarah

29. He it is Who created for you all that is in the earth. Then turned He to the heaven, and fashioned it as seven heavens. And He is Knower of all things.

30. And when your Lord said unto the angels: Lo! I am about to place a viceroy in the earth, they said: Will You place therein one who will do harm therein and will shed blood, while we, we hymn Your praise and sanctify You? He said: Surely I know that which you know not.

31. And He taught Adam all the names, then showed them to the angels, saying: Inform me of the names of these, if you are truthful.

32. They said: Be glorified! We have no knowledge saving that which You have taught us. Lo! You, only You, are the Knower, the Wise.

33. He said: O Adam! inform them of their names, and when he had informed them of their names, He said: Did I not tell you that I know the secret of the heavens and the earth? And I know that which you disclose and that which you used to hide.

34. And when We said unto the angels: Prostrate yourselves before Adam, they fell prostrate, all save Iblīs. He demurred through pride, and so became a disbeliever.

35. And We said: O Adam! dwell you and your wife in the Garden, and eat you freely (of the fruits) thereof where you will; but come not near this tree lest you become of the wrongdoers.

36. But the Devil caused them to deflect therefrom and expelled them from the (happy) state in which they were; and We said: Fall down, one of you a foe unto the other! There shall be for you on earth a habitation and a provision for a time.

37. Then Adam received from his Lord words (of revelation), and He relented toward him. Indeed! He is the Relenting, the Merciful.

38. We said: Go down, all of you, from hence; so when there comes unto you from Me a guidance; whoso follows My guidance, there shall no fear come upon them neither shall they grieve.

39. But those who disbelieve, and deny our revelations, such are rightful owners of the Fire. They will abide therein forever.

Women

Surah 4: Al Nisā

Revealed at Madinah

In the name of Allah, the Beneficent, the Merciful.

1. O mankind! Be careful of your duty to your Lord. Who created you from a single soul and from it created its mate and from the two has spread abroad a multitude of men and women. Be careful of your duty toward Allah in Whom you claim (your rights) of one another, and toward the wombs (that bore you). Lo! Allah has been a Watcher over you.

Surah 7: Al A'raf

11. And We created you, then fashioned you, then told the angels: Fall you prostrate before Adam! And they fell prostrate, all save Iblīs, who was not of those who made prostration.

12. He said: What hindered you that you did not fall prostrate when I bade you? (Iblīs) said: I am better than him. You created me of fire while him You did create of mud.

13. He said: Then go down hence! It is not for you to show pride here, so go forth! Lo! you are of those degraded.

14. He said: Reprieve me till the day when they are raised (from the dead).

15. He said: Lo! you are of those reprieved.

16. He said: Now, because You have sent me astray, surely I shall lurk in ambush for them on Your Right Path.

17. Then I shall come upon them from before them and from behind them and from their right hands and from their left hands, and You will not find most of them thankful.

18. He said: Go forth from hence, degraded, banished. As for such of them as follow you, surely I will fill Hell with all of you.

19. And O Adam! Dwell you and your wife in the Garden and eat from whence you will, but come not near this tree lest you become wrongdoers.

20. Then the Devil whispered to them that he might manifest unto them that which was hidden from them of their shame, and he said: Your Lord forbade you from this tree only lest you should become angels or become of the immortals.

21. And he swore unto them (saying): Lo! I am a sincere adviser unto you.

22. Thus did he lead them on with guile. And when they tasted of the tree their shame was manifest to them and they began to hide (by heaping) on themselves some of the leaves of the Garden. And their Lord called them, (saying): Did I not forbid you from that tree and tell you: Lo! the Devil is an open enemy to you?

23. They said: Our Lord! We have wronged ourselves. If You forgive us not and have not mercy on us, surely we are of the lost!

24. He said: Go down (from hence), one of you a foe unto the other. There will be for you on earth a habitation and provision for a while.

25. He said: There shall you live, and there shall you die and thence shall you be brought forth.

26. O Children of Adam! We have revealed unto you raiment to conceal your shame, and splendid vesture, but the raiment of restraint from evil, that is best. This is of the revelations of Allah, that they may remember.

. . .

189. He it is who did create you from a single soul, and therefrom did make his mate that he might take rest in her. And when he covered her she bore a light burden, and she passed (unnoticed) with it, but when it became heavy they cried unto Allah, their Lord, saying: If you give unto us aright we shall be of the thankful.

190. But when He gave unto them aright, they ascribed unto Him partners in respect of that which He had given them. High is He exalted above all that they associate (with Him).

Surah 15: Al Hijr

26. Surely We created man of potter's clay of black mud altered,

27. And the jinn did We create aforetime of essential fire.

28. And (remember) when your Lord said unto the angels: Lo! I am creating a mortal out of potter's clay of black mud altered.

29. So, when I have made him and have breathed into him of My spirit, do you fall down, prostrating yourselves unto him.

30. So the angels fell prostrate, all of them together

31. Save Iblīs. He refused to be among the prostrate.

32. He said: O Iblīs! What ails you that you are not among the prostrate?

33. He said: I am not going to prostrate myself unto a mortal whom You have created out of potter's clay of black mud altered.

34. He said: Then go you forth from hence, for surely you are outcast.

35. And lo! The curse shall be upon you till the Day of Judgment.

36. He said: My Lord! Reprieve me till the day when they are raised.

37. He said: Then lo! You are of those reprieved

38. Till an appointed time.

39. He said: My Lord, Because You have sent me astray, I verily shall adorn the path of error for them in the earth, and shall mislead them every one.

40. Save such of them as are Your perfectly devoted slaves.

41. He said: This is a right course incumbent upon Me:

42. Lo! as for My slaves, you have no power over any of them save such of the froward as follow you,

43. And lo! for all such, hell will be the promised place.

44. It has seven gates, and each gate has an appointed portion.

Surah 20: Tā Hā

115. And surely We made a covenant of old with Adam, but he forgot, and We found no constancy in him.

116. And when We said unto the angels: Fall prostrate before Adam, they fell prostrate (all) save Iblīs; he refused.

117. Therefore We said: O Adam! This is an enemy unto you and unto your wife, so let him not drive you both out of the Garden thus you come to toil.

118. It is (vouchsafed) unto you that you hunger not therein nor are naked,

119. And you thirst not therein nor are exposed to the sun's heat.

120. But the Devil whispered to him, saying: O Adam! Shall I show you the tree of immortality and a Kingdom that wastes not away?

121. Then they two ate thereof, so that their shame became apparent unto them, and they began to hide by heaping on themselves some of the leaves of the Garden. And Adam disobeyed his Lord, so went astray.

122. Then his Lord chose him, and relented toward him, and guided him.

123. He said: Go down hence, both of you, one of you a foe unto the other. But if there come unto you from Me a guidance, then who follows My guidance, he will not go astray nor will be unhappy.

124. But he who turns away from remembrance of Me, his will be a narrow life, and I shall bring him blind to the assembly on the Day of Resurrection.

125. He will say: My Lord! Wherefore have You gathered me (hither) blind, when I was wont to see?

126. He will say: So (it must be). Our revelations came unto you but you did forget them. In like manner you are forgotten this Day.

127. Thus do We reward him who is prodigal and believes not the revelations of his Lord; and surely the doom of the Hereafter will be sterner and more lasting.

128. Is it not a guidance for them (to know) how many a generation We destroyed before them, amid whose dwellings they walk? Lo! therein surely are signs for men of thought.

Surah 38: Sād

71. It is revealed unto me only that I may be a plain warner.

72. When your Lord said unto the angels: lo! I am about to create a mortal out of mire,

73. And when I have fashioned him and breathed into him of My spirit, then fall down before him prostrate,

74. The angels fell down prostrate, every one.

75. Saving Iblīs, he was arrogant and became one of the disbelievers.

76. He said: O Iblīs! What hinders you from falling prostrate before that which I have created with both My hands? Are you too proud or are you of the high exalted?

77. He said: I am better than him. You created me of fire, whilst him You did create of clay.

78. He said: Go forth from hence, for lo! you are outcast,

79. And lo! My curse is on you till the Day of Judgment.

80. He said: My Lord! Reprieve me till the day when they are raised.

81. He said: Lo! you are of those reprieved

82. Until the day of the time appointed.

83. He said: Then, by Your might, I surely will beguile them every one,

84. Save Your single-minded slaves among them.

85. He said: The Truth is, and the Truth I speak.

Questions for Review and Discussion

1. What is significant about the description of the creation of the first two humans in the *Qur'an*? How does it differ from the Judeo-Christian version?
2. Some Islamic scholars describe the gendered relationship between Adam and Hawwa as being complementary, equal, and not disfigured by an adversarial competitiveness or contentious hierarchy. Find evidence in the text to support or refute this position.
3. What significance do you attribute to the fact that Hawwa is never mentioned by name in the *Qur'an*?
4. What are the privileges given to Adam that are denied to Hawwa?
5. How might the endowment of Adam's privileges render him more morally culpable than Hawwa?
6. What evidence can you find in the Qur'anic version of temptation that Hawwa is less culpable than Eve in Genesis?
7. What indication can you find in the text that Hawwa has autonomy and agency?
8. Adam and Hawwa experience an identical punishment for their transgression: expulsion from the Garden of Eden. What is the significance of the total absence of gender-specific punishments?
9. Of the two, do you think Eve or Hawwa serves as a better role model for women today? Why?

Chapter 15

Maryam

Glossary of Names and Terms

ALLAH   The Arabic word for God

AR-RAHIM   The compassionate; one of the attributes of Allah; derived from the Arabic word for womb (see Raham below)

HAWWA   The Arabic name for Eve and from which the name Eve is derived

IMRAN   Family of Moses, Aaron, and Maryam

IBLIS   Arabic name for Satan

'ISA   Arabic name for Jesus; a prophet of Islam

MARYAM   Arabic name for Mary; the mother of 'Isa

QUR'AN   The sacred text of Islam; revealed to the Prophet Muhammad

RAHAM   Arabic word for womb

SURAH   Chapters in the *Qur'an*

SURAT MARYAM   Chapter 19 of the *Qur'an*; known as Maryam's chapter

YAHYA   Arabic name for John the Baptist

ZACHARIAH   Husband of Elizabeth, Maryam's cousin; acts as Maryam's guardian; father of Yahya

The Virgin Mary, known in Arabic as Maryam, has a unique and honored place in the Islamic tradition. She is the only female in the *Qur'an* to be identified by name and to have a surah (chapter) named after her. That fact, coupled with her noble ancestry from a line of prophets, is considered a refutation of those who would accuse her of illicit conduct in the birth of her son. Maryam's name appears more frequently in the *Qur'an* than in the entire New Testament. Only the names of Moses, Abraham, and Noah are mentioned more frequently in the *Qur'an* than is the name Maryam. Her story is invoked as a sign of Allah. And as is the case with the story of Adam and Hawwa, the story of Maryam, the mother of 'Isa (the Arabic name for Jesus), appears intermittently throughout the *Qur'an*.

Maryam's story begins while she is still in her mother's womb (Surah 3: 31). Her mother is referred to as a woman from the house of Imran, a reference that traces Maryam's lineage to Moses and Aaron, descendents from the family of Imran. Her ancestry from the line of prophets is thereby firmly established. The family of Imran receives special recognition in the Islamic tradition because it can be traced back to Moses and Aaron, and through Maryam and Elizabeth, it boasts 'Isa and Yahya (the Arabic name for John the Baptist).

The *Qur'an* tells us that while carrying Maryam in her womb, her mother dedicates her child exclusively to the service of God. The narrative unfolds with the birth of Maryam when her mother names her and seeks Allah's protection from Satan for her daughter and for her daughter's progeny. As a young girl, Maryam serves in the inner temple or sanctuary. Zachariah, the husband of her cousin Elizabeth, is appointed as her guardian. The story of Zachariah and his son, Yahya, (John the Baptist) intertwine the story of Maryam and 'Isa. Zachariah's prayer for a child in his old age followed by the declaration that Allah has granted his prayer generally precede the Qur'anic passages that declare Maryam's chaste conception of 'Isa. The events leading up to the two births share many similarities. Both Zachariah and Maryam question the possibility of having a child: Zachariah because his wife is past child-bearing age; Maryam because she is a virgin. Both receive assurances that all is possible for Allah. And both are given a sign: Zachariah is told he will not converse with anyone for three consecutive nights; Maryam vows a temporary silence and points to the infant 'Isa to speak on her behalf when confronted by her family. These parallels establish an affinity between Zachariah and Maryam on the one hand and Yahya and 'Isa on the other. Overall, however, the *Qur'an* grants greater prominence to Maryam and 'Isa than to Zachariah and Yahya.

As her guardian, Zachariah is responsible for Maryam's maintenance. The *Qur'an* states that when Zachariah enters the shrine to bring Maryam food, he finds that she already has ample provisions. Questioned as to how she has obtained the food, Maryam replies that it comes from Allah. This reinforces her privileged position as an individual who has found favor in the eyes of God.

Chapter 19, known as the Surah of Maryam (Surat Maryam), relates Maryam's withdrawal from her people to an eastern place, probably for the purpose of meditation and spiritual guidance. The East is symbolic of illumination and of new beginnings in many world traditions. While she is there, an angel appears to her and announces that she has been chosen by God to give birth to 'Isa. The angel, who assumes the guise of an adult male, is identified in later Islamic tradition as the angel Gabriel. Maryam's vulnerability at finding herself unprotected and in the presence of what appears to be an adult male is readily apparent. She seeks protection from Allah. The angel reveals his identity and delivers his message. Upon hearing the angel's announcement, Maryam questions her ability to bear a child while she is still a virgin. The response is that Allah can bring about anything He wishes through His word.

The *Qur'an* does not indicate how Maryam conceived, nor does it specify the length of her pregnancy. Instead, we are told that Maryam withdraws to a remote place to give birth to the child. Isolated, afraid, and in the throes of labor pains, she cries out in anguish: "Oh, would that I had died before this and had become a thing forgotten and out of sight" (19:23). It is not clear if she is crying out because of the severity of her labor pangs or because she anticipates the harsh recriminations of society for giving birth to a child out of wedlock. However, her agony is short-lived, for she is soon comforted. A voice tells her that Allah has provided a rivulet at her feet and fresh, ripe dates on the date palm in front of her for the purpose of providing her with refreshment while she experiences the pangs of labor. Islamic scholars differ as to the origin of the voice. Some claim it comes from the baby 'Isa, while others argue that it is the voice of the angel Gabriel. Maryam is instructed to partake of these provisions in order to relieve her discomfort. Her need for sustenance is taken as proof by Muslim scholars that she experiences pain during childbirth and that she needs strength to push the infant out of her womb. This underscores the fact that 'Isa was a human being, born in a natural manner from a mother who experiences a natural delivery.

Surah 19 tells us that after delivering her baby, Maryam carries him back to her family. As anticipated, she is greeted with admonition, suspicion, and accusations of immoral conduct. Maryam responds by pointing to the infant. The *Qur'an* tells us that the infant 'Isa speaks from the cradle, declaring himself to be a servant of Allah and a prophet. 'Isa not only vindicates his mother in front of her people, but he is also enjoined to show kindness to his mother as well as perform prayer and acts of charity as part of God's teachings. He invites the human community to follow his example. 'Isa's speech (19: 30) serves the dual purpose of confirming his mother's innocence of sexual misconduct and affirming his status as a human prophet and servant of God.

The *Qur'an* holds Maryam up as an example for all believers to emulate. Muslims are enjoined to aspire to the high standards she sets through obedience to God, through faith, and through chastity. However, since Islam does not promote celibacy, chastity is generally interpreted as abstinence from sexual relations before marriage and the exclusive engagement in sexual relations with one's lawful spouse within marriage.

Additionally, Maryam achieves a high status in her capacity as a mother. Muslims regard motherhood as a metaphor for the guidance and compassion within Islam. One of the attributes or adjectives used for of God is *ar-Rahim,* the Compassionate, a word that is derived from the same root as *raham,* the Arabic word for womb. Many of the references to Maryam in the *Qur'an* point to her role as the mother of 'Isa. These references serve to establish her humanity and the humanity of her son. For example, passages from Surahs 4 and 5 denounce those who believe that 'Isa and Maryam formed part of a divine trinity. As we have seen in our discussion of Hawwa, Muslims believe that there is one God and that 'Isa was a human being who served as one of His prophets. To assign divine status to 'Isa is considered blasphemy in Islam.

The selections below are translated by M.M. Pickthall in *The Meaning of the Glorious Qur'an,* revised and edited in modern English by Arafat K. El-Ashi.

REFERENCES

Ali, Abdullah Yusuf. Trans. *The Holy Qur'an: English Translation of the Meanings of the Qur'an with Notes.* Indianapolis: H&C International, 1992.

Ali, Al-Hajj Ta'lim (T.B. Irving). Trans. *The Qur'an: The First American Version.* Vermont: Amana, 1985.

Badawi, Leila. "Islam." *Women in Religion.* Eds. Jean Holm and John Bowker. London: Pinter, 1999. 84–112.

Cleary, Thomas, and Sartaz Aziz. *Twilight Goddess: Spiritual Feminism and Feminine Spirituality.* Boston: Shambhala, 2000.

Geagea, Rev. Nilo. *Mary of the Koran: A Meeting Point Between Christianity and Islam.* Trans. Rev. Lawrence T. Fares. New York: Philosophical Library, 1984.

Hammad, Ahmad Zaki. *Mary, The Chosen Woman: The Mother of Jesus in the Qur'an: An Interlinear Commentary on Surat Maryam.* Illinois: Quranic Library Institute, 2001.

Murata, Sachiko. *The Tao of Islam: A Sourcebook on Gender Relationships in Islamic Thought.* Albany: State U of New York P, 1992.

Pickthall, M. M., trans. *The Meaning of the Glorious Qur'an: Explanatory Translation.* Ed. Arafat K. El-Ashi. Rev. ed. Maryland: Amana, 2002.

Schimmel, Annemarie. *Deciphering the Signs of God: A Phenomenological Approach to Islam.* Albany: State U of New York P, 1994.

———. *Mystical Dimensions of Islam.* Chapel Hill: U of North Carolina P, 1975.

Sells, Michael, trans. *Approaching The Qur'an: The Early Revelations.* Ashland, Oregon: White Clouds P, 1999.

Smith, Huston. *The Religions of Man.* New York: Harper and Row, 1965.

Smith, Jane I., and Yvonne Y. Haddad. "The Virgin Mary in Islamic Tradition and Commentary." *The Muslim World* 79 (1989): 161–187.

Stowasser, Barbara Freyer. *Women in the Qur'an, Traditions, and Interpretation.* New York: Oxford UP, 1994.

Wadud-Muhsin, Amina. *Qur'an and Woman.* Kuala Lumpur: Penerbit Fajr Bakti Sdn. Bhd., 1992.

Selections from the *Qur'an*

Surah 3: Al 'Imran

31. Say, (O Muhammad, to mankind): If you love Allah, then follow me; Allah will love you and forgive you your sins; for Allah is Forgiving, Merciful.

32. Say: Obey Allah and the Messenger. But if they turn away, Lo! Allah loves not the disbelievers (in His guidance).

33. Lo! Allah preferred Adam and Noah and the Family of Abraham and the Family of 'Imrān above the worlds.

34. They were descendants one of another. And Allah is Hearer, Knower.

35. (Remember) when the wife of 'Imrān said: My Lord I have vowed unto You that which is in my belly as a consecrated (offering). So accept it from me. Lo! You, only You, are the Hearer, the Knower!

36. And when she was delivered she said: My Lord! O! I am delivered of a female—Allah knew best of what she was delivered and the male is not as the female; and Lo! I have named her Mary, and Lo! I crave Your protection for her and for her offspring from the outcast devil.

37. Thus her Lord accepted her with full acceptance and vouchsafed to her a goodly growth; and made Zachariah her guardian. Whenever

Zachariah went into the sanctuary where she was, he found that she had food. He said: O Mary! Whence comes unto you this (food)? She answered: It is from Allah. Allah gives without stint to whom He will.

38. Then Zachariah prayed unto his Lord and said: My Lord! Bestow upon me of Your bounty goodly offspring. Lo! You are the Hearer of supplication.

39. And the angels called to him as he stood praying in the sanctuary: Allah gives you glad tidings of (a son whose name is) John (Yaḥyā), (who comes) to confirm a word from Allah, lordly, chaste, a Prophet of the righteous.

40. He said: My Lord! How can I have a son when age has overtaken me already and my wife is barren? (The angel) answered: So (it will be). Allah does what He will.

41. He said: My Lord! Appoint a token for me. (The angel) said: The token unto you (shall be) that you shall not speak unto mankind three days except by signs. Remember your Lord much, and praise (Him) in the early hours of night and morning.

42. And when the angels said: O Mary! Lo! Allah has chosen you and made you pure, and has preferred you above (all) the women of creation.

43. O Mary! Be obedient to your Lord, prostrate yourself and bow with those who bow (in worship).

44. This is of the tidings of the unseen. We reveal it unto you (Muhammad). You were not present with them when they threw their pens (to know) which of them should be the guardian of Mary, nor were you present with them when they quarreled (thereupon).

45. (And remember) when the angels said: O Mary! Allah gives you glad tidings of a word from Him, whose name is the Messiah, Jesus son of Mary illustrious in the world and the Hereafter, and one of those brought near (unto Allah).

46. He will speak unto mankind in his cradle and in his manhood, and he is of the righteous.

47. She said: My Lord! How can I have a child when no mortal has touched me? He said: So (it will be). Allah creates what He will, if He decrees a thing, He says unto it only: Be! and it is.

48. And He will teach him the Scripture and wisdom, and the Torah and the Gospel.

49. And will make him a messenger unto the children of Israel, (saying): Lo! I come unto you with a sign from your Lord. Lo! I fashion for you out of clay the likeness of a bird, and I breathe into it and it is a bird, by Allah's leave. I heal him who was born blind, and the leper, and I raise the dead, by Allah's leave. And I announce unto you what you eat and what you store up in your houses. Lo! herein surely is a portent for you, if you are believers.

50. And (I come) confirming that which was before me of the Torah, and to make lawful some of that which was forbidden unto you. I come unto you with a sign from your Lord, so keep your duty to Allah and obey me.

51. Lo! Allah is my Lord and your Lord, so worship Him. That is a straight path.

52. But when Jesus became conscious of their disbelief, he cried: Who will be my helpers in the cause of Allah? The disciples said: We will be Allah's helpers. We believe in Allah, and bear you witness that we have surrendered (unto Him).

53. Our Lord! We believe in that which You have revealed and we follow him whom You have sent. Enroll us among those who witness (to the truth).

54. And they (the disbelievers) schemed, and Allah schemed (against them): and Allah is the best of schemers.

55. (And remember) when Allah said: O Jesus! Lo! I am gathering you and causing you to ascend unto Me, and am cleansing you of those who disbelieve and am setting those who follow you above those who disbelieve until the Day of Resurrection. Then unto Me you will (all) return, and I shall judge between you as to that wherein you used to differ.

56. As for those who disbelieve I shall chastise them with a heavy chastisement in the world and the Hereafter; and they will have no helpers.

57. And as for those who believe and do good works, He will pay them their wages in full. And Allah loves not wrongdoers.

Mary

Surah 19: Maryam

Revealed at Makkah

In the name of Allah, the Beneficent, the Merciful

1. *Kāf. Hā'. Yā'. 'Ayn. Sād.*

2. A mention of the mercy of your Lord unto His servant Zachariah.

3. When he cried unto his Lord a cry in secret,

4. Saying: My Lord! Lo! the bones of me wax feeble and my head is shining with grey hair, and I have never been unblessed in prayer to You, my Lord.

5. Lo! I fear my kinsfolk after me, since my wife is barren. Oh, give me from Your presence a successor

6. Who shall inherit of me and inherit (also) of the house of Jacob. And make him, my Lord, acceptable (unto You).

7. (It was said unto him): O Zachariah! Lo! We bring you tidings of a son whose name is John; We have given the same name to none before (him).

8. He said: My Lord! How can I have a son when my wife is barren and I have reached infirm old age?

9. He said: So (it will be). Your Lord says: It is easy for Me, even as I created you before, when you were nothing.

10. He said: My Lord! Appoint for me some token. He said: Your token is that you shall not speak unto mankind three nights with no bodily defect.

11. Then he came forth unto his people from the sanctuary and signified to them: Glorify your Lord at break of day and fall of night.

12. (And it was said unto his son): O John! Hold the Scripture. And We gave him wisdom when a child.

13. And compassion from Our presence, and purity; and he was devout,

14. And dutiful toward his parents. And he was not arrogant, rebellious.

15. Peace on him the day he was born, the day he dies and the day he shall be raised alive!

16. And make mention of Mary in the Scripture, when she had withdrawn from her people to a chamber looking East,

17. And had chosen seclusion from them. Then We sent unto her Our spirit and it assumed for her the likeness of a perfect man.

18. She said: Lo! I seek refuge in the Beneficent One from you, if you are God fearing.

19. He said: I am only a messenger of your Lord, that I may bestow on you a faultless son.

20. She said: How can I have a son when no mortal has touched me, neither have I been unchaste!

21. He said: So (it will be). Your Lord says: It is easy for Me. And (it will be) that We may make of him a miracle for mankind and a mercy from Us, and it is a thing ordained.

22. She conceived him, and she withdrew with him to a far place.

23. The pangs of childbirth drove her unto the trunk of the palm tree. She said: Oh, would that I had died before this and had become a thing forgotten and out of sight.

24. Then (one) cried unto her from below her, saying: Grieve not! Your Lord has placed a rivulet beneath you.

25. And shake the trunk of the palm tree toward you, it will cause ripe dates to fall upon you.

26. So eat and drink and be consoled. And if you meet any human, say: Lo! I have vowed a fast unto the Beneficent, so I shall not speak this day to any mortal.

27. Then she brought him to her own folk, carrying him. They said: O Mary! You have come with an amazing (unprecedented) thing.

28. Oh sister of Aaron! Your father was not a wicked man nor was your mother a harlot.

29. Then she pointed to him. They said How can we talk to one who is in the cradle, a little child?

30. He spoke: Lo! I am the slave of Allah. He has given me the Scripture and has appointed me a Prophet,

31. And has made me blessed wheresoever I may be, and has enjoined upon me prayer and almsgiving so long as I remain alive,

32. And (has made me) dutiful toward my mother, and has not made me arrogant, unblessed.

33. Peace on me the day I was born, the day I die, and the day I shall be raised alive!

34. Such was Jesus, son of Mary: (this is) a statement of the truth concerning which they doubt.

35. It befits not (the Majesty of) Allah that He should take unto Himself a son. Glory be to Him! When He decrees a thing, He says unto it only: Be! and it is.

36. And lo! Allah is my Lord and your Lord. So worship Him. That is a straight path.

37. But the sects among them differed: woe unto the disbelievers from the meeting of an awful Day.

38. How much they will see and hear on the Day they come unto Us! Yet the evildoers are today in error manifest.

39. And warn them of the Day of anguish when the case has been decided. Now they are in a state of carelessness, and they believe not.

40. Lo! We inherit the earth and all who are thereon, and unto Us they are returned.

41. And make mention (O Muhammad) in the Scripture of Abraham. Lo! he was a saint, a Prophet.

42. When he said unto his father: O my father! Why worship you that which hears not nor sees, nor can in anything avail you?

43. O my father! Lo! there has come unto me of knowledge that which came not unto you. So follow me, and I will lead you on a straight path.

44. O my father! Worship not the Devil. Lo! the Devil is a rebel unto the Beneficent.

45. O my father! Lo! I fear lest a punishment from the Beneficent overtake you so that you become a comrade of the Devil.

46. He said: Will you reject my gods, O Abraham? If you cease not, I shall surely stone you. Depart from me a long while!

47. He said: Peace be unto you! I shall ask forgiveness of my Lord for you. Lo! He was ever gracious unto me.

48. I shall withdraw from you and that unto which you pray beside Allah, and I shall pray unto my Lord. Perchance, in prayer unto my Lord, I shall not be unblessed.

49. So, when he had withdrawn from them and that which they were worshipping beside Allah, We gave him Isaac and Jacob. Each of them We made a Prophet.

50. And We gave them of Our mercy, and assigned to them a high and true renown.

51. And make mention in the Scripture of Moses. Lo! he was chosen, and he was a messenger (of Allah), a Prophet.

52. We called him from the right slope of the Mount, and brought him near in communion.

53. And We bestowed upon him of Our mercy his brother Aaron, a Prophet (likewise).

54. And make mention in the Scripture of Ishmael. Lo! he was a keeper of his promise, and he was a messenger (of Allah) a Prophet.

55. He used to enjoin prayer upon his people and alms giving, and was acceptable in the sight of his Lord.

56. And make mention in the Scripture of Idrīs. Lo! he was a saint, a Prophet;

57. And We raised him to high station.

58. These are they unto whom Allah showed favor from among the Prophets, of the seed of Adam and of those whom We carried (in the ship) with Noah, and of the seed of Abraham and Israel, and from among those whom We guided and chose. When the revelations of the Beneficent were recited unto them, they fell down, adoring and weeping.

59. Now there has succeeded them a later generation who have missed Prayer and have followed lusts. But they will meet deception,

60. Save him who shall repent and believe and do right. Such will enter the Garden and they will not be wronged in anything—

61. Gardens of Eden, which the Beneficent has promised to His slaves in the Unseen. Lo! His promise is ever sure of fulfillment—

62. They hear therein no idle talk, but only Peace; and therein they have food for morn and evening.

63. Such is the Garden which We cause the devout among Our bondmen to inherit.

64. We (angels) come not down save by commandment of your Lord. Unto Him belongs all that is before us and all that is behind us and all that is between those two, and your Lord was never forgetful—

65. Lord of the heavens and the earth and all that is between them! Therefore, worship you Him and be you steadfast in His worship. Do you know one that can be named along with Him?

66. And man says: When I am dead, shall I really be brought forth alive?

67. Does not man remember that We created him before, when he was nothing?

68. And, by your Lord, surely We shall assemble them and the devils, then We shall bring them, crouching, around Hell.

69. Then We shall pluck out from every sect whichever of them was most stern in rebellion to the Beneficent.

70. And surely We are best aware of those most worthy to be burned therein.

71. There is not one of you but shall approach it. That is a fixed ordinance of your Lord.

72. Then We shall rescue those who kept from evil, and leave the evildoers crouching there.

73. And when Our clear revelations are recited unto them those who disbelieve say unto those who believe: Which of the two parties (yours or ours) is better in position, and more imposing as an army?

74. How many a generation have We destroyed before them, who were more imposing in respect of gear and outward seeming!

75. Say: As for him who is in error, the Beneficent will surely prolong his span of life until, when they behold that which they were promised, whether it be punishment (in the world), or Hour (of Doom), they will know who is worse in position and who is weaker as an army.

76. Allah increases in right guidance those who walk aright, and the good deeds which endure are better in your Lord's sight for reward, and better for resort.

77. Have you seen him who disbelieves in Our revelations and says: Assuredly I shall be given wealth and children!

78. Has he perused the Unseen, or has he made a pact with the Beneficent?

79. Nay, but We shall record that which he says and prolong for him a span of torment.

80. And We shall inherit from him that whereof he spoke, and he will come unto Us, alone (without his wealth and children).

81. And they have chosen (other) gods beside Allah that they may be a power for them.

82. Nay, but they will deny their worship of them, and become opponents unto them.

83. Do you not see that We have set the devils on the disbelievers to confound them with confusion?

84. So make no haste against them (O Muhammad). We do but count to them a (limited) number (of days).

85. On the Day when We shall gather the righteous unto the Beneficent, a goodly company.

86. And drive the criminals unto Hell, a weary herd,

87. They will have no power of intercession, save him who has made a covenant with the Beneficent.

88. And they say: The Beneficent has taken unto Himself a son.

89. Assuredly you utter a disastrous thing,

90. Whereby the heavens are almost torn, and the earth is split asunder and the mountains fall in ruins,

91. That you ascribe unto the Beneficent a son,

92. When it is not consonant with (the Majesty of) the Beneficent that He should choose a son.

93. There is none in the heavens and the earth but comes unto the Beneficent as a slave.

94. Surely He knows them and numbers them with (right) numbering.

95. And each one of them will come unto Him on the Day of Resurrection, alone.

96. Lo! those who believe and do good works, the Beneficent will appoint for them love.

97. And We make (this Scripture) easy in your tongue, (O Muhammad) only that you may bear good tidings therewith unto those who ward off (evil), and warn therewith the froward folk.

98. And how many a generation before them have We destroyed! Can you (Muhammad) see a single man of them, or hear from them the slightest sound?

Questions for Review and Discussion

1. What is the significance of Maryam's lineage and upbringing?
2. What are some of the similarities and differences between the Islamic tradition and the Christian tradition concerning the announcement and birth of 'Isa/Jesus?
3. Maryam is instructed to partake of refreshments in order to alleviate her labor pangs. What does this concern with minimizing the distress of childbirth reflect about Muslim attitude toward labor and delivery? How does this attitude differ from the attitude towards labor and delivery as told in Genesis 3?
4. What are the similarities and differences in the depiction of the Virgin Mary in Luke 1–2 and the selections on Maryam in the *Qur'an*?
5. What are the similarities and differences in the depiction of Jesus in Luke 1–2 of the New Testament and the selections on 'Isa in the *Qur'an*?
6. What are the parallels in the Qur'anic story of Yahya and the story of John the Baptist in Luke 1–2?
7. Chapter 19:23 of the *Qur'an* tells us that Maryam cries out, "Oh, would that I had died before this and had become a thing forgotten and out of sight." What do you think Maryam means by this?
8. According to the Islamic tradition, one of the attributes of God is compassion (*rahma*), a word that is derived from the same root as *raham*, the Arabic word for womb. What is the significance of this connection?
9. Describe Maryam's qualities.

Chapter 16

Oshun

Glossary of Names and Terms

AJE   Power emanating from a feminine source

BABALAWOS   High priests or principal diviners of the Yoruba

DIVINATION   Mystical communion with spirits, ancestors, and divinities to learn of Olodumare's intentions, to learn of the future, and to seek spiritual guidance

IFA CORPUS   Body of scriptures of the Yoruba

IPONRI   Heavenly consciousness

IRIN AJO   Quest to unite earthly consciousness (ori) with heavenly consciousness (iponri)

IWE-PELE   Balanced character and attitude that results from successful quest to achieve unity with Olodumare

ODU   Sixteen prophets; also known as Ancients or Elders; disciples of Orunmila

ODU IFA   Teachings of Orunmila; instruct aspirant on how to arrive at state of divine unity

OLODUMARE   Also known as Olorun; supreme deity of Yoruba religion; creator and sustainer of universe

ORI   Earthly/human consciousness

ORISHA   Spiritual forces/energies within nature; spirits; manifestations of Olodumare

ORUNMILA   Prophet of Yoruba religion; god of divination; eldest son of Olodumare

OSE-TURA   Also known as Esu; son of Oshun

OSHUN/ỌṢUN   Revered goddess of the Yoruba people; river divinity; only female orisha present at creation; introduced to art of divination by her spouse, Orunmila

YORUBA   Tribe of over 20 million people in Nigeria, West Africa

The goddess Oshun is a revered and prominent deity in the indigenous religion of the Yoruba people of Nigeria, West Africa. The Yoruba is a large tribe of over 20 million that speak various dialects of the Yoruba language. People of Yoruba descent constitute the greatest percentage of Africans enslaved for labor in the Americas. A large percentage of enslaved Yoruba came from the elite classes of soldiers, priests, diviners, and medicine persons—individuals who had been initiated into and instructed with knowledge of their culture and religion. They carried that knowledge with them as they were transported to their destinations in the West Indies and the Americas. But the slave trade and interaction with Christianity caused distortions within the indigenous Yoruba religion. As a result, some Yoruba either rejected their traditional religion or simultaneously maintained and practiced their traditional beliefs with Christianity, with each tradition supplementing and complementing the other, and with elements of the Yoruba indigenous culture frequently being transfigured to accommodate European and American religious sensibilities. In some cases, the Yoruba were able to keep their deities alive by masking them behind Christian saints and rituals—a task that was made easier in Catholicism than in Protestantism.

The Yoruba religion and culture continue to thrive in Nigeria and are flourishing in the diaspora. The religion is multifaceted, plural in nature, multivocal, and fluid. Its practice in the Americas may differ somewhat from the Yoruba religion as it was originally practiced in Nigeria, in so far as the former may emphasize the occult aspect of Yoruba while the traditional religion stressed the mystical aspect of a divine journey to the supreme deity, known simultaneously as Olodumare or Olorun, the deity credited with the creation and sustenance of the universe.

The "prophet" of Yoruba religion and culture is Orunmila. He is recognized everywhere as the god of divination. In some traditions, Orunmila is a deity who holds the position equivalent to the son of god since he is the eldest son of Olodumare. He is present in his divine form when Olodumare creates the universe. In his human manifestation, Orunmila exhibits such prodigious intelligence and wisdom that he becomes recognized as a deity. As the omnilinguist god, he travels across the African continent and the diaspora sharing his wisdom, guidance, and knowledge. His teachings, known as the *Odu Ifa,* provide religious aspirants with the means to arrive at a state of divine oneness that comes from elevating one's earthly consciousness, known as *Ori,* with one's heavenly consciousness, known as *Iponri,* so the two become unified as one. This quest, known as *irin ajo,* is long, difficult, and fraught with perils, and should be undertaken only by those who are determined and pure of heart. Success depends on a number of factors: the study of the *Ifa corpus,* the scriptures that have been transmitted orally from one generation to the next by the *Babalawos* (High Priests/Principal Diviners); knowledge of the divinatory processes bequeathed by ancestors; rituals and sacrifices to the spirits that impact human development and evolution; and adherence to a moral code of ethics in order to vanquish oppressive human and spiritual forces.

Orunmila's disciples are the Ancients or Elders, known as the *odu,* sixteen heavenly prophets whose mission is to impart their celestial essence and to engage in prophecy. Each odu is signified by a series of unique marks, patterns, rituals, ethics, and morals. Access to the heavenly knowledge that the odu embody is manifested in the ability to divine. Through the process of divination, initiates learn of the forces that shape people's past, present, and future lives, and the means to overcome the forces that deter them from aligning with their heavenly selves.

The Yoruba believe that nature is to be viewed as a manifestation of the divine essence of Olodumare. This essence is inherent in all of creation as a life force that assumes material form in a natural object. The Yoruba do not worship a specific object in nature but the energy within it, an energy that permeates all of creation, including human beings, and connects us with each other as well as with the divine essence.

The act of divination forms the central core of Yoruba religious practice and belief. Divination consists of mystical communion with the divinities, spiritual beings, and ancestors for the purpose of revealing the intentions of Olodumare and the supernatural world, for knowing one's future and the future of others, for seeking scriptural messages of Ifa (the body of scripture that has been transmitted orally for centuries), for determining what offerings are expected by the orisha (spiritual forces), and for inquiring if those offerings are accepted by the orisha. There are various systems of divination, the most important of which is the *Ifa Divination*. Each type of divination employs different paraphernalia, including kola-nuts, cowrie shells, and palm nuts. One's level in the priestly hierarchy also determines which paraphernalia can be used for divination.

The Yoruba pantheon consists of the orisha, entities that embrace a variety of meanings, depending on the particular culture or tradition. They can be angelic spirits or deities that play a prominent role in human life. Some orisha personify natural forces and phenomena. The term can also mean a divinely revealed aspect of Olodumare, with each orisha signifying a different path to knowing god. Some orisha may have been historical figures or cultural heroes and heroines who were later deified. The term orisha combines *ori*, which designates human consciousness, with *sha*, which designates the ability of human consciousness to arrive at its ultimate potential of assimilating itself with the divine. In some traditions, the orisha are credited with assisting in the development of human consciousness as it goes through the stages of enlightenment, with each stage corresponding to a different orisha, and with each stage reflecting and informing human behavior and attitude.

The orisha act as messengers or guides to assist humanity in its spiritual quest to achieve a unitive state with Olodumare, a goal reflected in *iwe-pele*, a balanced character and attitude. Belief in the existence and function of the orisha is a prerequisite condition for achieving this state. The orisha can be induced to intervene on behalf of human beings through divination, faith, prayer, song, dance, ritual, and sacrifice that are performed by both priest and devotee. The Yoruba believe themselves to be descended from the orisha.

There are numerous orisha, each of which requires a special form of worship, song, and sacrifice, and each of which bears a different name. In some traditions, the goddess Oshun is one of the most prominent among them. She plays a central role in Yoruba religious thought and practice. She is the only female present at creation, and some traditions credit her with providing Obatala (also called Orishanla) with the water for smoothing the clay that he uses to mold human beings. She marries Orunmila who introduces her to the art of divination.

Oshun is multidimensional, complex, and fluid. She is revered in different cultural traditions, assuming a variety of manifestations and associations. She is as diverse as her devotees and the geographical locations where she is worshipped. Her presence during creation coupled with her participation in the formation of human beings endows her with the ability to influence human destiny. Among her attributes are unconditional love, receptivity, clarity, beauty, sensuality, graceful-ness, and an artistic sensibility. As a river divinity (the Oshun river in Southwestern Nigeria bears her name), she is associated with flowing movement and healing through cool waters. When used ritualistically, water, Oshun's primary curative agent, is purported to induce harmony, peace, and balance, to eradicate tension, and to reduce heat.

Oshun's name means source—the perpetually renewing source of life that underlies the visible realm. As a fertility divinity, she is aligned with the female and feminine processes. Her assistance is sought for tasks traditionally associated with the female: childbearing, child rearing, healing of children, nurturing, and alleviat-ing the discomfort of female disorders. Some traditions claim that without her, the other orishas are powerless and that divining becomes impossible. Oshun can alter-nate between being young and old, irritable and calm, depending upon the circum-stances and the nature of the devotee who seeks her assistance. She is associated with the color yellow, with objects made of brass, with the number five, and with rivers and lakes in the natural environment. Her physical correspondences are the circulatory system, the digestive organs, the elimination system, and the female pubic area.

Oshun is also revered as the preeminent hair-plaiter. Through practicing the decorative arts of beautifying the head, Oshun is reputed to hold the power to influ-ence destiny. The Yoruba tradition places great religious significance on beautifying the human head since the head is perceived as a reflection of one's personality and destiny as well as of the divinity or *ori* within. The head becomes a physical mani-festation of one's spiritual essence. Hence, hair-plaiting holds great symbolic value for the Yoruba people, and the hairdresser or hair-plaiter, since it is her task to beautify the head, is a well-respected member of the community.

Oshun centers and shrines are found in West Africa, Europe, and the Americas. Because the Yoruba tradition is currently experiencing a renewed interest in the United States, Oshun's devotees are growing in numbers. Devotion to Oshun enables African American priestesses to connect with their religious traditions and develop a spirituality that articulates strong, black womanhood. It provides them with a historical and spiritual foundation that links them to Africa, the ancestral home of the African diaspora. Oshun is celebrated in festivals in Nigeria and the Americas, including the Osogbo festival, the largest festival in Nigeria in honor of an indigenous deity.

The mythology of Africa is as vast and as diverse as its inhabitants. Stories from different cultures were transmitted orally for centuries before they were written down in European languages. Because the culture of Africa was oral, locating reliable sources of indigenous materials can be a challenging task, especially due to the pervasiveness of ethnic and cultural inflections. The *Ifa Divination* below, translated by Rowland Abiodun, contains the story of Oshun at the time of creation, her initial rejection by the odu, and their ultimate reconciliation. Its authenticity is generally accepted by the different traditions. Oshun's son, Ose-Tura, also known as Esu, forms the link between his mother and the remaining odu.

REFERENCES

Abimbola, 'Wande. "The Bag of Wisdom: Osun and the Origins of the Ifa Divination." *Osun Across the Waters: A Yoruba Goddess in Africa and the Americas.* Eds. Joseph M. Murphy and Mei-Mei Sanford. Bloomington: Indiana UP, 2001. 141–154.

Abiodun, Rowland. "Hidden Power: Osun, the Seventeenth Odu." *Osun Across the Waters: A Yoruba Goddess in Africa and the Americas.* Eds. Joseph M. Murphy and Mei-Mei Sanford. Bloomington: Indiana UP, 2001. 10–33.

Abrahams, Roger D. *African Folktales: Traditional Stories of the Black World.* New York: Pantheon, 1983.

Awolalu, Omosade J. *Yoruba Beliefs and Sacrificial Rites.* New York: Athelia Henrietta, 1996.

Badejo, Dierdre L. "Authority and Discourse in the *Orin Odun Osun.*" *Osun Across the Waters: A Yoruba Goddess in Africa and the Americas.* Eds. Joseph M. Murphy and Mei-Mei Sanford. Bloomington: Indiana UP, 2001. 128–140.

Courlander, Harold. *Tales of Yoruba Gods and Heroes: Myths, Legends, and Heroic Tales of the Yoruba People of West Africa.* New York: Crown, 1973.

———. *A Treasury of African Folklore: The Oral Literature, Traditions, Myths, Legends, Epics, Tales, Recollections, Wisdom, Sayings, and Humor of Africa.* New York: Crown, 1975.

Dorson, Richard M., ed. *African Folklore.* New York: Anchor, 1972.

Duane, O.B. *African Myths and Legends.* London: Brockhampton, 1998.

Fama, Chief. *Fundamentals of the Yoruba Religion (Orisha Worship).* San Bernardino: Ile Orunmila Communications, 1993.

Hackett, Rosalind I. J. "Women in African Religions." *Women and World Religions.* Ed. Lucinda Joy Peach. New Jersey: Prentice Hall, 2002. 309–327.

Karade, Baba Ifa. *The Handbook of Yoruba Religious Concepts.* Maine: Samuel Weiser, 1994.

Matateyou, Emmanuel. *An Anthology of Myths, Legends, and Folktales From Cameroon: Storytelling in Africa. Studies in African Literature.* Vol. 4. New York: Edwin Mellen, 1997.

Murphy, Joseph M., and Mei-Mei Sanford, eds. *Osun Across the Waters: A Yoruba Goddess in Africa and the Americas.* Bloomington: Indiana UP, 2001.

Tembo, Mwizenge. *Myths of the World: Legends of Africa.* New York: Metro, 1996.

Weaver, Lloyd, and Olurunmi Egbelade. *Maternal Divinity Yemonja: Tranquil Sea, Turbulent Tides: Eleven Yoruba Tales.* New York: Athelia Henrietta P, 1998.

Ifa Divination

It was divined for the sixteen Odù
Who were coming from heaven to earth
A woman was the seventeenth of them.
When they got to earth,
5   They cleared the grove for Orò,
Orò had his own space.
They cleared the grove for Ọpa,
Ọpa's abode was secure.
They prepared a grove for Eégún,
10 Eégún had a home.
But they made no provision for Ọ̀ṣun,
Also known as "Ṣẹ̀ẹ̀gẹ̀sí, the preeminent hair-plaiter with the coral-beaded
    comb."
So, she decided to wait and see
How they would carry out their mission successfully;
15 Ọ̀ṣun sat quietly and watched them.
Beginning with Èjì-Ogbè and Ọ̀yẹ̀kú méjì,
Ìwòrí méjì, Odi méjì, Ìròsùn méjì
Ọ̀wònrín méjì, Ọ̀bàrà méjì, Ọ̀kànràn méjì,
Ògún-dá, Òsá, Ọ̀ràngun méjì and so on,
20 They all decided not to countenance Ọ̀ṣun in their mission.
She, too, kept mute,
And carried on her rightful duty,
Which is hair-plaiting.
She had a comb.
25 They never knew she was an *"àjé."*
When they were coming from heaven,
God chose all good things;
He also chose their keeper,
And this was a woman.

30 All women are *àjé*.
And because all other Odù left Ọ̀ṣun out,
Nothing they did was successful.
They went to Eégún's grove and pleaded with him,
That their mission be crowned with success.
35 "Eégún, it is you who straightens the four corners of the world,
Let all be straight."
They went to Àdàgbà Òjòmù
Who is called Orò
"You are the only one who frightens Death and Sickness.

40   Please help drive them away."
      Healing failed to take place;
      Instead epidemic festered.
      They went to Ọ̀ṣẹ́ and begged him
      To let the rain fall.
45   Rain didn't fall.
      Then they went to Ọ̀ṣun
      Ọ̀ṣun received them warmly,
      And entertained them,
      But shame would not let them confide in Ọ̀ṣun,
50   Whom they had ignored.
      They then headed for heaven
      And made straight for Olódùmarè,
      Who asked why they came
      They said it was about their mission on earth.
55   When they left heaven,
      And arrived on earth
      All things went well;
      Then later things turned for the worse,
      Nothing was successful.
60   And Olódùmarè asked
      "How many of you are here?"
      They answered, "Sixteen."
      He also asked,
      "When you were leaving heaven, how many were you?"
65   They answered, "Seventeen."
      And Olódùmarè said, "You are all intriguers.
      That one you left behind
      If you do not bring her here,
      There will be no solution to your problem.
70   If you continue this way,
      You will always fail."
      They then returned to Ọ̀ṣun,
      And addressed her, "Mother, the preeminent hair-plaiter with the coral-
          beaded comb.
      We have been to the Creator
75   And it was there we discovered that all Odù were derived from you [Ọ̀ṣun],
      And that our suffering would continue
      If we failed to recognize and obey you [Ọ̀ṣun]."
      So, on their return to the earth from the Creator,
      All the remaining Odù wanted to pacify and please Ọ̀ṣun.
80   But Ọ̀ṣun would not go out with them.
      The baby she was expecting might go out with them,

But even that would depend on the gender of the baby
For she said that if the baby she was expecting
Turned out to be male,
85   It is that male child who would go out with them
But if the baby turned out to be female,
She [Òṣun] would have nothing to do with them.
She said she knew of all they [the Odù] had eaten and enjoyed without her,
Particularly all the delicacies and he-goat they ate.
90   As Òṣun was about to curse them all,
Òṣẹ́ covered her mouth
And the remaining Odù started praying
That Òṣun might deliver a male child.
They then started to beg her.
95   When Òṣun delivered
She had a baby boy
Whom they named Òṣẹ-Túrá.

Questions for Review and Discussion

1. The *Ifa Divination* makes it clear that Oshun's power and influence are greater than that of any other odu or orisha. She is the conduit through which all of life flows. Without her cooperation, life would cease to exist. The divination also tells us that Oshun is the only female among them. What indications do we have that her gender may be the source of her overwhelming power?

2. Why did the sixteen odu originally ignore Oshun?

3. Oshun knows that even though she has been ostracized by the odu, she is indispensable to the success of their mission. Yet she chooses not to confront them. Instead, she continues to engage in hair-plaiting with equanimity, knowing that the odu will eventually have to acknowledge her presence and seek her assistance. What does her conduct and demeanor in this situation reveal about her personality?

4. What is the significance of Oshun's insistence that she will work with the odu only if she has a male child? Why would she choose to shun them if her child is female?

5. Based on your understanding of this *Ifa Divination,* how important is the role of women in the Yoruba culture?

6. The divination describes Oshun as an "aje" and then reveals, "All women are aje." The word "aje" is generally translated to mean beings possessing a power that emanates from a uniquely feminine or female source. Aje are mysterious, ubiquitous, and powerful forces that can advance or hinder human goals. Discuss Oshun as a metaphor for the power, influence, and presence of the female and of the mother.

7. What does Oshun contribute to the powers of the other odu and to life in general?

8. How does Oshun exercise both sacred and secular agency?

9. In what ways can Oshun serve as a role model for women today?

Chapter 17

White Buffalo Woman

GLOSSARY OF NAMES AND TERMS

LAKOTA Collective name of over 30 different peoples from at least six language stocks who inhabited prairies and plains in North American

LILA WAKAN Very sacred

TUNKASHILA Grandfather; Great Spirit

WAKAN Sacred, holy, powerful; also ancient and enduring

WANBLEE GALESHKA Spotted eagle; sacred bird that acts as Tunkashila's messenger; twelve of his feathers hang from sacred pipe

WHITE BUFFALO WOMAN Central divinity in Lakota mythology; very sacred; mediator, messenger, and teacher

White Buffalo Woman features prominently in the myths and legends of the Lakota of North America. The Lakota are one of over 30 different peoples from at least six language stocks that inhabit the prairies and the plains in North America. Among them are the Pawnee, the Kansa, the Dakota, the Crow, and the Mandan. Originally from the Great Lakes area, they were eventually forced out and moved on to the plains to become a plains people. The plains people populate a region which stretches from Alberta to the Mexican border, flanked by the Rocky Mountains to the west and the Missouri River to the east. They share a significant number of similarities in their way of life, similarities which are land-based and which distinguish them from communities living on land that supports other types of activities and with whom they have little in common.

The Plains Indians exemplify native traditions in the minds of many. They have captured the imagination of Americans and Europeans more so than any other group of indigenous peoples. This is probably because they were the most effective in opposing the expansion of white settlers. The Lakota, for example, fought heroic battles defending themselves against conquest, white encroachment, and land appropriation. They boast Black Elk, Sitting Bull, Crazy Horse, John Lame Deer among their members, and White Buffalo Woman as a prominent *Wakan* being. In her story, White Buffalo Woman is identified as *Wakan*, a word that has been variously translated to mean "sacred," "powerful," "holy," in addition to "ancient" and "enduring."

Until recently, Native American literature was exclusively oral. It is generally recognized that translations from any one language to the next are at best approximations which are hampered by one's own language and its concomitant predispositions and perceptions. This is especially true in the case of English translations of America Indian texts because it is extremely difficult to convey the spirit and cultural context of the original while adhering to a faithful translation of the words. Compounding the problem is the fact that there is a performative aspect to native storytelling. It has a ceremonial function through song, dance, gesticulation, pause, and interaction between storyteller and audience. These elements, considered an integral part of the story-telling process, cannot be replicated in print.

The life and survival of the Plains Indians was so dependent upon and shaped by the buffalo that their fates were inextricably intertwined. For the Lakota, the buffalo contained all the ingredients necessary for the sustenance and nurture of life. Manifesting all the elements of creation, the buffalo were endowed with spiritual significance and revered as symbols of the universe. They provided the food and raw materials required for making shelter, clothing, utensils, and weapons. Every part of the buffalo was put to good use. Their abundant meat was eaten; their dung was used as cooking fuel; their hides were made into clothing and shelter; their horns into utensils; their bones into tools; their bladders into containers; their hair into ropes; their tendons into bowstrings; and their hooves into ceremonial rattles.

Since the buffalo played such a prominent role in the lives of the Lakota, it is not surprising that the most significant figure in their mythology is associated with the buffalo. White Buffalo Woman assumes multiple roles in the myth bearing her name. Through her manifestation as a buffalo, White Buffalo Woman mediates the connection between the two-legged and the four-legged creatures. By teaching the people how to raise crops, she provides them with a means to feed themselves. By teaching the women how to make fire, she helps them transform raw foodstuff into edible food. By mediating between the people and Grandfather, known as *Tunkashila,* she assumes the role of a messenger. By giving the people the sacred pipe and instructing them in its use, she aids them in communicating with Tunkashila.

The story of White Buffalo Woman constitutes a point of intersection between the sacred and profane, and as the central divinity in the story, White Buffalo Woman articulates the connection between the two realms. The story begins with a crisis in the community: the people are starving because of the shortage of game. Scouts repeatedly come back empty handed. One day, two scouts climb a mountain, looking for game. They see a beautiful woman approaching them who appears to be floating instead of walking. Her attire and demeanor define her as *lila wakan* (very sacred). In spite of that, one of the scouts approaches her with lust in his heart. He reaches out to touch her and is promptly annihilated for attempting to violate the proper relationship between humans and the sacred, between men and women, and between the natural world and the spiritual world. The woman then gives instructions to the remaining scout to prepare the camp for her arrival.

After four days, White Buffalo Woman approaches the camp and delivers her teachings. She provides the materials necessary for the sacred pipe ceremony, a ceremony that is designed to restore balance and harmony to all that exists. She instructs the people on the proper way to conduct the ceremony, rendering all her actions and objects cosmologically and symbolically as she does so. She makes it a point to honor women and children, recognizing and acknowledging the unique and vital contribution of each group. After imparting her message, White Buffalo Woman walks into the distance. She stops and rolls over four times, each time emerging as a buffalo of a different color. Her final transformation is in the form of a white buffalo calf, considered to be the most sacred living creature among the Lakota. Upon her disappearance, great herds of buffalo appear who allow themselves to be killed in a mutually reciprocal relationship with the two-legged creatures in order that the people may survive.

The story of White Buffalo Woman reveals the spiritual vibrancy of Native Americans as a whole, and the Plains people in specific. Theirs is not a compartmentalized spirituality but a spirituality that informs and saturates their everyday lives. Native American spiritual traditions so permeate their songs, stories, ceremonies, and art—in short, all aspects of their culture—that it may be difficult for a nonnative audience which has been steeped in a culture of secularism and materialism to comprehend the extent of the spiritual influence. Traditional works of art among Native American peoples embody the sacred: they constitute a metaphorical rendering of a spiritual reality and serve as a connection with a spiritual center.

Native American people are diverse, boasting many traditions and a plurality of views and spiritual practices. However, they share some fundamental similarities, one of which is their recognition of the sacred and spiritual dimension that exists in the natural world. For indigenous communities, cosmic order is manifested and experienced in the material world. Every aspect and action of our lives should reflect and reinforce the balance, harmony, and unity of the cosmic order, symbolized by the sacred cycle of seasons of growth and decay and periods of order and disorder. Native Americans perceive nature as a living, sacred being which is informed by spiritual significance and from which they derive their spiritual values and sustenance. They seek to establish a harmonious relationship with the spirit world, with the earth, and with all that resides in it by restoring proper relationships.

Accordingly, since nature is replete with occurrences and objects that happen in fours, the number four conveys great significance and plays a considerable role in Native American ceremonies and rituals. Four represents wholeness, completion, and the cycle. It is the sacred circle and all within it. The story of White Buffalo Woman attests to the importance of the number four since this number occurs intermittently and prominently throughout the story and is woven into the fabric of the ceremony and ritual that she introduces to the Lakota. White Buffalo Woman waits for four days after her initial appearance before she visits the tribe, carrying her sacred bundle and spiritual teachings. She circles the lodge four times. She spends four days imparting her teachings. She lifts the pipe towards each of the four directions. She refers to the buffalo as representing the universe, the four directions, and the four ages of creation. And as she departs, she rolls over four times, each time emerging as a buffalo in a different color.

White Buffalo Woman introduces the sacred pipe to the Lakota and teaches them how to pray with it. The sacred pipe acts as a vehicle for communicating with Tunkashila in a ritual that unifies and binds together all the elements, directions, and creatures of the earth. Through its agency, the people restore proper relationships. According to tradition, the Lakota had previously made their ceremonial pipes from ceramic clay, but after White Buffalo Woman introduced them to the red pipe made from the red pipestone quarries of Minnesota, they incorporated the red pipe into their ceremonies as a way of honoring her and respecting her message.

White Buffalo Woman identifies each part of the pipe and renders it symbolically. The red stone of the bowl represents the buffalo as well as the flesh and blood of the red man. The wooden stem represents all that grows on earth. The seven circular engravings on the bowl represent the seven sacred ceremonies and seven sacred campfires of the Lakota. And the twelve feathers that hang from where the stem joins the bowl are from *Wanblee Galeshka,* the spotted eagle—a sacred bird that acts as Tunkashila's messenger. Through the pipe, the Lakota are situated in harmony and proper relationship with all the things in the universe.

The Lakota sit in a circle and pass the pipe from one person to the next in a clockwise direction during a ceremony. Before taking a puff on the pipe, each smoker points the pipe to the above (sky), to the below (earth), and to the four directions. The smoke emanating from the pipe represents the breath of the Great Spirit. The pipe's stem is considered male and the bowl is considered female. The two parts are kept separate until needed for a ceremony, at which time their unification symbolizes the unification of male and female, an act that is considered to increase the pipe's potency and restore harmony and balance to all that exists.

An essential part of White Buffalo Woman's message consists of reminding people of the unitary nature of reality: all life is interrelated and that we are all part of an intricate tapestry of holiness and wholeness. She urges a respect for the connectedness of life and stresses individual and collective responsibility for maintaining harmony, balance, and a spirit of cooperation in our relationships with each other and with all those who reside within the sacred circle of life. Central to her message is that the Great Spirit informs all of life. As the children of the Great Spirit and Mother Earth, we are all brothers and sisters. Each one of us has a different contribution to make to the well being of the people, and each contribution should be recognized as valuable and necessary for the survival of the whole.

White Buffalo Woman remains such a powerful figure that many indigenous people affirm her continued presence and voice in their visionary experiences. Her story below is from *American Indian Myths and Legends,* selected and edited by Richard Erdoes and Alfonzo Ortiz.

REFERENCES

Allen, Paula Gunn. *Grandmothers of the Light: A Medicine Woman's Source Book.* Boston: Beacon, 1991.

———. *The Sacred Hoop: Recovering the Feminine in American Indian Traditions.* Boston: Beacon, 1986.

Caduto, Michael J., and Joseph Bruchac. *Native American Stories Told by Joseph Bruchac.* Colorado: Fulcrum, 1991.

Carlson, Paul H. *The Plains Indians.* College Station: Texas A & M UP, 1998.

Deloria, Vine. *God is Red.* New York: Grosset and Dunlap, 1973.

Demallie, Raymond J., and Douglas R. Parks, eds. *Sioux Indian Religion.* Norman: U of Oklahoma P, 1989.

Demallie, Raymond J., and James R. Walker, eds. *Lakota Society.* Lincoln: U of Nebraska P, 1982.

Driver, Harold E. *Indians of North America.* Rev. 2nd ed. Chicago: U of Chicago P, 1969.

Farb, Peter. *Man's Rise to Civilization: The Cultural Ascent of the Indians of North America.* Rev. 2nd ed. New York: E.P. Dutton, 1978.

Hultkrantz, Ake. *The Religions of the American Indians.* Trans. Monica Setterwall. Berkley: U of California P, 1979.

———. "The Religion of the Goddess in North America." *The Book of the Goddess, Past and Present: An Introduction to Her Religion.* Ed. Carl Olson. New York: Crossroad, 1990. 202–216.

Huntsman, Jeffrey F. "Traditional Native American Literature: The Translation Dilemma." *Smoothing the Ground: Essays on Native American Oral Literature.* Ed. Brian Swann. Berkeley: U of California P, 1983. 87–97.

Irwin, Lee, ed. *Native American Spirituality: A Critical Reader.* Lincoln: U of Nebraska P, 2000.

Lame Deer, John (Fire), and Richard Erdoes. *Lame Deer: Seeker of Visions.* New York: Washington Square P, 1972.

Neihardt, John G. *Black Elk Speaks: Being the Life Story of a Holy Man of the Oglala Sioux.* 1932. Lincoln: U of Nebraska P, 1989.

Swann, Brian, ed. *Smoothing the Ground: Essays on Native American Oral Literature.* Berkley: U of California P, 1983.

Tedlock, Dennis, and Barbara Tedlock, eds. *Teachings From the American Earth: Indian Religions and Philosophy.* New York: Liveright, 1975.

Versluis, Arthur. *The Elements of Native American Traditions.* Boston: Element, 1993.

Walker, James R., and Elaine Jahner, eds. *Lakota Myth.* Lincoln: U of Nebraska P, 1983.

Walker, James R., Raymond J. Demallie, and Elaine Jahner, eds. *Lakota Belief and Ritual.* Lincoln: U of Nebraska P, 1991.

Williamson, Ray A. *Living the Sky: The Cosmos of the American Indian.* Oklahoma: U of Oklahoma P, 1984.

Zak, Nancy C. "Sacred and Legendary Women of Native North America." *The Goddess Reawakening: The Feminine Principle Today.* Ed. Shirley Nicholson. Illinois: Quest Books, 1989. 232–245.

The White Buffalo Woman

[Brule Sioux]

The Sioux are a warrior tribe, and one of their proverbs says, "Woman shall not walk before man." Yet White Buffalo Woman is the dominant figure of their most important legend. The medicine man Crow Dog explains, "This holy woman brought the sacred buffalo calf pipe to the Sioux. There could be no Indians without it. Before she came, people didn't know how to live. They knew nothing. The Buffalo Woman put her sacred mind into their minds." At the ritual of the sun dance one woman, usually a mature and universally respected member of the tribe, is given the honor of representing Buffalo Woman.

Though she first appeared to the Sioux in human form, White Buffalo Woman was also a buffalo—the Indians' brother, who gave its flesh so that the people might live. Albino buffalo were sacred to all Plains tribes; a white buffalo hide was a sacred talisman, a possession beyond price.

One summer so long ago that nobody knows how long, the OcetiShakowin, the seven sacred council fires of the Lakota Oyate, the nation, came together and camped. The sun shone all the time, but there was no game and the people were starving. Every day they sent scouts to look for game, but the scouts found nothing.

Among the bands assembled were the Itazipcho, the Without-Bows, who had their own camp circle under their chief, Standing Hollow Horn. Early one morning the chief sent two of his young men to hunt for game. They went on foot, because at that time the Sioux didn't yet have horses. They searched everywhere but could find nothing. Seeing a high hill, they decided to climb it in order to look over the whole country. Halfway up, they saw something coming toward them from far off, but the figure was floating instead of walking. From this they knew that the person was *wakan*, holy.

At first they could make out only a small moving speck and had to squint to see that it was a human form. But as it came nearer, they realized that it was a beautiful young woman, more beautiful than any they had ever seen, with two round, red dots of face paint on her cheeks. She wore a wonderful white buckskin outfit, tanned until it shone a long way in the sun. It was embroidered with sacred and marvellous designs of porcupine quill, in radiant colors no ordinary woman could have made. This *wakan* stranger was Ptesan-Wi, White Buffalo Woman. In her hands she carried a large bundle and a fan of sage leaves. She wore her blue-black hair loose except for a strand at the left side, which was tied up with buffalo fur. Her eyes shone dark and sparkling, with great power in them.

The two young men looked at her open-mouthed. One was overawed, but the other desired her body and stretched his hand out to touch her. This woman was *lila wakan,* very sacred, and could not be treated with disrespect. Lightning instantly struck the brash young man and burned him up, so that only a small heap of blackened bones was left. Or some say that he was suddenly covered by a cloud, and within it he was eaten up by snakes that left only his skeleton, just as a man can be eaten up by lust.

To the other scout who had behaved rightly, the White Buffalo Woman said: "Good things I am bringing, something holy to your nation. A message I carry for your people from the buffalo nation. Go back to the camp and tell the people to prepare for my arrival. Tell your chief to put up a medicine lodge with twenty-four poles. Let it be made holy for my coming."

This young hunter returned to the camp. He told the chief, he told the people, what the sacred woman had commanded. The chief told the *eyapaha,* the crier, and the crier went through the camp circle calling: "Someone sacred is coming. A holy woman approaches. Make all things ready for her." So the people put up the big medicine tipi and waited. After four days they saw the White Buffalo Woman approaching, carrying her bundle before her. Her wonderful white buckskin dress shone from afar. The chief, Standing Hollow Horn, invited her to enter the medicine lodge. She went in and circled the interior sunwise. The chief addressed her respectfully, saying: "Sister, we are glad you have come to instruct us."

She told him what she wanted done. In the center of the tipi they were to put up an *owanka wakan,* a sacred altar, made of red earth, with a buffalo skull and a three-stick rack for a holy thing she was bringing. They did what she directed, and she traced a design with her finger on the smoothed earth of the altar. She showed them how to do all this, then circled the lodge again sunwise. Halting before the chief, she now opened the bundle. The holy thing it contained was the *chanunpa,* the sacred pipe. She held it out to the people and let them look at it. She was grasping the stem with her right hand and the bowl with her left, and thus the pipe has been held ever since.

Again the chief spoke, saying: "Sister, we are glad. We have had no meat for some time. All we can give you is water." They dipped some *wacanga,* sweet grass, into a skin bag of water and gave it to her, and to this day the people dip sweet grass or an eagle wing in water and sprinkle it on a person to be purified.

The White Buffalo Woman showed the people how to use the pipe. She filled it with *chan-shasha*, red willow-bark tobacco. She walked around the lodge four times after the manner of Anpetu-Wi, the great sun. This represented the circle without end, the sacred hoop, the road of life. The woman placed a dry buffalo chip on the fire and lit the pipe with it. This was *peta-owihankeshni*, the fire without end, the flame to be passed on from generation to generation. She told them that the smoke rising from the bowl was Tunkashila's breath, the living breath of the great Grandfather Mystery.

The White Buffalo Woman showed the people the right way to pray, the right words and the right gestures. She taught them how to sing the pipe-filling song and how to lift the pipe up to the sky, toward Grandfather, and down toward Grandmother Earth, to Unci, and then to the four directions of the universe.

"With this holy pipe," she said, "you will walk like a living prayer. With your feet resting upon the earth and the pipestem reaching into the sky, your body forms a living bridge between the Sacred Beneath and the Sacred Above. Wakan Tanka smiles upon us, because now we are as one: earth, sky, all living things, the two-legged, the four-legged, the winged ones, the trees, the grasses. Together with the people, they are all related, one family. The pipe holds them all together.

"Look at this bowl," said the White Buffalo Woman. "Its stone represents the buffalo, but also the flesh and blood of the red man. The buffalo represents the universe and the four directions, because he stands on four legs, for the four ages of creation. The buffalo was put in the west by Wakan Tanka at the making of the world, to hold back the waters. Every year he loses one hair, and in every one of the four ages he loses a leg. The sacred hoop will end when all the hair and legs of the great buffalo are gone, and the water comes back to cover the Earth.

The wooden stem of this *chanunpa* stands for all that grows on the earth. Twelve feathers hanging from where the stem—the backbone—joins the bowl—the skull—are from Wanblee Galeshka, the spotted eagle, the very sacred bird who is the Great Spirit's messenger and the wisest of all flying ones. You are joined to all things of the universe, for they all cry out to Tunkashila. Look at the bowl: engraved in it are seven circles of various sizes. They stand for the seven sacred ceremonies you will practice with this pipe, and for the Ocheti Shakowin, the seven sacred campfires of our Lakota nation."

The White Buffalo Woman then spoke to the women, telling them that it was the work of their hands and the fruit of their bodies which kept the people alive. "You are from the mother earth," she told them. "What you are doing is as great as what the warriors do."

And therefore the sacred pipe is also something that binds men and women together in a circle of love. It is the one holy object in the making of which both men and women have a hand. The men carve the bowl and make the stem; the women decorate it with bands of colored porcupine quills. When a man takes a wife, they both hold the pipe at the same time and red trade cloth is wound around their hands, thus tying them together for life.

The White Buffalo Woman had many things for her Lakota sisters in her sacred womb bag—corn, *wasna* (pemmican), wild turnip. She taught them how to make the hearth fire. She filled a buffalo paunch with cold water and dropped a red-hot stone into it. "This way you shall cook the corn and the meat," she told them.

The White Buffalo Woman also talked to the children, because they have an understanding beyond their years. She told them that what their fathers and mothers did was for them, that their parents could remember being little once, and that they, the children, would grow up to have little ones of their own. She told them: "You are the coming generation, that's why you are the most important and precious ones. Some day you will hold this pipe and smoke it. Some day you will pray with it."

She spoke once more to all the people: "The pipe is alive; it is a red being showing you a red life and a red road. And this is the first ceremony for which you will use the pipe. You will use it to keep the soul of a dead person, because through it you can talk to Wakan Tanka, the Great Mystery Spirit. The day a human dies is always a sacred day. The day when the soul is released to the Great Spirit is another. Four women will become sacred on such a day. They will be the ones to cut the sacred tree—the *can-wakan*—for the sun dance."

She told the Lakota that they were the purest among the tribes, and for that reason Tunkashila had bestowed upon them the holy *chanunpa.* They had been chosen to take care of it for all the Indian people on this turtle continent.

She spoke one last time to Standing Hollow Horn, the chief, saying, "Remember: this pipe is very sacred. Respect it and it will take you to the end of the road. The four ages of creation are in me; I am the four ages. I will come to see you in every generation cycle. I shall come back to you."

The sacred woman then took leave of the people, saying: *"Toksha ake wacinyanktin ktelo—*I shall see you again."

The people saw her walking off in the same direction from which she had come, outlined against the red ball of the setting sun. As she went, she stopped and rolled over four times. The first time, she turned into a black buffalo; the second into a brown one; the third into a red one; and finally, the fourth time she rolled over, she turned into a white female buffalo calf. A white buffalo is the most sacred living thing you could ever encounter.

The White Buffalo Woman disappeared over the horizon. Sometime she might come back. As soon as she had vanished, buffalo in great herds appeared, allowing themselves to be killed so that the people might survive. And from that day on, our relations, the buffalo, furnished the people with everything they needed—meat for their food, skins for their clothes and tipis, bones for their many tools.

—*Told by Lame Deer at Winner, Rosebud Indian Reservation, South Dakota, 1967.*

Two very old tribal pipes are kept by the Looking Horse family at Eagle Butte in South Dakota. One of them, made from a buffalo calf's leg bone, too fragile and brittle with age to be used for smoking, is said to be the sacred pipe which the Buffalo Maiden brought to the people. "I know," said Lame Deer. "I prayed with it once, long ago."

The turtle continent is North America, which many Indian tribes regard as an island sitting on the back of a turtle.

John Fire Lame Deer was a famous Sioux "holy man," grandson of the first Chief Lame Deer, a great warrior who fought Custer and died during a skirmish with General Miles. Lame Deer's son, Archie, is carrying on his work as a medicine man and director of the sun dance.

Questions for Review and Discussion

1. The intent of traditional Native American storytelling is never purely self-expression because that would suggest an imposition of one's personal perspective on to the collective—a practice that is deemed unworthy and shamefully self-promoting. Instead, the intent of narrative, ceremony, song, and legend is to reconcile and bring into balance and harmony all that exists in the universe. Identify each of the elements that is being integrated and restored through proper relationship in the story of White Buffalo Woman.

2. How is this proper relationship restored?

3. White Buffalo Woman punishes the young scout who approaches her by transforming him into a skeleton. What is he being punished for?

4. In the process of imparting her teachings, White Buffalo Woman designates gender specific tasks. But gender differentiation does not necessarily equate with gender hierarchy. How does White Buffalo Woman describe the gender-specific tasks? Are they complementary, mutually beneficial, and equally essential? Or are they ranked hierarchically? Support your answer with concrete examples from the text.

5. Why does White Buffalo Woman direct specific areas of her message to women and children? What purpose does this serve?

6. Native American societies have been described as gynocentric, that is to say, non-hierarchical, woman-centered, supportive of life, and celebrants of powerful female and male sacred beings. Identify elements of gynocentrism in the story of White Buffalo Woman. Which of her actions and words are designed to promote respect for women and reinforce a woman-centered perspective?

7. For audiences raised in the western tradition of rationalism and secular materialism, stories from an oral tradition pose some unique challenges. One such chal-

lenge in the story of White Buffalo Woman, for example, is the tacit assumption that humans, animals, and supernatural beings communicate freely with each other. What other challenges does the story of White Buffalo Woman pose for a western audience?

8. One fundamental assumption of Native American thought is that no clear line of demarcation exists between the material world and the spiritual world. Instead, the two are perceived as different and interchangeable manifestations of the same reality, with the sacred intermittently making its presence felt on the profane. How is this assumption articulated in the story of White Buffalo Woman?

9. What can we learn from the story and message of White Buffalo Woman?

Chapter 18

Corn Mother

GLOSSARY OF NAMES

CORN MOTHER Also known as First Mother; a manifestation of Mother Earth; born of plant, water, and sun; embodies sacred powers of the earth

KLOSKURBEH All-Maker

PENOBSCOT Native Americans of New England

GREAT NEPHEW Corn Mother's spouse; born of wind, water, and sun

The concept of the earth as Mother is rooted in areas of North America where the planting and harvesting of food substances, primarily by women, constituted the main economic activity. According to scholars of Native American religious traditions and cultures, Mother Earth has experienced a variety of manifestations and transformations. In some traditions, she is synonymous with Corn Mother. The presence of Corn Mother or some form of a corn goddess is ubiquitous throughout Mexico and among the planting people of the East and Southwest in North America. Her role is symbolically equivalent to the role played by the buffalo for the Plains Indians. Just as the buffalo willingly gives itself in order that the people may live, Corn Mother willingly gives herself in order that the people may cultivate corn for their survival.

Indian corn or maize was developed by Native Americans and was the most cultivated and significant food plant in North America and Mexico. It is estimated that at the time of the first European contact, maize provided more food for the indigenous peoples than all the other cultivated plants combined. Native Americans were resourceful in using every part of the crop. Some of the corn was dried and preserved for consumption during winter. Some was ground into cornmeal for bread, pudding, syrup, or dessert. And some was also eaten in soups. Corn husks were braided and woven to make masks, moccasins, mats, baskets, and dolls. Corncobs were used for fuel and as rattles for ceremonies. And corn meal and corn pollen figure prominently in ceremonies and rituals because of their sacred origin.

This story of Corn Mother comes from the Penobscot of New England. It begins with Kloskurbeh, the "All-Maker," leading a solitary life on earth. One day, he is joined by Great Nephew, a young man, born of the commingling of wind, water, and sun. The young man becomes Kloskurbeh's helper, and the two participate in creating "all manner of things." They are joined by a young woman, born of the union between a green plant, water, and sun. The young woman announces her presence as the provider of strength and nourishment for humans and animals. She joins in union with Great Nephew, and having conceived a child, she becomes First Mother. After teaching the couple and their children all they need to know in order to live, Kloskurbeh moves to the north. The people proliferate, but since they live by hunting and have not yet learned the importance of cultivating a reciprocal relationship between humans and animals and humans and plants, they gradually deplete the animal population and begin to starve.

Seeing her children crying from hunger, First Mother instructs her husband to kill her. She provides specific instructions as to the manner and timing of her death. She must be killed at high noon. Her body must be dragged across an empty patch of earth until no flesh remains on her bones. Her bones must be buried in the middle of a clearing. The site is then to be left undisturbed for seven months.

Great Nephew follows her instructions, and when he returns seven months later, he finds the earth covered with tasseled green plants—corn. First Mother's flesh is the gift of corn, a gift she gives to her children so that they may live. Following her instructions, the people deposit kernels back into the earth in order to renew her flesh and spirit in an ongoing, seven month cycle. In this way, corn serves a dual function: it is at once nourishing food for the body and, originating as it did from First Mother's flesh, it is also sacred food for the spirit. At the spot where her bones had been buried now grew tobacco. This represents First Mother's breath, also imbued with her sacred spirit. The people are instructed to smoke the tobacco for spiritual renewal and mental replenishment. And as they eat First Mother's flesh and inhale First Mother's breath, they participate in the ongoing, transformational cycle of renewal and reciprocity between humans and plants.

Corn Mother's origins from foliage, water, and sun associate her with a long tradition of earth goddesses who are responsible for the fertility and fecundity of the earth. Her birth from the union of plant, water, and sun symbolizes her embodiment of the sacred, life-generating powers of the earth. Her declaration that she provides strength and nourishment to humans and animals reinforces her spiritual and physical dimensions. Once her status as an embodiment of the sacred powers of the earth has been established, Corn Mother uses her body as the vehicle to transfer those sacred powers to her people. Through the consumption of her flesh and bones, the people get to eat. But they also ingest the life-generating qualities of the earth that she embodies. The earth's sacred powers are thus transferred to humans through the medium of Corn Mother. Like White Buffalo Woman who mediates between humans and animals, Corn Mother mediates between humans and plants. Both figures provide humans with food as well as access to the sacred powers embodied in living things.

The Penobscot story of Corn Mother illustrates many of the qualities, values, and traditions of Native Americans evidenced in the story of White Buffalo Woman. In the beginning, Kloskurbeh and Great Nephew participate in creating "all manner of things." Participatory creation where two or more deities collaborate to bring into being other living things is fairly common in Native American creation stories where the culture of individualism and self-aggrandizement is highly suspect. These qualities are replaced by power-sharing, knowledge-sharing, and cooperation. This spirit of cooperation reflects the same values and principles evident in the story of White Buffalo Woman: the stress on the unity of life, the importance of sharing knowledge and skills for the common good, and the essential contribution each has to make in order to sustain the balance and harmony within all that exists and on behalf of all that exists.

Another quality illustrated in the Penobscot story of Corn Mother is the perception of the earth as sacred and life-sustaining. This perception cultivates a respect for the earth as a vital and sacred being on which all life depends. The responsibility for renewing the earth through engagement in reciprocal relationships reflective of the intimate connection between humans, animals, and plants falls upon the human community. Consequently, Corn Mother specifically instructs the people not to eat all the corn. They are told to bury some kernels back into the earth in order to renew their supply of corn on an annual basis. Humans have cultivated corn to such a degree that it can no longer grow without their assistance as it once did. In order for corn to return and provide the food that people are dependent upon, Corn Mother has to be treated appropriately. Inappropriate treatment of Corn Mother results in her failure to reemerge and feed the people. The relationship between corn and humans is interrelated, mutually beneficial, and reciprocal. Each needs the other in order to survive.

Once again, the values that are being promulgated are those of generosity in word and deed, collaboration, recognition of the spiritual dimension of all things, and acknowledgement of individual and collective responsibility to keep the world in balance and harmony. All of these values emerge through cultivating a proper relationship with corn. In order to reap Corn Mother's benefits for both body and spirit, one must give something back to Corn Mother. One must plant her. The relationship is based on reciprocity and mutual benefit. Just as in the story of White Buffalo Woman where the buffalo establish a reciprocal and mutually beneficial relationship between humans and animals, so, too, the story of Corn Mother illustrates a reciprocal and mutually beneficial relationship between humans and plants. This relationship is at variance with a dominator/acquisitor model whereby the dominant partner continues to take without giving anything back. Instead, it is based on the knowledge that in order for all life to survive and flourish, the needs of animals, plants, and humans must be balanced, reciprocal, and respectful of the intimate relatedness of all life.

This story of Corn Mother is from *American Indian Myths and Legends*, selected and edited by Richard Erdoes and Alfonzo Ortiz.

REFERENCES

Allen, Paula Gunn. *Grandmothers of the Light: A Medicine Woman's Source Book.* Boston: Beacon, 1991.

———. *The Sacred Hoop: Recovering the Feminine in American Indian Traditions.* Boston: Beacon, 1986.

Beck, Peggy V., Anna Lee Walters, and Nia Francisco. *The Sacred: Ways of Knowledge, Sources of Life.* Arizona: Dine College, 2000.

Caduto, Michael J., and Joseph Bruchac. *Native American Stories Told by Joseph Bruchac.* Colorado: Fulcrum, 1991.

Deloria, Vine. *God is Red.* New York: Grosset and Dunlap, 1973.

Driver Harold E. *Indians of North America.* Rev. 2nd ed. Chicago: U of Chicago P, 1969.

Farb, Peter. *Man's Rise to Civilization: The Cultural Ascent of the Indians of North America.* Rev. 2nd ed. New York: E.P. Dutton, 1978.

Gill, Sam D. *Native American Religions: An Introduction.* California: Wadsworth, 1982.

Hultkrantz, Ake. *The Religions of the American Indians.* Trans. Monica Setterwall. Berkley: U of California P, 1979.

———. "The Religion of the Goddess in North America." *The Book of the Goddess, Past and Present: An Introduction to Her Religion.* Ed. Carl Olson. New York: Crossroad, 1990. 202–216.

Huntsman, Jeffrey F. "Traditional Native American Literature: The Translation Dilemma." *Smoothing the Ground: Essays on Native American Oral Literature.* Ed. Brian Swann. Berkeley: U of California P, 1983. 87–97.

Irwin, Lee, ed. *Native American Spirituality: A Critical Reader.* Lincoln: U of Nebraska P, 2000.

Kidwell, Clara Sue, Homer Noley, and George E. Tinker. *A Native American Theology.* New York: Orbis, 2001.

Martin, Joel W. *The Land Looks After Us: A History of Native American Religion.* New York: Oxford UP, 2001.

Swann, Brian, ed. *Smoothing the Ground: Essays on Native American Oral Literature.* Berkeley: U of California P, 1983.

Tedlock, Dennis, and Barbara Tedlock, eds. *Teachings From the American Earth: Indian Religions and Philosophy.* New York: Liveright, 1975.

Versluis, Arthur. *The Elements of Native American Traditions.* Boston: Element Books, 1993.

Williamson, Ray A. *Living the Sky: The Cosmos of the American Indian.* Oklahoma: U of Oklahoma P, 1984.

Zak, Nancy C. "Sacred and Legendary Women of Native North America." *The Goddess Reawakening: The Feminine Principle Today.* Ed. Shirley Nicholson. Illinois: Quest Books, 1989. 232–245.

Corn Mother

[Penobscot]

What the buffalo represented to the nomadic tribes of the Plains, corn was to the planting people of the East and the Southwest—the all-nourishing sacred food, the subject of innumerable legends and the central theme of many rituals. Derived from a wild grass called teosintl, *corn was planted in Mexico's Tehuacan Valley as early as 8,000 years ago. The oldest corn found north of the border was discovered in New Mexico's Bat Cave. It is about 5,500 years old. The Hopis say: "Moing'iima makes corn. Everything grows on his body. He is short, about the height of a boy. He has a female partner. Every summer he becomes heavy, his body is full of vegetables: watermelon, corn, squash. They grow in his body. When the Hopi plant, they invariably ask him to make the crop flourish; then their things come up, whether vegetables or fruit. When he shaves his body, the seeds come out, and afterward his body is thin. He used to live on this earth and go with the Hopi. When things grow ripe, he becomes thin and is unhappy. He stays in the west." Corn had equal significance for tribes in the East, as we see in this tale from a New England Tribe.*

When Kloskurbeh, the All-maker, lived on earth, there were no people yet. But one day when the sun was high, a youth appeared and called him "Uncle, brother of my mother." This young man was born from the foam of the waves, foam quickened by the wind and warmed by the sun. It was the motion of the wind, the moistness of water, and the sun's warmth which gave him life—warmth above all, because warmth is life. And the young man lived with Kloskurbeh and became his chief helper.

Now, after these two powerful beings had created all manner of things, there came to them, as the sun was shining at high noon, a beautiful girl. She was born of the wonderful earth plant, and of the dew, and of warmth. Because a drop of dew fell on a leaf and was warmed by the sun, and the warming sun is life, this girl came into being—from the green living plant, from moisture, and from warmth.

"I am love," said the maiden. "I am a strength giver, I am the nourisher, I am the provider of men and animals. They all love me."

Then Kloskurbeh thanked the Great Mystery Above for having sent them the maiden. The youth, the Great Nephew, married her, and the girl conceived and thus became First Mother. And Kloskurbeh, the Great Uncle, who teaches humans all they need to know, taught their children how to live. Then he went away to dwell in the north, from which he will return sometime when he is needed.

Now the people increased and became numerous. They lived by hunting, and the more people there were, the less game they found. They were hunting it out, and as the animals decreased, starvation came upon the people. And First Mother pitied them.

The little children came to First Mother and said: "We are hungry. Feed us." But she had nothing to give them, and she wept. She told them: "Be patient. I will make some food. Then your little bellies will be full." But she kept weeping.

Her husband asked: "How can I make you smile? How can I make you happy?"

"There is only one thing that will stop my tears."

"What is it?" Asked her husband.

"It is this: you must kill me."

"I could never do that."

"You must, or I will go on weeping and grieving forever."

Then the husband traveled far, to the end of the earth, to the north he went, to ask the Great Instructor, his uncle Kloskurbeh, what he should do.

"You must do what she wants. You must kill her," said Kloskurbeh. Then the young man went back to his home, and it was his turn to weep. But First Mother said: "Tomorrow at high noon you must do it. After you have killed me, let two of our sons take hold of my hair and drag my body over that empty patch of earth. Let them drag me back and forth, back and forth, over every part of the patch, until all my flesh has been torn from my body. Afterwards, take my bones, gather them up, and bury them in the middle of this clearing. Then leave that place."

She smiled and said, "Wait seven moons and then come back, and you will find my flesh there, flesh given out of love, and it will nourish and strengthen you forever and ever."

So it was done. The husband slew his wife and her sons, praying, dragged her body to and fro as she had commanded, until her flesh covered all the earth. Then they took up her bones and buried them in the middle of it. Weeping loudly, they went away.

When the husband and his children and his children's children came back to that place after seven moons had passed, they found the earth covered with tall, green, tasseled plants. The plants' fruit—corn—was First Mother's flesh, given so that the people might live and flourish. And they partook of First Mother's flesh and found it sweet beyond words. Following her instructions, they did not eat all, but put many kernels back into the earth. In this way her flesh and spirit renewed themselves every seven months, generation after generation.

And at the spot where they had burned First Mother's bones, there grew another plant, broad-leafed and fragrant. It was First Mother's breath, and they heard her spirit talking: "Burn this up and smoke it. It is sacred. It will clear your minds, help your prayers, and gladden your hearts."

And First Mother's husband called the first plant *Skarmunal*, corn, and the second plant *utarmur-wayeh*, tobacco.

"Remember," he told the people, "and take good care of First Mother's flesh, because it is her goodness become substance. Take good care of her breath, because it is her love turned into smoke. Remember her and think of her whenever you eat, whenever you smoke this sacred plant, because she has given her life so that you might live. Yet she is not dead, she lives: in undying love she renews herself again and again."

—*Retold from three nineteenth-century sources, including Joseph Nicolar.*

Questions for Review and Discussion

1. Corn Mother embodies the sacred, life generating powers of the earth that nourish the body and rejuvenate the spirit. Through the consumption of her flesh and bones, humans eat food and experience a corresponding renewal of body and spirit. In some ways, this experience parallels the Christian Eucharist whereby humans symbolically ingest the body of Jesus to experience a renewal of spirit. What are some other similarities and differences in the story of Corn Mother and the story of Jesus?

2. Corn Mother's body is dragged over the earth and emerges in spring as corn and tobacco. Locate parallels with other figures in this text where a deity "dies" annually and emerges in spring as food substances.

3. First Mother's husband urges the people to take good care of her flesh "because it is her goodness become substance." Similarly, he urges them to take care of her breath "because it is her love turned into smoke." What does it mean to take care of Corn Mother's flesh?

4. Corn Mother's spirit tells the people that the tobacco is sacred. She encourages them to smoke it because it generates clear-headedness, a sense of well being, and acts as an aid to prayer. Does the use of tobacco in this story serve the same function as in the story of White Buffalo Woman? Compare and contrast the use of tobacco in both stories.

5. How does Corn Mother ensure that the sacred powers she embodies will be renewed on a continuous basis?

6. The Penobscot story of Corn Mother attributes sacred origins to tobacco. How does this story's regard for tobacco differ from contemporary society's conceptions about tobacco and smoking?

7. Find evidence in the story of White Buffalo Woman and Corn Mother of the value Native Americans placed on earthly renewal and reciprocity.

8. What challenges does the story of Corn Mother pose for a western audience raised in a tradition of secular materialism?

9. What can we learn from the story of Corn Mother?

Bibliography

Abimbola, 'Wande. "The Bag of Wisdom: Osun and the Origins of the Ifa Divination." *Osun Across the Waters: A Yoruba Goddess in Africa and the Americas*. Eds. Joseph M. Murphy and Mei-Mei Sanford. Bloomington: Indiana UP, 2001. 141–154.

Abiodun, Rowland. "Hidden Power: Osun, the Seventeenth Odu." *Osun Across the Waters: A Yoruba Goddess in Africa and the Americas*. Eds. Joseph M. Murphy and Mei-Mei Sanford. Bloomington: Indiana UP, 2001. 10–33.

Abrahams, Roger D. *African Folktales: Traditional Stories of the Black World*. New York: Pantheon, 1983.

Agha-Jaffar, Tamara. *Demeter and Persephone: Lessons From A Myth*. North Carolina: McFarland, 2002.

Ahmed, Leila. *Women and Gender in Islam: Historical Roots of a Modern Debate*. New Haven: Yale UP, 1992.

Al-Hibri, Azizah. "A Study of Islamic Herstory: Or How Did We Ever Get Into This Mess?" *Women and Islam*. Ed. Azizah Al-Hibri. Oxford: Pergamon, 1982. 207–219.

Ali, Abdullah Yusuf. Trans. *The Holy Qur'an: English Translation of the Meanings of The Qur'an with Notes*. Indianapolis: H&C International, 1992.

Ali, Al-Hajj Ta'lim (T.B. Irving). Trans. *The Qur'an: The First American Version*. Vermont: Amana, 1985.

Al-Khattab, Huda. *Bent Rib: A Journey Through Women's Issues in Islam*. London: Ta-Ha, 1997.

Allen, Paula Gunn. *Grandmothers of the Light: A Medicine Woman's Source Book*. Boston: Beacon, 1991.

———. *The Sacred Hoop: Recovering the Feminine in American Indian Traditions*. Boston: Beacon, 1986.

Andersen, Sarah, ed. *Heaven's Face Thinly Veiled: A Book of Spiritual Writing by Women*. Boston: Shambhala, 1996.

Ann, Martha, and Dorothy Myers Imel. *Goddesses in World Mythology: A Biographical Dictionary*. Oxford: Oxford UP, 1993.

Anthes, Rudolf. "Mythologies in Ancient Egypt." *Mythologies of the Ancient World*. Ed. Samuel Noah Kramer. New York: Anchor/Doubleday, 1961. 15–92.

Armour, Robert A. *Gods and Myths of Ancient Egypt*. 2nd ed. New York: American U of Cairo P, 1986.

Armstrong, Karen. *The Gospel According to Woman*. New York: Anchor, 1986.

———. *A History of God: The 4000-Year Quest of Judaism, Christianity, and Islam*. New York: Ballantine, 1993.

———. *In the Beginning: A New Interpretation of Genesis*. New York: Ballantine, 1997.

Aschkenasy, Nehama. *Woman At the Window: Biblical Tales of Oppression and Escape*. Detroit: Wayne State UP, 1998.

Ashe, Geoffrey. *The Virgin*. London: Routledge and Kegan Paul, 1976.

Austen, Hallie Iglehart. *The Heart of the Goddess: Art, Myth, and Meditations of the World's Sacred Feminine*. Berkeley: Wingbow, 1990.

Awolalu, Omosade J. *Yoruba Beliefs and Sacrificial Rites.* New York: Athelia Henrietta, 1996.

Babbitt, Frank Cole, trans. *Plutarch's Moralia.* The Loeb Classical Library. Vol. V. Massachusetts: Harvard UP, 1962. 15 vols.

Bach, Alice, ed. *Women in the Hebrew Bible: A Reader.* New York: Routledge, 1999.

———, ed. *The Pleasure of Her Text: Feminist Readings of Biblical and Historical Texts.* Philadelphia: Trinity P, 1990.

Badawi, Leila. "Islam." *Women in Religion.* Eds. Jean Holm and John Bowker. London: Pinter, 1999. 84–112.

Badejo, Dierdre L. "Authority and Discourse in the *Orin Odun Osun.*" *Osun Across the Waters: A Yoruba Goddess in Africa and the Americas.* Eds. Joseph M. Murphy and Mei-Mei Sanford. Bloomington: Indiana UP, 2001. 128–140.

Bates, William Nickerson. *Euripides: A Student of Human Nature.* Philadelphia: U of Pennsylvania P, 1930.

Beck, Peggy V., Anna Lee Walters, and Nia Francisco. *The Sacred: Ways of Knowledge, Sources of Life.* Arizona: Dine College, 2000.

Bhattacharyya, Narendra Nath. *Indian Mother Goddess.* Calcutta: Indian Studies, 1971.

———. *History of the Śakta Religion.* New Delhi: Munshiram Manoharlal, 1974.

Bleeker, C. J. "Isis and Hathor: Two Ancient Egyptian Goddesses." *The Book of the Goddess, Past and Present: An Introduction to Her Religion.* Ed. Carl Olson. New York: Crossroad, 1990. 29–48.

Blofeld, John. *Bodhisattva of Compassion: The Mystical Tradition of Kuan Yin.* Boulder: Shambhala, 1978.

Blundell, Sue. "The Play Explores Social Conflict Between Men and Women." *Readings on Medea: The Greenhaven Press Literary Companion to World Literature.* Ed. Don Nardo. San Diego: Greenhaven, 2001. 68–75.

Bolen, Jean Shinoda. *Goddesses in Every Woman: A New Psychology of Woman.* New York: Harper Colophon, 1984.

Bottero, Jean. *Religion in Ancient Mesopotamia.* Trans. Teresa Lavender Fagan. Chicago: U of Chicago P, 2001.

Breen, John, and Mark Teeuwen, eds. *Shinto in History: Ways of the Kami.* Honolulu: U of Hawaii P, 2000.

Brockington, John. "India." *World Mythology.* Gen. Ed. Roy Willis. New York: Henry Holt, 1993. 68–87.

Brown, C. Mackenzie. "Kali, The Mad Mother." *The Book of the Goddess, Past and Present: An Introduction to Her Religion.* Ed. Carol Olson. New York: Crossroad, 1990. 110–123.

Brown, Raymond E., Karl P. Donfried, Joseph A. Fitzmyer, and John Reumann, eds. *Mary in the New Testament: A Collaborative Assessment by Protestant and Roman Catholic Scholars.* Philadelphia: Fortress P, 1978.

Bruteau, Beatrice. "The Unknown Goddess." *The Goddess Re-Awakening: The Feminine Principle Today.* Ed. Shirley Nicholson. Illinois: Quest, 1989. 68–80.

Budge, E. A. Wallis. *Egyptian Religion.* New York: Barnes and Noble, 1994.

Burkert, Walter. *Ancient Mystery Cults.* Massachusetts: Harvard UP, 1987.

Bynum, Caroline Walker, Steven Harrell, and Paula Richman, eds. *Gender and Religion: On the Complexity of Symbols.* Boston: Beacon, 1986.

Caduto, Michael J., and Joseph Bruchac. *Native American Stories Told by Joseph Bruchac.* Colorado: Fulcrum, 1991.

Caldwell, Sarah. "Margins at the Center: Tracing Kali Through Time, Space, and Culture." *Encountering Kali: In the Margins, At the Center, In the West.* Ed. Rachell Fell McDermott and Jeffrey J. Kripal. Berkeley: U of California P, 2003. 249–272.

Campbell, Joseph, and Charles Muses, eds. *In All Her Names: Explorations of the Feminine in Divinity.* San Francisco: HarperCollins, 1991.

Campbell, Joseph. *The Masks of God.* 4 Vols. New York: Viking, 1959.

———. *The Mythic Image.* Princeton: Princeton UP, 1974.

Cantor, Aviva. "Lilith, The Woman Who Would Be A Jew." *Which Lilith: Feminist Writers Re-Create The World's First Woman.* Eds. Enid Dame, Lilly Rivlin, and Henny Wenkart. New Jersey: Jason Aronson, Inc., 1998. 17–22.

Carlson, Kathie. *In Her Image: The Unhealed Daughter's Search For Her Mother.* Boston: Shambhala, 1990.

———. *Life's Daughter/Death's Bride: Inner Transformations Through the Goddess Demeter/Persephone.* Boston: Shambhala, 1997.

Carlson, Paul H. *The Plains Indians.* College Station: Texas A & M UP, 1998.

Carmody, Denise Lardner. *Religious Woman: Contemporary Reflections on Eastern Texts.* New York: Crossroad, 1991.

———. *Women and World Religions.* 2nd ed. Englewood Cliffs, NJ: Prentice Hall, 1989.

Chinnery, John. "China." *World Mythology.* Gen. Ed. Roy Willis. New York: Henry Holt and Co., 1993. 88–101.

Christ, Carol P. *Laughter of Aphrodite: Reflections on the Journey to the Goddess.* San Francisco: Harper and Row, 1987.

Clauss, James J., and Sarah Iles Johnston, eds. *Medea: Essays on Medea in Myth, Literature, Philosophy, and Art.* Princeton: Princeton UP, 1997.

Cleary, Thomas, and Sartaz Aziz. *Twilight Goddess: Spiritual Feminism and Feminine Spirituality.* Boston: Shambhala, 2000.

Coburn, Thomas B. "Devi: The Great Goddess." *Devi: Goddesses of India.* Ed. John Stratton Hawley and Donna Mari Wulff. Berkeley: U of California P, 1996. 31–48.

———, trans. *Encountering the Goddess: A Translation of the Devi-Mahatmya and a Study of Its Interpretation.* New York: SUNY P, 1991.

Cooey, Paula M., William R. Eakin, and Jay B. Daniel, eds. *After Patriarchy: Feminist Transformations of the World Religions.* New York: Orbis, 1993.

Corti, Lillian. *The Myth of Medea and the Murder of Her Children.* Connecticut: Greenwood, 1998.

Cotterell, Arthur. *A Dictionary of World Mythology.* Rev. Ed. New York: Oxford UP, 1986.

Courlander, Harold. *Tales of Yoruba Gods and Heroes: Myths, Legends, and Heroic Tales of the Yoruba People of West Africa.* New York: Crown, 1973.

———. *A Treasury of African Folklore: The Oral Literature, Traditions, Myths, Legends, Epics, Tales, Recollections, Wisdom, Sayings, and Humor of Africa.* New York: Crown, 1975.

Dame, Enid, Lilly Rivlin, and Henny Wenkart, eds. *Which Lilith: Feminist Writers Re-Create The World's First Woman.* New Jersey: Jason Aronson, Inc., 1998.

Darling, Pamela W. *New Wine: The Story of Women Transforming Leadership and Power in the Episcopal Church.* Boston: Cowley, 1994.

Decharme, Paul. *Euripides and The Spirit of His Dramas.* Trans. James Loeb. New York: Macmillan, 1906.

Delaney, Janice, Mary Jane Lupton, and Emily Toth. *The Curse: A Cultural History of Menstruation.* New York: E.P. Dutton, 1976.

Deloria, Vine. *God is Red.* New York: Grosset and Dunlap, 1973.

Demallie, Raymond J., and Douglas R. Parks, eds. *Sioux Indian Religion.* Norman: U of Oklahoma P, 1989.

———, and James R. Walker, eds. *Lakota Society.* Lincoln: U of Nebraska P, 1982.

Devlin-Glass, Frances, and Lyn McCredden, eds. *Feminist Poetics of the Sacred: Creative Suspicions.* Oxford: Oxford UP, 2001.

Dharma, Krishna, trans. *Ramayana: India's Immortal Tale of Adventure, Love, and Wisdom.* California: Torchlight Publishing, Inc., 2000.

Dorson, Richard M., ed. *African Folklore.* New York: Anchor, 1972.

Downing, Christine. *The Goddess: Mythological Images of the Feminine.* New York: Crossroad, 1981.

———, ed. *The Long Journey Home: Re-Visioning the Myth of Demeter and Persephone for Our Time.* Boston: Shambhala, 1994.

Drèze, Jean, and Amartya Sen. *India: Economic Development and Social Opportunity.* Oxford: Oxford UP, 1999.

Driver, Harold E. *Indians of North America.* Rev. 2nd ed. Chicago: U of Chicago P, 1969.

Drury, Clare. "Christianity." *Women in Religion.* Ed. Jean Holm and John Bowker. London: Pinter, 1999. 30–58.

Duane, O.B. *African Myths and Legends.* London: Brockhampton, 1998.

Dudbridge, Glen. *The Legend of Miao-Shan.* London: Ithaca, 1978.

Easwaran, Eknath, trans. *The Upanishads.* California: Nilgiri, 1987.

Edinger, Edward F. *The Eternal Drama: The Inner Meaning of Greek Mythology.* Ed. Deborah A. Wesley. Boston: Shambhala, 1994.

Ehrenreich, Barbara, and Deirdre English. *Witches, Midwives, and Nurses: A History of Women Healers.* Glass Mountain Pamphlet No. 1: The Feminist Press, 1973.

Ehrman, Bart D. *The New Testament: A Historical Introduction to the Early Christian Writings.* 2nd ed. New York: Oxford UP, 2000.

———. *The New Testament and Other Early Christian Writings: A Reader.* New York: Oxford UP, 1998.

Eisler, Riane. *The Chalice and the Blade: Our History, Our Future.* San Francisco: HarperCollins, 1988.

Eliade, Mircea. *Myth and Reality.* Trans. Willard R. Task. New York: Harper Colophon, 1975.

———. *The Sacred and the Profane: The Nature of Religion: The Nature of Religious Myth, Symbolism, and Ritual Within Life and Culture.* Trans. Willard R. Task. San Diego: Harcourt Brace and Co., 1959.

Eller, Cynthia. *Living in The Lap of The Goddess: The Feminist Spirituality Movement in America.* New York: Crossroad, 1993.

Ellwood, Robert S. and Barbara A. McGraw. *Many Peoples, Many Faiths: Women and Men in the World Religions.* 6th ed. New Jersey: Prentice Hall, 1999.

Engelsman, Joan Chamberlain. *The Feminine Dimension of the Divine.* Philadelphia: Western Press, 1979.

Erdoes, Richard and Alfonso Ortiz, eds. *American Indian Myths and Legends.* New York: Pantheon, 1984.

Erndl, Kathleen M. *Victory to the Mother: The Hindu Goddess of Northwest India in Myth, Ritual, and Symbol.* New York: Oxford UP, 1993.

Estes, Clarissa Pinkola. *Women Who Run With Wolves: Myths and Stories of the Wild Woman Archetype.* New York: Ballantine, 1992.

Exum, J. Cheryl. *Plotted, Shot, and Painted: Cultural Representations of Biblical Women.* Sheffield: Sheffield Academic P, 1996.

———. "Murder They Wrote: Ideology and the Manipulation of Female Presence in Biblical Narrative." *The Pleasure of Her Text: Feminist Readings of Biblical and Historical Texts.* Ed. Alice Bach. Philadelphia: Trinity P, 1990. 45–67.

Fama, Chief. *Fundamentals of the Yoruba Religion (Orisha Worship).* San Bernardino: Ile Orunmila Communications, 1993.

Farb, Peter. *Man's Rise to Civilization: The Cultural Ascent of the Indians of North America.* Rev. 2nd ed. New York, Dutton, 1978.

Faulkner, Raymond O., trans. *The Ancient Egyptian Book of the Dead.* Ed. Carol Andrews. New York: Macmillan, 1984.

Fiorenza, Elisabeth Schussler. *In Memory of Her: A Feminist Theological Reconstruction of Christian Origins.* New York: Crossroad, 1992.

Fitzmyer, S.J. Joseph A. *The Dead Sea Scrolls and Christian Origins.* Grand Rapids, Michigan: William B. Eerdmans, 2000.

Foley, Helene P., trans. and ed. *The Homeric Hymn to Demeter: Translation, Commentary, and Interpretive Essays.* Princeton: Princeton UP, 1994.

———. "The Conception of Women in Athenian Drama." *Reflections of Women in Antiquity.* Ed. Helene P. Foley. Philadelphia: Gordon and Breach Science Publishers, Inc., 1981. 127–168.

Fox, Matthew, ed. *Hildegaard of Bingen's Book of Divine Works with Letters and Songs.* Santa Fe: Bear and Co., 1987.

Franzmann, Majella. *Women and Religion.* New York: Oxford UP, 2000.

Friedman, Richard Elliott. *Who Wrote the Bible?* New York: HarperCollins, 1997.

Frymer-Kensky, Tikva. *In the Wake of the Goddesses: Women, Culture, and the Biblical Transformation of Pagan Myth.* New York: Fawcett Columbine, 1992.

Fuller, C.J. *The Camphor Flame: Popular Hinduism and Society in India.* Princeton: Princeton UP, 1992.

Gadon, Elinor W. *The Once and Future Goddess: A Symbol for Our Time.* San Francisco: Harper, 1989.

Gagne, Laurie Brands. *The Uses of Darkness: Women's Underworld Journeys, Ancient and Modern.* Indiana: U of Notre Dame P, 2000.

Gardini, Walter. "The Feminine Aspect of God in Christianity." *Women in the World's Religions, Past and Present.* Ed. Ursula King. New York: Paragon House, 1987. 56–67.

Gaventa, Beverly Roberts. *Mary: Glimpses of the Mother of Jesus.* Minneapolis: Fortress P, 1999.

Geagea, Rev. Nilo. *Mary of the Koran: A Meeting Point Between Christianity and Islam.* Trans. Rev. Lawrence T. Fares. New York: Philosophical Library, 1984.

Gill, Sam D. *Mother Earth: An American Story.* Chicago: U of Chicago P, 1987.

———. *Native American Religions: An Introduction.* California: Wadsworth, 1982.

Gimbutas, Marija. *The Goddesses and Gods of Old Europe: Myths and Cult Images: 6500–3500 B.C.* Berkeley: U of California P, 1982.

———. *The Language of the Goddess.* London: Thames and Hudson, 1989.

Graves, Robert. *The White Goddess: A Historical Grammar of Poetic Myth.* New York: Farrar, Straus and Giroux, 1948.

Gross, Rita M. "Buddhism." *Women in Religion.* Eds. Jean Holm and John Bowker. London: Pinter, 1999. 1–29.

———. "Hindu Female Deities as a Resource For The Contemporary Rediscovery of the Goddess." *The Book of the Goddess, Past and Present: An Introduction to Her Religion.* Ed. Carl Olson. New York: Crossroad, 1990. 217–230.

Gupta, Lina. "Kali, The Savior." *After Patriarchy: Feminist Transformations of World Religions.* Ed. Paula M. Cooey, William R. Eakin, and Joy B. Daniel. New York: Orbis, 1993. 15–38.

Gupta, Roxanne Kamayani. "Kali Maya: Myth and Reality in a Banaras Ghetto." *Encountering Kali: In the Margins, At the Center, in the West.* Ed. Rachel Fell McDermott and Jeffrey J. Kripal. Berkeley: U of California P, 2003. 124–142.

Hackett, Rosalind I. J. "Women in African Religions." *Women and World Religions.* Ed. Lucinda Joy Peach. New Jersey: Prentice Hall, 2002. 309–327.

Hall, Nor. *The Moon and the Virgin: Reflections on the Archetypal Feminine.* New York: Harper and Row, 1980.

Hamilton, Edith. *Mythology: Timeless Tales of Gods and Heroes.* New York: Mentor, 1969.

Hammad, Ahmad Zaki. *Mary, The Chosen Woman: The Mother of Jesus in the Qur'an: An Interlinear Commentary on Surat Maryam.* Illinois: Quranic Library Institute, 2001.

Harris, Kevin. *Sex, Ideology and Religion: The Representation of Women in the Bible.* New Jersey: Barnes and Noble, 1984.

Hartz, Paula R. *Native American Religions: World Religions.* New York: Facts on File, Inc., 1997.

Harvey, Andrew, and Anne Baring. *The Divine Feminine: Exploring the Feminine Face of God Throughout the World.* Berkeley: Conari, 1996.

Hassan, Riffat. "The Issue of Woman-Man Equality in the Islamic Tradition (1993)." *Eve and Adam: Jewish, Christian, and Muslim Readings on Genesis and Gender.* Ed. Kristen E. Kvam, Linda S. Schearing, and Valarie H. Ziegler. Bloomington: Indiana UP, 1999. 464–476.

———. "Muslim Women and Post-Patriarchal Islam." *After Patriarchy: Feminist Transformations of the World Religions.* Faith Meets Faith Series. Ed. Paula M. Cooey, William R. Eakin, and Jay B. Daniel. New York: Orbis, 1994. 39–64.

———. "Muslim Feminist Hermeneutics." *In Our Own Voices: Four Centuries of American Women's Religious Writing.* Eds. Rosemary Skinner Keller and Rosemary Radford Ruether. San Francisco: Harper, 1994. 455–459.

Hawley, John S. and Donna M. Wulff, eds. *Devi: Goddesses of India.* Berkeley: U of California P, 1996.

Heidel, Alexander. *The Babylonian Genesis: The Story of Creation.* 2nd ed. Chicago: U of Chicago P, 1951.

Henderson, Joseph L., and Maud Oakes. *The Wisdom of the Serpent: The Myths of Death, Rebirth, and Resurrection.* Princeton: Princeton UP, 1963.

Holm, Jean, and John Bowker, eds. *Women in Religion.* London: Pinter, 1999.

Homer. *The Odyssey.* Trans. Robert Fitzgerald. New York: Anchor, 1963.

Hori, Ichiro, Alan L. Miller, and Joseph Mitsuo Kitagawa, eds. *Folk Religion in Japan: Continuity and Change.* Reissued edition. Chicago: U of Chicago P, 1994.

Houston, Jean. *The Hero and the Goddess: The Odyssey as Mystery and Initiation.* New York: Ballantine, 1992.

Hultkrantz, Ake. *The Religions of the American Indians.* Trans. Monica Setterwall. Berkeley: U of California P, 1979.

————. "The Religion of the Goddess in North America." *The Book of the Goddess, Past and Present: An Introduction to Her Religion.* Ed. Carl Olson. New York: Crossroad, 1990. 202–216.

Huntsman, Jeffrey F. "Traditional Native American Literature: The Translation Dilemma." *Smoothing the Ground: Essays on Native American Oral Literature.* Ed. Brian Swann. Berkeley: U of California P, 1983. 87–97.

Irving, T.B. (Al-Haj Ta'lim Ali), trans. *The Qur'an: The First American Version.* Vermont: Amana Books, 1985.

Irwin, Lee, ed. *Native American Spirituality: A Critical Reader.* Lincoln: U of Nebraska P, 2000.

Jacobsen, Thorkild. *The Harps That Once . . . Sumerian Poetry in Translation.* New Haven: Yale UP, 1987.

————. *The Treasures of Darkness: A History of Mesopotamian Religion.* New Haven: Yale UP, 1976.

————. *Toward the Image of Tammuz and Other Essays on Mesopotamian History and Culture.* Ed. William L. Morgan. Massachusetts: Harvard UP, 1970.

Johnson, Elizabeth A. *Truly Our Sister: A Theology of Mary in the Communion of Saints.* New York: Continuum, 2003.

Jones, Alexander, Gen. Ed. *The Jerusalem Bible: Reader's Edition.* New York: Doubleday and Co., Inc., 1968.

Juschka, Darlene M., ed. *Feminism in the Study of Religion: A Reader.* London and New York: Continuum, 2001.

Karade, Baba Ifa. *The Handbook of Yoruba Religious Concepts.* Maine: Samuel Weiser, Inc., 1994.

Keller, Rosemary Skinner, and Rosemary Radford Ruether, eds. *In Our Own Voices: Four Centuries of American Women's Religious Writing.* San Francisco: Harper, 1994.

Kerenyi, Carl. *Eleusis: Archetypal Image of Mother and Daughter.* Trans. Ralph Manheim. Princeton: Princeton UP, 1967.

————. *Goddesses of Sun and Moon.* Trans. Murray Stein. Dallas: Spring, 1979.

Kidwell, Clara Sue, Homer Noley, and George E. Tinker. *A Native American Theology.* New York: Orbis, 2001.

Kimelman, Reuven. "The Seduction of Eve and the Exegetical Politics of Gender." *Women in the Hebrew Bible: A Reader.* Ed. Alice Bach. New York: Routledge, 1999. 241- 269.

King, Urusla, ed. *Women in the World's Religions, Past and Present.* New York: Paragon House, 1987.

King, Karen L., ed. *Women and Goddess Traditions: In Antiquity and Today.* Minneapolis: Fortress, 1997.

Kinsley, David R. *The Goddesses' Mirror: Visions of the Divine From East and West.* Albany: SUNY P, 1989.

————. *Hindu Goddesses: Visions of the Divine Feminine in the Hindu Religious Tradition.* Berkeley: U of California P, 1988.

————. "Kali." *Encountering Kali: In the Margins, At the Center, In the West.* Ed. Rachel Fell McDermott and Jeffrey J. Kripal. Berkeley: U of California P, 2003. 23–38.

————. "The Portrait of the Goddess in the *Devi-Mahatmya.*" *Journal of the American Academy of Religion* 46 (1978): 489–506.

Kitagawa, Joseph M. *Religion in Japanese History.* New York: Columbia UP, 1966.

————, ed. *The Religious Traditions of Asia.* London: Macmillan, 1989.

Kitto, H.D.F. "The *Medea* of Euripides." *Medea: Myth and Dramatic Form.* Eds. James L. Sanderson and Everett Zimmerman. Boston: Houghton Mifflin, 1967. 286–297.

Klostermaier, Klaus K. *Hindu Writings: A Short Introduction to the Major Sources.* Oxford: One World, 2000.

Knapp, Bettina L. *Women, Myth, and the Feminine Principle.* New York: State U of NY, 1998.

Knox, Bernard. "Euripides Prophecies a World of Violence and Disorder." *Readings on Medea: The Greenhaven Press Literary Companion to World Literature.* Ed. Don Nardo. San Diego: Greenhaven, 2001. 59–63.

Kolenda, Pauline. "Pox and the Terror of Childlessness: Images and Ideas of the Smallpox Goddess in a North Indian Village." *Mother Worship: Themes and Variations.* Ed. James J. Preston. Chapel Hill: U of North Carolina P, 1982. 227–250.

Koltuv, Barbara Black. *The Book of Lilith.* Maine: Nicolas-Hays, Inc., 1986.

Kramer, Samuel Noah, ed. *Mythologies of the Ancient World.* New York: Anchor, 1961.

———. *The Sacred Marriage Rite: Aspects of Faith, Myth, and Ritual in Ancient Sumer.* Bloomington: Indiana UP, 1969.

———. *Sumerian Mythology: A Study of Spiritual and Literary Achievement in the Third Millennium B.C.* Rev. Ed. Philadelphia: U of Pennsylvania P, 1972.

Kvam, Kristen E., Linda S. Schearing, and Valarie H. Ziegler, eds. *Eve and Adam: Jewish, Christian, and Muslim Readings on Genesis and Gender.* Bloomington: Indiana UP, 1999.

Lame Deer, John (Fire), and Richard Erdoes. *Lame Deer: Seeker of Visions.* New York: Washington Square P, 1972.

Larrington, Carolyne, ed. *The Feminist Companion to Mythology.* London: Pandora, 1992.

Lattimore, Richmond, trans. *The Odyssey of Homer.* New York: Harper Perennial, 1991.

Lauter, Estella, and Carol Schreier Rupprecht. *Feminist Archetypal Theory: Interdisciplinary and Re-Visions of Jungian Thought.* Knoxville: U of Tennessee P, 1985.

Layton, Bentley, trans. *The Gnostic Scriptures: Ancient Wisdom For the New Age.* New York: Doubleday, 1987.

Leeming, David, and Jake Page. *Goddess: Myths of the Female Divine.* New York: Oxford UP, 1994.

Lerner, Gerda. *The Creation of Patriarchy.* Oxford: Oxford UP, 1986.

Lincoln, Bruce. *Emerging From the Chrysalis: Rituals of Women's Initiation.* New York: Oxford UP, 1991.

Littleton, C. Scott. "Japan." *World Mythology.* Gen. Ed. Roy Willis. New York: Henry Holt and Co., 1993.

———. *Shinto: Origins, Rituals, Festivals, Spirits, Sacred Places.* New York: Oxford UP, 2002.

Long, Asphodel P. *In a Chariot Drawn by Lions: The Search for the Female in Deity.* Freedom: Crossing P, 1993.

Lyons, Deborah. *Gender and Immortality: Heroines in Ancient Greek Myth and Cult.* Princeton: Princeton UP, 1997.

Martin, Joel W. *The Land Looks After Us: A History of Native American Religion.* New York: Oxford UP, 2001.

Mascetti, Manuela Dunn. *Goddesses: An Illustrated Journey Into the Myths, Symbols, and Rituals of the Goddess.* New York: Barnes and Noble, 1998.

Matateyou, Emmanuel. *An Anthology of Myths, Legends, and Folktales From Cameroon: Storytelling in Africa. Studies in African Literature.* Vol. 4. New York: Edwin Mellen, 1997.

Matter, E. Ann. "The Virgin Mary: A Goddess?" *The Book of the Goddess Past and Present: An Introduction to Her Religion.* Ed. Carl Olson. New York: Crossroad, 1990. 80–96.

McDermott, Rachel Fell. "Kali's New Frontiers: A Hindu Goddess on the Internet." *Encountering Kali: In the Margins, At the Center, In the West.* Ed. Rachell Fell McDermott and Jeffrey J. Kripal. Berkeley: U of California P, 2003. 273–295.

McDermott, Rachel Fell, and Jeffrey J. Kripal, eds. *Encountering Kali: In the Margins, at the Center, In the West.* Berkeley: U of California P, 2003.

McDonald, Marianne. "Medea as Politician and Diva: Riding the Dragon Into the Future." *Medea: Essays in Medea in Myth, Literature, Philosophy, and Art.* Ed. James L. Clauss and Sarah Iles Johnston. Princeton: Princeton UP, 1997. 297–323.

McFarlane, Stewart. "Chinese Religions." *Women in Religion.* Ed. Jean Holm and John Bowker. London: Pinter, 1999. 158–167.

McGaa Eagle Man, ed. *Mother Earth Spirituality: Native American Paths to Healing Ourselves and Our World.* New York: Harper Collins, 1990.

Medicine Eagle, Brooke. *Buffalo Woman Comes Singing: The Spirit Song of a Rainbow Medicine Woman.* New York: Ballantine, 1991.

Menon, Ramesh, trans. *The Ramayana.* New York: North Point, 2001.

Mernissi, Fatima. *The Veil and the Male Elite: A Feminist Interpretation of Women's Rights in Islam.* Trans. Mary Jo Lakeland. Massachusetts: Addison-Wesley, 1987.

Meyer, Marvin W., ed. *The Ancient Mysteries, A Sourcebook: Sacred Texts of the Mystery Religions of the Ancient and Mediterranean World.* San Francisco: Harper and Row, 1987.

Meyers, Carol, General Ed. *Women in Scripture: A Dictionary of Named and Unnamed Women in the Hebrew Bible, The Apocryphal/Deuterocanonical Books, and The New Testament.* Boston: Houghton Mifflin, 2000.

Miles, Jack. *God: A Biography.* New York: Vintage, 1996.

Monaghan, Patricia. *The Book of Goddesses and Heroines.* Minnesota: Llewellyn, 1990.

Mookerjee, Ajit. *Kali: The Feminine Force.* Rochester: Destiny, 1988.

Murata, Sachiko. *The Tao Of Islam: A Sourcebook on Gender Relationships in Islamic Thought.* Albany: SUNY P, 1992.

Murphy, Joseph M., and Mei-Mei Sanford, eds. *Osun Across the Waters: A Yoruba Goddess in Africa and the Americas.* Bloomington: Indiana UP, 2001.

Nakamura, Kyoko Motomochi. "The Significance of Amaterasu in Japanese Religious History." *The Book of the Goddess Past and Present: An Introduction to Her Religion.* Ed. Carl Olson. New York: Crossroad, 1990. 176–189.

Narayan, R.K., trans. *The Ramayana: A Shortened Modern Prose Version of the Indian Epic.* New York: Viking, 1972.

Nardo, Don, ed. *Readings on Medea: The Greenhaven Press Literary Companion to World Literature.* San Diego: Greenhaven, 2001.

Neihardt, John G. *Black Elk Speaks: Being the Life Story of a Holy Man of the Oglala Sioux.* 1932. Lincoln: U of Nebraska P, 1989.

The New Oxford Annotated Bible With the Apocryphal/Deuterocanonical Books: New Revised Standard. 3rd ed. Ed. Michael D. Coogan. Oxford: Oxford UP, 2001.

Nicholas, Ralph W. "The Village Mother in Bengal." *Mother Worship: Themes and Variations.* Ed. James J. Preston. Chapel Hill: U of North Carolina P, 1982. 192–209.

Nicholson, Shirley. *The Goddess Re-Awakening: The Feminine Principle Today.* Illinois: The Theosophical Publishing House, 1989.

Nunnally-Cox, Janice. *Foremothers: Women of the Bible.* New York: Seabury, 1981.

Olson, Carl, ed. *The Book of the Goddess Past and Present: An Introduction to Her Religion.* New York: Crossroad, 1990.

Ono, Sokyo. *Shinto: The Kami Way.* Boston: Charles E. Tuttle Co., 1994.

Pagels, Elaine. *Adam, Eve, and the Serpent.* New York: Random House, 1988.

———. *Beyond Belief: The Secret Gospel of Thomas.* New York: Random House, 2003.

———. *The Gnostic Gospels.* New York: Vintage, 1989.

Panadian, Jacob. "The Goddess Kannagi: A Dominant Symbol of South Indian Tamil." *Mother Worship: Themes and Variations.* Ed. James J. Preston. Chapel Hill: U of North Carolina P, 1982. 177–191.

Pargiter, F. Eden., trans. *The Markandeya Purana.* The Asiatic Society of Bengal, 1904. Reissued by Delhi: Indological Book House, 1969.

Patai, Raphael. *The Hebrew Goddess.* USA: KTAV Publishing House, Inc., 1967.

Paul, Diana Y. "Kuan-Yin: Savior and Savioress in Chinese Pure Land Buddhism." *The Book of the Goddess, Past and Present: An Introduction to Her Religion.* Ed. Carl Olson. New York: Crossroad, 1990. 161–175.

———. *Women in Buddhism: Images of the Feminine in the Mahayana Tradition.* 2nd ed. Berkeley: U of California P, 1985.

Peach, Lucinda Joy, ed. *Women and World Religions.* New Jersey: Pearson Education, Inc. 2002.

Pereira, Filomena Maria. *Lilith: The Edge of Forever.* Texas: Ide House, 1998.

Perera, Sylvia Brinton. *Descent to the Goddess: A Way of Initiation for Women.* Canada: Inner City, 1981.

———. "The Descent of Inanna: Myth and Therapy." *Feminist Archetypal Theory: Interdisciplinary Re-Visions of Jungian Thought.* Ed. Estella Lauter and Carol Schreier Rupprecht. Knoxville: U of Tennessee, 1985. 137–186.

Perkell, Christine G. "On Creusa, Dido, and the Quality of Victory in Virgil's *Aeneid.*" *Reflections of Women in Antiquity.* Ed. Helene P. Foley. Philadelphia: Gordon and Breach Science Publishers, Inc., 1981. 355–377.

Philippi, Donald L., trans. *Kojiki.* Princeton and Tokyo: Princeton UP and U of Tokyo P, 1968.

Phipps, William E. *Assertive Biblical Women.* Connecticut: Greenwood P, 1992.

Pickthall, M. M., trans. *The Meaning of the Glorious Qur'an: Explanatory Translation.* Ed. Arafat K. El-Ashi. Rev. ed. Maryland: Amana, 2002.

Pintchman, Tracy. *The Rise of the Goddess in the Hindu Tradition.* Albany: SUNY P, 1994.

Plaskow, Judith. "Lilith Revisited (1995 CE)." *Eve and Adam: Jewish, Christian, and Muslim Readings on Genesis and Gender.* Ed. Kristen E. Kvam, Linda S. Schearing, and Valarie H. Ziegler. Bloomington: Indiana UP, 1999. 425–430.

Plaskow, Judith, and Carol P. Christ, eds. *Weaving the Visions: New Patterns in Feminist Spirituality.* San Francisco: Harper, 1989.

Plaskow, Judith and Joan Arnold Romero, eds. *Women and Religion: Papers of the Working Group on Women and Religion.* Montana: American Academy of Religion and Scholars Press, 1974.

Pomeroy, Sarah B. *Goddesses, Whores, Wives, and Slaves: Women in Classical Antiquity.* New York: Schocken, 1975.

Powell, Barry B. *Classical Myth.* Englewood Cliffs: Prentice Hall, 1995.

Powers, Meredith A. *The Heroine in Western Literature: The Archetype and her Reemergence in Modern Prose.* North Carolina: McFarland, 1991.

Pratt, Annis. *Archetypal Patterns in Women's Fiction.* Bloomington: Indiana UP, 1981.

———. *Dancing With Goddesses: Archetypes, Poetry, and Empowerment.* Bloomington: Indiana UP, 1994.

Preston, James J. *Cult of the Goddess: Social and Religious Change in a Hindu Temple.* Prospect Heights: Waveland P, 1985.

———. "The Goddess Chandi as an Agent of Change." *Mother Worship: Themes and Variations.* Ed. James J. Preston. Chapel Hill: U of North Carolina P, 1982. 210–226.

———, ed. *Mother Worship: Theme and Variations.* Chapel Hill: U of North Carolina P, 1982.

Pritchard, James B., ed. *Ancient Near Eastern Texts: Relating to the Old Testament.* 3rd ed. Princeton: Princeton UP, 1969.

Qualls-Corbett, Nancy. *The Sacred Prostitute: Eternal Aspect of the Feminine.* Toronto: Inner City, 1988.

Rabuzzi, Kathryn Allen. *Motherself: A Mythic Analysis of Motherhood.* Bloomington: Indiana UP, 1988.

Reader, Ian. *Religion in Contemporary Japan.* Honolulu: U of Hawaii P, 1991.

Reid, D. "Japanese Religions." *Handbook of Living Religions.* Ed. John R. Hinnells. New York: Penguin, 1985. 365–391.

Rivlin, Lilly. "Lilith." *Which Lilith: Feminist Writers Re-Create The World's First Woman.* Ed. Enid Dame, Lilly Rivlin, and Henny Wenkart. New Jersey: Jason Aronson, Inc., 1998. 4–14.

Rosenberg, Donna, ed. *World Mythology: An Anthology of the Great Myths and Epics.* 2nd ed. Illinois: NTC Publishing Group, 1994.

Ruether, Rosemary Radford. *Gaia and God: An Ecofeminist Theology of Earth Healing.* San Fransisco: Harper Collins, 1992.

———, ed. *Religion and Sexism: Images of Women in the Jewish and Christian Traditions.* New York: Simon and Schuster, 1974.

———. *Woman Guides: Readings Toward a Feminist Theology.* Boston: Beacon, 1996.

Russell, Letty M., ed. *Feminist Interpretation of the Bible.* Philadelphia: Westminster P, 1985.

Russell, Letty M., and J. Shannon Clarkson, eds. *Dictionary of Feminist Theologies.* Kentucky: Westminster John Knox, 1996.

Salmonson, Jessica Amanda. *The Encyclopedia of Amazons: Women Warriors From Antiquity to the Modern Era.* New York: Anchor, 1991.

Sandars, N.K., trans. *Poems of Heaven and Hell From Ancient Mesopotamia.* London: Penguin, 1971.

Schaberg, Jane. *The Illegitimacy of Jesus: A Feminist Theological Interpretation of the Infancy Narratives.* San Francisco: Harper and Row, 1987.

Schimmel, Annemarie. *Deciphering the Signs of God: A Phenomenological Approach to Islam.* Albany: State U of New York P, 1994.

———. *Mystical Dimensions of Islam.* Chapel Hill: U of North Carolina P, 1975.

Schotroff, Luise. *Let the Oppressed Go Free: Feminist Perspectives on the New Testament.* Trans. Annemarie S. Kidder. Louisville: Westminster/John Knox P, 1993.

Sells, Michael, trans. *Approaching The Qur'an: The Early Revelations.* Ashland, Oregon: White Clouds P, 1999.

Sered, Susan Starr. *Priestess, Mother, Sacred Sister.* New York: Oxford UP, 1994.

Sharma, Arvind, ed. *Women in World Religions.* Albany: State U of New York P, 1987.

Shlain, Leonard. *The Alphabet Versus The Goddess: The Conflict Between Word and Image.* New York: Penguin/Compass, 1999.

Shulman, David. "Fire and Flood: The Testing of Sita in Kampan's *Iramavataram.*" Ed. Paula Rickman. *Many Ramayanas: The Diversity of a Narrative Tradition in South Asia.* Berkeley: U of California P, 1991. 89–113.

Smith, Huston. *The Religions of Man.* New York: Harper and Row, 1958.

Smith, Jane I. "Islam." *Women in World Religions.* Ed. Arvind Sharma. Albany: SUNY P, 1987. 235–250.

Smith, Jane I., and Yvonne Haddad. "Eve: Islamic Image of Woman." *Women and Islam.* Ed. Azizah Al-Hibri. Oxford: Pergamon, 1982. 135–144.

Smyers, Karen A. "Women and Shinto: The Relation Between Purity and Pollution." *Women and World Religions.* Ed. Lucinda Joy Peach. New Jersey: Pearson Education, Inc., 2002. 117–125.

Soskice, Janet Martin, and Diana Lipton, eds. *Feminism and Theology.* Oxford: Oxford UP, 2003.

Spretnak, Charlene, ed. *The Politics of Women's Spirituality: Essays on the Rise of Spiritual Power Within the Feminist Movement.* New York: Anchor, 1982.

Stanton, Elizabeth Cady. *The Woman's Bible: Parts I and II.* New York: Arno, 1972.

Stern, David, and Mark J. Mirsky, eds. *Rabbinic Fantasies: Imaginative Narratives From Classical Hebrew Literature.* New Haven: Yale UP, 1990.

Stone, Merlin. *Ancient Mirrors of Womanhood: A Treasury of Goddess and Heroine Lore from Around the World.* 1979. Boston: Beacon, 1990.

———. *When God Was a Woman.* New York: Harcourt Brace Jovanovich, 1976.

Stowasser, Barbara Freyer. *Women in The Qur'an, Traditions, and Interpretation.* New York: Oxford UP, 1994.

Stuckey, Johanna H. "Inanna and the Huluppa Tree: An Ancient Mesopotamian Narrative of Goddess Demotion." *Feminist Poetics of the Sacred: Creative Suspicions.* Ed. Frances Devlin-Glass and Lyn McCreddon. Oxford: Oxford UP, 2001. 91–105.

Sugirtharajah, Sharada. "Hinduism." *Women in Religion.* Ed. Jean Holm and John Bowker. London: Pinter, 1999. 59–83.

Swann, Brian, ed. *Smoothing the Ground: Essays on Native American Oral Literature.* Berkeley: U of California P, 1983.

Tedlock, Dennis, and Barbara Tedlock, eds. *Teachings From the American Earth: Indian Religions and Philosophy.* New York: Liveright, 1975.

Tembo, Mwizenge. *Myths of the World: Legends of Africa.* New York: Metro, 1996.

Trible, Phyllis. *God and the Rhetoric of Sexuality.* Philadelphia: Fortress, 1978.

———. "Eve and Adam: Genesis 2–3 Reread (1993 CE)." *Eve and Adam: Jewish, Christian, and Muslim Readings on Genesis and Gender.* Ed. Kristen E. Kvam, Linda S. Schearing, and Valarie H. Ziegler. Bloomington: Indiana UP, 1999. 430–438.

———. "Not a Jot, Not a Tittle: Genesis 2–3 After Twenty Years (1995 CE)." *Eve and Adam: Jewish, Christian, and Muslim Readings on Genesis and Gender.* Ed. Kristen E. Kvam, Linda S. Schearing, and Valarie H. Ziegler. Bloomington: Indiana UP, 1999. 439–444.

Turner, Frederick, ed. *The Portable North American Indian Reader.* New York: Penguin, 1974.

Versluis, Arthur. *The Elements of Native American Traditions.* Boston: Element, 1993.

Via, E. Jane. "Women in the Gospel of Luke." *Women in the World's Religions, Past and Present.* Ed. Ursula King. New York: Paragon House, 1987. 38–55.

Wadud-Muhsin, Amina. *Qur'an and Woman.* Kuala Lumpur: Penerbit Fajar Bakti Sdn. Bhd., 1992.

Walker, Barbara G. *The Crone: Woman of Age, Wisdom, and Power.* San Francisco: Harper and Row, 1985.

———. *The Woman's Encyclopedia of Myths and Secrets.* San Francisco: Harper Collins, 1983.

Walker, James R., and Elaine Jahner, eds. *Lakota Myth.* Lincoln: U of Nebraska P, 1983.

———, Raymond J. Demallie, and Elaine Jahner, eds. *Lakota Belief and Ritual.* Lincoln: U of Nebraska P, 1991.

Warner, Marina. *Alone of All Her Sex: The Myth and The Cult of the Virgin Mary.* New York: Alfred A. Knopf, 1976.

Warner, Rex, trans. "The Medea." *The Complete Greek Tragedies: Euripides 1.* Ed. David Grene and Richmond Lattimore. Chicago: U of Chicago P, 1955. 56–108.

Weaver, Lloyd, and Olurunmi Egbelade. *Maternal Divinity Yemonja: Tranquil Sea, Turbulent Tides: Eleven Yoruba Tales.* New York: Athelia Henrietta P, 1998.

Wilkinson, Tanya. *Medea's Folly: Women, Relationships, and the Search For Identity.* Berkeley: Pagemill, 1998.

———. *Persephone Returns: Victims, Heroes and the Journey From the Underworld.* Berkeley: Pagemill, 1996.

Williamson, Ray A. *Living the Sky: The Cosmos of the American Indian.* Oklahoma: U of Oklahoma P, 1984.

Wolkstein, Diane, and Samuel Noah Kramer, trans. *Inanna, Queen of Heaven and Earth: Her Stories and Hymns From Sumer.* New York: Harper and Row, 1983.

Woodman, Marion, and Elinor Dickson. *Dancing in the Flames: The Dark Goddess in the Transformation of Consciousness.* Boston: Shambhala, 1996.

Wright, Alexandra. "Judaism." *Women in Religion.* Ed. Jean Holm and John Bowker. London: Pinter, 1999. 113–140.

Yamani, Mai, ed. *Feminism and Islam: Legal and Literary Perspectives.* New York: New York UP, 1996.

Yarnall, Judith. *Transformations of Circe: The History of an Enchantress.* Urbana: U of Illinois P, 1994.

Young, Serenity, ed. *An Anthology of Sacred Texts By And About Women.* New York: Crossroad, 1993.

Yü, Chün-fang. *Kuan-Yin: The Chinese Transformation of Avalokiteśvara.* New York: Columbia UP, 2000.

Zabkar, Louis V. *Hymns to Isis in Her Temple at Philae.* Hanover: UP of New England, 1988.

Zak, Nancy C. "Sacred and Legendary Women of Native North America." *The Goddess Re-Awakening: The Feminine Principle Today.* Illinois: Quest, 1989. 232–245.

Credits